The Jewish Legion and the First World War

The Jewish Legion and the First World War

Martin Watts

© Martin Watts 2004

All rights reserved. No reproduction, copy or transmission of this publication may be made without written permission.

No paragraph of this publication may be reproduced, copied or transmitted save with written permission or in accordance with the provisions of the Copyright, Designs and Patents Act 1988, or under the terms of any licence permitting limited copying issued by the Copyright Licensing Agency, 90 Tottenham Court Road, London W1T 4LP.

Any person who does any unauthorised act in relation to this publication may be liable to criminal prosecution and civil claims for damages.

The author has asserted his right to be identified as the author of this work in accordance with the Copyright, Designs and Patents Act 1988.

First published 2004 by
PALGRAVE MACMILLAN
Houndmills, Basingstoke, Hampshire RG21 6XS and
175 Fifth Avenue, New York, N. Y. 10010
Companies and representatives throughout the world

PALGRAVE MACMILLAN is the global academic imprint of the Palgrave Macmillan division of St. Martin's Press, LLC and of Palgrave Macmillan Ltd. Macmillan® is a registered trademark in the United States, United Kingdom and other countries. Palgrave is a registered trademark in the European Union and other countries.

ISBN 1–4039–3921–7

This book is printed on paper suitable for recycling and made from fully managed and sustained forest sources.

A catalogue record for this book is available from the British Library.

Library of Congress Cataloging-in-Publication Data

Watts, Martin, 1953-
The Jewish Legion and the First World War / by Martin Watts.
    p. cm.
    Includes bibliographical references and index.
    ISBN 1-4039-3921-7
    1. Jewish Legion. 2. Great Britain. Army–History–World War, 1914-1918. 3. World War, 1914-1918–Regimental histories–Great Britain. 4. Zionism–History–20th century. 5. Great Britain–Ethnic relations–History–20th century. I. Title.

D568.7.W28 2004
940.4′1241′089924–dc22   2004049120

10 9 8 7 6 5 4 3 2 1
13 12 11 10 09 08 07 06 05 04

Printed and bound in Great Britain by
Antony Rowe Ltd, Chippenham and Eastbourne

*This book is dedicated to the memory of David Englander,
Reader in History, the Open University*

'Shalom, haver'

Contents

List of Illustrations	viii
List of Maps	ix
List of Tables	x
Acknowledgements	xi
List of Abbreviations	xiii
Brief Biographies	xiv
1 Introduction: a Matter of Record	1
2 The Zion Mule Corps	20
3 The Founding of the Legion: Part One	48
4 The Founding of the Legion: Part Two	76
5 Raising the Battalions: Great Britain	117
6 Raising the Battalions: the United States	138
7 Preparation and Prejudice	160
8 The Legion at War	182
9 Disturbance and Decline	201
10 Conclusions: Legacy of the Legion	239
Appendix I: Strength Returns March 1918–May 1921	244
Appendix II: Maps	248
Notes	250
Bibliography	270
Index	279

Illustrations

1.1 ZOA citation, Capt. Philip Jacobs, 1968 (courtesy of Mr and Mrs Herbert Goldsmith, London, UK)   16
7.1 Recruits for the 40th (Palestine) Battalion, Royal Fusiliers, summer 1918 (by permission of the Imperial War Museum. IWM, No. Q12670)   175
7.2 Major James (de) Rothschild at Jaffa with recruits for the 40th (Palestine) Battalion, summer 1918 (by permission of the Imperial War Museum. IWM, No. Q12680)   175
7.3 Recruits for 40th (Palestine) Battalion, Jerusalem, summer 1918 (by permission of the Imperial War Museum. IWM, No. Q12671)   176
7.4 Recruits for the 40th (Palestine) Battalion, *en route* from Jaffa to Helmieh (Egypt), summer 1918 (by permission of the Imperial War Museum. IWM, No. Q12679)   176
7.5 Letter to Harry Levine from Levi Eshkol, 1964 (courtesy of Mrs Helen Finkel, New Jersey, USA)   180
8.1 Platoon of 'A' Company 38th at Giza, 1918. Pte. Berger is fourth from right, front row (courtesy of L. Berger, Edinburgh, UK)   199
9.1 Private Aaron Gitelson, 1919 (courtesy of Mr and Mrs Ash, New York, USA)   206
9.2 Private Aaron Gitelson and comrades, 1919 (courtesy of Mr and Mrs Ash, New York, USA)   207
10.1 Letter to Harry Levine from D. Ben-Gurion, 1964 (courtesy of Mrs Helen Finkel, New Jersey, USA)   240

Maps

A.II.1 The landings at Gallipoli (courtesy of the Imperial War Museum) 248
A.II.2 Megiddo 1918 (courtesy of the Imperial War Museum) 249

Tables

9.1 Disposition October 1918   205
9.2 Courts martial summary August 1919   225
A.I.1 Strength returns March 1918–May 1921   244

Acknowledgements

This work would not have been possible without the assistance, co-operation and patience of the curators, librarians and staff of the following institutions (located in London, unless otherwise stated):

Anglo-Jewish Archives, University of Southampton
Bodleian Library, Oxford
Bishopsgate Institute
British Library
Guildhall Library
House of Lords Record Office
Imperial War Museum
Institute of Historical Research
The Jewish Legion Museum, Avichail, Israel
Jews College
Kent County Central Library, Maidstone
Liddell Hart Archives, Kings College, University of London
London Metropolitan Record Office
Maidstone Library
Mocatta Library, University College, University of London
National Army Museum
National Register of Archives
Public Record Office
Rothschild Archive
SOAS Library, University of London
Wiener Library

Particular acknowledgment is reserved for Lt.-Col. Pettifar (retd.), Major Bowes-Crick and Jim Kelleher at the Regimental Headquarters of the Royal Regiment of Fusiliers, HM Tower of London. They were introduced to me by Fred Baker (ex-RSM), my colleague and friend, to whom I owe a great deal.

I also wish to pay a personal tribute to those who have made it possible, through their friendship and support, for this work to be completed over the past eight years. They include the late Dr David Englander (an inspiration), the late Dr John Herman, Pat Upward, Tony Sawyer, Ralph Coney, Liz Fox and Robin Leach. I am indebted to

Dr Bernard Waites for his friendly encouragement, patience and wise advice. Thanks, too, to Julian Putkowski, Dr Gerard Oram and Dr Buck Ryan.

Indebtedness and gratitude are also due to the correspondents and interviewees listed in the Bibliography. The photographs supplied by the Ash family of New York, the Finkel family of New Jersey, the Berger family of Edinburgh and the Goldsmith family of London are particularly appreciated. Warm thanks also to the Gildesgame Foundation and Laurence Hoppen, who succeeded in finding the resting place of the Legionnaire grandfather he never knew.

Finally, I wish to thank my wife Denise, daughters Helen and Laura, my Mum Vera and brother Nigel without whose love and unstinting faith I would have given up long ago. My only regret and sadness is that my Dad, Ron, did not live to see the completion of this research; I like to think there is a part of him in it.

Abbreviations

AAG	Assistant Adjutant-General
AJA	Anglo-Jewish Archives
BAPIP	British Association of Palestine Israel Philatelists
BDBJ	Board of Deputies of British Jews
Bod. Lib.	Bodleian Library
CAB	Cabinet papers
CUP	Cambridge University Press
CZA	Central Zionist Archive, Jerusalem
EEF	Egyptian Expeditionary Force
FJPC	Foreign Jews Protection Committee
FO	Foreign Office papers
GHQ	General Head Quarters
GLRO	Greater London Record Office
GOC-in-C	General Officer Commanding-in-Chief
GS	General Staff
HO	Home Office papers
IWM	Imperial War Museum
JC	*Jewish Chronicle*
LHA	Liddell Hart Archives
MEF	Mediterranean Expeditionary Force
NCO	Non-Commissioned Officer
OUP	Oxford University Press
PRO	Public Record Office
QMG	Quartermaster-General
USSD	United States State Department
WO	War Office papers
ZMC	Zion Mule Corps
ZOA	Zionist Organisation of America

Brief Biographies

Allenby, Edmund Henry Hynman, Viscount (1861–1936)
A career soldier and cavalryman in the British Army, Edmund Allenby commanded the 1st Cavalry Division in 1914, and was promoted to command the Third Army on the western front in 1915. In 1917 he was sent to Egypt as commander-in-chief, where he earned his reputation during two campaigns that resulted in taking Jerusalem and then defeating the Turks at Megiddo and Damascus. Allenby commanded a multi-national army and managed to gain the respect not only of his troops but also of Arab and Jewish leaders. After a short spell as military governor and leave at home, Allenby was made high commissioner to Egypt in 1919 until his retirement in 1925.

Amery, Leopold Charles Maurice Stennett (1873–1955)
Leopold Amery was a Conservative MP from 1911 to 1945, who served as an assistant-secretary to the War Cabinet of Lloyd George. An advocate of the British Empire and Commonwealth, Amery was a pro-Zionist who considered that British support for an independent Jewish state in Palestine would be of benefit to Britain's imperial and strategic interests. He was responsible for the first draft of the Balfour Declaration and campaigned for the establishment of the Jewish Legion on behalf of Jabotinsky. Later colonial secretary, Amery's final ministerial post was as secretary of state for Burma and India during Winston Churchill's premiership 1940–1945.

Ben-Gurion, David (1886–1973)
Born David Green in Poland, Ben-Gurion emigrated to Palestine in 1906 and, working on the land, joined Poale Zion, the Zionist Socialist group. Before the First World War he went with Isaac Ben-Zvi to university in Constantinople to study law but returned to Palestine on the entry of Turkey into the conflict. Expelled by the Turks, Ben-Gurion and Ben-Zvi (collectively known as the 'Benim') went to the USA where they assisted in the foundation and recruitment of the American contingent of the Jewish Legion. Ben-Gurion served as a corporal in the Legion despite upsetting his superiors by delivering political speeches to his comrades. As a labour leader after the war, involved with the Histradut (Jewish Workers Federation) and the Haganah (Jewish self–defence group), Ben-Gurion's influence grew until, in 1948, he announced the founding of

the state of Israel. He was prime minister between 1948 and 1953, and again between 1955 and 1963 when he was succeeded by another former Legionnaire, Levi Eshkol.

Jabotinsky, Vladimir (1880–1940)
Vladimir Jabotinsky's background was distinctly middle class and he received a Russian education in his hometown of Odessa, before moving on to study law in Italy and Rome. He became an international correspondent for home newspapers and had a gift for languages; skills that made him a powerful propagandist and speaker. His interest in Zionism began with the Russian pogroms of 1903, and he became a regular attendee at Zionist Congresses and meetings. Jabotinsky's commitment to the founding of an independent Jewish state was absolute and, in the First World War, he poured his energy into founding the Jewish Legion. His views were not shared by other Zionist leaders, including his personal friend Chaim Weizmann, but he did succeed with the Jewish Legion project and was commissioned into the 38th Battalion and saw active service at the battle of Megiddo in September 1918. After the war Jabotinsky had a brief period as political officer to the Zionist commission, but quit after becoming disillusioned with what he saw as the British authorities' failure to implement the promises of the Balfour Declaration. As a leader of the Haganah (self-defence) he took part in the Arab–Jewish riots in 1920, was arrested and subsequently released. Afterwards, he served with the Zionist Executive and went on to become the founder of the Zionist youth movement Betar (Brit Trumpeldor) and led the revisionist movement in opposition to the socialist Zionist groups that existed throughout the mandate period. In 1940, after being banned from Palestine by the mandatory authority, Jabotinsky succumbed to a heart attack whilst visiting the Betar movement in New York.

Patterson, John Henry (1867–1947)
Originally a civil engineer from a middle-class Anglo-Irish protestant family, Patterson made his name during the second Boer war as volunteer in the Imperial Yeomanry. He was promoted from lieutenant to lieutenant-colonel in less than six months and earned a DSO and several mentions. During this campaign he gained the acquaintance of the future Lord Allenby and remained listed in the territorial force until he resigned in 1913 over Irish home rule. In the meantime he worked in East Africa building bridges and becoming a famous big game hunter; his clients included the former president of the United States, Theodore Roosevelt. He was able to resume his military career in

1915 and commanded the Zion Mule Corps and, subsequently, the 38th Battalion Royal Fusiliers – the first unit of what was to become known as the Jewish Legion. He left the Legion at the end of 1919 and remained a friend of Jabotinsky throughout the inter-war period.

Rothschild, Lionel Walter, 2nd Lord (1868–1937)
Succeeding to the title in 1915, Lord Rothschild took over as the widely recognised leader of the Jewish community in Britain, at a time when questions raised by the war and its influence on the future had a profound effect upon Anglo-Jewish relations. Although originally opposed to the Jewish Legion idea, Rothschild adapted to the inevitable and attempted to provide a bridge between the opposing factions. The combination of compulsion, and the transfer of some Jewish soldiers from other regiments, persuaded Rothschild to support the Jewish battalions. He was also extremely influential in ensuring that the battalions would not bear a Jewish name until distinction in the field had been achieved. It should also be noted that Rothschild had to deal with the welfare issues arising out of the Military Service Convention, and that it was to him that the note containing the Balfour Declaration was addressed.

Sokolow, Nahum (1859–1936)
A historian and journalist from eastern Poland, Sokolow was an able linguist and scholar who became general secretary of the Zionist Organisation from 1906 to 1909. A colleague and supporter of his friend Chaim Weizmann, he worked for the Zionist cause in Britain during the First World War, preparing diplomatic support for the Balfour Declaration and placing pressure on the British government over the Jewish Legion question. He played a leading part at the peace conference and then became chairman of the Zionist executive and was later president during Weizmann's 'interregnum' following the publication of the Passfield report in 1931.

Swaythling, Edwin Samuel, 2nd Baron (Lord Montagu) (1879–1924)
Second son of the 1st Baron, Edwin Montagu was a Liberal MP prior to taking his seat in the House of Lords, serving as secretary of state for India from 1917 to 1922. Before this appointment he was financial secretary and the minister for munitions. Lord Swaythling was a leading anti-Zionist Jew who regarded himself as an Englishman first and foremost, and did not recognise the Jewish people as comprising a separate state. He led the delegations to the War Office that nearly succeeded in having the Jewish battalions scrapped before they were formed, and was also instrumental in softening the original drafts of the Balfour Declaration.

Sykes, Sir Mark (1879–1919)
A Conservative MP, Mark Sykes' diplomatic skills were used to provide the British government with advice on Middle-Eastern matters during the First World War. He was responsible for negotiating a secret agreement with the French foreign minister, François Georges Picot, in 1916 (the Sykes–Picot agreement), that set out post-war Anglo-French spheres of control and influence in the Middle East. After this work had been completed, Sykes became interested and supportive of Zionism and the Jewish Legion, and contributed to the drafts that went on to become the Balfour Declaration. He believed that Arabs and Jews would be able to happily co-exist and was therefore disappointed to discover, on a visit to Palestine prior to his early death, the extent of Arab resentment to the implications of the declaration.

Trumpeldor, Joseph (1880–1920)
Joseph Trumpeldor is believed to be the first Jew to receive a commission in the Tsarist army following his bravery at the defence of Port Arthur in 1904 during the Russo-Japanese war. Although severely wounded, losing his left arm, he survived and was sent to Japan as a prisoner of war. Whilst in the camp he conducted classes in Zionism and established a Jewish prisoners organisation accompanied by a newsletter. After his repatriation he emigrated to Palestine in 1912 and met Jabotinsky in Alexandria in 1915. Together they played the leading roles in organising the Zion Mule Corps and, when Jabotinsky left following a disagreement over the military employment of the corps, Trumpeldor served as second-in-command to Patterson before taking over for the final stages of the Gallipoli campaign. He then came to Britain and assisted Jabotinsky in his fight to raise the Jewish battalions, but left when it became apparent that he would not be offered a commission in the new unit. Trumpeldor then accepted an offer by the Provisional Government in Russia to raise a Jewish army for deployment against the Turks in the Caucasus, but this came to naught with the overthrow of Kerensky. Returning to Palestine in 1919, Trumpeldor took an active part in Jewish self-defence of the settlements, and became a hero when killed by Arabs during the massacre at Tel Hai on 1 March 1920. Jabotinsky founded the nationalist youth movement Brit Trumpeldor (Betar) in his name.

Weizmann, Chaim (1874–1952)
Born and raised in the Pale of Settlement, Chaim Weizmann initially pursued an academic career as a chemist, which led him to work at Manchester University from 1904. By then he had also become leader of

a Zionist opposition group from where he first attempted to combine the theoretical and practical elements of Zionism he had encountered at congress and during his visits to Zionists across Russia. Introduced, early in the First World War, to members of the British establishment such as David Lloyd George and C.P. Scott, Weizmann again combined his activities as a research scientist and Zionist leader with remarkable effect. He solved the acetone supply problem for the munitions minister (then Winston Churchill) and, despite his opposition to the official Zionist policy of neutrality, nurtured his political relationships to the extent that he advised on the wording of the Balfour Declaration and suggested that it be addressed to Lord Rothschild. In obtaining the support of the British government in this matter his influence was seen to have outweighed that of the traditional Anglo-Jewish establishment as represented by Lucien Wolf. In addition, despite his disapproval of Jabotinsky's methods, Weizmann befriended and supported him in his endeavours to raise a Jewish Legion, something he himself tried to do early in the Second World War. Chaim Weizmann was at the forefront of Zionist politics throughout the inter-war period and his pragmatism and diplomacy were characterised by moderation and realism. Whilst this caused him to lose the leadership of the Zionist Congress for four years in the early 1930s, and again in late 1946, his outstanding work on behalf of the Jewish people was recognised when he was invited to become the first president of Israel, a post he held from 1948 until his death in 1952.

Wolf, Lucien (1857–1930)

By profession a historian and journalist, being the founder and president of the Jewish Historical Society of England and the editor of the *Jewish World*, Lucien Wolf also acted as secretary of the Conjoint Committee Foreign Branch. This influential committee, often consulted by the government, included representatives of the Board of Deputies of British Jews and the Anglo-Jewish Association. As a leading anti-Zionist he was central to the Jewish opposition to the Jewish Legion idea and the Balfour Declaration. Although defeated on both issues, it remains the case that both fell short of the expectations of their advocates and this was due in no small part to the work of Wolf, who went on to assist in the drafting of the Minorities Treaties at the peace conference of 1919.

1
Introduction: a Matter of Record

In early 1986 I was spending my lunchtimes in the archives of the Royal Regiment of Fusiliers in the Tower of London, helping to assist a professional archivist, Frances Devereaux, who was cataloguing records on behalf of Lt.-Col. George Pettifar. During one session a number of handwritten ledgers were discovered which were nominal rolls for three battalions raised towards the end of the First World War. Amongst the names those of Privates Ben-Gurion and Ben-Zvi stood out from the page, and the great majority of the remainder were clearly of Jewish origin. Lt.-Col. Pettifar confirmed that the regiment did indeed have three Jewish battalions, raised for service in Palestine, and he mentioned their existence in *The Fusilier* magazine.[1] Thus began an extended period of research leading to this work, which is intended as a contribution to military, political and social (as well as Jewish) history.

The First World War provided an opportunity for a distinct form of Jewish military service, which found its outlet in the British Army. General Allenby's forces in the final campaign in Palestine and Syria during the late summer of 1918 included two battalions of, in the overwhelming majority, Jewish soldiers serving in the British Army as the 38th and 39th Battalions, Royal Fusiliers. The 40th Battalion arrived in Egypt from the United Kingdom at the end of August, and the three sister battalions were known unofficially as the Jewish Legion.

The Legion's formation represented the culmination of various efforts, which had begun soon after the war's commencement, to create a Jewish military force quite distinct from the military units in which Jews served alongside their fellow countrymen. Service in Palestine gave it a specific purpose, as well as furthering the objectives of the Egyptian Expeditionary Force (EEF) of which it formed part.

The existence of a Jewish Legion in the British Army raises some fundamental questions regarding its composition, organisation and purpose. For instance, without a Jewish nation state to defend where had the idea for such a force come from? How was it possible that this Jewish force, serving in the army of a world power, eventually came officially to be regarded as the 'father' of the modern Israeli Army?[2] Is it true that the essence of this matter lay in the brute fact of the Jewish Diaspora and the lack of a national state with which to identify? Did the creation of the Legion signal the increasing association of militant Zionism with the project for an armed sovereign state, capable of defending itself, and by extension, offering a measure of protection from anti-Semitism?

In addition to these questions, the service and performance of Jewish formations in the British Army require examination and analysis, which will establish their military efficiency and value, consider their relations with other troops and comment upon the treatment they received from the military and political establishments. The existence and performance of the Legion will also be seen in relation to British policy, from the point of view of both strategy and the lived experience of the Jewish 'legionnaires'.

The importance of this study lies in the fact that no such fundamental examination of the Legion has yet been attempted, and that it incorporates hitherto unused primary sources, such as public records (military and political) and veterans' testimonials. The result provides a new perspective on Anglo-Jewish relations in the early twentieth century, and contributes to the analysis of the attitudes and values that characterised anti-Semitism and philo-Semitism in Britain.

Jewish soldiers were to be found in all the participating armies during the Great War but only in Britain were specifically Jewish units raised. The crucial factor in the origin of Jewish forces was the increasing attraction of Zionism for many Eastern European Jews, who sought security and freedom in Palestine after the Tsarist regime had imposed civil restrictions throughout the Pale of Settlement and condoned the pogroms of the 1880s and 90s. It has been argued that this policy of Zionist emigration was particularly favoured by working-class Jews, who were less likely than their middle-class contemporaries to have achieved a high degree of assimilation.[3] Thus, even before Turkey's entry into the war in November 1914 made conflict in Palestine likely, some Zionists realised that serving the victorious side might lead to a reward in the way of territorial gain and to some form of independence. This could be quickly achieved by the gift of the victors or through the participation of Zionists in the peace process that would decide the shape of the post-war world. Moreover, the Zionists were aware that the formation of a Jewish fighting body could provide a nucleus for a self-protection force for the increasing number of Jewish settlers in Palestine.

To be weighed against these benefits, however, the supporters of a Jewish military force had to consider the fears of many Zionists, including those who had already settled in Palestine through the unofficial purchase of land. These fears included the possibility of retribution against the settlers by the Turks, should the Jewish soldiers fight on the side of the Triple Entente or, in the event of them doing so, ending the war on the defeated side. Furthermore, service alongside the forces of the entente would place the Jews who had fled from the Tsarist pogroms on the same side as their erstwhile tormentors. On the other hand, co-operation with the Turks meant collaboration with the imperial occupiers of Palestine. In either case, post-war independence could not be guaranteed, nor could Palestinian Arab and Christian acquiescence in mass Jewish settlement in the wake of Allied victory. Taking these factors into account, the executive of the Zionist Council, which had moved from Berlin to Copenhagen on the outbreak of war, decided in December 1914 to adopt a policy of strict neutrality. The Zionists who were to support the idea of a Legion therefore found themselves at odds with their international leadership, and this added to the difficulties they faced.

The Jewish Legion idea was first aired in Britain in the autumn of 1914, amongst a small group of intellectual Russian Jews who were active in the Zionist movement, having attended international Zionist Congresses as delegates from the Pale, and subsequently settled in Britain.[4] They included Chaim Weizmann, an academic scientist at Manchester University and later the first president of Israel, and Asher Ginsberg, better known by his pen-name of Ahad Ha'am – literally 'one of the people'. Ahad Ha'am was a writer and activist, who came to London in 1907 as a director of a Russian tea company. He believed that achieving Zion required more than the physical occupation of the land; it would involve spiritual and cultural emancipation to ensure its viability. This philosophy complemented Weizmann's political skills and his pragmatic ability to distinguish the possible from the impossible, without losing sight of moral principle.

Both in his autobiography[5] and in correspondence with Ahad Ha'am,[6] Weizmann referred to his contact in early September 1914 with Pinhas Rutenberg, who arrived without invitation at Weizmann's house in Manchester. A Russian Jew, he had come from Italy, where he had fled after engaging in revolutionary activity in Russia. He told Weizmann of his dream of a Jewish army to fight on the Allied side, which would secure a seat at the peace conference and so obtain a Jewish state in Palestine. On 29 September, Weizmann again met Rutenberg at Ahad Ha'am's London home, but it would appear Rutenberg was given no further encouragement to promote his ideas in Britain. This was because the Zionist movement was officially neutral, despite Weizmann's commitment to furthering Zionist interests within the Triple Entente. Additionally, Weizmann had formed a low opinion of Rutenberg and considered his views on the Jewish problem and on Palestine 'superficial'.[7] Rutenberg later visited New York to promote the Legion idea among the Russian Jewish community, and eventually returned to Russia. He became governor of Petrograd in Kerensky's provisional government, then, following the Bolshevik revolution, found his way to Palestine where he became responsible for developing the hydro-electricity system.[8]

Despite his failure to raise a Jewish Legion, Rutenberg undoubtedly saw the war as an opportunity to emancipate Russian Jews through settlement in their own state in Palestine, and he has a rightful claim to be one of the earliest to express these ideas. In a letter to Viscount Allenby, dated 27 April 1933, Rutenberg wrote:

> I am proud to state now the fact, known to few, that I am the author of the idea of the Jewish Battalions to fight with the allies in the Great War. To redeem with Jewish blood Jewish Palestine. That was in August 1914 ... It was the privilege of Jabotinsky to make the dream a reality.[9]

Rutenberg had concluded that a direct approach to the British Government, without the assistance of influential Zionists living in Britain, was unlikely to gain an official hearing.

To contextualise the Legion, something should be said about the origins of Zionism. Put simply, it emerged as an organised political ideal in the late nineteenth century, as a direct result of the Russian pogroms, when the need for a safe haven for displaced Jews became tragically evident. This goal was investigated and supported by the Anglo-Jewish elite. In *The Origins of Zionism*, David Vital describes the development of Zionism up to the conclusion of the first Zionist Congress held in Basle in 1897, and makes a very important point that explains the appeal of Zionism to Jews from diverse traditions and personal backgrounds:

It [the first Congress] established a precedent – and the principle – of unity, bringing together virtually all the diverse strains of which the movement was composed: romanticists and pragmatists, orthodox and secularists, socialists and bourgeois, easterners and westerners, men whose minds and language were barely influenced by the non-Jewish world and those who were largely products of it ...[10]

Eugene Black agrees with Vital's assertions by acknowledging how Zionism transcended the religious and social divides between the Jewish sub-communities. But in concentrating on its impact on the Anglo-Jewish establishment, Black argues that Zionism challenged the assumptions on which Anglo-Jewish institutions had been constructed and the goals Anglo-Jewry defined and pursued. He concludes:

Zionism, however, did succeed in dividing Anglo-Jewry itself, appealing, for various reasons, to limited numbers among the elite. Zionism more quickly attracted restive spirits within the Jewish middle classes. No more effective club was available with which professionals could smite their pretentious betters.[11]

Thus Zionism is presented as both a force for unity and a force for division, dependent upon the background and social standing of the Jewish community concerned. Anglo-Jewish assumptions, based upon the desirability of assimilation, are indicative of the aspirations of a longer established community that had achieved a measure of emancipation and security within its host society. Recently arrived immigrants from the Pale of Settlement, however, would not have felt as secure and, in a general sense, can have been expected to be more attracted to Zionism than their settled co-religionists. The complicating factor in addressing Zionism in the period leading up to the First World War is that the positions of the two Jewish communities were not mutually exclusive. Stuart Cohen has demonstrated that not all immigrant Jews were devoted Zionists, neither were all members of Anglo-Jewry opposed to Zion. A lack of political activity among the mass of immigrants meant that they were not the driving force behind the transfer of power from the Anglo-Jewish establishment to the Zionist leadership. This transfer involved the infiltration and taking over of the institutions that had been set up by Anglo-Jewry, with Cohen asserting that this was a communal and not a political revolution.[12]

Ben Halpern describes a different situation in the United States, where relations between the settled and emancipated Jewish community and the new immigrants were also developed to the point where the Zionists became the dominant part. Halpern outlines the notions of nationalism and religion which were of greater pertinence to the immigrant community there as a whole, and provides an explanation for the evolvement of 'a thoroughly American version of Zionism'.[13]

The types of support for Zionism were, in fact, similar in Britain and the USA. From all traditions and backgrounds these ranged from the provision of philanthropic support for the Jews settled in the Yishuv – in Palestine – itself, through to the preparation of what could almost be termed a Jewish national government in exile.[14] These two extremes recognised the vulnerability of the Jewish settlers and were aware of the Ottoman treatment of other minorities, especially the persecution of the Armenians. The protection and sustenance of the Yishuv was dependent upon financial support from the Diaspora, but those Zionists who favoured establishing a nation state used the circumstances of the war to assert their communal leadership. Thus, the greatest single achievement of the Zionists came about with the securing of the Balfour Declaration from the British government in November 1917. The declaration was issued after lengthy negotiations between leading Zionists such as Chaim Weizmann, and sympathetic members of Lloyd George's administration. Original drafts were altered under pressure from influential assimilationists Jews, like Edwin Montagu, and the resulting declaration contained ambiguities that would lead to differing interpretations and trouble throughout the post-war mandatory period in Palestine. Perhaps the most obvious example of this is the change from 'Palestine should be constituted as the national home of the Jewish people', to 'the establishment in Palestine of a home for the Jewish people'. The declaration itself was put in the form of a letter addressed to Lord Rothschild by the foreign secretary, Arthur Balfour and dated 2 November 1917:

> Dear Lord Rothschild,
> I have much pleasure in conveying to you, on behalf of His Majesty's Government, the following declaration of sympathy with Jewish Zionist aspirations which has been submitted to, and approved by, the Cabinet.
> 'His Majesty's Government view with favour the establishment in Palestine of a national home for the Jewish people, and will use their best endeavours to facilitate the achievement of this object, it

being clearly understood that nothing shall be done which may prejudice the civil and religious rights of existing non-Jewish communities in Palestine, or the rights and political status enjoyed by Jews in any other country.' I should be grateful if you would bring this declaration to the knowledge of the Zionist Federation.
Yours sincerely,
Arthur James Balfour.[15]

This event cemented the pre-eminence of the Zionist movement in the eyes of the Allied powers and had the effect of uniting many of its own factions. The active diplomacy of Chaim Weizmann worked on fertile ground in Britain where, as will be seen, the importance of Jewish power and influence was recognised.[16]

The Balfour Declaration was, in effect, the British endorsement of a Jewish national home, and its publication must be viewed in the light of Britain's strategic objectives and war-time international relations in the Middle East. These are central to Isaiah Friedman's *The Question of Palestine*, which is a thorough treatment of the advent of the Balfour Declaration and provides an updated analysis of Leonard Stein's seminal work.[17] Friedman argues that the Balfour Declaration resulted from the deliberate pursuit of a foreign policy designed to support Zionism within an overall framework of the protection of British interests and aims in the Middle East. These interests and aims, and the measures taken to safeguard them, predated the war and had developed largely as the result of the need to control imperial trade routes, particularly to India, and to secure the supply of oil from the Arabian Gulf. (The Royal Navy was converting to oil burning at this time.) The region had also become part of the pre-war division of spheres of influence between the great powers, which encouraged the emergence of 'Young Turk' nationalism and led to a deterioration of Anglo-Turkish relations.

Friedman notes that, after the March revolution in 1917, British interests focused on the immediate, strategic necessities of keeping Russia in the conflict, and dismembering the Ottoman Empire through the military defeat of Turkey. This does not mean that Friedman discounts what might be termed the religious or sentimental sympathy for Zionism amongst British gentiles. The roots of Protestant support for the return of the Jews to Palestine extended back to the sixteenth century; it was the reluctance of the Jews themselves, until the Russian pogroms of the early 1880s, which prevented such a return from taking place.[18] However, Friedman emphasises the preponderance of political over religious and idealistic factors. As he puts it, when discussing the desire to attract the support of world Jewry for Allied war aims:

> It was however not until World War One that Zionism finally triumphed ... It was the competition among the warring powers to win the sympathy of world Jewry, those in the United States in particular, that put Zionism on the map.[19]

Rashid Ismail Khalidi provides another invaluable analysis of war-time international relations in the Middle East by examining the strategic issues from an Arab perspective. He describes how Palestine had become strategically vital to the protection of British-occupied Egypt and the Suez Canal, following the Aqaba crisis of 1906 and the threat posed by railway construction across the region. In order to prepare the defence of the canal's eastern bank and of Sinai and the approaches to Palestine, Kitchener arranged for a clandestine survey to be undertaken by officers who were later to play an important role in the Arab Bureau during the war, including Colonel Newcombe and T.E. Lawrence. One concern of the British staff was that projected railway links between Germany, Turkey and the Arabian Gulf would have outflanked the Canal and Egypt from the East. According to Khalidi this threat was met in part by negotiation and, in a very detailed examination of the Anglo-French railway agreements relating to Syria of 1909–10, he establishes that these agreements pre-empted post-war boundaries. In a passage that reinforces Friedman's view, Rashid Khalidi argues that British support for Zionism succeeded in forming a mandated Palestine that split the Arabs territorially and weakened the influence of Syria upon Egypt. British rulers of Egypt, particularly Lord Kitchener, had identified and feared the unifying nature of Syrian influence in the decade before 1914. In the conclusion to his monograph, Khalidi depicts the position of Arab peoples as pawns in an international strategic struggle:

> However, all Arab nationalists in 1914 like the people of Palestine, faced the same dilemma: their understandable inclination to appeal to another Power for assistance against the Turks was necessarily tempered by the knowledge that their benefactor would be sure to demand something in return.[20]

Zionists were also aware that western support came at a price.

British support for the Jews, justified by the strategic considerations discussed above, may have been brought about by misconceptions as

Introduction: a Matter of Record 9

to the extent of the power and influence of Jewish communities in the west. Mark Levene, in an article written in 1992, has argued that these misconceptions were created by anti-Semitism, citing the Foreign Office's concerns about access to American finance, and the campaign of *The Times* accusing Jewish financiers of attempting to keep Britain out of the war, to the benefit of Germany.[21] After debunking the misconceptions, Levene argues that the Balfour Declaration was motivated by a desire, itself driven by anti-Semitism and fear of defeat, to secure Jewish support to the prosecution of the war. Thus he is able to offer a consistent explanation as to why the western Allies strove to reverse Jewry's perceived support for Germany and later, why they sought to reduce the threat to the alliance with Russia posed by the activities of the Bolsheviks, who were also perceived to be part of yet another Jewish conspiracy.[22] Levene concludes that the prejudiced perceptions about the Jews, which were generally held by the ruling class in Britain, provide a more plausible reason for the Balfour Declaration than a rational, strategic assessment. He does, however, recognise that David Lloyd George was a major exception to this rule, and this book will argue that without Lloyd George there would have been no Balfour Declaration or Jewish Legion: his motivation coming from personal beliefs, sympathies and an overwhelming desire to achieve strategic success.

Over the last twenty years research into Anglo-Jewish history has been revitalised after years of accepting a relatively uncritical assimilationist viewpoint. David Cesarani remarked, in 1990, on the lack of published research into the history of Anglo-Jewry and the apologetic nature of the previously received history exemplified by the work of Cecil Roth.[23] In the introduction to a collection of essays, Cesarani describes how the authors highlight the pervasiveness of anti-Semitism in Britain and the restrictive effect it had on the behaviour and development of the Jewish community. The pressure to assimilate is also discussed and Cesarani argues that the success of the Zionists belittled the standing of the Diaspora with similar, 'apologetic' consequences, which again had the effect of inhibiting historical debate until the modern revisionists published their research.[24]

Peter Stansky has delineated several points to illustrate the historical dilemmas which modern research has sought to address. These include the question of it being possible to be Jewish and English, and the existence of an implicit social contract by which Jews agreed to conduct themselves within the norms of the host society, in return for emancipation.[25] The price of toleration seems to have been a tacit agreement on the part of Jews to 'Anglicise' themselves. This 'contractarian' account makes the existence of an apologetic approach more understandable. Furthermore, it aids appreciation of the fact that, some decades after having gained emancipation, Anglo-Jewry felt that their position within British society was threatened by the mass immigration of Jews from Eastern Europe in the 1880s. Indeed, it was almost as if their own history had come to an end with emancipation, a point well made by David Katz in an essay written in 1991.[26] That this denial was effective, in a cultural sense, has been acknowledged by Tony Kushner, who argues convincingly that heritage in Britain is seen as something relating to and grown out of the host culture only, and it is one of the benefits of the new history that the cultural price Jews had to pay for making a contribution to British society is now acknowledged.[27]

The existence and extent of anti-Semitism in Britain is a major concern of this book. The older Anglo-Jewish historiography rather colluded with the notion that British anti-Semitism was relatively innocuous because it lacked the visceral hatred of, say, Edouard Drumont on the French right or the genocidal ambition of German National Socialism. More recent scholarship rejects these comforting and slipshod comparisons, and attempts to penetrate the fog of national self-congratulation that has occluded British attitudes to Jews. Todd Endelman has observed that the new history is bleaker in that it recognises that anti-Semitism was more blatant and damaging than previously accepted; Cesarani and Kushner, for example, have shown that it existed as part of the cultural and social mainstream.[28] Similarly, Colin Holmes, in his ground-breaking account written in 1979, argued that anti-Semitism was a continuing and hostile tradition in British society. Whilst acknowledging the mildness of anti-Semitism in Britain, when compared to Russia and Germany, and the absence of 'official governmental anti-Semitism', he established the presence of social discrimination across political boundaries and within all socio-economic classes.[29]

Holmes also noted the existence of literary anti-Semitism, a phenomenon studied by Bryan Cheyette who, by demonstrating how literary representations of Jews met the authors' particular concerns with race and politics, explains why there are contradictions among the various stereotypes that were constructed in this way. Cheyette argues that these contradictions created a 'Semitic discourse' based on the assumption that 'good' Jewish traits were acceptable whereas 'bad' traits were not. Hence Jews could be seen as capitalist financiers on the one hand and communist agitators on the other or, in Cheyette's own words 'as both within *and* without; a stranger *and* familiar; an object of esteem *and* odium; a progressive universalist *and* a racial particularist'.[30] The exposure of this 'Semitic discourse' is extremely valuable in the analysis of Anglo-Jewish history, as it allows us to see how both anti-Semitic *and* philo-Semitic attitudes drew upon stereotypes of Jewish identity and power.

By avoiding a stereotypical approach it is possible to appreciate the diversity of the Jewish communities that existed in Britain before the war, and the conflicts that arose within and between them. An excellent survey and analysis of this diversity and the nature of intra-communal differences can be found within David Feldman's work.[31] Feldman used three themes in his history: the relation of Jews to the nation and its institutions; the changing ways in which Jews tried to establish a collective identity; and the economic, social and political history of Jewish immigrants, with emphasis on the working class.

There can be little doubt that the progress made by the current generation of Anglo-Jewish historians has succeeded in opening up the debate over anti-Semitism (and anti-alienism), and allowed for an analysis that has not been overshadowed by the Holocaust. This assessment is supported by the latest critical treatment of pre-1914 anti-Semitism, provided in an article by Thomas Weber. After summarising modern research, Weber addresses the question of the extent of early twentieth-century anti-Semitism, noting that the Holocaust effect had been used to burnish the image of British tolerance. In a study of Jewish admissions to Oxford and Heidelberg universities, Weber casts doubt over the prevalent picture of Oxford as tolerant and assimilationists: Heidelberg was more accessible to Jews, though it combined greater opportunities for Jewish scholars with more violent expressions of anti-Semitism. Weber also provides evidence that overt prejudice in Germany did not prevent Jewish academic attainment in Germany, whereas in Britain it was difficult for Jewish academics to progress in their careers. The pervasive anti-Semitism in British academia, as identified by Weber, clearly supports the views of Cesarani, and Kushner but he also notes the recent criticism of the revisionist arguments, expressed most notably by William Rubinstein.[32]

Rubinstein does not deny a tradition of anti-Semitism, and argues that it acquired a 'class based' form in left-wing politics and a racially charged form on the right. But he insists that there was a continuous history of admiration and support for Jews in diverse Gentile circles, going back to the campaign to admit Jews to parliament and remove other civil disabilities. Rubinstein is correct to point to a philo-Semitic strain in British culture, deriving from Protestant fundamentalism and classical liberalism, and this book adds significantly to his account by documenting how Gentile admiration and support for Jews found a war-time focus in the Jewish Legion. Nevertheless, there are problems with Rubinstein's approach. By concentrating on what he sees as the 'success story' of Anglo-Jewry, Rubinstein uncritically accepts the assimilationists' argument, and provides trivialising explanations for hostility towards Jews that do not address the revisionists' case for pervasive anti-Semitism in British society. For example, he contends against ample evidence that writers such as Goldwin Smith, J.A. Hobson and G.K. Chesterton could not have been anti–Semitic, because this would have contradicted their belief in liberalism. He then goes on to provide individual analyses, involving their personal lives and experiences, to explain the paradox between their beliefs and their writing.[33]

Rubinstein's analysis includes the question of the experience of Jews in Britain during the First World War and again he finds himself in disagreement with David Cesarani. The conclusion Rubinstein reaches from Jewish participation in the war is that it led to greater acculturation of Jews in British society, whereas Cesarani considers that wartime tensions arising out of the conscription of 'aliens' resulted in an increase in anti-Semitic behaviour and eroded the position of Jews in British society.[34] This difference in historical interpretation turns on the issue of military service as applied to the Russian Jews in the East End of London and other, smaller centres in the north of Britain. Rubinstein is dismissive of the Russian Jews' failure to volunteer on the same basis as Anglo-Jewry, and condones the hatred this aroused as 'a perfectly natural widespread hostility and contempt, from Gentile and Jew alike'.[35] When it comes to the actual military experience of the Jews, Rubinstein concentrates on the significant contribution of Anglo-Jewry, and sees the formation of the Russian Jewish regiment (Jewish Legion) as a means of assimilation.[36]

This book seeks to contribute to the historians' debate over the presence of Jews in British society through a study and analysis of the experience of the officers and men of the Jewish Legion. This will involve an examination of prejudice against Russian Jewish immigrants, their willingness or otherwise to serve in the British Army and the army's attitude towards them. By such means it should also be possible to gauge the extent and effect of pre-war anti-Semitism, and describe the ways in which the events of the war affected Jewry in terms of identity and nationalism. However, this research has not disclosed a picture of unmitigated anti-Semitism: it has also revealed what the Rubinsteins call 'admiration and support' for Jews in the highest political circles and even within the army officer corps.[37]

The sources used in this work include four accounts by leading participants who covered the Legion's history in some detail. These are: Lt.-Col. J.H. Patterson's *With the Zionists in Gallipoli* (1918)[38] and *With the Judeans in the Palestine Campaign* (1922),[39] Vladimir Jabotinsky's *The Story of the Jewish Legion* (1945)[40] and Elias Gilner's *War and Hope: a History of the Jewish Legion* (1969).[41] Patterson was the Legion's first commander, Jabotinsky its effective founder, and Gilner a Russian-American who served in the Legion. These have proved invaluable but have deficiencies I have sought to correct. It should also be noted that, apart from these accounts, no detailed military history exists covering Jewish unit participation in Gallipoli and Palestine, and in all of the appropriate books and articles cited in the bibliography, the Jewish units receive only a passing mention at most; an omission this research attempts to address. Jabotinsky's book was published five years after his death, and reflected its author's single-minded determination in the pursuit of his dream – a Jewish Legion. It would be unfair to criticise this memoir for partisanship because it was written solely from one point of view. From his own words, he appears an uncompromising zealot. His forthright and abrupt dismissal of any opposition, and failure to listen to the arguments of those that opposed him, help to explain the difficulties he experienced in dealing with Allied diplomats. It is easy to appreciate from his writing how his fervour could have been – and was – interpreted as fanaticism, in fascinating contrast with the conduct and style of his friend and colleague Chaim Weizmann.

Jabotinsky's influence on Lt.-Col. Patterson is clearly discernible through the latter's portrayal of the events and circumstances surrounding his own participation with the Zion Mule Corps and the Legion. Although a Gentile, Patterson shared Jabotinsky's militant Zionism, and dismissed the alternative views of Zionists who favoured neutrality, whilst admitting his limited knowledge of the Zionist debate. His accounts convey his forthright opinions about still recent controversies. He bitterly criticised the General Staff of the EEF in *With the Judeans*, for example, although he used initials to disguise the identity of some senior military and political figures, including certain names which were not released in public records until fifty or seventy-five years later. In some cases, I have been able to identify the individuals involved and describe some controversial events more fully. Gilner's work is a more professional and comprehensive account of the

14 The Jewish Legion and the First World War

Legion and its precursor, the Zion Mule Corps. He relied heavily on Jabotinsky, Patterson and the diaries of Captain Joseph Trumpeldor, a key figure in the Mule Corps and the founding of the Legion. Despite its scholarly appearance, Gilner's work is understandably partisan and written before many of the official papers were released. None of these earlier histories conveyed the experience of the Legion within the wider context of Britain's war policies. Mention must also be made of Harold Pollins's article published in 1995, in which he described the sources consulted in trying to quantify the number of Jewish war dead who served in the British Army between 1914 and 1918.[42] By comparing synagogue records with official lists of the war dead and the British Jewry Book of Honour, Pollins was able to point out the difficulties of interpretation and validation of these sources, particularly as far as declaration of religion and change of name is concerned. This small but valuable work has been used to assist in the interpretation of other corroborative sources, such as war diaries and unit histories, which form a central part of this book.

I have also made use of veterans' personal testimonies, made available through the generous co-operation of the Jewish Legion's own museum, 'Beit Hagudim', in Avichail, Israel. The museum was founded by veterans on a site where homes had been built for them; finance was raised from surviving members who lived mainly in the USA, Canada, Great Britain and Israel. The founding of the museum and the remembrance of the Legion's brief active existence is evidence of the depth of feeling that it aroused amongst the participants. The Zionist Organisation of America honoured those who returned to the USA after the war, and a network of veteran's associations was established. They also recognised the participation of the veterans from Britain, as shown in the copy of the certificate issued to Captain Philip Jacobs in 1968 (Figure 1.1). In Britain, a commemorative dinner was held to mark the 50th anniversary of the Legion on 25 November 1967, the same year Gilner's history was published and Israel's defence ministry took over Beit Hagudim. Such commemoration served to reinforce, especially as far as American veterans were concerned, the links between the Legion, the creation of a Jewish army and the founding of the state of Israel. To commemorate in this fashion is to mythologise in the sense of creating a stock of public memories that overlay, conventionalise and distort the recollection of personal experience.

The first tranche of testimonies were collected by the museum between 1957 and 1961, being compiled either by veterans or their families, and additional testimonies have since been provided by family members. The number of usable records received from the museum amounted to 804, of which 637 were written in English, and it is these that have been used in this research. Of these records sixteen relate to the Zion Mule Corps (including the testimonies of five who also served in the Legion), 236 to the 38th Battalion, 324 to the 39th Battalion and sixty-one to the 40th. The number attributable to the three Legion battalions, 626, represents about 7 per cent of the 10,000 or so who enlisted, according to War Office records, Jabotinsky and Gilner.[43]

The testimonies mostly record the age, date of enlistment, place of origin, service and later life of each individual soldier; although in some instances only sparse details have been given. Others have commented at length on particular incidents at which they were present, thus providing indicators for further research and investigation. Noteworthy, too, is the inclusion of genealogical data and the progress of successive generations, which provide a small but interesting insight into the development of the Jewish population of the Diaspora and Palestine, in the early years of the twentieth century.

It is appropriate at this juncture to comment upon the use and validity of personal testimony as primary source material. Any critical interpretation of such evidence must take into account the context in which it was written, and appreciate the personal perspective involved in the description of events and incidents that may not be supported by corroborating evidence. In other words, the analytical treatment of any personal diary or memoir must be sensitive to the point of view of its creator. In any event the biographical information contained in these particular records does provide a valid (albeit brief) record of the age, origins and service of many of the soldiers concerned. Where incidents are remarked upon, care has been taken to check, where possible, dates against public documents (although these are limited), official diaries, nominal rolls – the originals of which are retained at the Regimental Headquarters – and the sources mentioned earlier. Naturally, it is never possible to guarantee fully the accuracy of narrative compiled from these sources, but the greater the range and weight of evidence, then the greater the likelihood of producing a full and objective history.

In this context, it is appropriate to add a further note of caution. Although fortunate in gaining access to the veterans' testimonials I have not over-exploited their content, and they constitute only a small part of the primary material on which this book is based. Care has also been taken not to generalise from narrow and sometimes contradictory evidence. For example, the Imperial War Museum has an

Figure 1.1 ZOA citation, Capt. Philip Jacobs, 1968

audio recording of Private J. Plotzker's reminiscences in which he asserted that anti-Semitism was worse in the war-time army than in the Merchant Navy, in which he previously served. This contrasts with the experience of another former merchant seaman, Adler Bandall, who changed his name from Cohen because life for Jews in the Merchant Navy was 'rough in those days'.[44]

Another primary source that has been consulted is the unpublished memoir of Major Henry Myer, a professional, middle-class Anglo-Jewish officer, who writes candidly about his attitude towards working-class Russian Jewish immigrants.[45] Mark Levene has published a critique of Myer's manuscript, contrasting his 'negative' assessment of the immigrants with his respect for the volunteers from the USA and Palestine. Myer's contact with Zionist activists also seems to have made him more aware of anti-Semitism at home.[46]

As far as public records are concerned, aside from pertinent Cabinet, Home Office and Foreign Office papers, a voluminous general series of War Office files that no previous researcher has exploited have been used to update earlier accounts. Though incomplete, these files allow for a new and fuller analysis of the creation of the Legion, and provide an insight into relations between the government, Anglo-Jewry and the Zionist supporters of the Legion.[47]

The historiography of the First World War has evolved away from the preoccupation with military strategy in the official histories and the pioneer works of Cyril Falls, Basil Liddell Hart and John Terraine towards greater emphasis upon the personal experience of the common soldier, as exemplified by such historians as Lyn Macdonald, John Keegan and Martin Middlebrook.[48] Peter Simkins, in commenting on this trend, classified the use of personal records to convey the experience of the war as 'battle studies' and called for a greater convergence of the sub-disciplines of military and social history, which implied that their exclusivity precluded a comprehensive understanding of the war.[49] It should be noted, however, that before Simkins wrote this, Trevor Wilson's *The Myriad Faces of War: Britain and the Great War, 1914–18* (1985) had brilliantly synthesised personal experience and grand strategy. Simkins' own study of the raising of the New Armies in 1914–16 was a model of the 'new' social history of the armed forces.[50] Modern military history tries to overcome scholarly parochialism by both analysing strategy and recreating the lived experience of war, as in Antony Beevor's studies of Stalingrad and Berlin.[51]

This work aims to contribute to a genre of historical studies known as 'war and society', and is thus indebted to Arthur Marwick who has argued for a broader understanding of the relationship between total war and social change.[52] According to Marwick, participation in war has brought political and social gains, and it could be argued that the Jewish Legion represented an eminently successful example of that process. This study of the Jewish Legion seeks to combine historical sub-disciplines by placing the Jewish soldiers' experience in the broader context of military recruitment policy, Zionist politics, Anglo-Jewry and the origins of the Palestine mandate. It is also intended to be a valuable addition to the study of minorities in war-time, in which context a comparison is made with the experience of another minority group, the British West Indies Regiment.[53]

Finally, this book takes the form of an analytic narrative that explains why events followed a certain sequence and not another, and permits questions to be addressed in a chronological order. Chapter 2 deals with the Zion Mule Corps, the precursor to the Legion, and assesses its importance and relevance to the latter's founding. Questions regarding the conduct of the Dardanelles campaign and the military status of the foreign-born muleteers are also examined. Chapters 3 and 4 cover the military, political and social background to the founding of the Legion, providing analysis and explanation of the obstacles faced by Jabotinsky. These included the difficulties encountered by the alien immigrant community with both the host population and the Anglo-Jewish establishment. In addition, the influence of anti-Semitism and philo-Semitism upon the creation of the Legion is reviewed. Chapters 5 and 6 deal with the raising of the battalions in Britain, the United States and Palestine and address questions regarding the nature of recruitment and the reaction to events such as the Balfour Declaration, the Bolshevik Revolution and the impact of the withdrawal of Russia from the war. The active service of the Legion with the Egyptian Expeditionary Force, and the treatment it received from the high command of that force, form the substance of Chapters 7 and 8. These chapters contain an assessment of the experience of the legionnaires, including the extent of anti-Semitism, and answer questions regarding military capability and effectiveness, and the expectations of individual soldiers with regard to their future after the war.

Chapter 9 reviews the Legion's post-war employment and the events leading to its eventual disbandment. The presence of Jewish soldiers in Palestine created difficulties for the British military authority, and matters such as demobilisation, deployment and relations between the command and the Jewish units are addressed. Furthermore, the question of Jewish self-defence is explored, with reference to the association of the Legion with the development of an independent, underground force, and the construction of the myths and reality that have given this unique unit a significant place in the history of modern Israel.

This work concludes with Chapter 10, which attempts to answer the questions posed at the beginning, and describes the memory and legacy of the Legion.

2
The Zion Mule Corps

The origin of the Zion Mule Corps and its association with the founding of the Jewish Legion is an important and vital part of the history of Russian Jewish service in the British Army. In Chapter 1 mention was made of Pinhas Rutenberg and Vladimir Jabotinsky, who shared the idea of raising a Jewish force under the aegis of the western Allies. They were not alone. Russian Jewish exiles living in Palestine and Turkey were also considering Zionist participation in the war, but on the Ottoman side. Two of the leading activists, David Ben-Gurion and Isaac Ben-Zvi (the pair were known as the 'Benim'), both of whom were to play a crucial part in the formation of an independent Israel, then saw the future interests of Zion as being best served by assisting the Turks. They feared that the neutrality officially espoused by the Zionist movement could discredit and endanger the Jews who had settled in Palestine under a benign Ottoman regime.[1]

The 'Benim' were socialist writers, journalists and publishers who had practised what they preached. By working on the land in Palestine following the rise of the 'Young Turks' in 1908, they demonstrated their belief that some sort of Jewish self-government in Palestine was more likely to be acquired by living there rather than by pursuing the cause at a distance through slow and complex diplomatic means. This was in marked contrast to the appreciation formed by Ahad Ha'am following his visits to Palestine. He understood that local Arabs benefited from Jewish agricultural settlement, and that the Ottoman authorities were perfectly aware of the bribery and corruption of local Turkish officials that enabled the settlers to bypass some of the legal restrictions imposed upon them. Nevertheless, he concluded that the Turks would only permit a certain amount of Jewish settlement, and as soon as the threshold was crossed, and the Turks felt threatened, then vigorous action against the Jews was bound to follow.[2]

As part of their commitment to working for Zion from within the Ottoman Empire, the 'Benim' spent a couple of years before 1914 studying law at the university in Constantinople, where they discussed using their qualifications, knowledge and experience so that 'Maybe someday we can sit as representatives of the Jewish people in the Turkish Parliament.'[3]

After their return to Palestine and, following Turkey's entry into the war, the Benim volunteered for service in the Turkish Army. They proposed to the Turkish military commander in Jerusalem that Jews be allowed to form a fighting force to assist in the defence of Palestine, presumably in the event of an Allied attack from Egypt. Not surprisingly, this proposal was turned down, although a small number of Jewish volunteers (forty according to one source)[4] were permitted to train as a militia, before the authorities closed it down.

The extent of Ben Gurion's and Ben Zvi's misjudgement regarding Turkey's attitude towards the future of Jewish settlers in Palestine was soon made apparent, however, for in December 1914 the Ottoman authorities began arresting Jews, and the Benim found themselves in prison in Jerusalem before being deported to Alexandria, in British-controlled Egypt. Here they were arrested as enemy aliens by the British authorities, although this was strictly not the case, as they did not possess Turkish citizenship. Eventually they obtained, like many similar exiles, travel papers that enabled them to proceed to the United States, finally arriving in New York in May 1915.

During their time in Alexandria, Ben-Gurion and Ben-Zvi witnessed the efforts of Vladimir Jabotinsky and Joseph Trumpeldor to raise a Jewish military unit from among local and exiled Jewish refugees for service with the British Army. Trumpeldor, whom they had first met in Constantinople during his journey back to Palestine from the Zionist congress in Vienna, had been a Russian army hero during the Russo-Japanese war, when he lost an arm at Port Arthur. Following a year as a prisoner of war in Japan, where he organised Zionist classes and a 'Jewish Prisoners' Organisation', Trumpeldor and his comrades were returned to Russia. In recognition of his military services he was both decorated for gallantry and commissioned into the Army Reserve; it is probable that he was the only Jewish officer in the Tsarist army. By December 1914 Trumpeldor was living in Alexandria on a Russian military pension.[5]

Vladimir Jabotinsky was a roving journalist employed by the *Russian Monitor* whose profession gave him an opportunity for extensive travel, an opportunity denied the vast majority of Russian Jews. In 1909 he had been the editor of a number of Zionist journals in Constantinople, and formed an opinion of the Turkish authorities that was in stark contrast to the original appreciation of the Benim. In short, he believed that the breakup of the Ottoman Empire was a prerequisite for the establishment of a Jewish state in Palestine, a development that also required the co-operation of the (victorious) western powers.

When Turkey entered the war, Jabotinsky, who was then in France, immediately reckoned that Turkey would be defeated, and calculated that a Jewish force raised to fight on the side of the western Allies against the Turks could play a vital role in achieving Zionist objectives. This puts Jabotinsky about two months behind Rutenberg in thought, but not in deed. He obtained permission from his editor to tour the Muslim countries of North Africa to report on the effect of the extension of hostilities. *En route* to Morocco he visited Dr Max Nordau, one of Zionism's elder statesmen, then living in exile in Madrid. In conversation Jabotinsky clearly expressed his anti-Turkish views, even to the extent of dismissing the widely held Jewish view of Turks as Semitic cousins. Such sympathy, which was implicit in the pro-Turkish stance of the Benim, played no part in the Zionist thinking of Vladimir Jabotinsky:

> 'Doctor,' I said, 'we cannot let idiots (Jews regarding Turks as their cousins) dictate our policy. Not only are the Turks no cousins of ours; even with the real Ishmael [i.e. Arabs] we have nothing in common. We belong to Europe, thank God; for two thousand years we helped to build European civilisation. And here comes another quotation from one of your speeches: "We are going to Palestine to extend the moral boundaries of Europe as far as the Euphrates. Our worst enemy in this undertaking is the Turk. Now that the hour of his downfall has struck, we cannot possibly stand by and do nothing, can we?"'[6]

Jabotinsky then travelled to Alexandria where, in December 1914, he saw the plight of the Jewish refugees from Turkey. The British authorities set up two refugee camps at Gabbari and Mafruza, in close proximity, which contained an estimated 1,200 inmates, of whom three-quarters were Russian Ashekenazim, and the remainder Sephardim of local and Palestinian origin.[7]

Jabotinsky devoted his time to relief work in the camps, and to establishing, with others, a Hebrew community. For example, he enlisted the assistance of Edgar Suares, a banker and local Sephardi leader, in prevailing upon the British authorities not to co-operate with the Russian consul, Count Petrov, who was obliged by his government to secure all Russian citizens in Egypt for military service in the Russian Army. Petrov's efforts ended in vain, but this was not the first time that he had experienced difficulty in dealing with Jews because, somewhat ironically, he had unsuccessfully attempted to force the local Sephardim to surrender Pinhas Rutenberg for arrest following his revolutionary activities in Russia.[8]

Count Petrov did, however, perform one very valuable service for Jabotinsky by introducing him to Joseph Trumpeldor. The journalist and the soldier worked to form a military unit from the Russian Jews in the camps, in anticipation of a British advance from Egypt to Palestine. News of further Turkish restrictions and actions against Jews remaining in Palestine continued to be received in the camps. A meeting was held in the evening of (Tuesday) 2 March 1915, attended by Jabotinsky, Trumpeldor, Mordecai Margolis an Oil Company representative, Dr Weitz a Jerusalem doctor, Victor Gluskin a wine grower, Z.D. Levontin a banker and Akiva Ettinger an agronomist. They duly resolved 'To form a Jewish Legion and to propose to England to make use of it in Palestine.'[9]

A week later nearly 200 Jewish refugees had pledged to join the Legion, and the next step for Jabotinsky and Trumpeldor was to take a delegation to the British civil and military authorities in Cairo, represented by Ronald Graham, the minister of interior and the general officer commanding, General Sir John Maxwell. The delegation included Levontin, Gluskin and a local Sephardi leader named Kattawi Pasha. Unfortunately, their proposal was not welcomed with the enthusiasm that Jabotinsky in particular had expected. General Maxwell pointed out that he was unable, under the Army Acts, to recruit alien soldiers as a unit into the British army, but he was willing to consider employing the Jewish volunteers in a transport and supply unit. Again, and much to Jabotinsky's disgruntlement, General Maxwell informed the delegation that there was no planned British offensive in Palestine and he could only hint at employment on 'another Turkish front'.[10] Jabotinsky took this as a rebuff, and left Egypt to pursue his cause in the capitals of the western Allies.

Joseph Trumpeldor, who had a greater understanding of the military and did not share Jabotinsky's impatience, continued to meet with the British civil and military authorities. Even so, whilst he appreciated the importance of supply, he too was perturbed by Maxwell's proposal that the refugees provide a transport unit rather than a fighting formation.

This matter was finally resolved at a meeting in Alexandria between Trumpeldor and Mr Hornblower, the inspector of refugees, who was accompanied by General Maxwell's staff officer, Captain H. Holdich. Trumpeldor, when giving evidence to the Dardanelles Commission in January 1917, summarised this event as follows:

> They told us that in the British Army it is just the same, transport or fighting unit, just the same conditions. They told us that now it is necessary to organise a transport unit, especially pack mules and they said that our people came from Palestine, that many of our people were workmen in Palestine, and worked with mules in Palestine. Therefore they could very quickly organise pack mules, and pack mules would be necessary on the expedition. Therefore they offered us to accept service in this transport unit and to organise. After they told us that it was the same honour and just the same conditions we accepted it.[11]

Trumpeldor also knew that in practice the Mule Corps' role would be far from non-combatant: it would operate within range of the enemy, often in support of units actually engaged with the Turks. Whilst it is easy to appreciate Jabotinsky's impatience with what he perceived to be the relegation of his Jewish Legion to a mere Mule Corps, it is clear that Trumpeldor recognised that this unit could be the beginning of a Jewish force and not the end of a glorious idea.

As far as deployment was concerned, General Maxwell was in no position to promise service in Palestine to the Jewish volunteers, but he was nevertheless keen to take early advantage of their services: his Egyptian Command was becoming increasingly involved in the Allied operations in the Dardanelles. Maxwell's efforts to provide support to General Hamilton's Mediterranean Expeditionary Force (MEF) included his offer to Jabotinsky, Trumpeldor et al. for the creation of a transport unit utilising the services of the Jewish refugee volunteers. It is as well to state here that, given his knowledge of the limited time available before the MEF went into action, Maxwell must have realised that there would be barely enough time to train the Jewish refugees as a transport unit, let alone as infantry familiar with British Army field tactics. This would have reinforced his need to persist with the original notion of a transport role. He was also aware that 'another Turkish front' meant Gallipoli, but he was not, of course, in a position to reveal the actual theatre of operations. This had the unfortunate effect of allowing some of the volunteers to believe that they would in fact be taking part in an invasion of Palestine and, following Jabotinsky's departure, probably aided Maxwell in his next and final attempt to persuade the volunteers to join the mule transport unit he was proposing. This attempt took the form of a further meeting, on 19 March, at which Maxwell, Major General Godley, Trumpeldor and Lt.-Colonel John Henry Patterson, the commanding officer designate, addressed several hundred volunteers.

In his speech to the meeting, Maxwell read out a telegram of support from Israel Zangwill in London. Zangwill was a popular novelist and respected Jewish intellectual who had founded the Jewish Territorial Organisation, which endeavoured to find places where Jews could thrive and be protected from persecution. As Eugene Black has suggested,[12] Zangwill, although obviously in favour of Zionism, considered that an independent Jewish state in Palestine was too distant a prospect to provide immediate relief for persecuted Jews. Nevertheless his nationalist credentials were impeccable and his endorsement of Maxwell's proposals was both important and welcome. Notwithstanding Maxwell's appeal and Zangwill's support the volunteers were still not convinced that they should accept the offer; the lack of a firm promise of service in Palestine created an air of uncertainty that was only dispelled when Godley, an ebullient and impressive public speaker, spoke to the assembly and made this dramatic appeal, 'The English people is now speaking through me to the Jewish people, seeking friendship which will undoubtedly continue in Jewish Palestine. Do you have it in your hearts to shake the extended hand or to reject it?'[13]

On what authority Godley made this offer with its specific reference to Jewish Palestine is not known, and there is no mention of this episode in either Godley's papers or autobiography.[14] In any event, Godley's appeal swayed the meeting and, for the first time since the age of the Maccabeans, a Jewish military force came into being. One of the veterans of the Zion Mule Corps, Israel Korman, later recalled his own experience:

> I went to Palestine in 1912 from Russian Poland and worked in orange groves and vineyards in Rehovot until war broke out. The Turkish Government at the time rounded up foreign nationals and sent them to Damascus. I and several more escaped to Alexandria in Egypt, where were [sic] in a refugee camp. There we met Vladimir Jabotinsky and Capt. J. Trumpeldor and the Zion Mule Corps was formed *with the object of taking Palestine from the Turks* (Martin

Watts' italics). Instead we were sent to Gallipoli. When this was over, we returned to Egypt. From there I was sent to England and joined the 5th Royal Berks. Regt with whom I served until the war ended. I was demobilised in 1919 in England where I have lived ever since.[15]

The Assyrian Refugee Mule Corps, as it was first known, was officially formed in Alexandria on 23 March 1915, when the Grand Rabbi of Alexandria, Raphael della Pergola, administered the oath of obedience to about five hundred volunteers. Gilner writes that the swearing in took place on 1 April, but this is contradicted by Patterson's account, which states that 23 March was the date. This is substantiated by the war diary of the Directorate of Transport, which has its first report on the mule depot dated 30 March, clearly showing that the unit had been formed and that enlistment was continuing.[16] In a general note at the end of this report mention is made of the unit's difficulty in carrying out normal military routine, due to the observance of Passover – an early example of the friction that marked the experience of Jewish formations in the British Army. The formation of the corps was reported in Britain in the *Jewish Chronicle* of 30 April, which also included brief notes on the careers of Patterson and Trumpeldor; no other newspaper carried the story.

Meanwhile, General Maxwell had confirmed Lt.-Colonel Patterson in his appointment as commanding officer. Patterson was a forty-seven year old Irish protestant with an interesting and well-connected background, having been a civil engineer in Africa before gaining an international reputation as a big-game hunter. This gave him the opportunity to meet and develop friendships with influential people, including the American President Theodore Roosevelt, who subsequently entertained him at the White House. Patterson's military experience was gained in South Africa where he commanded a Regiment of Imperial Yeomanry during the second Boer War, receiving the DSO and three mentions in despatches, as well as rapid promotion (from lieutenant to Lt.-Colonel in five months). Among his friends during this period was the future Field Marshal Edmund Allenby.

After the war Patterson was listed as a major in the Essex Imperial Yeomanry of the Territorial Force, with the honorary army rank of Lt.-Colonel having been granted on 11 February 1903.[17] He sought to return to active service on the outbreak of the First World War, but his return was not straightforward, as he had resigned his commission in 1913, in protest at the government's Ulster policy. As he later explained when giving evidence to the Dardanelles Commission, being frustrated with the repeated failure of the War Office to find him an appointment, he eventually travelled to Egypt at his own expense to seek military employment.[18] Given his age and connections with the Ulster Volunteers (a Unionist paramilitary force equipped with small arms bought in Germany), perhaps it is hardly surprising that the War Office were reluctant to offer Patterson an appointment, thus obliging him to rely on his own resources and contacts overseas.

In March 1915, Patterson was in Cairo when General Maxwell approached him, on the recommendation of another of Patterson's friends, General Godley, in order to offer him command of the Jewish volunteers. Whether or not Maxwell was aware of Patterson's background or interest in Jewish history is unclear, but his appointment was certainly a fortuitous one for the troops he commanded. Patterson himself, in a later interview with the *Jewish Chronicle,* stated in answer to the question 'Was there any special reason you were selected for command?' that 'No, I happened to be in Cairo at the time and General Maxwell asked me [...] I had been a student of Jewish history and tradition and felt the deepest interest in the race, and so I readily accepted the offer.'[19] The roots of Patterson's empathy with Eastern European Jews remain to be explored but, as with other philo-Semites involved in this history, they may well have lain in a type of protestant upbringing that exalted the common roots of the Jewish and Christian traditions.[20]

There is a lack of primary source material covering the activities of the Mule Corps, mainly due to the fact that there appears to be no official unit records such as war diaries, intelligence and signal logs. The unusual circumstances under which the Jewish muleteers were recruited placed the organisation and administration of their unit outside the normal military framework, hence the lack of records. Nevertheless, arrangements had to be made for the purposes of command, pay and administration, and the surviving War Office records covering administration in Egypt, the MEF, transport arrangements and divisional war diaries, as well as the reports, statements and proceedings of the Dardanelles Commission, have been extensively searched to provide primary sources for the following account.

It is important to note that the War Office considered the ZMC to have been constituted as a locally raised colonial force, and so required the enlisted men to sign contracts for a twelve months service.[21] The corps was supplied with standard issue British Army uniform, a cap badge depicting the Shield of David and issued with Mauser rifles captured from the Turkish troops who had crossed the Sinai in February. In his foreword to Jabotinsky's book *The Story of the Jewish Legion*, Lt.-Colonel Patterson stated:

> We were not only a transport corps but a fighting corps to boot, and every man was equipped and trained to take his place on the battle-front – where in the rough and tumble of trench warfare the men of Zion often came to grips with their old enemies, the Turks.[22]

The strength of the Assyrian Refugee Mule Corps at the time of swearing-in was five British officers, five Jewish officers and 366 other ranks. The official record notes that the rank and file, 'consists *in toto* of Jews from Russia, Palestine and Egypt',[23] and since Patterson had decided to organise the corps into four troops consisting of 120 men commanded by one British and two Jewish officers, the establishment strength of the corps was to be set at 500 officers and men, with a mule strength of around 700 pack animals. Unfortunately, no official records survive that would permit a detailed analysis of the origin and background of the Jewish volunteers. General comments from the secondary sources indicate that the volunteers mainly consisted of 'students and workmen'[24] with the majority being of Russian origin. The British Jewry Book of Honour contains a nominal roll of 727 members of the Mule Corps (inclusive of replacements), but some of the names are duplicated and corrupted in the manner described by Harold Pollins. A count of Sephardi type names contained in this roll indicates that some 15 to 20 per cent of the total were of non-Russian origin, and therefore confirms the general picture in the available literature.

With the exception of Patterson and Trumpeldor, neither the British nor Jewish officers had any previous military service, which had severe implications for the conduct of the unit in combat, particularly in view of the brief period of training – less than one month – that was afforded to the corps. All five British officers were recruited locally: Lieutenant Gye having previously been an official with the Egyptian ministry of finance, Lieutenants Carter, Maclaren and the two brothers Rollo coming from banking and cotton broking. Patterson took upon himself the appointment of Jewish officers from among the volunteers, initially selecting Dr Levontin as medical officer and promoting 2nd Lieutenant Alexander Gorodissky, an academic from the Lycée Academy in Alexandria, from the ranks.

On 5 April General Maxwell wrote to General Hamilton detailing the progress he had made in recruitment of local support forces:

MULE TRANSPORT CORPS

The Zion Mule Corps composed of about 375 Jewish refugees from Palestine, mostly Russian veterans of the Russo-Japanese War, with 650 good pack mules, has been formed to assist in solving the difficulty of transport in the roadless theatre of operations. They can be equipped with mausers as soon as you wish. At present located in Alexandria under Lt-Col Patterson late Essex Yeomanry.[25]

Not only does this report provide further evidence as to the preponderance of Russian Jews within the corps, but it also raises the otherwise uncorroborated issue of the volunteers' previous military experience. With the obvious exception of Trumpeldor, there is no hard evidence to support Maxwell's assertion of mass participation in the Russo-Japanese War of 1904/05, and perhaps his remarks were designed to impress Hamilton who had been the official British War Office observer in Manchuria.[26]

General Hamilton saw the Mule Corps for himself when travelling to join his headquarters ship, the SS *Arcadian* in Alexandria on 7 April, and recorded the event in an entry in his diary:

On my way down to the harbour overhauled the Assyrian Jewish Refugee Mule Corps at the Wardian Camp. Their Commander, author of that thrilling 'The Man Eaters of Tsavo' finds Assyrian and Mules rather a mouthful and is going to tabloid bipeds and quadrapeds [sic] into THE ZION CORPS. The mules look very fit so do the Assyrians and, although I did not notice that their cohorts were gleaming with purple or gold, they may help us to those habliments [sic]. They may in fact serve as ground bait to entice the big Jew journalists and bankers towards our cause. The former will lend us the colour, the latter the coin. Anyway, so far as I can, I mean to give the chosen people a chance.[27]

Hamilton's remarks appear to be sarcastic; the use of the term 'chosen people' and the reference to 'big Jew journalists and bankers' seem to reveal an anti-Semitic attitude. Hamilton repeated similar views in a letter to Winston Churchill, the First Lord of the Admiralty, on 26 May 1915, when he remarked on the poor performance of some French Zouaves in the opening month of the campaign, stating that they consisted of 'Martinique half-castes and Algerian Jews'.[28] He repeated these disparaging remarks to Lord Kitchener in a letter of the same date, thereby indicating that such comments were a normal part of everyday communication.

On 14 April 1915 the Zion Mule Corps passed from the command of General Maxwell GOC Egypt, to General Hamilton, C.-in-C. Mediterranean Expeditionary Force.[29] Lt.-Col. Patterson and Captain Trumpeldor, as commandant and assistant commandant respectively and their British officers received British Army pay, as did the NCOs and men, ranging from 12/6 per day for a captain, to 3/6 per day for a sergeant, 2/- for a corporal farrier and 1/- per day for private soldiers.[30] Patterson granted local, temporary commissions to Jewish officers who received less than their British counterparts and were also required to mess separately. Although this distinction was blurred under field service conditions, it reinforced the 'Colonial Corps' philosophy that underpinned the general British attitude towards foreign-raised units and their administration under the Army Acts. The exception made for Trumpeldor (through the use of an 'honorary' British commission), demonstrated the unique nature of the Zion Mule Corps.

Training was completed on 16 April and the Zion Mule Corps was divided into two parts, with its headquarters and A and B Troops embarking on HM Transport *Hymettus*, and C and D Troops joining HM Transport *Anglo Egyptian* for the voyage from Alexandria to an unknown destination. Secrecy was a normal security precaution, even if the Turks had been alerted by the naval attacks in the Dardanelles Straits, and many of the men believed that they were *en route* to Palestine. Patterson and Trumpeldor knew that landing elsewhere would impose a strain upon discipline, despite their earlier efforts to convince the volunteers that service with the British Army anywhere in the region would assist in the defeat of the Turks. In any event the short, two-day voyage from Alexandria ended at the logistic staging post at Mudros Bay on the island of Lemnos in the Aegean Sea, some seventy miles from the assault beaches on the Gallipoli peninsula. There was now no concealing the truth as plans for the landing of the assault forces were put into action, with the British 29th Division detailed to land at beaches on Cape Helles, and the ANZAC Corps at beaches twenty miles to the north-west, past Gaba Tebe. Both landings, and a diversionary French action at Kum Kale on the Asiatic shore of Turkey, near the ruins of Troy, were to take place on 25 April, with the support troops, including transport and supply units, to follow as soon as practicable.

Whilst at Mudros the *Hymettus* became grounded for two days, thereby disrupting preparations, and on 23 April Patterson received orders that the Zion Mule Corps was to be divided into two parts, with Troops A and B allocated to the 29th Division, and Troops C and D attached to the ANZAC Corps. Patterson protested at the splitting of his force, which involved removing the 200 members of C and D Troops from his direct command and influence, a situation made worse by the short notice and physical separation of the two halves of the ZMC, which prevented him from transferring Trumpeldor to the *Anglo Egyptian*. Both he and Trumpeldor were well aware that C and D Troops consisted mainly of Alexandrian Jews and were led by Lieutenants Maclaren, Carver and I. Rollo, three very inexperienced officers. Despite his protests, Patterson was informed that C and D Troops were urgently required by ANZAC and that, since the main objective was to link up the British and ANZAC forces within a few days, his objections were overruled – with disastrous consequences.

The ANZAC landings began poorly, with the initial assault wave being landed north of their planned destination, and the subsequent confusion and disruption combined with the narrow beaches and fierce Turkish resistance to create a desperate situation. Groups of soldiers who managed to surmount the cliffs became isolated, and stragglers found their way back to the beaches where officers and NCOs had to reorganise, encourage and cajole them in order to restore their military effectiveness. The ANZAC line was so confused that no artillery could be landed and fire support from the warships patrolling offshore was withheld, to avoid the inflicting of casualties upon Allied forces. The coming of nightfall further reduced the ANZAC commanders' ability to control their soldiers and General Birdwood, the corps commander, was obliged to signal Hamilton requesting a decision on the possibility of withdrawal. Hamilton, who had fortuitously arrived off the ANZAC beaches on board the flagship, HMS *Queen Elizabeth*, sent a strongly worded – and now famous – reply which ordered the troops ashore to 'dig, dig, dig, until you are safe'.

This put paid to any idea of withdrawal, but did little to bring immediate order to the chaos on the beaches, where C and D Troops of the Zion Mule Corps were tasked with carrying ammunition, food and water to the front line. The war diary of the administrative staff of the New Zealand and Australian Division records that, between 28 April and 2 May, a total of 196 mules and 213 officers and muleteers of the Zion Mule Corps were disembarked. During this period, as the ANZAC infantry struggled to consolidate their positions, the muleteers of the ZMC strove to establish lines of supply by moving mainly at night. Unfortunately, their lack of training and poor communications were cruelly exposed by the horrific conditions onshore, and it became increasingly difficult for them to carry out their duties. The war diary entry for 3 May records the inevitable result:

> Owing to difficulty of working with Zion Mule Corps drivers, who are unable to speak English, and, who have had little or no previous training[,] it has been decided to embark them all (213) on various transports to replace ASC (Army Service Corps) drivers in looking after Div. Train Mules on board ship.[31]

By 17 May the muleteers of C and D Troops had been completely replaced by men of the Indian Mule Corps, who had previously served in the trenches of the western front, and were returned to Alexandria without taking any further part in the campaign.

A rather different story is revealed in Hamilton's letter to Maxwell dated 15 July:

> I have just been very much annoyed by the stupidity of a very stupid man, my Director of Transport. You know the Jewish Mule Corps was divided into two portions. The portion at Helles under Patterson is happy, has done well and is doing well. The portion at ANZACS did not receive consideration from the Australians, and I fear some of the men were shot or bayonetted under the impression they were Turks owing to their being unable to reply to challenges. I had heard something of this and had meant to bring them out for a rest, and to get them into good fettle, when I would have probably joined them on to the Helles lot. Now they tell me that these discontented, unhappy fellows have all been sent back to Alexandria, staright [sic]. There they, being the unhappy section of the Corps[,] will spread unhappy rumours and kill recruiting. Who can combat such stupidity as this? I feel it badly because just at this moment I wanted to recruit up the Corps again. Patterson thinks he can get half a dozen good recruiters from his lot at Helles who would explain to the men how much better the conditions were there, and try to get them to come on. Probably I shall cable you about this during the course of the day.[32]

The Zion muleteers' lack of English no doubt accounts for any confusion regarding their response to challenges from Australian pickets and sentries, but there are no references to any casualties inflicted by friendly forces in the available sources, with the exception of the anecdotal remarks contained in Hamilton's letter. One indubitable point, however, is that ANZAC troops were made painfully aware from the outset of the courage of their Turkish foes, and it is quite possible that they mistook the unfamiliar muleteers for enemy soldiers. The Turks frequently employed ruses to entice soldiers from cover or to provoke undisciplined rifle fire that revealed their positions, particularly at night. Evidence of this activity is recorded as early as the afternoon of 26 April when, according to the war diary of the General Staff, 1st Australian Division, 'Troops warned against enemy ruses. These consist in passing orders and reports e.g. the troops at so and so are Indians don't fire.'[33] This warning was soon followed by a divisional order from Major General William Bridges, commanding the 1st Australian Division: 'Very few of the Indian troops can speak English and none of them are in the least likely ever to say "Don't shoot we are Indians." Any men advancing and coming forth with such a cry should be shot at once as enemies.'[34]

Under all these circumstances it is hardly surprising that C and D Troop became so quickly demoralised and disorganised. The same fate had befallen a number of the ANZAC troops soon after landing, and nine days later, on 6 May, more than fifty mules were killed by Turkish shelling and half of the Indian muleteers fled, leaving their commanding officer, Captain Alexander and his officers to restore the situation by leading the surviving mules to safety.[35]

The physical and moral condition of the members of C and D Troops was noted on their arrival back in Alexandria where, of the 190 who landed, sixty-two were discharged on medical grounds, fifty-seven were placed under arrest for refusing to obey orders and, by 11 June, only twenty were available for duty, the balance of fifty-one having deserted.[36] According to one of their Jewish officers, 2nd Lieutenant Zlotnic, who was to later join the ZMC at Cape Helles, the men of C and D troops received brutal treatment at the hands of their British officers in Alexandria, and the mass desertion was provoked by the stoppage of leave which prevented them from visiting their families in the refugee camps. On 16 June Patterson, who had been advised of the situation regarding his men in Alexandria, agreed with the director of supplies and transport MEF (Colonel F. Koe) that the remaining elements of C and D Troops be disbanded.[37]

The grounding of the *Hymettus* in Mudros harbour resulted in the transfer of Patterson, Trumpeldor and A and B Troops to the transport vessel *Dundrennan*. Already embarked on this vessel was the Indian mule detachment under the command of the aforementioned Captain

Alexander, which was landed at ANZAC after the ZMC were put ashore in support of the 29th Division at Cape Helles. The assault landings on Cape Helles took place at five beaches located on either side and at the base of the Cape. Beginning with the most easterly beach on the southern side and then proceeding in a clockwise direction, they were codenamed S, V, W, X and Y. The attacking forces were sent into the beaches early on 25 April and the flanks (S and Y) were rapidly secured, due to the degree of surprise they achieved. This was denied to the forces on the other beaches because they were attacking more heavily defended positions, and used a preparatory naval bombardment that served to warn the Turks of their approach. Patterson and Trumpeldor, on board *Dundrennan*, observed the landings at V beach, the most significant point of attack on the Cape. They saw, with their men, the slaughter of the infantry disembarking from the *River Clyde*, a hastily converted collier that had been deliberately grounded on the beach, and watched the day-long struggle to establish a beachhead under constant enemy fire.

The lack of progress in moving inland prevented the landing of supply and transport echelons for nearly two days, during which the ZMC witnessed the horrors of the fighting onshore. This experience, when added to the realisation amongst the muleteers that they were not going to Palestine, contributed to a wavering in morale, but Patterson and Trumpeldor were equal to the challenge this presented to their authority, and the corps was duly prepared for disembarkation.

The *Dundrennan* unloaded the ZMC into barges for transportation to V beach where they deployed during the night of the 27/28 April. By this time the infantry had begun a cautious advance inland following the clearing out of the Turkish defenders from Sedd el Bahr fort, and were in urgent need of resupply. Major J. Gillam of the Army Service Corps, in local command of the 29th Divisional Train was: 'Ordered to make a small advanced depot just behind the firing line using packmules under Colonel Patterson of the Zion Mule Corps. The drivers are Syrian refugees from Syria, and curiously enough speak Russian as their common language.'[38]

The ZMC were the first transport unit to be sent ashore and, despite the Turkish shelling and sniping, their mules and all personnel were landed without loss. The lack of cover on V beach resulted in half – about 200 – of their mules being moved almost immediately to W beach, nearly a mile to the west, where they were loaded with ammunition and water. This was a period of frenetic activity for the men of the 29th Divisional Train, with the dispersed nature of the front line imposing extreme demands upon the supply units who were hampered by an overall shortage of mules. For a day and a half the muleteers struggled through the scrub of the terrain, often caught in the no-man's land between the British and Turkish front lines, as they endeavoured to locate the infantry in desperate need of the supplies that they carried.

Private David Muscovitz became the ZMC's first casualty by going missing during the first night ashore, at the height of the confusion caused by the relocation to W beach. His fate has never been established but he was eventually listed as having been killed in action and commemorated accordingly.[39] Some respite from the shelling was obtained when the corps occupied a gully just behind the firing line, which provided shelter for both animals and men and a supply of fresh water from a well in a nearby, abandoned Turkish farm.

As the front line of the 29th Division solidified, preparations were made for a major advance towards the dominant feature of the peninsula, Achi Baba, and the taking of Krithia village at its foot. Krithia was well defended and heavily reinforced by the Turks and it was necessary to accumulate large amounts of stores in order to undertake an assault upon this strongpoint. The supply system that was set in place to achieve this consisted of wheeled transport from the beaches to selected dumping grounds, from where transport to the front lines was carried out by pack animals.

The operations conducted in early May towards Krithia proved to be a testing time for the men of the Zion Mule Corps, during which they began to exhibit a willingness to join in the frontline fighting. Whilst unloading ammunition in the Gully ravine area on 1 May, a party of mules and their drivers, commanded by 2nd Lt. Claude Rollo, came under particularly heavy shellfire. This caused a number of the mules to stampede and created a tremendous noise in the ensuing chaos. The stampede proved fortuitous for the British soldiers in the area because, not only did the disturbance raise the alarm within their positions, but it also convinced a number of infiltrating Turkish soldiers, who had advanced under the cover of the bombardment, that they were being charged by British cavalry, thereby obliging them to reveal their positions. Standing-to with their comrades in the infantry, the muleteers opened fire and the startled Turks withdrew.

As fighting in the area escalated, up to fifty muleteers petitioned Patterson for permission to take a more offensive role alongside the British infantry. Patterson passed on the request to the divisional commander, General Hunter-Weston, but it was denied on the grounds that the men could not be spared from the vital duties they were already performing. This fact was also confirmed by General Hamilton who wrote, in a letter to General Maxwell in Cairo dated 4 May: 'What we would have done without the Zion Mule Corps I do not know.'[40]

Despite their disappointment at having their request turned down, the fighting spirit of some of the muleteers remained undiminished. Private M. Groushkovsky, leading a team of fully laden mules to the front near Krithia on 5 May, suffered shrapnel wounds to both of his arms when his column was shelled. Refusing to let go of his charges, he prevented a stampede and went on to deliver the urgently needed ammunition to the British trenches, whilst under continuous Turkish fire. For his bravery in the face of the enemy Private Groushkovsky was promoted corporal and recommended for the Distinguished Conduct Medal by General Hamilton. This recommendation raised questions in London as to the status of the Zion muleteers, but, in any event, this well-deserved award was duly confirmed and Corporal Groushkovsky was decorated in the field.

General Hunter-Weston launched a further assault on Krithia on 6 May and when the 1st Royal Inniskilling Fusiliers were counter-attacked by Turkish forces, a group of Zion muleteers joined them in the trenches and helped to repel the enemy in a further demonstration of their fighting capability. Corporal E. Hildesheim, who had been supervising the delivery of ammunition and food to the Fusiliers, led the group. After the war, Hildesheim changed his name to Leon L. Gildesgame, and later settled in Mount Kisco, New York. Originally one of the students ejected from Palestine by the Turks, he wrote in correspondence with the author in 1987:

> Due to the fact that the story of the Zion Mule Corps is over 70 years old, since the early part of World War 1, I do not remember everything concerning this volunteer Jewish Battalion. I was one of the founders, with the rank of Corporal and Acting Sergeant, and one of the actual fighters in the trenches on the Gallipoli Peninsula ... A number of my buddies were killed or wounded and the rest were transferred to other regiments, mainly the Royal Fusiliers ... Palestine was then under the rule of Turkey and Turkey was allied with Germany and Austria. And since most of the students at the school were either Russian or British, the Turks arrested us all and subsequently expelled us to Egypt and the desert. That is when we decided to found a Jewish Brigade and that is how the Zion Mule Corps was founded.[41]

Corporal Hildesheim/Gildesgame's enlistment number on the corps roll was 28, a fact that certainly supports his claim to be one of its founder members. Leon Gildesgame was one of many Zion Mule Corps veterans to be later awarded the Gallipoli Star.

The attack on Krithia failed on 7 May and the campaign at Helles became bogged down, with the exhausted remnants of the 29th Division left with no option but to entrench and await the arrival of reinforcements from Egypt and the United Kingdom. On the eastern slopes of Achi Baba, on the opposite side from Krithia, a new permanent base was found for the Zion Mule Corps, from which they operated until evacuation at the end of the year. Regular shelling in the morning and late afternoon became part of the Zion Mule Corps' base routine, and both men and mules suffered casualties as a result. Private Hirsch Stein was killed on 13 May, and Farrier-Corporal Abram Frank, who had a wife and five children back at the refugee camp near Alexandria, died from shellfire on the 14th. A particularly heavy bombardment on 20 May wounded five men, two seriously, and caused the death of a dozen animals. Outside of their camp muleteers continued to deliver supplies to the firing lines, always operating at night and initially aided by the powerful searchlights of the warships that were anchored close inshore off Cape Helles. The torpedoing and sinking of three elderly battleships led to the withdrawal of close naval support, and forced the muleteers to rely even more on their own resources.

Between 30 May and 15 June the ZMC suffered a further five fatalities. Privates B. Katzelenjohn, Jacob Rottman and Samuel Bargman were killed outright, their bodies brought back to camp for ceremonial burial. Private Joseph Rouah died from disease on 3 June and Private I. Kirzner succumbed to his wounds on the 15th. During this time Colonel Patterson and his officers developed the habit of frequently visiting the front line units that their men were supplying, and struck up a particularly friendly relationship with Lt.-Colonel Bruce and the officers and men of the Gurkha Battalion he commanded. This gave them the opportunity to gauge the effectiveness of the ZMC and witness the lack of progress of the general campaign. On the evening of 2 June whilst returning to camp, Patterson and Claude Rollo had a narrow escape when they were seen by the Turks and bombarded with artillery and small arms fire.

Meanwhile the climate of Gallipoli, with its warm spring and hot summer months, combined with poor sanitation to produce an epidemic of dysentery and other diseases, spread by the multitudes of flies throughout the Allied armies on the peninsula, and the ZMC suffered like the rest. As its own sick list and casualty numbers grew, the strain on morale increased and discipline wavered amongst some of the muleteers through late May and the first half of June. Patterson attributed the origins of the indiscipline to the fact that the men broadly consisted of two types, Russians and Alexandrians: in the former, the combination of a European discipline and zeal for their cause resulted in a strong will to fight; the latter exhibited an Arab temperament unconducive to soldiering. According to Gilner, who used extracts from Trumpeldor's diary, Trumpeldor's assessment coincided with that of his commanding officer: he thought the one hundred Sephardi Jews who committed various offences, ranging from falsely reporting sick to failing to deliver supplies as ordered, were ignorant of the purpose of Zionism, and were not sufficiently committed to the oath they had taken on enlistment.[42]

The recalcitrant muleteers were dealt with severely by their officers, who did not hesitate to administer floggings and other brutal field punishments. Although he understood, as a professional soldier, that such treatment was necessary to restore unit discipline, Trumpeldor was nevertheless unhappy with the zeal with which some of the British officers, particularly Claude Rollo, administered the punishment, and subsequently fell out with Patterson over this issue. For his part, Patterson was inclined to blame Trumpeldor for the episodes of poor discipline, and went so far as to threaten him with dismissal back to Alexandria. Such a threat was wasted on a character like Trumpeldor who immediately offered his resignation. Patterson realised that this would have disastrous consequences for the corps and apologised; both were men of strong conviction and enjoyed mutual respect, but neither were immune from the strain of the campaign in which they were so heavily engaged.[43]

With normal relations thus restored they were able to face the muleteers and give them the opportunity to air their underlying grievances. These included alleged discrimination on the part of their British officers, for treating them like Egyptian labourers rather than soldiers, and a general questioning of their status within the army and its effect on their entitlements to maintenance allowances for their wives and families in Alexandria, including pensions in the event of death in service. It is easy to understand the resentment that a group of volunteers would have felt towards inexperienced officers who did not respect their cultural background; a resentment fuelled by the lack of recognition from higher military authorities who appeared to be ignorant of their situation. By agreeing to put these matters in writing to General Headquarters, Patterson managed to defuse the situation, but only temporarily for, on 15 June, he found himself facing a militant deputation insisting on repatriation to Alexandria. According to Gilner there were three unnamed ringleaders and a total of seventy-five men involved in this near mutiny, which finally brought matters to a head by making Patterson take drastic action:

> The Colonel arrived, followed by several British soldiers from neighbouring units, who carried whips. Three well-known troublemakers were taken out of the Muleteer ranks, stripped to the waist and tied to posts. Turning to the most notorious of the three, the Colonel asked 'For the last time: will you obey orders?' 'No,' said the man as the other two looked on sullenly. 'My feet hurt.' The Colonel nodded, and the three received twelve lashes each. Some of the men surged forward in protest but were shoved back. Afterwards, the three were taken from the whipping posts, tied to wagon wheels for three hours, and then confined for three days on bread and water.[44]

Patterson's punishment achieved its objective of restoring unit cohesion and maintaining military discipline in the field. If a mutiny had occurred it could be assumed that the participants would have received absolutely no mercy at the hands of higher authority; desertion within the confines of the peninsula was simply not viable. Trumpeldor supported Patterson's actions notwithstanding his sympathy with some of the grievances that were expressed, because of the absolute priority of preserving the corps as an effective unit. Any future expectations Trumpeldor may have nursed with regard to the raising of a larger Jewish Legion would have been permanently destroyed had the muleteers broken up in disarray.

The ZMC had come close to breakdown but it should be noted in mitigation that the men involved had only been subjected to military discipline and training for four weeks, prior to their embarkation. They were then exposed to a daily round of bombardment, nightly deliveries to the front lines, sniping and disease, without prospect of relief or respite from the Turkish guns. It is therefore to their credit that they survived the ordeals of the first two battles of Krithia without major disruption, and there can be no doubt that their response to the field leadership of Patterson and Trumpeldor was crucial to this fact. The ultimate test of this leadership was the breaking of the ringleaders and the restoration of discipline, which led to a settled period when the ZMC buckled down to its supply duties and attracted the acclamation of the units that it served. It was about this time that the British soldiers involved began to express their respect and affection for the Jewish foreigners who fought alongside them by coining the nickname of the 'Allied Cavalry' and creating a famous but strictly unofficial motto 'No Advance Without Security'.

The instigation of mule races and other sporting competitions also testifies to the raising of morale during this time. Despite the proximity of the Turkish troops such sporting activities – which had long been recognised for their positive effect on the well-being of all concerned – were encouraged throughout the peninsula. Mule races provided an opportunity for gambling as well as leisure, and the prevalence of inter-unit soccer matches throughout the campaign has been recorded.[45] Patterson's satisfaction with the performance of the majority of his men was confirmed by letters of thanks from troops who were being supplied by sections of muleteers on detachment. Unfortunately none of these letters or testimonials has been traced. In his own book, however, Patterson recorded that the section led by Corporal Nehemiah Yehuda was very much in demand, and Major A.H. Mure, of the 5th Battalion The Royal Scots, wrote:

> I ran across Col. Patterson who had equipped, at his own expense, a corps of Zionist Jews from Palestine, to carry water. They did excellent and merciful work all through the campaign, and one or two got mentioned.[46]

There is no evidence to suggest that Patterson personally paid for his men's equipment, although it was by no means unknown for commanding officers to do so.

Despite the transformation in morale that Patterson achieved, discipline remained under threat from the treacherous and dangerous circumstances facing the ZMC. In early July, a number of muleteers abandoned their charges and ran for the beach when the Allied line was rushed and partly broken by Turkish infantry, but Private Nissel Rosenberg restored the reputation of the ZMC by rounding up the mules and delivering, under fire, the ammunition and supplies they were carrying. Rosenberg was promoted in the field to Sergeant and recommended by Patterson for the Distinguished Conduct Medal, but actually received a Mention in Dispatches for his brave conduct. In later operations further decorations were awarded to Sergeant Meyer Erchovitz, who earned both a Mention in Despatches and the ZMC's second Distinguished Conduct Medal, and Lt. Claude Rollo who gained a Mention.

By the end of July, the ZMC in Helles had lost more than half its effective strength, mainly because of disease. Although casualties due to enemy fire were few, with eight deaths and an estimated sixty wounded, the reduction of about 50 per cent is in line with the diminution in strength of all of the forces under Hamilton's command.[47] To remedy the situation Hamilton ordered Patterson to Alexandria to recruit replacements and establish a depot and training base. Hamilton's keenness to exploit the propaganda value of the existence of this Jewish unit has already been mentioned, and he had himself written to the New York press confirming its good work. Supporting correspondence had also been received at GHQ from both the United Kingdom and the United States, including a communication from former president Theodore Roosevelt.

Armed with this knowledge and accompanied by Trumpeldor, Claude Rollo and Corporal Groushkovsky, Patterson sailed for Alexandria on 25 July, leaving Lt. Gye in command of the remaining fit muleteers and animals. Patterson was well aware of the difficulties he would face in Alexandria as a result of the disaffection of men from C and D Troops, which had finally been disbanded in the middle of June. At recruitment meetings held at Camp Wardian both Patterson and Trumpeldor had great difficulty in countering the accusations of racism and ill treatment that had been spread about by the discharged muleteers, and had to deal with the persistent petitioning for the payment of pensions by the widows of those who had been killed.

The matter of pension and other welfare arrangements revolved about the uncertain status of the Zion Mule Corps. By virtue of its unique nature, the corps did not fit into the British Army's rigid classification system, particularly with regard to colonial and native corps that were primarily classed as labour battalions. Fortunately, there are a number of War Office administrative files available which contain much of the official argument and correspondence relating to compensation and pension arrangements for the ZMC. The following passage is based on these files.

It has already been established that the ZMC was raised under the auspices of the GOC Egypt, General Sir John Maxwell, and transferred to Hamilton's command on 15 April 1915. In a letter of 13 April, Maxwell advised Hamilton that his command would be willing to pay to the Egyptian civil government money for the subsistence of dependants of members of the ZMC. Those dependants living in the refugee camps were to continue to be supported by the civil authorities and, at a meeting in Alexandria on the 15 April, between the MEF command paymaster (Colonel Armstrong) and the inspector of refugees Mr Hornblower, an agreement was reached for allowances to be paid to non-refugees of the Jewish community. These allowances were calculated on the basis of:

> 1/- per day for each family of three persons or less. 1 PT (piastre) per day for each dependant above 3. Dependants under 5 years old to be entitled to $\frac{1}{2}$ piastre. Male dependants of 16 years and over not entitled to subsistence.[48]

The arrangements for payment of these allowances and the continuing support of muleteers' families in the refugee camps were finalised on the day that the ZMC received its embarkation orders, 15 April 1915. No mention was made of pension arrangements and when GHQ Cairo received notification of the death in action of the ZMC's first confirmed fatality, Corporal Frank, General Maxwell requested the War Office to make a payment to Mrs Frank of between £50 and £60. The Army Council finally sanctioned a payment of £38, the equivalent of one year's pay, a principle it had applied in granting Maxwell discretion to pay compensation to the widows of men of the Egyptian and Greek Labour Corps, and which reflected the twelve month contract that the muleteers had signed.

This did not find favour, however, with Maxwell who felt strongly that the Zion Mule Corps, by virtue of its front line service, deserved greater entitlements. In this he clearly supported Patterson, who had written in with a list of the men's grievances, and included his own request for pensions on their behalf, a request that Hamilton endorsed. In a letter to the War Office, written in Cairo on 13 September 1915, Maxwell stated the case for special consideration and revealed that:

> No authorised mention of pensions [was] made to them on joining, but they undoubtedly consider themselves eligible for the same consideration as soldiers ... The payment of such pensions to other ranks would present insuperable difficulties, I therefore recommend that they be made eligible for gratuities based on the capitalised values of these pensions.[49]

In support of his argument General Maxwell pointed out that the majority of the muleteers were subjects of Russia or Egypt, and would be entitled to the benefits he was requesting on their behalf, if serving in the military forces of those two countries. The response of the War

Office in mid-October was to reject the capital value idea as being 'unduly liberal', and to maintain the one-year principle as applied to Mrs Frank. A temporary end to the debate on pensions resulted from this reply, until Patterson raised it again in the spring of 1916 following his return to the United Kingdom, when he finally managed to persuade the War Office to make a special case of the Zion Mule Corps. This resulted in the official sanction, in July 1916, of an increase in the widow's pension entitlement from one to three years pay, subject to a maximum of £75 for NCO's, a welcome development but apparently too late for Mrs Frank.[50]

The Jewish officers appointed by Patterson were not so privileged. Unlike their British colleagues they had no entitlement to pensions and compensation. Only one Jewish officer, Lt. Gorodissky, died during the campaign and a case for compensation was argued by the Adjutant-General of the MEF who wrote to the War Office in the summer of 1916:

> Mr. Gorodissky died on 11/9/15 of acute pancreatis on board the hospital ship DUNLUCE CASTLE (then off Cape Helles). He left a mother dependent on him, now resident in Alexandria, but it appears she has another son who earns his own living. It has been further ascertained that apart from British officers with the ZMC there were two Hebrew officers per troop, appointed by the OC without reference to higher authority and liable to reversion by him to the rank of NCO if found inefficient. In these circumstances I am of the opinion that Mr. Gorodissky cannot be regarded as an officer for the purpose of compensation [...] but I recommend, seeing that he performed the duties of an officer for four months and belonged to a well educated middle class family, that the maximum compensation (£75) allowed for a NCO of the corps be increased to £200, in this, a very special case.[51]

The War Office endorsed this request to the Treasury which sanctioned an 'exceptional grant' of £150, a sum that represented less than a year's pay. In fairness there can be no argument that this treatment compared well with that given to NCO's and other ranks, but the mention of the class and educational background of the officer concerned does betray the social attitudes of the time.

Patterson's concern for the well-being of his men and their dependants was understandable, but his zeal in pursuit of pensions rankled higher authority. Such was the strength of his conviction that he chose to submit evidence to the Dardanelles Commission in January 1917, in a further attempt to gain full army pensions for the Zion Mule Corps dependants. In this he was supported by Trumpeldor and the commission decided to recommend that the War Office give 'favourable consideration' to the granting of pensions, but it is apparent that this issue was never officially raised again.

Colonel Patterson's recruiting party remained in Alexandria until the end of September but failed to reignite the spark of enthusiasm that had fired the original volunteers. Two months of unrelenting effort resulted in the enlistment of only 150 mainly Sephardi recruits, who were formed into 'Cairo Troop' in a deliberate move designed to keep them apart from the veterans and enable them to serve under their own NCOs. Segregation of this type proved to be justified, for Patterson and Trumpeldor had learned a painful lesson from their earlier experiences and were now very firm in their handling of the 'Alexandrians'.

Not all of the new recruits were local Sephardim. The Cairo troop's baker was 21 year old Hanoch Gabrilevitz who, as a teenager, had found his way to Palestine from his family home at Wielien, Russia. After the campaign was over, Hanoch worked his passage to Britain as a stoker on board a merchant ship, and settled in East London, where he married and raised five children. He continued to work as a baker, and his colleagues and friends in the Jewish Baker's Union always referred to him as 'Dardanelles'.[52]

Meanwhile at Gallipoli the failure to exploit the opportunities created by the successful landing at Suvla Bay on the 6/7 August presaged the final stalemate of the campaign and its ultimate failure. On the 26th, whilst the new recruits were preparing for embarkation, the ZMC base back at Helles underwent an inspection by the assistant director of transport, MEF. His very revealing report endorsed the differences between 'Russians' and 'Alexandrians', and contrasted sharply with his earlier reports on the excellent condition of the men and animals of the Indian Mule Corps.[53] The report speaks for itself:

> MULES: Those in regular work in trenches in fair condition. Remainder poor and neglected due lack of drivers. Regular, daily exercise ordered.
>
> PERSONNEL: Russian Jews are satisfactory. Most of these are on detachment with regimental units, or are NCO's. Alexandrian Jews are reported by all concerned to be of little use. They make trouble in camp, and go sick as soon as they are told to do any work. Col. Patterson is away recruiting in Alex, but from reports received by the Junior Officers, he has not had much success in enlisting

Russians there. The Corps is certainly not doing much useful work at present. There are about 35 Russians and 60 Alexandrians at present here, and I understand nearly all of them want to get away.
GENERAL: The mules are dug in and the men also. The lines are dirty and untidy compared with those of other units. Lt. Gye has done his best with the very bad material at his disposal.[54]

This inspection only covered the men and mules actually at the depot, and confirms the view that the Russian muleteers were more popular with front line units. Unfortunately the report does not mention that the inspection was carried out at a time when the ZMC was at its most run down, and deprived of the leadership of Patterson and Trumpeldor.

Arriving at Helles on 3 October, Cairo Troop and their officers immediately commenced supply duties in cold and wet weather. The stalemated campaign was by now doomed to an ignominious end and General Hamilton was relieved of his command on 15 October. His replacement, General Sir Charles Monro, informed the War Office on 1 November that he considered the peninsula should be abandoned and the troops evacuated. The War Office now found itself hoist by its own petard. Initially unwilling to commit the necessary resources to ensure success it now baulked at the prospect of evacuation, which it believed would result in great loss of life. Unable to make up its mind, Lord Kitchener was sent to Gallipoli to see for himself; he agreed with Monro and informed the War Cabinet accordingly on 22 November. The evacuation orders were issued on 8 December, by which time the peninsula was in the grip of a big freeze that inflicted further misery and death upon both sides.

During its last two months the tempo of the campaign slackened, and the officers and men of the ZMC entered a period of relative inactivity. Lt. Gye transferred to the Royal Horse Artillery and Colonel Patterson was taken sick on 25 November, his illness forcing him to leave for hospital in Alexandria. Command of the corps passed to Captain Trumpeldor who, despite a bullet wound to his left shoulder sustained on 19 December, remained with the ZMC, overseeing their evacuation on the last day of 1915. Their campaign over, the muleteers finally disembarked in Alexandria on 10 January 1916. On 3 March the muleteers erected a mausoleum to their fallen comrades in Alexandria, an event which was reported in the *Jewish Chronicle* three weeks later, when it also published a brief interview with Lt.-Col. Patterson, then convalescing in London.[55]

Trumpeldor did all he could to keep the corps together after its return to Alexandria but, despite his efforts to persuade the authorities to maintain the unit for a campaign in Palestine, the only offer he received concerned participation in the campaign in Ireland.[56] Unsurprisingly this offer was not taken up and the Zion Mule Corps was disbanded on 26 May 1916. The months of inactivity in Alexandria led to the loss of many of the men who simply abandoned camp. Nevertheless, Trumpeldor and about one hundred and twenty of his colleagues managed to remain attached to the British Army and find their way to Britain.

The volunteer soldiers of the Zion Mule Corps were in no doubt as to what they were fighting for. A poignant expression of this sentiment is to be found in a letter written by Trumpeldor to the father of a soldier, believed to be a Private Wortheimer, who died of his wounds in Alexandria. The letter was written in Hebrew and a translation reads as follows:

> Dear Sir, I have received your letter. When your son was wounded I was in Alexandria, and did'nt [sic] know where his things were sent to. I've looked for them but could'nt [sic] find them. [...] Your son was a good man and a good Jew as well as a good soldier. I know that your heart is breaking, but you should know that your son fell a hero for the people of Israel and for the Land of Israel.
> Signed: Captain Trumpeldor/Cape Hellis, [sic] 13th December 1915.[57]

The efforts of Patterson, Maxwell and Hamilton in representing the corps' activities to the War Office clearly resulted in it gaining an unique status, outside the normal regulations applied to locally raised labour units, which the granting of enhanced pensions as a 'special case' confirmed. Combat status is more difficult to determine. This account has shown that there were several episodes when the muleteers fought as infantry, with gallantry, despite their primary role as a transport and supply unit. Their efforts certainly earned praise from Hamilton, who later wrote to Jabotinsky, 'The men have done extremely well, working their mules calmly under heavy shell and rifle fire, and thus showing a more difficult type of bravery than the men in the front line who had the excitement of combat to keep them going.'[58]

Although Hamilton confirms by his wording that the muleteers were not in the front line, it is worth remembering that the confined nature of the Gallipoli theatre enabled the Turks to reach all Allied troops with artillery, and the close proximity of the front lines exposed every troop movement to observation. In this situation, notions of front and rear lines derived from the western front are inappropriate. The gallantry awards won by members of the corps in the face of the enemy further blur conventional distinctions between combatant and noncombatant troops. The War Office, in confirming the awards, again demonstrated the corps' special status and its military reputation, notwithstanding the débâcle at ANZAC and the near mutiny that required the utmost efforts of Patterson and Trumpeldor to quell.

The debate over the uncertain status of the ZMC has influenced the evaluation of its importance and relevance to the future founding of the Jewish Legion. Bernard Wasserstein for example, refers to the ZMC as a 'support unit' and regards the later Jewish Legion as the first Jewish combat unit, thus implying that the activities of the ZMC were strictly non-combatant and therefore of less importance.[59] This implication is refuted, both by the above evidence and by the influence the performance of the corps had upon people like Patterson and Hamilton, who appreciated the Russian Jew's effectiveness as a soldier and the propaganda value of a Jewish force amongst Jewry, particularly in Britain and the United States, to the benefit of the Allied war effort. There can be no doubt therefore that the Zion Mule Corps was of enormous value to those wishing to promote the formation of a larger Jewish force, a conclusion finally reached by Jabotinsky, who had left Alexandria when unable to support the raising of the corps. Writing several years later, in his book *The Story of the Jewish Legion*, Jabotinsky publicly recognised the wider role of the Zion Mule Corps, and generously acknowledged that 'Trumpeldor was right: though it was in the Jordan Valley that we were victorious, the way through Gallipoli was the right way.'[60]

The presence of Jabotinsky, Patterson and the Zion Mule Corps cadre in Britain in 1916, combined to ensure that efforts were made in Britain to raise a full Jewish Legion. Jabotinsky and Patterson were to find out that the Russian Jews of Whitechapel did not all share their zeal for Zionism and were not at all willing to undertake military service, particularly while Britain was allied to Russia. Furthermore, the Anglo-Jewish establishment preferred assimilation to separation and segregation, and the debate concerning Jewish military service polarised the Jewish community in Britain as never before. This debate and Jabotinsky's struggle must now be examined.

3
The Founding of the Legion: Part One

Whilst the Zion Mule Corps was engaged in the Dardanelles campaign, Vladimir Jabotinsky turned his attention towards securing the support of the western Allies for his Jewish Legion scheme. This task commenced even before Jabotinsky left Trumpeldor in Alexandria, when he received a telegram from Pinhas Rutenberg who had previously advised Chaim Weizmann of his own Jewish Legion idea. They met for the first time in Brindisi, Italy, during the middle of April 1915, and immediately explored their common interest in forming a Jewish Legion. They reasoned that there was massive potential for recruitment among Russian Jews living in western Europe and the United States, and that it would be necessary to approach all the western Allies with an interest in the Mediterranean region, in order to ensure sufficient support for their ideas. They finally decided to work together in Rome, after which Jabotinsky was to take their case to Paris and London whilst Rutenberg travelled to the United States, where he would work to recruit support from amongst New York's Jews.[1]

Jabotinsky's single-minded determination prevented him from fully appreciating the difficulties that support for his scheme would bring to the Allied governments and politicians he dealt with. His direct approach, whilst commendable for its honesty, was diplomatically naive and therefore unlikely to achieve the results he hoped for. This was amply demonstrated in Rome, where the Italians responded negatively to Jabotinsky's and Rutenberg's overtures. They were looking for a sponsor and paymaster, but Italy was still neutral and it would therefore have been most untoward for the Italian government to give any hint of support to such a scheme.

Jabotinsky duly travelled on to Paris where he renewed his acquaintance with Chaim Weizmann, whom he knew from various Zionist congresses. Weizmann, in the course of his own work for Zionism, was a frequent visitor to Paris and while he was personally convinced that a Jewish homeland should be a British protectorate, he also appreciated that Britain would be loath to upset relations with France. Weizmann's dealings with both governments were therefore circumspect at this stage of the war, and it is more than likely that he left Jabotinsky to sound out the French attitude to Palestine through the Jewish Legion proposal. This supposition is supported by the fact that Weizmann asked Jabotinsky to cable him in London with the results of his meeting with Delcassé, the French foreign minister. Jabotinsky offered the French the services of a Jewish Corps in their army, in return for assurances of French support for the Zionist cause. The quid pro quo for France would have been assistance in the war against Turkey and an increased regard for France by the future Jews of Palestine. Inevitably, French support was not forthcoming, and the impression the French minister left on Jabotinsky is perhaps best summarised by the following extract taken from the report he sent back to Weizmann: '(a) France is already aware that she will not be allowed to annex Palestine ; (b) The Government is not interested in Zionism.'[2]

The failures in Italy and France can be attributed to Jabotinsky's naivety and unwillingness to take into account the likely consequences of their agreement to endorse publicly his type of overt nationalist Zionism. Nevertheless, he could take considerable consolation from the fact that he had secured support from Weizmann, whose interests happily coincided with his own as far as the Legion was concerned. The blossoming of their friendship also materially assisted Jabotinsky, as he was able to operate from Weizmann's base in London, which then consisted of a small, rented property at 3 Justice Walk, Chelsea.

Unfortunately, Weizmann's support for his friend caused him much embarrassment within the international Zionist movement. On 10 June 1915, the World Zionist Organisation had passed a resolution affirming the official Zionist position of neutrality, a decision designed to protect the interests of Jews living in all combatant countries. Neutrality had also been reinforced by the decision of the organisation to relocate its headquarters from Berlin to Copenhagen (the Copenhagen Bureau), a move Weizmann opposed as futile and meaningless. He considered that the policy of neutrality was detrimental to the ultimate aims of Zionists; it gave no regard to the post-war future of the Middle East in the political settlement that was bound to follow the end of the war. Quite simply, Weizmann considered the neutral option to be soft, timid and defensive, promising nothing for the future, and he was prepared to back his own judgement and take a calculated risk to secure a stake in the peace.³

It was not only with the organisation, however that Weizmann had policy differences. On a more personal level, two of Weizmann's closest Zionist colleagues, Ahad Ha'am and Nathan Sokolow, were stoutly opposed to the Jewish Legion scheme. The whole situation required a delicate balancing and diplomatic act on Weizmann's part that he summarised as, 'To conduct Zionist policy during the First World War was to walk on eggs.'⁴

The early summer months of 1915 saw Jabotinsky on his travels once again, when he paid what proved to be his last visit to Russia where he secured continuing employment and sponsorship from the editor of the *Russian Monitor*, Professor Manuilov. This valuable support enabled Jabotinsky to maintain his official journalist's credentials and the earnings provided him with resources to continue to live and work in the United Kingdom. On his way back to Britain, he visited the Zionist Bureau at Copenhagen where senior members and officials in the shape of Tschlenow, Victor Jacobson and Henke tried to persuade him – without success – to drop the Jewish Legion idea.⁵

Jabotinsky arrived back in London in August 1915, and began to make preparations for the renewal of his campaign to convince the Government of the benefits of a Jewish Legion. Unfortunately, he discovered that the British authorities were not in the ideal frame of mind to consider a further development in the Mediterranean theatre, let alone pay prompt attention to a proposal for a Jewish Legion designed for service with the British Army in Palestine. The continuing disappointment of the Gallipoli expedition was exacerbating the argument between the military and political leadership over the direction of strategy, with regard to concentrating resources on the western or eastern front.

Against this unpromising background, Jabotinsky continued to cultivate the encouragement of committed individuals, both Jewish and Gentile. An example of the latter is Lt.-Col. Patterson who, in turn, secured the support of General Birdwood. Firm evidence confirming this endorsement is available in a letter Patterson wrote to Jabotinsky on 10 November 1915, in reply to Jabotinsky's proposals regarding the formation of a Jewish Brigade. In his letter Patterson mentioned that he had shown General Birdwood the proposals:

> and he at once saw how useful to our cause a Brigade of young Jewish soldiers would be, and he was of the opinion that I should

proceed to England to assist in the raising of the Corps, but of course this decision must rest with the War Office in London where the Case has now, as I understand been referred. Personally nothing would give me greater gratification than to raise, train and command a Jewish Fighting Unit, as, from what I have seen of the Jewish youth serving under me here, I am quite certain that I could lead them successfully anywhere.[6]

Meanwhile, Jabotinsky had formally approached the War Office in London with the proposal that the Zion Mule Corps be expanded into a Jewish Legion or Brigade. The War Office replied in a letter dated 18 November 1915:

The War Office consider that it would be better not to interfere with the Zion Mule Corps but leave it where it is doing good work. If you are confident of getting plenty of men, it is suggested that you should apply to the Foreign Office for permission to raise a Foreign Legion to fight for the allies. Signed Casgrain Major G.S. (General Staff).[7]

Jabotinsky's term 'Jewish Legion', although unrecognised by the authorities, would later become the colloquial title used by the recruiters in Britain and the United States, and by the soldiers who served in it.

Jabotinsky was nothing if not single-minded, but the beliefs and attitudes of the various Jewish communities in Britain during the autumn of 1915 tested his resolve to the utmost. Three important difficulties needed to be addressed if the Legion was to progress from idea to reality. The first of these was the obstructive attitude of several leading members of the official Zionist organisations. Jabotinsky was well aware of the deep-seated nature of their objections through the difficulties caused to his friend Chaim Weizmann. Secondly, there was the antipathy of the individuals the Legion was designed to recruit, the Russian Jews resident in Britain, and their negative attitude towards enlistment and participation in the British war effort. Thirdly, Jabotinsky had to contend with the opposition of the major part of the Anglo-Jewish establishment, which believed his ideas constituted a threat to the position of Jews in British society. In addition to dealing with these difficulties, Jabotinsky had to influence British opinion and patiently develop arguments that would encourage the Government, through the Foreign and War Offices, to support his scheme.

Exactly how Jabotinsky coped with British politics and procedure, and succeeded in obtaining official sanction for the formation of a Jewish fighting unit, is well documented in primary source material from public records and Anglo-Jewish archives. Before reviewing these papers and tracing the development of the Legion, it is necessary to analyse the three factors mentioned above, so as to appreciate the Jewish context and perspectives which Jabotinsky and his supporters had to take into account.

The most comprehensive survey of Britain's Jewish community including its sub-communities in the period is to be found in Eugene C. Black's *The Social Politics of Anglo-Jewry 1880–1920*. In this work, Black uses an institutional and organisational approach which clearly identifies the three main elements of Jewish society in Britain as being firstly, the original Sephardi immigrants who entered Britain in the century following Cromwell's re-admittance of the Jews, secondly the Ashkenazi families who came to Britain mainly in the late seventeenth and eighteenth centuries, and finally the Russian (Ashkenazi) immigrants who, having fled the pogroms in Tsarist Russia, arrived in Britain in great numbers between 1880 and 1905. The first two groups had become, by the time of the arrival of the third, politically emancipated and established as an Anglo-Jewish community that was British by nationality and outlook. By the pre-war decade, Anglo-Jewry was represented in high levels of government, banking and commerce, and Black describes and analyses the efforts made by this established community, known colloquially as 'West End' Jewry, to deal with the social and economic problems presented by their alien co-religionists who had mainly settled in the East End of London.[8]

The main thrust of their efforts was to encourage the assimilation of these Russian Jews, most of whom retained their Russian nationality, despite being second- or even third-generation immigrants by 1914. Other efforts were made to encourage the resettlement of the Russian immigrants, particularly in Palestine, an idea involving, in part, the doctrine of Zionism examined in greater detail below. It must be said that this dual policy, a curious mixture of acceptance and rejection, is likely to have been both a source of contention among Jews, and of confusion for British Gentiles when dealing with the Jews. Black succinctly summarises the divide between British Jews and alien Jews and explains the basic difference in their respective view of military service, emphasising the difficulty of requiring aliens to serve at a time when conscription for British citizens had not yet been introduced. British Jews had volunteered for service since the beginning of the war and served throughout the various branches of the armed services. The Russian Jews, however, regarded service as an ally of the Tsarist regime that had treated them so appallingly as unacceptable and, as Black points out; 'For their part, the alien Jews, almost exclusively Russian, regarded recruitment as a thinly disguised scheme to take away their hard-won East End homes, jobs and sanctuary.'[9]

David Cesarani agrees with Black's observations and goes further:

> British-born Jews were deeply embarrassed by the behaviour of their co-religionists [Russian immigrant Jews]. They sympathised broadly with the various experiments which the government undertook in an effort to induct immigrant Jews into military service in 1916–17 and became increasingly intolerant of the opposition aroused by these schemes.[10]

David Feldman's analysis of the behaviour of established Anglo-Jewry towards the immigrants acknowledges that assimilation of the late arrivals was seen as a means of placating the host population, which was generally antipathetic to immigration. Like the earlier development of Reform Judaism, which attempted to mirror, in Jewish society, the position of religion in British society, this was a defensive strategy designed to align Jews in Britain with the indigenous community.[11]

Nationality and patriotic obligations were not the only factors determining differences of opinion both within and between the various Jewish groups. Political and class factors were also important causes of dissension within the Jewish community as a whole, and reflected not only the cultural and economic differences between British and alien Jews, but also the social changes that were taking place in Britain generally. This was because assimilated Jews, particularly those who had been accepted into the upper and middle classes, adopted elite social values, and saw their Jewishness more as a devotional practice than a whole way of life. This separation of religion from other aspects of identity, and the adoption of Anglicised clerical titles for Rabbis, was anathema to many Russian immigrants for whom their religion provided social and cultural sustenance as well as spiritual fulfilment.

The most important political factor was the growth of Zionism which, under the pressures created by the war, quickly became the focal point of many of the internal arguments regarding Jewish national identity and the political future of the Jewish people. It has already been noted that many British Gentiles, such as Hamilton, Birdwood and Patterson, supported Jabotinsky's cause out of certain sympathy for Zionist aims. A similar sympathy was also instrumental in securing the later support of Lloyd George, Balfour, Amery, C.P. Scott and others for a Jewish homeland, under British protection, which was crucial to the issuing of the Balfour Declaration in November 1917 (see Chapter 5).

International relations, political aspirations and considerations of race, religion and war can each be seen as having an impact upon Jabotinsky's activities. In his quest for a Jewish Legion, Jabotinsky, despite his single-mindedness, did not attempt to surmount the obstacles in his path alone. Whilst he remained the driving force behind the scheme, other personalities, some of whom were mentioned earlier, supported and encouraged his efforts to overcome the inertia caused by the difficulties referred to above.

Of fundamental importance was his relationship with Chaim Weizmann, through whom Jabotinsky began to develop a network of important contacts and supporters, both Jewish and Gentile, such as Joseph Cowen, Montague Eder and C.P. Scott, the editor of the *Manchester Guardian*. Cowen had become the owner of the *Jewish Chronicle* in 1907, had been introduced to Zionism by his relative, Israel Zangwill, and was a founder of the British Zionist Federation. Another relative of Zangwill's, and incidentally Cowen's brother-in-law, was Dr Montague Eder, a practising physician and psychoanalyst. Both Cowen and Eder were closely associated with Weizmann's efforts to secure British support for a Jewish homeland in Palestine against the policy of the World Zionist Organisation.

Weizmann and Scott had met, by chance, at a party in Manchester in the autumn of 1914. Their friendship grew quickly and Weizmann indicated the high level of trust that sprang up between them by recording that:

> He [Scott] was so unaffected, so open, so charming that I simply could not help pouring out my heart to him. I told him of my hatred for Russia, of the internal conflicts of the Jews, of our universal tragedy, of our hopes and aspirations for Palestine, of the little we had already done there, and of our almost Messianic dreams – such as they appeared then – for the future.[12]

Scott enthusiastically studied Palestine and the Jewish question with Weizmann and, in return, provided a valuable service by arranging meetings with Lloyd George, then Chancellor of the Exchequer, Herbert Samuel, also in government, and others, thus opening some of the key doors to Whitehall. As an accredited journalist, Jabotinsky developed other avenues to the corridors of power, though his way was made easier by the fact that the Zion Mule Corps had become known in London via Russian and British diplomatic channels.

Another friendship, begun in correspondence and destined to become the closest and most important relationship throughout this whole chain of events, was affirmed in December 1915 when Lt.-Col. Patterson and Jabotinsky finally met in London. Their meeting was arranged when Patterson (prompted by General Birdwood), arrived in London on convalescent leave, and wrote to Jabotinsky requesting they get together to discuss their common interests. Soon after their initial meeting Patterson took Jabotinsky to the House of Commons to meet Captain Leopold Amery, a Unionist Member of Parliament who was to become an influential and important advocate of the Jewish Legion scheme. Amery and Patterson's acquaintance had its roots in the Boer War, where Amery had been a military correspondent of *The Times*. Amery had recently returned from a War Office liaison appointment in the Balkans and Gallipoli, and was critical of Asquith's leadership. Now armed with personal knowledge of the reality of war on the eastern and western fronts, and convinced that Britain needed a fully resourced and co-ordinated strategy, Amery used his parliamentary position to promote the pursuit of the eastern option and advocate the introduction of conscription.

When Jabotinsky returned to Britain in the late summer of 1915, voluntary enlistment was still in force but it was becoming clear that the unprecedented numbers needed for a war of attrition would require, sooner or later, a system of compulsion. Prime Minister Asquith was personally opposed to conscription, and its delayed and gradual introduction has been ascribed to the premier's dilatory and ineffective leadership, though scholars have contested this interpretation.[13]

The National Registration Act was duly enacted in July 1915, and required all men between the ages of fifteen and forty-one to register their names on lists that would be made available to recruiting offices. This was itself soon followed by a final effort to secure the army's supply of men through voluntary means, when the government introduced the Derby Scheme between October 1915 and January 1916. Under it, men were invited to pledge their services by 'attestation'; in practice they joined up for the day of their attestation and then returned to their usual occupation to await call up from the 'reserve' they were deemed to have joined.

Whether an appeal for volunteers, based on harsh but true information, would have succeeded in attracting sufficient numbers cannot be known though it seems highly unlikely. In the context of Jewish military service, established British Jewry had broadly supported the war effort and British Jews had volunteered as eagerly as their countrymen,[14] but the Government had prevented resident aliens from enlisting, under the Defence of the Realm Act and the Aliens Restriction Act, both of 1914. One of the complications involved in the administration of these acts was the distinction between enemy, neutral and friendly aliens. David Cesarani has argued that the prevailing anti-alienism made the application of these acts somewhat impracticable, as the powers they contained 'rested on the premise that friendly and enemy aliens could be distinguished. This proved difficult in practice.'[15]

Despite this difficulty, the search for manpower and the continuing unease over the unwillingness of most Russian Jews in the East End of London to volunteer, encouraged Lord Derby to examine means of including aliens in his scheme. In an interview with the *Jewish Chronicle*, on 19 November 1915 he confirmed that he was 'looking to arrange enlistment of foreign born men who have been in Britain since infancy'.[16]

The Anglo-Jewish community was also seeking to use the Derby Scheme to promote the recruitment of their co-religionists. The Board of Deputies discussed the question of recruiting at a meeting on 21 November 1915 where it was stated, 'British born sons of Russian Jews were not being permitted to enlist if fathers not naturalized.' Various members of the board made statements citing examples, and David Lindo Alexander, the president, referred to correspondence between Leopold Rothschild and Lord Derby where the latter had written that he 'hoped to be able to alter affairs'. Alexander also advised the committee that Lord Derby's public statements were encouraging, and the item was concluded by H.S.Q. Henriques stating that 'the Board was doing its best to claim for Jews the rights (to enlist) that were refused them in this society'. The outcome of this dialogue between Anglo-Jewry and Lord Derby was the establishment of a Jewish Recruiting Committee that was described by the *Jewish Chronicle* of 10 December as a 'medium between Jews and the military'.[17]

The War Office announced the formation of the Jewish Recruiting Committee on 18 December 1915, and confirmed that a British-born Jew of friendly alien parentage was now eligible for service. Being 'eligible for service' was not the same as joining up, however, and it was now becoming increasingly evident that the Derby scheme was but a stepping-stone between voluntarism and compulsion. In January 1916, conscription was introduced for single men and, in May, extended to their married fellows. The atmosphere of compulsion produced a heightened public awareness of the question of Russian Jewish military service, and greatly increased internecine tension within the Jewish community.

Against this background C.P. Scott and Leo Amery gave Jabotinsky and Patterson the opportunity to present their case for a Jewish Legion directly to the Foreign and War Offices in Whitehall. Scott wrote to Lord Robert Cecil at the Foreign Office on 11 December 1915, formally introducing Jabotinsky and reminding the minister of the services of the Zion Mule Corps. Jabotinsky followed this up with a letter to Cecil dated 22 December referring to Scott's introduction, and requesting a meeting at the Foreign Office. He also enclosed his own credentials as an accredited Russian journalist together with testimonials regarding the Zion Mule Corps from General Hamilton and Lt.-Col. Patterson. In order to present his proposal Jabotinsky included a memorandum entitled 'Jewish Eastern Legion'. The Legion, he explained, was 'to consist of foreign subjects only as British Jews have naturally to serve their country at any front or operation'. Furthermore, government assistance was asked for, in the form of a London Central recruitment office. A Foreign Office note on the file clearly shows that it was of the opinion that the question of foreign recruitment must be left to the War Office, and there is no record of a reply, at this stage, to Jabotinsky from Cecil.[18]

Three weeks later on 11 January 1916, Patterson wrote to Cecil enclosing a letter of introduction from Leo Amery at the War Office, and requesting a meeting. Cecil replied confirming that an appointment had been made for Patterson at the Foreign Office on Tuesday 18 January; a prompt response in contrast to the treatment of Jabotinsky. This difference was unsurprising, for Jabotinsky was a known Zionist and Russian journalist introduced by the editor of a radical newspaper, whereas Patterson was a senior serving officer with an introduction from a sitting MP. At their meeting, Cecil must have asked Patterson for further information because, on the following day, Patterson wrote to Cecil giving him a brief account of the Zion Mule Corps. Patterson also mentioned that many letters of support for the corps had been received from Jews and Gentiles alike, with, 'The most important of the latter coming from President Roosevelt who was keenly interested in this move to counter Jewish sympathy for Germany – which exists mainly owing to hatred of Russia.'[19] In this context it should be noted that, according to Weber, there were some 615,000 Jews in Germany in 1914, compared with 240,000 in Britain.[20] The anti-Russian feeling of Eastern European Jews in Germany, Britain and Russia should not be underestimated; in the battle to secure Jewish support it was a crucial factor.

Clearly, Patterson was not shy of using his position, and was aware of the difficulties that Britain was having with pro-German propaganda in the United States, despite the nine-month-old furore over the sinking of the *Lusitania*. He also took the opportunity to point out to Cecil that Allied support for a Jewish Legion could lead to an uprising in Palestine, where 40,000 Jews could be mobilised against the Turks, and that the prestige of the British Government would be greatly enhanced amongst world Jewry. Finally, he urged the Foreign Office to force the issue as he feared that the War Office was 'always opposed to new schemes'.[21] These were all good points, strongly made, but unfortunately demonstrate that Patterson, no doubt influenced by Jabotinsky and Trumpeldor, did not appreciate the complexities and realities of international Zionist politics, and assumed that British foreign policy in the Middle East was ready to comply with Jabotinsky's dream. Cecil merely noted on the file that he thought 'there was a good deal in what Patterson says/proposes but FO must fall in with WO – it is their matter'.[22]

The Foreign Office were well aware of the War Office's position as they were in receipt of a minute written on 17 January 1916, headed 'Military objections and administrative difficulties of the scheme' which included the following statement that unequivocally confirms the official military opinion:

> Is it not likely that this corps may in someway be brought in connection with the Zionist movement? As a matter of fact Mr. Jabotinsky was told some ten months ago that we could not entertain a scheme of his to raise a corps of Jews for service in Palestine. On the whole therefore we are not in favour of this project.[23]

The mention of events 'ten months ago' obviously refers to Jabotinsky's initial recruiting activities in Alexandria, from where he originally attempted to persuade the British authorities to back his idea. A week after this War Office note was made, Patterson received a letter from Cecil, which confirmed that, due to the objections of the War Office, the Foreign Office could not offer its support.

Jabotinsky in the meanwhile was not content with sitting back to await a response from the Foreign Office, and set about cultivating a further influential relationship with Charles Masterman, another former *Times* man and ex-Cabinet minister who was now the head of the War

Propaganda Bureau. They met during the course of an official press visit to the Grand Fleet at Rosyth Naval Base. On 26 January 1916 Jabotinsky wrote to Masterman elaborating on the virtues of his scheme. In his letter he pointed out that there were one and a quarter million Jews in the United States with 'serious political influence', and emphasised the same propaganda factors that Patterson had referred to earlier. Jabotinsky also informed Masterman of Patterson's efforts and argued that 'Zionism is [the] anvil for scheme for Legion [sic]'[24] There is no record of a reply from Masterman or the Propaganda Bureau but a file note from the Foreign Office indicates that the scheme was not of sufficient interest to the War Office or the Foreign Office, and that 'there are no great benefits although perhaps it will upset US which likes all its citizens to serve under stars and stripes'.[25] This is an interesting comment that reveals a desire not to take any risks with Anglo-American relations.

On 10 February 1916, nearly a month after Patterson had received his unhelpful reply, Jabotinsky finally received a note from the Foreign Office confirming that it could not consider his proposal until the military authorities gave their approval. Shortly afterwards, an attempt was made to break the impasse by Leo Amery, whose persistence in this matter can be attributed to both his imperialist ambition to promote British interests in the middle east, and his pro-Zionism. The existence and importance of these beliefs have been made more understandable through the recent research of William D. Rubinstein, which has revealed that Amery's mother was Jewish, being a member of a Hungarian family that had converted to Protestantism, and that Amery made great efforts to disguise his origins, perhaps using his public support of the Zionist cause to camouflage his inner identity.[26]

Amery tabled a parliamentary question for Cecil asking whether or not the Foreign Office had any objection to the raising of the Legion, and suggesting that they might write to the War Office about it. The reply advised that the FO had 'no objection on political grounds to the raising of a Jewish Corps in England'.[27] This remark was immediately followed by a statement in parentheses '(We are not at all irrevocably opposed to Zionism)', which demonstrates that the FO was aware of the implications and motives of the scheme, and provides evidence of some sympathy for Zionism. Perhaps this is what Amery was trying to exploit in his next letter to Cecil, dated 26 February in which he wrote:

> (3) Jewish Corps ... as far as I can make out it was turned down by the WO not on military but on foreign policy grounds, because we don't want to get committed to, or entangled in, Zionist schemes ...

If the FO view is different and they don't fear Zionist complications and favour the scheme from the point of view of effect upon American Jews then it might be worth you writing a letter to the WO informally ... thus reopening the question.[28]

The FO replied to Amery, through Cecil, on 11 March in a carefully worded letter that confirmed that there were no political objections but:

> that if there is any intention of proceeding with the scheme, it must of course be understood that the Legion will be limited to British or Allied subjects, as the recruitment of Jews from neutral countries would land us in political complications, especially with the United States.[29]

This extract was entirely consistent with the sentiment expressed by the FO in their file note covering Jabotinsky's earlier correspondence with Masterman, and by specifically mentioning 'Allied subjects' included the recruitment of Russian Jews as envisaged by the scheme.

Political complications notwithstanding, the propaganda perspective had assumed significance in its own right. Masterman, despite the official response to Jabotinsky's overtures, did in fact fully appreciate the propaganda potential of the Jewish Legion idea and had arranged for Jabotinsky to meet with Lord Newton, the minister for propaganda at the Foreign Office, who was himself concerned with the pro-German views being put forward in the United States.[30] Jabotinsky used the remainder of the interview to advise Lord Newton of his belief that Jews loved Palestine more than they hated Russia, and that a British commitment to Zionism, supported by the raising of a Jewish Legion, would win the Jews over. Newton's response was necessarily cautious, but he did inform Jabotinsky that his proposals would be considered and discussed in the department, and that he would be interested in talking to Patterson. On 27 March Masterman wrote to Newton to thank him for seeing Jabotinsky and reiterated that:

> I am sure that a Jewish Legion, fighting as volunteers for us in Eastern Europe, would be an enormous asset for our propagandist work in America, and to oppose the continued stories of Jewish persecution and outrages on the Jews by the Russians which are printed by the pro-German newspapers.[31]

In a note written underneath his signature, Masterman suggested to Newton that if he required further information he should contact

Patterson, whose address could be obtained through the Foreign Office. As Jabotinsky had already passed on Newton's interest to Patterson, he (Patterson) did not wait to hear from the minister for propaganda, but wrote directly to Newton on 11 April. A meeting was arranged for the afternoon of the 12th, at the Foreign Office, after which Newton continued to develop his department's interest in the scheme.

Newton's department was not the only body to consider the propaganda value of an information campaign amongst 'the neutral Jewries' at this time. The Anglo-Jewish establishment was also aware of the potential benefits to the Allied cause that could be obtained by countering the German propaganda that was being circulated among the Jews of the United States. Lucien Wolf, the secretary of the Conjoint Committee Foreign Branch, compiled a 'confidential suggestion' for a counter-campaign in America supported by the following points:

(1) Jews more sympathetic since Lusitania.
(2) Majority are German Jews with two-thirds being second generation American – but their fathers and grandfathers do not remember an [sic] united Germany therefore tend to be liberal in outlook and anti-Prussian so only need a little push.
(3) The German immigrants are liberal but from the time of the German Empire are perhaps the most devout pro-Germans.
(4) Russian Jews – numerous and hostile to Russia thus resenting the triple entente. But they know nothing of modern Germany and could be converted to allied cause. Zionism is the key although the author deprecates this as Jewishness is not a nationality.[32]

In his fourth point, Wolf summarised the most difficult question faced by the Anglo-Jewish establishment in its affirmation of continued Jewish solidarity with the British and Allied war effort. He appreciated that the behaviour of Russian Jews in Britain would be seen by the host population as being representative of the attitude of the wider Jewish community. Unfortunately for Wolf, who was in effect, as noted by Eugene Black, the Anglo-Jewish 'Foreign Secretary',[33] the support of Russian Jews for the British war effort could only be secured by aligning them with Jabotinsky's form of Zionism. To support Jabotinsky, however, was plainly contrary to all that the Anglo-Jewish assimilationist leadership believed in and strived for. The two horns of the dilemma they faced were that they could neither work with Jabotinsky nor ignore the increasing public disquiet over the question of alien recruitment.

As far as Jabotinsky and the Jewish Legion were concerned, the significance of Wolf's work lay in the fact that he was recognised by the government as the representative of Anglo-Jewry, and frequently consulted as such by various ministers and officials. Surviving papers, in the Archive of the Board of Deputies of British Jews and the Anglo-Jewish Archive of Southampton University, contain some of the details of Wolf's diplomatic efforts and demonstrate, once more, the complexities of the Jewish community and the difficulties surrounding the question of military service and the Russian Jews.

Of particular relevance are the documents relating to the Conjoint Committee Foreign Branch, of which – as mentioned above – Wolf was the secretary. The Conjoint Committee consisted of leading representatives of the Board of Deputies of British Jews and the Anglo-Jewish Association, including David Lindo Alexander, H. Sq. Henriques and Claude G. Montefiore. The assimilationist credentials of the Conjoint Committee were impeccable. Alexander was a distinguished barrister and president of the Board of Deputies, Henriques a long-standing member of the board and Claude Montefiore was the president of the Anglo-Jewish Association. In many respects Montefiore was the embodiment of an assimilated British Jew, for whom nationality and religion were discrete identities, as in the case of a British Roman Catholic. In commenting upon the strength of this feeling within Claude Montefiore, Eugene Black quotes from a sermon in which he (Montefiore) asserts the case for the separation of race and religion – the precondition of Jewish emancipation having been met – and writes:

> Small wonder that Montefiore, more strongly than any Anglo-Jewish leader, would resist, denounce and fight the emergence of Jewish nationalism. For those who sought refuge from anti-Semitism and the tremors of his age in a Jewish state and Jewish nationalism, Montefiore argued the case for Jewish universalism.[34]

The Conjoint Committee recorded, in March 1915, its policy with regard to Zionism:

> Our present view is that the Zionist programme in Palestine can never offer any solution of the large practical questions that confront us in Russia, Poland and Roumania, and hence it must be regarded as essentially a sentimental question. Nevertheless, it is one which appeals to the historic sense of all Jews, and also to the religious hopes of many non-Jews.[35]

Given the composition of the committee, the above statement is slightly surprising in that, whilst it contained a dismissive recognition of Zionist activity, it did not overtly promote assimilation. The inference, however, is clear. Jews in Eastern Europe required emancipation before assimilation was possible. There is no doubt that, as far as Russia was concerned, the committee envisaged Jews earning emancipation through their contribution to the military and industrial war effort, and they even asked the British Government to exert pressure on their Russian allies so as to encourage and sustain Jewish involvement. This followed a report by Wolf that evidence existed, from a number of correspondents, which demonstrated that the Russian authorities were decrying the war services of their Jewish soldiers 'in order to prevent them from reaping the reward of their patriotic self sacrifice at the end of the war'.[36]

Lucien Wolf and the Conjoint Committee were fully aware that a similar anti-Semitic attitude could arise in Britain by the end of the war, if the question of military service by Russian Jews living in Britain was not settled. Indeed, proper recognition of the services and sacrifices of the 50,000 British Jews who had already volunteered was threatened by the inadequate response of East End Jews to the Jewish Recruitment Committee's pleadings. The introduction of conscription having brought this issue to a head, the Home Secretary Herbert Samuel, had to respond to the growing public resentment against the Russian Jews. As a Jew he was cogniscent of the internecine arguments that Zionism in general and the military service issue in particular, had provoked. Turkey's entry into the war had opened Samuel's mind to the possibility of a Jewish state in Palestine and, in his memoirs, he reproduced a conversation with Sir Edward Grey, the foreign secretary on 9 November 1914. Samuel recorded:

> I thought that British influence ought to play a considerable part in the formation of such a state, because the geographical situation of Palestine, and especially its proximity to Egypt, would render its goodwill to England a matter of importance to the British Empire. I suggested that the English and American Jews ought to take the leadership in such an enterprise, if it were undertaken. The Germans could do nothing in present circumstances; the French were not sufficiently influential, nor the Italians; it was important that the new state should be founded under the auspices of the most progressive countries in which the Jews found themselves.[37]

These remarks make clear that Samuel combined his Zionist sympathies with an appreciation of what he regarded as politically and strategically important for Britain's national and imperial interests. The complications that were to arise in 1916, over conscription and Russian Jewish recruitment, could not have been foreseen in 1914, and Bernard Wasserstein, in his biography of Samuel, has very neatly expressed the latter's dilemma in 1916 by commenting that:

> As minister responsible for Aliens, as a Jew, and as one who had championed the notion that Jewish nationalism could be realized in a form that would benefit British strategic interests, Samuel found himself confronted with a potentially embarrassing controversy.[38]

Samuel realised that voluntary recruitment efforts would probably fail to assuage public opinion and reassure the Anglo-Jewish establishment, and he began to develop a solution to the problem based on compulsion. In essence, Samuel's policy was to allow time for voluntary recruitment to operate, whilst raising the spectre of compulsion through the adoption of a Military Service Convention with Allied states. The convention when enacted would give the British Government the right to offer friendly aliens in Britain, who mainly consisted of Russian Jews, the option of conscription into the British Army, or passage home for enlistment in their own army. Implicit in the operation of the convention was the threat of deportation for those not complying with its requirements. The need to consult Allied states and secure their agreement to the convention, and to consider the effects of such legislation on existing regulations concerning aliens and military service, delayed its enactment until July 1917. Nevertheless, between early 1916 and the early summer of 1917, the convention scheme greatly influenced the debate over the proposal for a Jewish Legion.

As early as 7 April 1916, Samuel consulted with Wolf and received the wholehearted support of the Conjoint Committee for the convention policy. No such support, however, was forthcoming from the *Jewish Chronicle* which, on 14 April, commented that military service conventions with Allied states were just, but not for Russian Jews, because of their unequal status in their home country. The editorial went on to state:

> It [the convention] would be the exchange of freedom for oppression. The men referred to, all others similarly placed so far as residence in

allied countries is concerned have already been authorised to enlist in the army of the country where they reside. That or the formation of a Jewish Battalion on the lines of the Zion Mule Corps would adequately meet the case of the Russian Jews. The other would be unthinkable. It may perhaps be pointed out that according to the Labour party in the Duma, the Jews in Russia have already given over 400,000 men to the colours ...[39]

The inequality alluded to by the *Jewish Chronicle* was central to Jabotinsky's own rejection of the conventionist policy, and to his conviction that the formation of a Jewish military unit provided the best solution to the whole problem. Jabotinsky described the underlying factors of his reasoning in a conversation with Joseph King, a radical West Country Liberal Member of Parliament, who had brought Jabotinsky's activities to the notice of the House of Commons. The pair met in early 1916 and King, speaking on behalf of his 'Whitechapel friends', derided Jabotinsky's efforts and advised him that 'I have told them [my Whitechapel friends] that it would be best if a large number of foreign Jews were to join the British Army together with our own boys.' Jabotinsky replied:

> That is where you are mistaken. It is an unjust demand ... Because there is a vast difference between your boys and those East End boys. Your boys are British; if Britain wins their people is saved. Ours are Jews; if Britain wins, millions of their brothers will still remain in purgatory. You cannot demand equal sacrifices where the hope is not an equal one ... a compromise. In order to be just you can demand only two things from the foreign Jew: first 'Home defence,' to protect Britain itself, because he lives here; second, to fight for the liberation of Palestine, for that is to be the Heim of his people. 'Home and Heim' – that is my war motto for your Whitechapel friends.[40]

Joseph King continued to press Samuel and the government on their intentions respecting the convention and published, in late April, the result of his enquiries into the matter. He confirmed that a Russian citizen of good character could not be pressed into British service, and advised that the Russian government had yet to contact the British authorities regarding the proposed convention. Finally, he wrote that 'The proposal to raise a Jewish Battalion for definite service under British command presents a number of difficulties and need not be pressed at present.'[41] Thus, the position adopted by Joseph King reflected East End Jewish feeling. His view of the situation contrasted starkly with that of Jabotinsky, on the one hand, and Wolf and the Anglo-Jewish establishment on the other.

Despite this evidence of the differences within the Jewish community as a whole, Jabotinsky's 'compromise' offer to raise a Jewish Legion was further investigated by the government in an attempt to find a practical solution to the problem. Wolf reported to the Conjoint Committee that his views on the idea of a Jewish Legion had been canvassed by Hubert Montgomery, of the department of information at the Foreign Office, in May 1916. This approach and Wolf's response to it have been commented upon by Isaiah Friedman, who places particular emphasis on Wolf's opinion that the Jewish Legion idea needed to be discussed with Anglo-Jewish representatives, and that the formation of such a force would result in many unspecified difficulties for the Jewish community. Friedman does not, however, mention other parts of the letter that Wolf sent to Montgomery, which give a clear impression of the depth of his antipathy towards Zionists and Jabotinsky. In the letter, dated 22 May 1916 Wolf wrote:

> As far as I can see, it [the Legion idea] is almost universally disapproved. It originated with a hare-brained ex-Nihilist named Ruthenberg, who has lately become a violent Zionist. Jabotinsky, who now advocates it, has no position in the Jewish community at all, and I am told is disavowed even by the Zionists.[42]

Wolf's representation of the Zionist view was based on the official Zionist executive policy of neutrality, and he was clearly not aware of Jabotinsky's close relationship with Weizmann. This is important, because Weizmann's growing influence with the British Government gave him credibility as a Zionist representative, despite his holding no formal office in the official Zionist organisation (and disagreement with neutrality), and added weight to his support for Jabotinsky. Mark Levene, in describing Wolf's dealings with Weizmann throughout the war, has noted how the balance of representative power that existed between them had changed, in Weizmann's favour, by the middle of 1916.[43]

The continuing pressure that was being placed upon Russian Jews to volunteer, and the impact that it was having upon the fears of British Jews, was reflected in the *Jewish Chronicle* of 26 May. In a leader entitled 'Aliens and Enlistment', the newspaper acknowledged 'a certain moral validity to the agitation in the press in favour of compulsory service for allied citizens'. The leader went on to repeat the special case of the Russian Jews but concluded, 'With compulsion there is now no reason why the proposal of a special unit should not be reconsidered.'[44] War Office records of the same month show that the Army Council was not yet willing to endorse any such proposal. In reply to Major H. L. Nathan, a serving officer who had written to the War Office offering to raise and command a battalion of Russian and Polish Jews, the Army Council 'regretted they could not accept his offer or proposal'.[45]

Wolf was consulted by Samuel and Hubert Montgomery in late May, and discussed with David Lindo Alexander and Claude Montefiore the need to make some proposals to the government that would alleviate the problem of alien recruitment. In a letter, written on 2 June, to Leopold Rothschild, Wolf sought (successfully) endorsement for their main proposal which was that friendly aliens be subjected to compulsory enlistment, in return for which they would receive automatic – and thereby free – naturalisation as British subjects. Wolf assured Rothschild that the Yiddish press in the East End would support this initiative, and that like himself and his colleagues, the Zionists would be opposed to the formation of a specifically Jewish military unit.[46] Once again, this is entirely consistent with Wolf's understanding of the official Zionist position, and he went on, in an exchange of correspondence with Israel Zangwill, to attack vehemently the proponents of the Jewish Legion scheme. Zangwill had written:

> The East End Jewry seems considerably agitated about the possibility of aliens being deported to the Russian Army or conscription into our own. I remain of the opinion that the most desirable course is to collect them into a Jewish regiment.

This elicited the following response from Wolf, couched in terms that again betray the depth of his feelings:

> stormy meeting in East End yesterday re conscription of aliens. I am afraid the people are being deceived and misled by carpet bagging demagogues. As for a Jewish Regiment I can only say 'God Forbid'. As a matter of fact, the scheme has no friends at all, and even the Zionists are strongly opposed to it.[47]

Home Secretary Samuel agreed with Wolf's proposal that the voluntary enlistment of Russian Jews would be encouraged by the offer of free naturalisation at the end of the war, and persuaded his colleagues in government accordingly. On 8 June 1916 the War Office issued Army Council Instruction 1156 which confirmed that friendly aliens would now be permitted to join up. However, the restrictions imposed by the Army Act of 1908, that limited the ratio of aliens to British citizens within military units to no greater than one in fifty, remained in force. Although ACI 1156 was relevant to aliens of any friendly nationality, clause five of the Instruction explicitly covered Russian Jews, and stated:

> In the case of Russian Jews they may be recruited on production of a certificate from the Jewish War Services Committee, New Court, St. Swithins Lane, London E.C. and if they so desire, may be posted in batches to serve together in the same unit.[48]

Samuel was certainly confident that the introduction of ACI 1156 would result in the enlistment of friendly aliens, and thereby alleviate the social disorder their failure to participate in the military war effort had engendered. In correspondence with Asquith, Samuel wrote, on 9 June 1916, that such problems:

> will however, be greatly diminished as far as the competition of friendly aliens is concerned (specially serious in the East End of London) by the recent decision to enlist friendly aliens who are willing to serve in the British Army ... which is supplemented by the arrangements now in force for returning to their own country subjects of France, Belgium and Italy who are seeking to avoid military obligation by residence in this country.[49]

These comments make clear that the government had given Russian Jews the opportunity to volunteer before compulsion, through conscription or deportation, would be forced upon them, in contrast to the citizens of other allied countries. The relative importance of this concession, made in recognition of Jewish difficulties with the Tsar's regime, can be gauged by comparing it with the treatment of British born or naturalised sons of German or Austrian parentage. Following the introduction of compulsory service these British subjects were posted to Labour or Infantry Works Companies, as required by ACI 467 of 1 March 1916 and reinforced by ACI 582 of 15 March, which extended the scope of these postings to British subjects whose parents had been interned.[50] There can be no doubt therefore that the Russian Jews received special consideration with respect to conscription, but it was also clear that, unless a substantial voluntary effort was rapidly forthcoming, they could expect to be subject to the full powers available under the proposed Military Service Convention.

Throughout the remainder of June 1916, the *Jewish Chronicle* carried leading articles that supported compulsion, and doubted the success of the voluntary arrangements, but nevertheless appealed to East End co-religionists to come forward. On 23 June the newspaper, Anglo-Jewish in outlook and with some Russian readers, urged that 'the Board of Deputies and whole weight of Jewish leadership' be placed behind recruitment, as the Recruiting Committee was not succeeding in its efforts to attract a sufficient number of volunteers. This matter and correspondence critical of the Jewish war effort published in *The Globe* and *Pall Mall Gazette* was discussed by the Board of Deputies on 25 June, but the minutes of this meeting do not record whether or not specific action was considered or agreed.[51] In the same edition, the *Jewish Chronicle*, in a report reflecting its own lack of influence over the 'East End', stated that only 400 out of an estimated 10,000–12,000 Russian Jews of military age (government estimates at this time were double this figure)[52] had offered their services through the New Court Jewish Recruiting Committee. Within a week, these disappointing results forced Samuel to apply more public pressure to the reluctant Jews. This pressure was somewhat cautiously increased, because Samuel was in a dilemma throughout this episode. Speaking on 29 June, in the House of Commons, Samuel merely 'proposed to intimate' that compulsion to serve in either the British or Russian Armies would be introduced, if the voluntary scheme co-ordinated by the Jewish Recruiting Committee failed. It is significant that, at this stage, he stopped short of threatening actual deportation.[53]

Jabotinsky exhibited a similar willingness to compromise by writing to the *Jewish Chronicle*, the day after Samuel's statement, with a proposal that Russian Jews should be offered military employment only for the purpose of home defence of the United Kingdom. It is difficult to see how such a suggestion, if acted upon, would have done anything to alleviate the unrest in the East End. Moreover, the military and social difficulties that could have arisen from congregating large numbers of reluctant Russian Jewish soldiers in remote areas of Britain are easily envisaged. Perhaps Jabotinsky's proposal should be seen as evidence of frustration with the recruitment situation, and desperation as to the plight of the East End ghetto, for he finished his letter by writing:

> I must add that personally I cherished, in connection with the development of the Zion Mule Corps, a scheme of a Jewish unit for

wider national purposes. I have not given up the hope of seeing it realised, nor will I give up so long as the war lasts. But this letter is written for another purpose and represents simply an attempt to suggest a neat way out from a dangerous situation.[54]

The *Jewish Chronicle* itself criticised Jabotinsky's proposal on the grounds of its military impracticability, and argued once more for conscription, despite acknowledging that this outraged Russian Jewish readers.

This anger manifested itself, unsurprisingly, in the continued failure of the voluntary scheme, and left Samuel with no choice but to announce in parliament on 11 July that service in either the British or Russian Army would be compulsory. The announcement included the establishment of special tribunals to consider applications for exemption on grounds that were available, under the Military Service Acts, to British subjects. The most contentious issue arising from the operation of these proposals obviously revolved around their application to political refugees. Herbert Samuel gave an immediate and apparently unequivocal reply to a fellow MP's question on this very point, which Wasserstein has quoted, without comment, in his biography. Samuel said that, as far as political refugees were concerned: 'I see no reason why they should not serve in our Army.'[55] A different impression of Samuel's intentions, however, is evident in the minutes of the Law and Parliamentary Committee of the Board of Deputies, when this body met to consider the home secretary's statement. The meeting on 16 July noted that the (special) tribunals would be sympathetic to political refugees, and the board unanimously resolved to support Samuel and to offer their assistance in the composition of the tribunals.[56]

With the enforcement of compulsory service for the non-naturalised now a distinct probability, Jabotinsky wrote to both the *Jewish Chronicle* and *The Times* with yet another proposal. In a return to his original Jewish Legion idea, Jabotinsky pointed out that the Russian Jews were asking for a promise 'that if we fight we shall be helping to assure the freedom of the Jewish race?' then argued:

> It does not mean that the Russian Jews in this country ought to be free from military obligations. On the contrary, they ought to serve. But they should be treated as an old race with its own grievances and its own hopes deserves to be treated. The appeal must be made to their own enthusiasm, not to fear of 'deportation.' They should be given the privilege of serving in units which bear the Jewish name and of knowing that their merits will be recorded for the glory of their race.[57]

In support of Jabotinsky, an accompanying leading article in *The Times* agreed that 'deportation' would not provide a solution, and asserted that the formation of Jewish units would enable their willingness to serve to be tested in a fair and reasonable manner. Furthermore, this leader ended:

> Into the territorial aspirations of 'Zionism' we cannot now enter. But we believe the tendency represented by 'Zionism' to be healthy – the tendency, that is to say, for Jews to take, as Jews, their ethnic and religious stand in the world.[58]

The support of *The Times* must have encouraged Jabotinsky and, although there was no mention of the subject in the popular press, it presented his proposal to a wider and more influential audience.

By contrast, no such publicity could have influenced the anti-Zionist and anti-Legion views of Lucien Wolf. In a letter written on 24 July 1916, Wolf was frank and forthright on the matter of the failure of Russian Jews to come forward; his remarks leave the reader in no doubt as to his opinion and the rationale that lay behind it:

> I am afraid I do not agree that Russian Jews of military age living in this country have any right to object to serve in the british [sic] Army on the ground of Russian persecution of the Jews. Many non Jewish British subjects hold the internal policy of the Russian Empire in as much detestation ... but they do not on that account hesitate to serve in the British Army ... Nor do I see why there should be so much clamour against deportation. There need be no deportation if the Jew does his obvious duty.[59]

In his firm statement, Wolf denied that the hostility of East End Russian Jews towards the Tsarist regime was a legitimate motive for avoiding military service. He implied that they had a duty to Britain as a consequence of the refuge they had been given.

Nowhere was this concept, and the difficulties it involved, more clearly and passionately expressed than in a letter written by Edwin Montagu, a cabinet minister and cousin of Herbert Samuel, to Sir Eric Drummond of the Foreign Office on 3 August 1916. Unlike Samuel, who, as mentioned earlier, was in sympathy with Zionism, Montagu was an ardent and uncompromising assimilationist. The contents of this remarkable letter put the assimilationist case and the fears of Anglo-Jewry in frank and definitive terms. Its relevance to the circumstances surrounding the development of the Jewish Legion justify a near complete reproduction:

> It seems to me that Jews have got to consider whether they regard themselves as members of a religion or a race, world-wide in its habitat and striving to maintain in spite of geographical distribution an entity for political as well as religious consideration. For myself I have long made the choice. I saw with horror the aspiration of a national entity. Did I accept it, as a patriotic Englishman, I should resign my position on the Cabinet and declare myself neutral, or at any rate not primarily concerned in the present war ... I regard with perfect equanimity whatever treatment the Jews receive in Russia. I am convinced that the treatment meted out to Jews in Russia will be no worse or no better than the Russian degree of civilization ... For the moment the correspondence [with Sir George Buchanan, British Ambassador to Russia] seems to me to show clearly two things; first that the Russian Jews have not, in Buchanan's opinion, played a very distinguished part in the war. (I hope that they have played a more distinguished part in England, but be it said in passing, could anything be more disastrous than for Jewish Englishmen and Jewish Americans to be bracketed with the Jewish Russians, sharing the same verdict for their part in the war?!), secondly that Jewish nationalism, (which is to my mind horrible and unpatriotic) has already damaged or contributed to the damage of the Allied Cause by helping in the disappearance of Soyanoff [Actually S. Sasonov, the Russian Foreign Minister who resigned on 23 July 1916] I implore the Foreign Office to be content with that achievement and to discountenance this pro-German anti-civilisation tendency.[60]

Whatever the views of Jabotinsky, Wolf and Montagu, the fact remained that the voluntary scheme using the services of the New Court Jewish Recruiting Committee continued to fail to attract significant numbers. An indication of this failure was a report in the *Jewish Chronicle* of 4 August, which mentioned that three men had been jailed for publishing nearly two thousand copies of the *Workers Friend*, a Yiddish language newspaper distributed in the East End, which urged the Russian Jews to refuse to volunteer.

Herbert Samuel was left with no choice but to develop his proposals for compulsion, and so put into effect the threat of his 11 July announcement. However, whilst conscription and deportation drew ever nearer, the desperate nature of the situation elicited yet another attempt to reconcile the differences that existed in the Jewish community. This attempt was initiated by Gregory Benenson, the Russian managing director of the Russian and English Bank, based in the City of London, who contacted Wolf and informed him that the Russian Jews had no leadership and distrusted the New Court Recruiting Committee. Benenson and Wolf then set about constructing a new 'East End' recruitment committee, which would rely on both the endorsement of prominent Zionists and the support of the Anglo-Jewish establishment in order to succeed. Wolf was soon able to secure the latter from Samuel Rothschild and Edward Sebag Montefiore, whilst Benenson was able to confirm, on 1 August 1916, that he had obtained the former through Chaim Weizmann and Nathan Sokolow – both of whom had previously maintained a public silence on the subject of military service.

This bridge over the communal divide enabled Samuel to meet Benenson, Weizmann, Sokolow and Jabotinsky at the Home Office on 11 August. In agreeing with many of the proposals laid before him during this meeting, Samuel was able to confirm that he was prepared to allow a further period, until the end of September, for voluntary recruitment, and to offer free citizenship to volunteers and their child dependants after three month's service. Compulsion was not to be considered until 15 October and, in a concession to the representations made to him, Samuel agreed that no mention would be made of deportation or compulsion. Instead, he would make it clear that, should the scheme fail, further measures would be considered. He also agreed, however, that if compulsion became necessary, the government would apply the same criteria for conscription as existed in Russia, with a broader and more acceptable – to the Russian Jewish community – membership of the special tribunals originally announced in July. In return for these concessions, Gregory Benenson agreed to finance the new Recruiting Committee office. Samuel duly made the official announcement in the House of Commons on 22 August. With the Benenson scheme approved and his contribution complete, Wolf withdrew from this arrangement, his efforts being rewarded by a letter of thanks from Samuel.[61] Eugene Black has commented that Wolf was 'delighted to be quit of his role as middleman'[62] and referred to the letter Wolf wrote to Leopold Rothschild informing him of the details of Samuel's new policy announcement. In this letter Wolf expressed his satisfaction that he had been of use to the Home Office, but revealed his pessimism as to the outcome of the scheme:

> I will not conceal from you, [Rothschild] any more than I have concealed from Mr. Samuel, that I am still far from hopeful. The East End people really do not want concessions. What they want is unconditional exemptions. I believe the War Office is disposed to draft them all into labor [sic] Battalions, and not send them to the front at all, but, of course, this is a concession which cannot be published.[63]

It has already been established that the assimilationists were fearful of a poor military performance by the Russian Jews, and would have preferred the labour service option. But this would have done little to placate or satisfy those East End Gentiles whose menfolk were subject to the usual conditions of the Military Service Act, which classified conscripts (and volunteers) according to their medical status. In addition, if the War Office shared the fears of the assimilationists, then the main attraction of placing the Russians into labour battalions would have been to avoid the incorporation of substantial numbers of reluctant soldiers into fighting formations. In any event, the War Office in August 1916 had no intention of agreeing to the formation of a Jewish Legion.[64]

In conclusion, it can be stated that the complicated religious, racial, diplomatic and political considerations involved in this issue gave rise to confusion where clarity was required. But clarity was a luxury only enjoyed by the single-minded. Thus Jabotinsky and Trumpeldor viewed the formation of a Jewish Legion as a fundamental prerequisite for the establishment of an independent Zionist state that would be, in effect, a reward for war services rendered to the entente. It would also serve the secondary purpose of establishing a defence force for the Jewish settlers. This vision contrasted with that of Chaim Weizmann who acknowledged that, whilst the development of Zionism required the support of a sympathetic British Government, this support would never be allowed to threaten Britain's national and imperial interests. Nevertheless, Weizmann fully recognised the value of the Jewish Legion as a means of demonstrating British sympathy for Zionism, by indicating to the Jews of the Diaspora that their plight had not been forgotten, and he understood the symbolic importance of a specifically Jewish contribution to the war effort.

Finally, in spite of the unpromising situation of early August 1916, it is clear that the preceding eight months had seen some substantial, if occasionally faltering progress made towards the formation of a Jewish military unit as a constituent part of the British Army. At the very least the subject of the Legion had been discussed at the highest levels of the British Government, and had focused the minds of the Anglo-Jewish leadership on the whole question of Zionism and its relation to the wider strategic and political aspects of the war.

4
The Founding of the Legion: Part Two

At the end of August 1916, only one week after Wolf had written to Rothschild, Samuel asked him once more for his assistance in activating the Benenson Recruitment Committee which had made no progress whatsoever, despite Samuel's concessions. In response to this plea and as an indication of the seriousness of the situation, Wolf acted with great speed; so much so that he met Cowen and Jabotinsky on the morning of 1 September, Benenson and Weizmann in the afternoon, and arranged to see Henderson of the Home Office in the evening. Wolf prioritised his meeting with Cowen and Jabotinsky because he recognised that an immediate and forceful propaganda campaign had to be put in place in the East End, regardless of the activity – or lack of it – of the Benenson Committee. Wolf also accepted that, if Jabotinsky was to play a serious role for in securing recruitment, then the 'Home and Heim' rallying call had to be at the centre of the propaganda message.[1] This approach, particularly with regard to the necessity to provide Jabotinsky with 'fuel for his very useful enthusiasm' was explained in a letter from Wolf to Samuel, which ended with a paragraph that indicated his concern at the prospect of the reinstatement of the deportation policy:

> There is one word I want to say to you on the deportation question. I hope the Government will not make up its mind on this question for a few days. I have been looking into the treaties, diplomatic precedents, and International Law Treatises, so far as they relate to the military service of aliens, and I believe that you will be able to achieve your full purpose without troubling about deportation at all.[2]

The media chosen for the campaign was a new Yiddish newspaper established by Jabotinsky and entitled *Unsere Tribune*. Jabotinsky was keen to secure the services, as editor of this journal, of Meir Grossman, an old friend and colleague, who was working in Copenhagen as the editor and publisher of *Die Tribune* which supported Jabotinsky and the Jewish Legion despite official international Zionist policy. Although *Die Tribune* was banned by the British censor, it being regarded as a German publication, Grossman was able to obtain the required clearance to come to Britain after Wolf, in another concession to Jabotinsky, made representations to the Home Office on his behalf. With regard to their apparent co-operation in this matter, it is important to remember that Jabotinsky and Wolf retained their opposing views on Zionism. Jabotinsky, for instance, makes no mention at all of Lucien Wolf in *The Story of the Jewish Legion*, and merely comments 'I summoned Grossman from Copenhagen', when dealing with this episode.[3] In similar vein, it is worth recalling that Wolf had only recently referred to Jabotinsky as a 'carpet-bagging demagogue', and so the assistance he rendered to Jabotinsky can be viewed as having been motivated by expediency rather than goodwill. Another interpretation of Wolf's policy has been made by Mark Levene, who observed that:

> His [Wolf's] recognition that the Zionists might be most suited to do the work in the East End and his encouragement of their schemes were evidence of his desire to compromise, for the sake of 'the national interest'. Moreover, the lukewarmness of their [the Zionists'] efforts served only to magnify the traditional Anglo-Jewish leadership's reliability as government agents.[4]

If this is so, then it can be argued that Wolf's magnanimity towards Jabotinsky was driven by a desire to reinforce the relationship between the 'traditional Anglo-Jewish leadership' and the government, by capitalising on the weakness of the Benenson Committee. In simple terms, this would have enabled Wolf to place the assimilationists ahead of the Zionists in the contest to influence government policy, and to assert their communal authority over the Jewish community in Britain.

Evidence supporting this argument can be found in Wolf's letter to Leopold Rothschild, part of which was quoted earlier, written on 23 August on completion of his efforts to re-establish the Benenson Committee. After mentioning the thanks he had received from Samuel he wrote:

> In accordance with Baron Edmund's wishes, I have been in consultation with Dr. Weizmann and Mr. James Rothschild on the subject

of a concordat with the Zionists [...] For the moment, I will only say that Weizmann's conditions are absolutely inadmissible.[5]

Regardless of political strategy or ulterior motive, the Russian recruitment situation forced Jabotinsky and Wolf to continue their co-operation. Using Wolf as an intermediary, Jabotinsky obtained assurances from the government that volunteers would be accepted in batches of between fifty and one hundred men, and that they would be classified for service in accordance with the medical criteria laid down for British soldiers. In addition, Wolf informed Jabotinsky that the War Office had agreed to remove the exclusive labour battalion proposal, but he did not consider that the time was right to pursue the question of 'Home' service.[6] Unfortunately, this latter point caused embarrassment for Wolf because, as part of the recruitment publicity campaign he wrote an article for the *Daily Chronicle*, published on 6 September, which was designed to explain the 'Home and Heim' policy. As originally written, the article would have reassured the host population that Russian Jews were being offered service under comparable conditions to British servicemen, and that, in this context, home service could include deployment in India or Egypt. Regrettably, these explanations were removed by the official censor and, in the 8 September edition of the *Jewish Chronicle*, Wolf was severely criticised for advocating labour or non-combatant roles for Russian Jewish soldiers.[7] This dispute camouflaged the fact that both Wolf's and Jabotinsky's interests would have been served by the promise of service in Egypt. The assimilationists would have seen the mass of Russian Jews removed to an area of secondary military importance, thus reducing the risk of a poor performance tainting all British Jews. On the other hand, Jabotinsky and his supporters would have seen service in Egypt as being but one step away from having Jewish soldiers involved in the liberation of Palestine.

Shortly after the launch of Jabotinsky's campaign, he was joined in London by Joseph Trumpeldor, who had travelled from Alexandria with a view to joining the British Army, preferably in a Jewish unit. This was followed by another encouraging event when Herbert Samuel asked Jabotinsky if the Home Office could provide any further assistance to his recruiting efforts. Jabotinsky did not need a second invitation. He bluntly asked the Home Secretary to publish a statement endorsing 'Home and Heim', and promising to form a Jewish Regiment if a thousand signatures could be successfully petitioned. Samuel made it clear that only the 'whole cabinet' could decide on such an issue, given the known level of opposition to the scheme from both assimilationist and Zionist quarters. Jabotinsky's response was pessimistic: 'without an official statement from you I cannot guarantee success'.[8]

Such pessimism was well founded. In the same edition of the *Jewish Chronicle* that unfairly criticised Lucien Wolf, an article entitled 'Russian Born Jews and Military Service' reported that no recruitment committee had been formed. It also revealed that a Zionist conference had been arranged to take place, in the East End, later in September, presumably with the object of constructing yet another compromise that would remove the threat of deportation.[9]

Although a small, indeterminate number of Russian Jews did volunteer in 1914 and 1915, the failure to respond to the urgings of the Home Secretary, Wolf and Jabotinsky, prompted the authorities to observe and report on the activities of the Jewish population of the East End of London. Special Branch and other Metropolitan Police efforts in this field are documented in Home Office records, specifically the HO 45 series, which have been well researched by historians. In particular, Sharman Kadish's work takes into account the impact of police activities on the majority of this population. For example, Kadish has established that, whereas the police predictably focused their efforts on known activists, the great majority of Russian Jewish men took no part in political activities; day-to-day economic survival was of paramount importance.[10] This is a useful corrective to the accounts by Black, Stein, Friedman and Wasserstein,[11] which have quite legitimately concentrated on community leaders and political activists.

As Kadish appreciated however, there was an element of formally organised opposition to friendly alien recruitment. There were two groups in particular; the Foreign Jews Protection Committee against Conscription and Deportation, commonly referred to as the 'FJPC', formed in June 1916, and the Committee of Delegates of the Russian Socialist Groups in London, which first met on 13 March 1916. The FJPC was closely monitored by the Metropolitan Police Special Branch, commanded by Basil Thomson who employed, amongst others, a Jewish constable from Leman Street Police Station, Stepney, named Greenberg, and a Yiddish-speaking sergeant by the name of Albers.[12]

The Special Branch also maintained a watch on Jabotinsky, presumably to check on the opponents who heckled and disrupted the meetings he held during October 1916, and also perhaps to ensure that his efforts were indeed directed towards the encouragement of voluntary recruitment. For example, Sergeant Albers, reporting on such meetings held on 16 and 17 October stated:

> The audience at both these places consisted of the Jewish element, chiefly Russians of military age. From the commencement of the proceedings in each case, they were antagonistic towards the speakers and a considerable amount of booing and hissing greeted them ... At both the meetings it was found necessary to have the hall cleared by Police. In my opinion it appears useless to hold these gatherings as the Jewish folk seem to greatly resent the arguments put forward, and in view of the hostile attitude of the crowd, no good purpose could be served by continuing to advocate Mr. Jabotinsky's propaganda.[13]

In fact, Jabotinsky's 'Home and Heim' campaign, encouraged by Wolf and seen as a final bid for successful voluntary recruitment, lasted for just one month and, in his own words was a 'complete failure. We obtained altogether three hundred signatures – and Whitechapel life in those days was one interminable tumult.'[14] As a result of this failure the propaganda campaign was also halted and Meir Grossman returned to Copenhagen; by November 1916 'Home and Heim' had come to naught.

Home Secretary Samuel now took the matter of Russian Jewish recruitment to a committee of the Cabinet, having ascertained from the Foreign Office that international law would permit the conscription of aliens, provided that they were citizens of a fellow belligerent with whom an appropriate agreement had been signed. The committee took into account the moral position involved in the deportation of persons who could argue that they held refugee status, and acknowledged that the efficacy of deportation was threatened by severe transport problems. After their deliberations were concluded, at the end of the first week in November, the committee proposed that legislation be introduced that would establish a Military Service Convention with Russia, so that all Russian Jews in Britain who met the qualifying criteria for military service, would be conscripted into the British Army or deported to Russia to meet similar obligations there. In an acknowledgment of the moral argument, the committee also recommended that those affected be given a chance to leave Britain, implying that it was their intention not to force through swift legislation. It is interesting to note that whereas the committee's proposals were accepted by the full Cabinet, Asquith did not agree, being himself strongly supportive of the moral argument against deportation.[15]

Despite its failure the 'Home and Heim' campaign was not without its positive aspects, and one of its lasting legacies was that Jabotinsky had found encouragement from the press including the *Manchester Guardian*, the *Jewish Chronicle* and *The Times*, whose supportive leaders had been written by its foreign editor, Henry Wickham Steed. Although a Gentile, Steed's enthusiasm for the Jewish Legion project emanated from his belief in Zionism, with which he had become acquainted during his years in Central and Eastern Europe as a *Times* correspondent. In 1917 Steed struck up a friendship with Chaim Weizmann that resulted in *The Times* playing a leading role in the press campaign urging the government to recognise Zionism and ignore the assimilationists' arguments. This had the practical effect of aligning the formation of a Jewish Legion with public sympathy for Zionism; both Jabotinsky and Weizmann were suitably grateful in their memoirs. For example, Jabotinsky wrote of Steed in sentimental and glowing terms:

> He understood the mentality of Zionism as few Christians can understand it – the inner, spiritual, anti-assimilation aspect, just as incisively and deeply as the Herzlian thirst for political statehood. Naturally – as with any non-Jew who 'talks like a Zionist' – many Jews accused him of anti-Semitism. This tendency among my fellow Jews – to see a Haman in every Gentile who permits himself to tell a 'Jewish' anecdote – has always been completely incomprehensible to me. Mr Steed spoke of Jews just as a Zionist would speak ... And he crystallised his friendship in real, influential service at the greatest moment of our new history.[16]

And Weizmann wrote:

> He [Steed] was not only glad to publish the Zionist statements but expressed downright annoyance with the heads of the Conjoint Committee. For a good hour or so we discussed the kind of leader which was likely to make the best appeal to the British public, and when it appeared ... it caused something like consternation among the assimilationists. It was a magnificent presentation of the Zionist case.[17]

These feelings were reciprocated by Steed, who wrote of Weizmann:

> It was natural that we should 'hit it off' from the outset. I was one of the very few British non-Jews with first-hand knowledge and experience of central European Jewry; and he was relieved to find that I

needed no conviction in regard to the Zionist ideal. I had also a point of comparison that was not unfavourable to him. I had known Theodore Herzl, first in 1896 at Breslau, and later in Vienna from the end of 1902 until his death in 1904. Instinctively I measured the vigorous, positive Weizmann against the somewhat dreamy, poetic Herzl – and found Weizmann the bigger and bolder.[18]

In spite of this mutual admiration it has been demonstrated by Stein and Kadish that the basis of Steed's pro-Zionist beliefs was fundamentally anti-Semitic. During his time as correspondent in Vienna, Steed had noted the disproportionate influence of the Jews upon the economy and culture of the countries in which they lived. Zion, as a home for all Jews, could therefore be seen as a means of removing this influence, and this is the argument that Sharman Kadish persuasively uses to explain the difference between *The Times* leader's support for Zionism and the anti-Semitic tone of their Petrograd correspondent during the course of the revolution in 1917.[19] Leonard Stein described Steed's position 'as illustrating the civilised type of anti-Semitism – to be distinguished from paranoiac judaephobia – characteristic of some Gentile pro-Zionists'.[20] Regardless of personal belief or motivation, Henry Steed was added to the list of important and influential figures whose advocacy of the Legion idea, combined with other events, was to bring Jabotinsky closer to the realisation of his dream.

The first such event came to Jabotinsky's attention through Joseph Trumpeldor, who received a telegram from ex-Sergeant Nissel Rosenberg of the Zion Mule Corps advising that 120 former members of the corps had arrived in Britain and had volunteered for the army. Rosenberg was well known to Trumpeldor, whose assistance he now sought to prevent the Jewish volunteers from being scattered throughout the British Army. Jabotinsky and Trumpeldor immediately realised that these 120 Jewish volunteer soldiers, with creditable war service behind them, provided a focal point on which another bid to create a Jewish Legion could be founded. They consulted with Patterson and Amery through whose influence, and with the co-operation of Lt.-Col. Assheton Pownall, the War Office ultimately agreed to place the 120 Jewish volunteers in a single company in Pownall's battalion, the 20th London, stationed at Haseley Down barracks near Winchester. Although this arrangement was permissible under a broad interpretation of the terms of clause five of Army Council Instruction 1156 (which dealt with the proportion of alien troops permitted to serve together), it did not indicate that the War Office viewed a specifically Jewish formation any more favourably. Indeed, it was reported in the *Jewish Chronicle* that the government in a parliamentary answer to a question regarding alien Jewish military service, stated that 'the formation of these men into a separate unit is not considered desirable'.[21] Nevertheless, it was a beginning – a small beginning based on the solid foundation of the Zion Mule Corps.

Jabotinsky was further encouraged by the resignation of Asquith and the change of government on 7 December 1916. Whilst Herbert Samuel remained loyal to Asquith and left office, Lloyd George became Prime Minister. As munitions minister, he had already become acquainted with Chaim Weizmann, whose chemical work for the ministry had been responsible for his move to London from Manchester. Another supporter and friend of Jabotinsky, Leo Amery, became a member of the influential 'kitchen cabinet' that advised the prime minister on the conduct of the war. Lloyd George was sympathetic to Zionism and had advocated an eastern strategy which involved holding the front in France whilst actively fighting the Central Powers elsewhere. In accordance with this strategy Lloyd George urged General Murray, the commander-in-chief of the Egyptian Expeditionary Force, to seek early success against the Turks across Sinai. Although his resources were limited, due to the needs of the western front, Murray's forces did manage to cross Sinai and in two actions at Magdhaba and Rafa on 23 December 1916 and 9 January 1917 respectively, finally removed the last remaining Turkish forces from Egyptian territory.[22]

As a result of political developments in Britain and military events abroad, Jabotinsky and his supporters faced dramatically altered circumstances at the turn of the year. We must now consider how Zionists and anti-Zionists and the various factions within the Jewish community exploited and manipulated these circumstances during 1917, using the voluminous general series of War Office files which no previous researcher has consulted. Though incomplete, these files allow for a fuller analysis of the final phase of the creation of the Jewish Legion than hitherto undertaken.[23]

In January 1917, Jabotinsky decided to volunteer and enlist with the Zion Mule Corps cadre in the 20th Battalion of the London Regiment. Acting on Amery's advice, and taking full advantage of his increased influence as a newly appointed assistant secretary to the War Cabinet, Jabotinsky and Trumpeldor wrote to the prime minister on the 21 January 1917, the day before Jabotinsky presented himself for enlistment. They proposed raising a Jewish Legion for service in Palestine and

Egypt, and described the success of the Zion Mule Corps in Gallipoli. They pointed out that Jabotinsky had worked throughout 1916 to raise such a force, and said they understood that the Foreign Office was sympathetic but the War Office had not been encouraging. In this summary the authors may have been correct, but it is clear that they were less than frank when they went on to blame the failure of the 'Home and Heim' campaign on a lack of official support. Whilst it was understandable that they did not mention the general reluctance of the Russian Jews to volunteer, they must have realised that this fact would be brought to the attention of the prime minister when consideration was given to their proposals. Perhaps in an effort to overcome this disadvantage, they concluded with an emotional appeal to Lloyd George: 'We ask for the Jew the privilege the Welshman has – to fight for his country; to fight like the Welshman does – in Regiments of his own, not scattered and nameless.'[24] It is reasonable to assume that the symbolic effects of the formation of the Welsh Guards in 1915 would not have been lost on the recipient of this appeal.

A number of enclosures and attachments accompanied Jabotinsky's and Trumpeldor's text, including copies of testimonials from Generals Hamilton and Birdwood, together with a memorandum that contained five specific points on recruitment and organisation. In summary, these points urged the government to establish a Jewish Regiment for Palestine, comprised of Russian Jewish volunteers from Britain, Egypt, Palestine, France and other neutral countries. British subjects who volunteered for the Jewish Regiment were also to be welcomed. A nucleus was to be formed from the Zion Mule Corps cadre and the 200 Russian Jews who had voluntarily attested (Jabotinsky's and Trumpeldor's figures, the Home Office estimate was about 400) before 25 October 1916, and augmented by the 280 Mule Corps veterans who remained in Alexandria. It was proposed that the government appoint commanding officers of any race or religion, but that other commissioned ranks should be filled by British Jews and 'from the educated elements of enlisted aliens'. Finally, Jabotinsky and Trumpeldor offered to staff and fund a recruiting campaign amongst the estimated 30,000 Russian Jews in Britain, to be followed by similar campaigns in the United States and Russia, where it was hoped that the recognition of Zionist ideals by western governments would ameliorate the condition in which Jews lived.

These proposals were initially referred to the War Office, whose reservations were recorded in an unsigned minute of MI (Military Intelligence) 2 dated 3 February 1917. This minute acknowledged that the creation of a Jewish force for service in Palestine would be successful in recruiting terms, but mainly concentrated on the strain that such a development would place upon Anglo-French relations. It was argued that difficulties would arise from the fact that the employment of such a corps would inevitably involve a British political commitment to Zionism that was incompatible with the 'intention of the Entente to internationalise Palestine'. Amery was criticised for placing the scheme before the War Cabinet without 'putting down the serious objections which undoubtedly exist'.[25] The French question was also paramount in the considerations of the General Staff. In a file entitled 'Proposed Jewish Legion – Reasons against', Colonel G.S. Buckley wrote a concluding summary which traced the rapid course of the Jewish Legion proposal through the offices of the director of military intelligence, the Adjutant-General (Sir Neville Macready) and the Chief of the Imperial General Staff (Sir William Robertson). It is recorded that the CIGS concurred with his colleagues that the formation of a Jewish unit could not be sanctioned without consultation with the French, owing to 'French susceptibilities in Palestine', and an administrative objection was also lodged by the adjutant-general, who disliked 'the formation of special individual units which could only be used for a limited purpose'.[26]

The Jewish Legion proposal was also considered by the Foreign Office where the government's principal adviser on the Middle East was Sir Mark Sykes, who had earlier been responsible with the French Minister, François Picot, for agreeing to the future internationalisation of the greater part of Palestine. Sykes appreciated the relevance of the Jewish Legion to the Zionist cause (which he generally supported), and wrote to Chaim Weizmann to indicate this. But he also advised Weizmann that he thought the time for such a unit had not yet arrived. Weizmann replied in agreement, and made clear his own priorities and the difference between his position and that of his friend Jabotinsky by stating 'it is a pity that the idea of a Jewish Legion has almost become his idée fixe and he has subordinated important Zionist interests to this idea'.[27] Weizmann informed Jabotinsky of Sykes' interest and opinion, and the Foreign Office itself sent a brief, formal letter to Jabotinsky merely acknowledging receipt of his proposals.

The cautious approach of both the War and Foreign Offices, particularly with regard to what might be termed the 'French Question', reflected the importance of maintaining entente solidarity. Whatever the merits of the Jewish Legion proposal and the sympathies of its supporters both in and out of government, its association with Zionism meant that it could not be properly considered without reference to the wider implications for current and post-war policy. This created a number of awkward dilemmas. For example, the known plight of the Jews in Russia gave moral impetus to British support for Zionism, but this had to be weighed against the vital strategic necessity of keeping the Russian Army fighting Germany. Similarly, the terms of the Sykes–Picot agreement, which had been signed in Petrograd in March 1916, had been designed to provide zones of influence for the entente partners in a post-war Middle East; thus any over-enthusiastic reference to British sponsorship of Zionism, at this stage, had to be avoided.

By contrast, the Jewish Legion proposal has obvious attraction in the propaganda struggle to influence Jewish opinion and counter pro-German publicity in the United States. Furthermore, it should be remembered that influential persons such as Leo Amery and Mark Sykes were pro-Arab as well as pro-Zionist, believing there to be scope in a post-war Middle East for Arabs and Jews to co-exist under some form of British hegemony that would protect British imperial trade. Again, the war-time need to sustain the entente could not permit open advocacy of such a policy, which also had to take into account the previously mentioned objections of assimilationist representatives such as Lucien Wolf. As far as British policy towards Zionism was concerned, Weizmann's 'walking on eggs' description was as apt for Gentiles as it was for Jews.

What then permitted the development of the Jewish Legion from proposal to fact, and enabled the proponents of the scheme to overcome the caution of the government and the arguments of its opponents?

Firstly, there was the increasing domestic pressure on the government to take action on Russian Jewish recruitment by concluding a Military Service Convention with Russia. On 26 January 1917 the *Jewish Chronicle* printed an article headed 'Action by Stepney Borough Council', which reported that this body had asked other local authorities to express regret at the failure to enlist of 'all able-bodied aliens of military age claiming nationality with this country's allies and resident in the UK', a clear reference to Russian Jews. Another public body, the Metropolitan Borough of Islington, wrote to the foreign secretary on 14 March, endorsing a resolution carried by the members of the Bethnal Green Local Tribunal. According to the Islington letter this resolution called the government's attention to:

> the serious position created by the large number of male aliens in this country who are enjoying immunity from military service and exceptional opportunities for commercial activities, and expressing

the hope that the Government will immediately take the necessary steps to compulsorily remedy this obvious injustice.[28]

Reports of the assistant provost marshal for the military district of London also contain references to the disturbances caused by the alien enlistment problem. For example, in his report of the 16 April 1917, addressed to the provost marshal, Home Force, the APM states:

> With regard to the disturbance last week among the Jewish soldiers in the Whitechapel Road I am credibly informed that a great deal of feeling exists in that quarter re the enlistment of Russian Jews. Unless some steps are taken to enlist these men further trouble will probably occur.[29]

Unfortunately, no other evidence has come to light with regard to the 'Jewish soldiers' mentioned in the report. It would be interesting to discover whether or not these were British Jewish soldiers who were attacking their co-religionists. However, street violence provoked by the recruitment situation clearly occurred and was well known to the authorities.[30]

Secondly, two major international events took place in February and early March that were to influence greatly the conduct of the war and the formation of the Jewish Legion. In February, the prospect of the United States of America entering the war was considerably enhanced by the severance of diplomatic relations with Germany, following the declaration of unlimited submarine warfare and the incident of the Zimmermann telegram. In early March revolution broke out in Petrograd, resulting in the abdication of the Tsar and the establishment of a dual government comprising the Petrograd Soviet and Prince Lvov's provisional government.

Jabotinsky and Trumpeldor did not hesitate to exploit the opportunity offered by these international developments to press the government to sanction a Jewish unit, and solve their domestic difficulties on the streets of the East End. By the middle of March, Trumpeldor and Jabotinsky had control of the 20th London cadre and requested that it be sent to Palestine. The War Office turned down this request and Jabotinsky realised that there was now every chance that the Jews of the 20th London would be sent to France with the next regimental draft. In order to avoid this situation Jabotinsky wrote to Sykes, on 25 March, arguing that 'the events in Russia have tremendously influenced the East End aliens, whom the Government seems to be so anxious to enlist.'[31]

Sir Mark Sykes was impressed by this argument and, as a result of deliberations in the Foreign Office, an official memorandum of 7 April was sent to the Secretary of the War Council, requesting a thorough examination of the Jewish Legion proposals. A copy of Jabotinsky's letter to Sykes was attached to the memorandum, which included the following statement:

> Mr. Balfour considers that the proposal might go far to meet the difficulties which have arisen in connection with the enlistment of Jews in this country and the scheme might indeed open fresh sources of recruiting in the British Dominions as well as the USA and Egypt. From a political point of view it will be important for HMG not to identify themselves too closely with the political objectives of a Zionist nation which clearly underlie this proposal, since by so doing they would be committing themselves to a definite course in a matter upon which the most representative Jews of the world are utterly divided.[32]

The wording of this memorandum confirmed the Foreign Office's acceptance of Jabotinsky's main point, summarised policy considerations and marked the breaking of the bureaucratic logjam in which the Jewish Legion proposals had been caught. Further momentum came from Leo Amery who wrote to Lord Derby, the secretary of state for war, on 5 April. Amery argued that compulsory service for the Russian Jews in Britain, combined with the formation of a Jewish Legion, would be the best way of proceeding, and had the potential of attracting Jews from 'America and South Africa'. With regard to the latter he referred to a conversation he had held with General Smuts, the South African leader and member of the War Cabinet, who also thought that 'he could get any number of Boers to volunteer for a campaign in the Holy Land, as the idea would appeal enormously to them'.[33] Regardless of their practicality, the significance of such remarks is that they emphasise the religious sympathy between Judaism and Protestantism, and reinforce the importance of this factor in the development of the Jewish Legion.

Jabotinsky, Trumpeldor and their supporters were not content to leave the matter solely in the hands of the Foreign and War Offices. On 3 April, four days before Sykes' memorandum was issued, Weizmann attended a breakfast meeting with the prime minister at which, according to notes made by C.P. Scott, he 'spoke in support of the Jewish Regiment to Lloyd George, who reacted enthusiastically'.[34] On the same day Jabotinsky and Trumpeldor wrote directly to the prime minister, adding the points they had made to Sykes to the arguments presented in their correspondence of January. They also argued that, despite the new situation in Russia, 'the adhesion of the Jewish factor to the Entente's cause is yet far from being complete ... the pacifist current is still very pronounced amongst the Jews in Russia and America', and that the best way of securing the full support and active participation of the Jewish people was to form a 'Jewish Regiment for Palestine'.[35]

The effect of these diverse appeals was immediate. Jabotinsky was summoned to the Foreign Office for a meeting with Sir Eric Drummond and Sir Mark Sykes, where he was informed that the Legion scheme was due to be discussed by the War Cabinet in the 'next few days'. After this meeting, Jabotinsky was questioned by General Smuts who remarked, according to Jabotinsky's notes 'that Jews should fight for the Land of Israel is the finest idea I have heard in my life'.[36]

The Foreign Office meetings were followed, on 9 April, by the incongruous sight of Private Jabotinsky, dressed in a drab khaki battledress uniform and accompanied by Trumpeldor, attending the War Office to meet Lord Derby and Major-General Woodward, the director of organisation, at the behest of the prime minister. Again, Jabotinsky and Trumpeldor outlined the details of their scheme but on this occasion, when Lord Derby asked about the chances of obtaining volunteers for service in a Legion, he received an answer from Trumpeldor which touched a political nerve: 'If it is to be just a regiment of Jews – perhaps. If it will be a regiment for the Palestine front – certainly. If, together with its formation, there will appear a government pronouncement in favour of Zionism – overwhelmingly.'[37] Derby did not respond directly to Trumpeldor's reply, and after General Woodward had been reassured as to the ability of Russian Jews to undertake an infantry role, he simply informed Jabotinsky that the Regiment's title, administration and insignia would be considered by General Geddes, the director of recruiting, who 'will send for you one of these days and talk it over'. At the conclusion of this extraordinary interview Jabotinsky and Trumpeldor travelled back to barracks to relate their experience to Lt.-Colonel Pownall, and await the call from General Geddes.

The interview with Lord Derby revealed three substantial indications of the Government's position with regard to the Russian Jewish question in general, and the Legion in particular. Firstly, the government were understandably coy about any formal association with

Zionism. Secondly, despite the work on a Military Service Convention, the use of voluntary recruitment to provide a quick solution to the difficulties of the East End had not been ruled out. Finally, the Army Council had decided to proceed with the formation of a Jewish unit, a fact which was later confirmed to the Foreign Office in a letter written on 16 April:

> I am commanded by the Army Council to inform you that they propose to proceed with the scheme for the formation of a Russian Jewish Battalion. I am to add that this decision has been taken on the distinct understanding that it is not to be regarded as in any way connected with, or in promotion of, the Zionist movement.[38]

The positive response of the War Office was in contrast to its previous reluctance, and the impetus for the change came about from Foreign Office support and, ultimately, War Cabinet instructions. A minute in the War Office files confirms that the secretary of state was instructed to investigate the implementation of the scheme, following the Imperial War Cabinet's consideration of Jabotinsky and Trumpeldor's memorandum of 24 January. This instruction led directly to their meeting with Lord Derby and so it appeared that, by the middle of April, the scheme was approved and that Jabotinsky had merely to await final administrative and recruitment details. Unfortunately for Jabotinsky and his supporters, this was not the case: at the end of the War Office minute referred to above it was noted that objections to the scheme had been received from 'English Jews', representatives of whom had already lobbied the War Office in an effort to prevent the formation of the Legion.[39]

The representatives in question were Major Lionel Rothschild, head of the failed Jewish Recruiting Committee, and Claude Montefiore, the leading assimilationist and president of the Anglo-Jewish Association. They attended a conference with senior officials at Horse Guards on 13 April, which resulted in a memorandum that was sent to General Woodward on the same day – four days after the general had accompanied Lord Derby in his meeting with Jabotinsky and Trumpeldor. This memorandum was signed by Major-General Tagart, Adjutant-General Home Forces who had been asked to consult with 'leading Jews' on the possibility of raising a volunteer Jewish Battalion in London, and had thus established contact with Major Rothschild and Claude Montefiore. Tagart's memorandum summarised the points made by Rothschild and

Montefiore, in unambiguous terms, which demonstrated their concern regarding the impact of Russian Jewish behaviour upon the standing of British Jews. To quote from the text:

> (1) There is no earthly use in touching the scheme unless it is made compulsory.
>
> The reason for this is that owing to the number of Englishmen and British Jews that have been withdrawn from the East End into the army, these alien Jews are now earning from £4 to £10 p. week, and no appeal to patriotism or duty will make one of them give up the money they are earning unless they are compelled.
>
> (2) The British Jews are all strongly in favour of compulsion, and they take it badly that they have had to give up their chances of amassing wealth when the alien is left to benefit. If a bill is introduced into parliament to conscript the alien Jews Rothschild and other Jews of importance will support it and speak in favour.[40]

In addition to these strongly worded remarks, it was also suggested that, when compulsion became effective, a special appeal tribunal be set up 'on which 2 or 3 observant British Jews (who should be selected by Major Rothschild and his committee) would sit'. By such means Rothschild and Montefiore were determined to ensure that there would be as few 'shirkers and slackers' as possible, and that maximum control over the Russian Jews by their Anglicised co-religionists would be exercised. It is not difficult to imagine the confusion and inertia caused in the War Office by these proposals from men of power and influence who represented a number of Anglo-Jewish organisations. Lord Derby, whilst appearing to be satisfied with the Jewish Legion scheme, had ensured that the Army Council's approval was very explicit about the fact that the government did not wish its support to be taken as an endorsement of Zionism. Given Jabotinsky's well-known commitment to Zionist aims, and the misgivings implicit in the proposals of Major Rothschild's delegation, there can be little doubt that the War Office realised that the scheme required further consideration, in conjunction with the Foreign Office, before becoming operative.

Jabotinsky's impatience at the War Office's delay resulted in a letter, written from his billet at Hazeley Down Camp on 20 April, to the Foreign Office. In this letter Jabotinsky reminded Sir Eric Drummond of their meeting, and sought his assistance in accelerating the implementation of the scheme. As an argument for renewed and urgent effort, Jabotinsky pointed out to Sir Eric:

> But [sic] I cannot help thinking that one of the greatest dangers of the moment is the pacifist demagogy in Russia ... This current in Petrograd is not a Jewish one ... But undoubtedly the Jewish element is represented in its ranks, and, I fear, by active and clever men ... I am absolutely sure that the creation of such a unit [the Jewish Legion] would immediately counter-balance the pacifist tendencies as far as Russian Jewry is concerned.[41]

To support his argument Jabotinsky mentioned that he was in receipt of correspondence from Russia and Denmark (where the wartime headquarters of the International Zionist Organisation were located) which indicated that Russian support for the war against Germany was weakening. This testimony demonstrated Jabotinsky's recognition and exploitation of the fact that the Allies feared Russian withdrawal from the war before an American army could be effectively deployed in Europe. It is also noteworthy that his letter contains no overt reference to Zionism or the possible role of the Legion in its promotion; again an indication that, by this time, he was very well aware of the difficulties facing the government over this issue.

Receiving no reply to his letter, Jabotinsky wrote directly to the prime minister, and in five pages of small manuscript, expressed his frustration at the delay in implementing the scheme. In concise and powerful terms he stressed that 'the impression [upon Russian Jewry] of the Russian change, America's entry and of the Palestine advance, is fresh and strong', and reiterated the arguments recorded above. Particular emphasis was placed on the propaganda effect in Russia of the formation of a Jewish Legion, and the importance of its speedy development so as to maximise the effect. The latter half of Jabotinsky's letter sought to assure the prime minister that the fears raised by Chaim Weizmann, concerning the possibility of Turkish recriminations against Jews living in Palestine, were largely exaggerated. Jabotinsky argued that the most obvious time for such reaction would have been during the setting up of the Zion Mule Corps. Since then, Jabotinsky continued, it had become well known in Turkey that a Jewish Legion was being actively promoted in Britain. In a passage that revealed the strength of his resolve and the firmness of his belief, he wrote:

But, besides all this, I disagree with the principle itself that the political diapason [sic] of an oppressed nation should be determined – in such a moment – by fear of massacre over a small portion of coreligionists ... They [Jews in Palestine] knew their dangers when they preferred to remain in the colonies after the outbreak of the war; they stayed not because of their property or business, but to fill a sentry post[42]

From the above it can be seen that Jabotinsky's view of the Jews in Palestine was based on the simple but suspect premise that the settlers were, by their very existence, fully committed, militant, Zionists.

Coincidentally with the receipt of Jabotinsky's letter at 10 Downing Street, the Turkish authorities embarked on a series of pogroms against the Jews of Jaffa and other areas of Tel Aviv. These attacks were reported in the British press as well as through official channels from Egypt, and the prime minister's office responded swiftly to Jabotinsky's pleas for action. On 5 May Lloyd George's private secretary, Philip Kerr, sent a note to the War Office confirming that the commencement of the pogroms, and the recognition of the propaganda value of the Jewish Legion scheme, had removed any remaining Foreign Office reservations. He added that Weizmann had also been in touch with the prime minister to make it clear that; 'in the light of recent events in Palestine, the opposition which had been manifested in Jewish quarters to this scheme in the past has now disappeared and that the plan ... would now receive the support of all prominent Jews.'[43] In concluding his note Kerr asked the War Office to reconsider the scheme, and pointed out that Weizmann, who was shortly to accompany Sir Mark Sykes on a government mission to Palestine, now believed that 'a great many thousand Jews' could be recruited locally.

Sykes was to take up the position of political adviser to General Allenby, the newly appointed commander-in-chief of the EEF. Significantly, he was fully briefed by Lloyd George and Lord Curzon on 3 April, immediately prior to the approach to Weizmann. Thus there was now an evident divergence in policy between the prime minister and the Foreign Office, with regard to the Middle East in general and Palestine in particular. On the one hand, the Foreign Office insisted that the establishment of a Jewish unit did not imply any official approval of Zionism, whereas the decision to permit Weizmann to accompany Sykes signalled the pro-Zionist intentions of the prime minister.[44] The Foreign Office desire to uphold the terms of the Sykes–Picot agreement was not going to be allowed to interfere with the exploitation of opportunities made possible by the EEF's advance into Palestine. In other words, Lloyd George's preference for support of Zionist aims over the claims of France, Italy and the Arabs underwrote the creation of the Jewish Legion.[45]

Inevitably, Jabotinsky's apparent victory over the Anglo-Jewish establishment proved to be far from swift and conclusive. Whilst the Military Service Convention was being prepared, further attempts at voluntary enlistment had been made through the Jewish Recruiting Committee, without success. On 23 May 1917 an exasperated Lord Derby reported to the War Cabinet that, despite all of these efforts:

> The enthusiasm of the over age Jews has found no counterpart in the willingness of Jews of military age to take up arms for the country of his [sic] adoption ... When the Military Service (Conventions with Allied States) Bill becomes law and if Russia enters into the agreement now proposed, these men will become available for the Army but not before.[46]

The continuing failure of Russian Jews to volunteer in significant numbers reinforced the arguments that Rothschild and Montefiore had presented to the War Office, and cast doubt on Jabotinsky's claims that Russian Jews of military age were willing to serve in a Jewish Legion. Nevertheless, while acknowledging Jabotinsky's inflexibility, it would be unfair to imply he was indifferent to the continuing dearth of volunteers. His earlier efforts in the East End had met with virtual humiliation, and he knew that governmental support for a Jewish Regiment meant nothing if no soldiers could be found to fill its ranks.

It is clear, therefore, that the only alternative to voluntary enlistment was compulsion, and evidence showing how Jabotinsky appreciated this fact and changed his approach, is contained in the records of his long awaited interview with Brigadier Geddes, director of recruitment, and the correspondence that followed. Geddes met with Jabotinsky at the War Office on the morning of Saturday 9 June 1917, and submitted a long report to the new director of organisation, General Hutchinson.[47] In this report, Geddes emphasised Jabotinsky's optimism that a guarantee permitting all aliens concerned to serve together, and the removal of the regulation that restricted commissioned rank to British subjects, would greatly encourage recruitment. Jabotinsky also took the opportunity to present his view of the assimilationists, in uncompromising terms, which further demonstrated the difficulties of trying to reach a compromise between the different Jewish positions:

> He (Jabotinsky) tells me that in the east end [sic] of London and in Manchester and in Leeds and in Glasgow the alien Jews regard the ultra British Jews as hardly of the same race as themselves. They say that these Jews have forgotten their Jewishness in an attempt to become British, and he says that they are always spoken of as diluted Jews ... He tells me that they would far sooner have British officers of undiluted British descent ... than have a British Jew on the Officers Staff unless he was a Jew who had already done outstandingly well in the war.[48]

Their discussion next turned to the question of a regimental badge or symbol. Jabotinsky informed Geddes 'that the badge of the Jew' was the Magen David (Shield of David), and Jewish colours were blue and white. Geddes envisaged these symbols being placed on uniform collars, and that they would provide another aid to recruitment. Unfortunately, what Jabotinsky failed to mention was that the Shield of David had been adopted by the Zionist Congress as its official symbol, a fact that would not have been lost on the assimilationist establishment. It remains open to speculation whether or not this was a deliberate deception on Jabotinsky's part.

Geddes responded positively to Jabotinsky's points and reported that he considered it would be possible to raise a full brigade. As far as the question of officer rank was concerned, Geddes indicated that a system of honorary rank, valid only within the alien unit, was a possible solution. These matters having been dealt with, Geddes concluded his report with remarks that prove that Jabotinsky had finally realised compulsion was necessary:

> He further told me that it was, in his opinion, of no use starting the movement until we had cleared up the various points and until we had statutory power under the new Act (which is now before the House) to form Corps of Aliens. My personal feeling is that his points are good ones and that as soon as we have the legal power to take these men compulsorily if we form some convention with the Russian Government, which will give us that power, we should proceed along the lines that he suggests.[49]

On 19 June the director of organisation put his written endorsement to these minutes, adding the suggestion that voluntary recruitment should continue in the meanwhile, using the cadre of the 20th Battalion London Regiment as a reception unit, and mentioning Patterson as a commander for the unit on the grounds that 'he understands these people'.[50]

Jabotinsky's own written record of his meeting with Geddes is contained in a very brief passage in his *The Story of the Jewish Legion*, in which he tellingly makes no mention of the Magen David or of his support for compulsion. Instead he states that it was agreed that the unit be named the Jewish Regiment, and that its badge was to be the Menorah (a seven branch candlestick), the base of which was to be inscribed Kadimah, a Hebrew word with the apt meaning of forward and eastward.[51] Eventually, but only after seeing active service in Palestine, the Jewish battalions obtained the right to their own title and did indeed adopt the Menorah badge as described. It is therefore intriguing that General Geddes' minute contained no reference to this particular symbol, and that his account was later supported by the memoirs of his superior, Sir Neville Macready the Adjutant-General, that mentioned 'a suitable badge, the Shield of David, I think was agreed to'.[52] In the same passage of his memoirs Sir Neville also commented on the fact that junior staff officers in the War Office produced 'many ribald proposals' in respect of a unit name and badge for the Legion. These remarks indicate a certain level of anti-Semitism in the army establishment that showed its time-honoured contempt for the foreigner was alive and well. The background to military anti-Semitism at this time has been demonstrated in Keith Surridge's recent study, which has shown how the officer class expressed contempt for Jewish capitalists in South Africa during the second Boer War. By the time of the First World War many of these officers had reached high rank and attained influential positions within the military establishment.[53]

We have already noted the importance Jabotinsky attached to securing commissions for aliens, so it is unsurprising that he sought Samuel's assistance in attempting to obtain the required concession. On 14 June Samuel wrote to Jabotinsky, advising him that he had discussed the matter with the Under-Secretary of State for War, and 'understood from him that the government was favourably disposed'. It was apparent, however, that the limited scope of the proposed Military Service Convention meant that a statement on commissions for aliens could not be incorporated, and Samuel informed Jabotinsky that a separate Act of Parliament would be required.[54] One unfortunate effect of this delay was that Jabotinsky lost the inspirational services of

Joseph Trumpeldor who, disappointed at being unable to obtain a full commission, accepted an offer from Kerensky's government to go to Russia for the purpose of raising a Jewish army. It was Trumpeldor's intention to recruit and train this army for deployment through the Caucasus, with the ultimate objective of defeating the Turks. The overthrow of the Provisional Government in November 1917 wrecked this scheme and Trumpeldor returned to Palestine.[55]

The Military Service Convention between Britain and Russia was agreed on 16 July 1917, and permitted the conscription or repatriation of Russian subjects of military age (18–41 years) living in Britain, with a reciprocal arrangement for British subjects in Russia. The convention required Russian subjects, who wished to return to that country, to register their intention by 9 August. The remainder became 'deemed to have been enlisted and transferred to the Reserve in the British Army for the duration of the war' and were entitled to the same appeal and exemption conditions that applied to British subjects, using specially constituted tribunals with Jewish representation. This latter element very much reflected the arrangements proposed earlier by Major Rothschild and the Jewish Recruiting Committee, who were determined that their Russian co-religionists would serve. Finally, the convention stipulated that naturalisation would be available, at no charge, to Russian soldiers on completion of three months satisfactory service.[56]

Predictably, reaction against the convention by such bodies as the Foreign Jews Protection Committee was immediate and forceful. Public meetings and rallies were organised by the FJPC, in what was effectively a continuation of the tactics it had adopted since Samuel's first intimation of a convention and Jabotinsky's subsequent 'Home and Heim' campaign in 1916. The leader of the FJPC was Abraham Bezalel – born Solly Abrahams – who, although originally from Eastern Europe, had served as a corporal in the French Army before arriving in Britain in the early part of the war. Bezalel had been under scrutiny from the Special Branch throughout the operation of the FJPC and, as a result of his activities and the interception of a telegram to Petrograd, condemning British treatment of Russian Jews, he was deported in early August 1917. Bezalel's arrest took place during a Metropolitan Police raid on the East London Headquarters of the FJPC on 27 July, an action that effectively terminated this organisation's existence.[57]

The conventionists – as those choosing to return to Russia were called, have been researched by Sharman Kadish. Her analysis of the incomplete statistics suggests that their total number was only about 10 per cent of the Russian Jewish population of military age. Kadish has also established that the idealists who returned to Russia were predominantly of the intellectual left and other radical movements.[58] In accepting Kadish's argument it is clear that the departure of this intellectual vanguard weakened the various socialist movements in the East End of London, and thus removed some of Jabotinsky's most avowed opponents amongst the Russian Jewish population. This means that Jabotinsky's concern about the loss of some of his supporters was balanced by the withdrawal of some of his opponents, and demonstrates once again the multi-factional nature of the Russian Jews and the disunity amongst the Jewish community as a whole. Kadish herself points out the divisive nature of this issue for both 'West End' and 'East End' Jews. For the latter, the advent of the Anglo-Russian Military Service Convention and the formation of the Jewish Regiment in the summer of 1917 exposed intra-communal dissension that left the former in an uncomfortable position. We also know, from Kadish's research, that the great majority of Russian Jews of military age were neither politically active nor concerned with their civil rights. Instead they sought to protect their livelihoods and homes by failing to register for service under voluntary or compulsory schemes, claiming exemption, and 'failing' medical examinations. Nor were they excited by the opportunity to return to Russia, understandably given that most were raised, if not actually born, in Britain and had little connection with Russia, the country their parents had fled.

After the convention was in force, newspapers frequently reported that Russian aliens were avoiding service or absenting themselves having earlier attested. This provoked violent indignation amongst local patriots. For example, a report in *The Times* on 17 July, which covered the fining (£10) at Old Street Magistrates Court of Isidore Borkov for absenteeism was entitled '4,000 Stepney Absentees – Avoiding Service by Every Conceivable Means' – a quote attributed to the recruiting officer for Stepney, who had testified in this case. The same newspaper, on 25 July, published a report on the various meetings held by the anti-conventionists in general, and the speaking activities of Bezalel in particular. Under the heading 'Service for Aliens – Tactics of Russian Jews in London', this report also contained the following passage quoting remarks attributed to 'British residents' that portrayed the strength of local feeling:

> Eight thousand Jewish aliens of military age are still living as civilians in Stepney and Hackney alone … 'The ferment down here,' a well-known Hackney resident said yesterday, 'is rapidly becoming

serious, and if the Government deal with the situation with a strong hand they will have the full support of the British population. The demand [from the Russian Jews] that families shall be sent back to Russia is very largely a bluff ... They do not want to go to Russia. They do not want to fight for anybody... Conscience has not prevented them from making money out of war contracts and war work.[59]

Occasionally the strong feelings of the local, indigenous population were exhibited in violence. One such incident resulted in the appearance on 8 August, again before Old Street magistrates, of Marcus Reubon, aged thirty-six, a watchmaker of Islington; Myer Smerna, aged thirty-seven; a warehouseman of Spitalfields, and Hyman Rosenfeld, aged thirty-six, a tailor's machinist of Stepney Green, on charges of using 'insulting words and behaviour'. Two policemen testified that the three were part of an estimated crowd of about 150 that had assembled outside the Alien's Registration Office in Commercial Street. It was alleged that Reuben had shouted '—— the Army, I am not going to join', to which Smerna had added, 'I won't join', the pair being promptly arrested. At this Rosenfeld called out 'Let them go, this is worse than Russia', a remark that set off a scuffle with the remainder of the crowd who appear to have been mainly British. It was only the prompt action of the police in taking them into custody that saved them from a beating, a fact commented upon by the magistrate when binding them over.[60]

Not all local British residents were hostile towards the Russian aliens, however, for support came from members of the anti-war left. An example can be found in a resolution from the Tottenham branch of the Independent Labour Party:

This meeting protests against the abrogation of the Right of Asylum in this country and points out that the Government, which now welcomes the Russian Revolution, was previously preparing to deliver into the hands of Tsarism these fighters for freedom ... who had sought shelter in Britain. This meeting condemns any forcible deportation of aliens to their native countries for political motives, including military service ... At the same time the meeting demands that every facility should be given to those Russians who wish voluntarily to return to Russia in order to assist the movement for the full democratisation of the country.[61]

These libertarian and democratic sentiments failed to take into account the real situation of most Russian Jews, to whom the term 'freedom fighter' was scarcely applicable. Furthermore, the ILP's pacificism was unrepresentative of the population at large, who co-operated with compulsory service, and would not tolerate behaviour they saw as provocative and unpatriotic.[62] Russian Jewish antipathy to military service was also responsible for widening the divide between the Anglo-Jewish establishment and their alien co-religionists. Even the *Jewish Chronicle* which, in 1916, had supported the voluntarist ethos implicit in the 'Home and Heim' campaign had, by the summer of 1917, come round to strongly advocating compulsion, the very policy which Lucien Wolf had always seen as the only practical solution to the Russian recruitment problem.

Military recruitment was not the only issue heightening intra-communal tension in the summer of 1917. Anglo-Jewish circles were increasingly aware of the government's alignment with Zionism, and this exposed the different viewpoints within them. The hard, anti-Zionist line of David Lindo Alexander, Claude Montefiore and Lucien Wolf represented an assimilationist (and Reform) tradition that accommodated their conception of Judaism solely as a religion. Nevertheless Wolf, on behalf of the Conjoint Foreign Committee, had been aware of the importance of dialogue with the Zionists and was sensitive to growing British (and French) support for their cause, but this balancing act by discussion could not be sustained. In what Black has described as a 'pre-emptive strike',[63] Alexander and Montefiore signed a letter, entitled 'Palestine and Zionism – Views of Anglo-Jewry', which *The Times* published on 24 May 1917. This sought to bring the Zionists out into the open and thereby discourage the government from pursuing the sympathetic policy that it had been developing with Weizmann and others. There is no denying that this was a risky strategy, but it should be remembered that the government had recently sought and accepted Wolf's advice, which was based on the premise that Zionist publicity was prejudicial to the safety of Jews in Palestine, as to the best means of contacting German Jews. The idea behind this contact was that influential German Jews might have persuaded their government to help prevent the persecution of Jews in Palestine, through discussion with their Turkish allies.[64]

Unfortunately for Wolf and his colleagues their strategy backfired, mainly because of Alexander's and Montefiore's failure to consult with all sections of Anglo-Jewry prior to the publication of *The Times* letter. In the ensuing internal debate the president of the Board of Deputies, Alexander, was forced to resign and this weakened further the board's influence with the government. This situation also raised the larger question of the board's claim to represent the interests of Anglo-Jewry. For example, Jewish friendly societies, which encompassed the largest group of Jews living in Britain, had no representation on the Board of Deputies and did not view kindly what they saw as the high-handed behaviour of the board in general and Alexander in particular.[65] This anger was directed at the board regardless of the fact that the United Council of Jewish Friendly Societies was itself firmly opposed to the Jewish Legion scheme, as confirmed by two unanimously adopted resolutions at its 1917 annual conference:

> 1. That the United Council of Jewish Friendly Societies make such representation to the proper authorities as will lead to the abandonment of the proposed formation of Jewish Battalions.
> 2. That the United Council take steps to redeem the prospect held out previously of securing representation on the Tribunals to be set up for Russian Jews.[66]

A further consequence of this public split amongst Anglo-Jewry was the dissolution, in the middle of July 1917, of the Conjoint Foreign Committee that had consisted of representatives of the Board of Deputies and the Anglo-Jewish Association. While it is true that a replacement body, again with Lucien Wolf as secretary and spokesman, was soon formed, the timing of this very public split amongst Anglo-Jewry was an important factor in securing victory for the Zionists in the struggle for government support.[67]

It has been seen that Zionists themselves were not a united group and, in concluding this brief section on the divisions between the Jewish sub-communities, it is important to reiterate that Weizmann's advocacy of an informal alliance with Britain ran contrary to the official Zionist policy of neutrality. Within the East End Russian Jewish community, the left-wing activists prominent in the Right to Asylum campaign mainly regarded Zionism as an opportunity to build a state on socialist principles, away from the religious, economic and social antagonism they faced in the Diaspora. They were, for the most part, also anti-war, seeing it as a class-based conflict, with the working-class masses sacrificed on the altar of capitalism.[68]

Ahad Ha'am, the Zionist intellectual, held another point of view, which he expressed in correspondence with Trumpeldor:

> your main argument is that the Legion will prove to whoever is in need of proof, that we are able to fight, and that, therefore we shall

be able to defend our Country. But I believe, that even without the Legion the Jews have sufficiently demonstrated their fighting capacity in all the armies that are at present engaged in the war.[69]

Finally, a more poignant and down to earth argument was made clear in a letter to the *Jewish Chronicle* from a Russian Jew named Horwich, from Plaistow, London E13, who wrote proposing a Jewish Legion to fight the Turks in Palestine because, 'Russian Jews see the war as not involving them as they didn't start it, and do not want to become cannon fodder for Gentiles who will continue to regard them as aliens after the war.'[70]

The public arguments within Anglo-Jewry and its East End counterpart did not escape the attention of the War Office, and the complexities of the situation presented grave difficulties when organising units specifically for Russian Jewish conscripts. However, with the decision already made at the political level to form a Jewish Regiment, and the convention a fact, the War Office issued a press release on 27 July 1917, duly announcing that:

Arrangements are now nearing completion for the formation of a Jewish Regiment of Infantry. Experienced British Officers are being selected to fill the higher appointments in the unit, and instructions have already been issued with a view to the transfer to this unit of Jewish soldiers, with a knowledge of Yiddish or Russian languages, who are now serving in British Regiments. It is proposed that the badges of the Regiment shall consist of a representation of King David's Shield. Further information as to the conditions of enlistment and service will be issued shortly, as soon as the necessary legal powers have been obtained.[71]

Service in Palestine was, as far as Jabotinsky was concerned, an essential prerequisite for the Legion. As he expressed in a later letter to the *Jewish Chronicle*: 'must fight in Palestine because Jew fighting against Jew in Europe could only do so as part of their national army'.[72]

The War Office announcement appears to represent a smooth transition from policy to action, but the records reveal that the decision to make this public announcement was only taken after pressure was applied by the Home Office, which was conscious of the urgent need to assuage public feelings. The same records show that the announcement was made some three weeks after the War Office sent out a general request, to all unit commanders, for a list of names of 'officers rank of Major or below who are desirous of transfer to such a Battalion'.[73]

To add to the confusion at the War Office, Major Rothschild and Claude Montefiore went to see Major-General Tagart, the Home Forces adjutant-general, on 3 August, in another attempt to preclude the formation of the Legion. In a memorandum to the director of organisation, Tagart reported:

> Major Rothschild and Mr. Montefiore represented to me on behalf of the Jewish community these facts:
>
> 1. That the arrest of the agitator Bezallel [sic] and the firm action of the Government had had an excellent effect.
> 2. That the Jews in the East End were now thoroughly cowed and prepared to accept anything.
> 3. That the impression now generally prevailed that it was the intention of the War Office to raise and train this Jewish Battalion, despatch it to France as soon as possible, put it in a most unhealthy part of the line, and get it exterminated. I believe this course however desirable from one point of view is not the intention, but that it is the intention to use the Battalion merely as a training centre and then despatch the Jews in drafts where required.[74]

It is abundantly clear from other evidence that the first two points made by Rothschild and Montefiore were untrue, and seriously misrepresented the actual situation in the East End. The very reason for the Home Office pressure referred to above was the continued agitation against the convention by the Russian Jews, and the reaction this provoked from the local British population. The third point demonstrated the assimilationists' wish to see the Russian Jews drafted and dispersed into the various units of the British Army, thus avoiding any possibility of their discrediting the reputation of Jews as a whole. Unfortunately, the appalling sentiments expressed in Tagart's comment on this point betray anti-Semitism directed towards Russian Jews of the poorer classes; it may have been understandable to deprecate their reluctance to serve, but the attitude revealed is of a more sinister nature. It is also notable that this was not commented upon in the War Office's brief acknowledgement and, in any event, the memorandum arrived too late to influence the Army Council's decision of 9 August, to the effect that 'It has been decided to go on with the formation of the 1st Battalion of the Jewish Regiment, it will be located at Plymouth.'[75] Patterson's appointment as commanding officer was also confirmed. News of these developments was released to the press, together with further information regarding the regiment, including its right to the same pay and conditions as the rest of the British Army, plus the provision of kosher food and synagogue facilities. Hence, under the heading 'The Jewish Corps' and the sub-title 'Anxiety to Fight for Britain', *The Times* was able to print the following details:

> There are 40,000 Jews in the British Army ... 32,000 are English Jews, the remaining 8,000 are from the Empire ... He [Patterson] is living in an atmosphere of Yiddish, Hebrew and Russian, and helping him is a most able Russian author and journalist ... There are 20,000 Jews of military age in London, so it will be seen that there is ample material to work on.[76]

Although the accuracy of these figures cannot be verified, for the reasons stated earlier, they indicate roughly the proportions of British to Russian Jews as far as military service was concerned and the extract demonstrates the distinction between the two in public discourse.

The official announcement of the establishment of the Jewish Regiment was presaged by Jabotinsky joining Patterson at the latter's office in an annexe to the War Office, where they worked on recruitment under the command of General Geddes. Given every facility by Geddes department, Jabotinsky reassembled the Zionist writing group that had helped him to publish recruiting pamphlets and Yiddish news-sheets during the ill fated 'Home and Heim' campaign. Jabotinsky also organised and spoke at recruitment rallies in the East End, where he encountered demonstrations often led by George [Grigory] Chicherin, a Bolshevik agitator who had played a major role in the disruption of the 1916 campaign. To counter these protests and to protect the meetings Jabotinsky resorted to employing Zion Mule Corps veterans, this escalation leading eventually to the internment of Chicherin who was later to become the Soviet commissar for external affairs.[77]

Patterson, for his part, called a meeting of senior figures, for 8 August, representing a broad cross-section of the various Jewish communities and factions, together with others with an interest in the regiment. They included Lord Rothschild, Sir Stuart Samuel (the new president of the Board of Deputies), Chaim Weizmann, L. Greenberg (editor of the *Jewish Chronicle*), Dr M. Eder (psychiatrist and leading Zionist), J. Ettinger (agriculturalist, founder of Jewish settlements in Eretz Israel and adviser to Weizmann), M. Landa (prominent author, journalist and moderate Zionist), Revd. S. Lipson (Chief Rabbi to the

Armed Services), Capt. R.N. Salaman (a distinguished medical doctor), D. Levontin (banker and a leading negotiator in the founding of Zion Mule Corps), Major Lionel Rothschild, Montefiore, Leo Amery, Major W. Schonfield, N. Primrose, J. Cowen, J. Hager, D. Ventir, Ormsby Gore, Sykes, Amery and, of course, Jabotinsky.

No minutes have been traced for this meeting, but references in War Office files and items in the Landa papers confirm that the Jewish representatives agreed to support Patterson and the regiment, but a minority noted their objection that it had been formed without what they regarded as full and proper consultation with the mainly assimilationist Anglo-Jewish organisations. Nevertheless, support for the regiment was secured, at least for the time being, no doubt because, faced with a *fait accompli*, some of those present felt it would have been disloyal to disrupt its development.[78] Furthermore, some may have agreed with Capt. Salaman, who told the meeting:

> The Zionists have played us Columbus egg-trick. They have confronted us with an accomplished fact and thus stopped all discussion. There is only one thing left for us – try to make the Regiment a success and a credit to the Jewish people.[79]

Whatever the reservations, having secured support for the regiment, Patterson left the meeting in the hands of Lord Rothschild, and he returned to his office from where, a short while afterwards, he was summoned to General Geddes and reprimanded for holding a Zionist meeting. Contemporary accounts show that, immediately following Patterson's departure from the meeting, Major Rothschild and Montefiore went to Geddes office to complain about the proceedings. Patterson denied the allegations made against him, and pointed out that it was the assimilationists who had raised the question of Zionism; he was merely attempting to carry out his orders to organise recruitment to the Regiment.[80]

Meanwhile Lord Rothschild, acting as chairman of the meeting, had overseen the setting up of a provisional executive committee for the promotion of the Jewish Regiment. Myer Landa, who had been offered medical, chaplaincy, band and welfare services from sympathetic Jews following the public announcement of the regiment, was appointed secretary, the other members being J. Cowen, L. Greenberg (who withdrew on 13 August), Dr Eder, J. Ettinger, D. Levontin, Revd. S. Lipson, Capt. R. Salaman, Sir Stuart Samuel and Major W. Schonfield. The committee decided to hold a general meeting of Jews in order to mobilise support from the wider Jewish community for recruitment and welfare. This decision was taken notwithstanding the remaining unease amongst assimilationists, and whilst mass demonstrations by Russian Jews opposed to conscription continued outside Commercial Street Police Station.

This general meeting was arranged for the evening of 13 August at Jews College, Queen's Square, and the same day that Sir Stuart Samuel withstood hostile anti-Legion questioning at a meeting of the Board of Deputies. Lord Rothschild presided over the proceedings that were attended by Patterson, who afterwards wrote a report to Lord Chichester, then serving as a deputy assistant Adjutant-General to the director of organisation. Patterson commented upon the details of the meeting and described, in simple terms, the differences of opinion that had divided Jewry in Britain over the question of Russian Jewish military service. In addition, Patterson was keen to bring to Chichester's attention the very real possibility that the hard-liners would intensify their efforts to wreck the scheme. Patterson's letter is invaluable evidence for conflicting attitudes towards the Legion and for this reason a substantial extract of is reproduced here:

> The decision of the War Office in calling the regiment 'a Jewish Regiment' was enthusiastically endorsed by practically everybody present. There were, I think, but two exceptions and these were elderly English Jews who had apparently lost touch with the living ideals which are at present held by Jewry ... I may say that Lord Rothschild himself, is in favour of the regiment being called 'a Jewish Regiment,' ... There are I know, a few so called English Jews, headed by the Montagues [sic] and some of the Montefiores who wish apparently to forget that they are Jews because forsooth they have been settled in England for two or three generations and what they say is, that they are afraid that this regiment might possibly not do them credit ... but it was strongly pointed out to them ... that their trumpery two or three generations reputation in England was but a very small thing indeed compared with the six thousand odd years which the Jewish Nation have behind them ... as I understand that these few monied Jews in England are attempting by subterranean political intrigue to put obstacles in the way of the formation of the regiment and do all they can to get the War Office to change their mind on the subject. I hope the Secretary of State will not listen to any of their suggestions ... PS I am inundated with applications for transfers from British Jews now serving in the Army.[81]

Patterson's warning was not without foundation for, after the events of 8 August, the anti-Zionist Major Lionel Rothschild and Claude Montefiore enlisted the participation of Lord Swaythling in a meeting they had arranged with Lord Derby on the 13th, in an effort at least to change the name of the Jewish Regiment. Lord Swaythling was the second baron and senior member of the Montagu family, being the elder brother of Edwin, with whom he shared a strong antipathy towards Zionism. Lord Derby's reaction to this powerful delegation is not recorded, but he did send Swaythling's deputation to see the director of organisation, General Hutchinson, the very next day. Hutchinson wrote a minute of this meeting to the adjutant-general (Macready) and its contents reveal that the War Office recognised that the naming of the unit was a very sensitive issue, and attempted to end the controversy by adopting a firm stance. After a sentence, endorsed in the margin by Macready with the words 'approved – 15.8.17', which read, 'It was more or less settled that the units were to be called 1st 2nd 3rd Etc. Jewish Regiment', Hutchinson advised:

> The above named (Lord Swaythling, Major Rothschild and Mr. Montefiore) strongly object to this name – whether they represent any large section of Jews I cannot say – they think the Jews we are going to enlist will disgrace the name of the Jew. I do not care what the unit is called but we have already called it the Jewish Reg. in a Communique. The name suggested are:
> Russian Jewish Reg.
> Zion Regiment (Taken from the Zion Mule Corps in Egypt).
> Macobean [sic] Reg.
> Perhaps you will get a decision as to what this unit is to be called.[82]

On the same date, 15 August, the adjutant-general responded to Hutchinson with the written confirmation that Lord Derby had 'decided that the unit be called "The Jewish Regiment"' and had written to Lord Swaythling to inform him of this decision.[83]

Despite the conveying of this decision to Lord Swaythling, the hard-line assimilationists continued in their attempts to change Lord Derby's mind. Lord Rothschild was well aware that the matter was far from settled and, contrary to the statement made by Patterson in his letter to the War Office, was unhappy about the name 'The Jewish Regiment'. Furthermore, in correspondence with Landa, he made it clear that he should not be associated with recruitment activities in the East End, as his name was linked with the failed efforts of 1916. He also informed Landa that he feared, due to the intervention of Lord Swaythling's delegation, that 'there is a possibility of the whole affair of coming to naught'. A very interesting postscript further advised 'I also think it wise to have nothing to do with the Recruiting Branch', which implied that the assimilationist lobby had secured the support of some members of that branch of the War Office.[84] Lord Rothschild's position seems to have placed him between the pro- and anti-Legion factions, but a letter he wrote to Lord Derby, on 22 August 1917, clearly shows that he had now adopted a pragmatic position. Thus, whilst he had always objected to a Jewish unit in principle, he now supported the idea for two reasons arising from changing circumstances. Firstly, there had been a large number of applications for transfer to the new regiment from Jewish officers and men currently serving the Crown, as confirmed by Patterson. Secondly, the conscription of Russian Jews made the formation of such a unit a practical necessity because language and other problems made integration into standard army units extremely difficult. In this letter Rothschild also confirmed his objection to the proposed name and suggested 'The Maccabean Regiment or Field Force'; his reasons being that the regiment would not be 'representative of all the Jews', and that the Russian government and Russian Jews both objected to 'any name at all symbolical of or suggestive of a "Foreign Legion".'[85]

Rothschild's suspicions of certain parts of the War Office were shared by Jabotinsky. In his impetuous way, Jabotinsky decided to use his contact at the Foreign Office, Sir Ronald Graham (who had been influential in the formation of the Zion Mule Corps), in order to vent his frustrations and place further pressure upon the military authorities. In a letter dated 19 August, Jabotinsky pointed out to Graham that:

> the two essential steps, the formation of a nucleus (we have already had applications for transfer in and a London Regt. cadre), and the appeal to Jewish 'manhood' to be published by the authorities, has not happened ... Although the official papers on the Jewish Regiment I saw bore the heading 'for service in Palestine'[,] the WO refused to confirm this publicly.[86]

Jabotinsky also accused the War Office of undermining the work of Lord Rothschild, by refusing to allow him (Jabotinsky) to deny publicly rumours suggesting the scheme was to be dropped, service in Palestine was to be denied and, most invidiously of all, that 'this is a scheme to substitute aliens in a Legion Estranger for British troops in dangerous areas'. This last point has strong echoes of the sentiments expressed in Major-General Tagart's earlier memorandum, and it is significant that no denial was issued or authorised by the War Office. In response to Jabotinsky's request Sir Ronald Graham approached the War Office, but apart from ascertaining that the matter was in the hands of Lord Derby, could only inform him that the War Office considered 'The differences that have arisen appear to be mainly due to the acute division of opinion in Jewish circles which the scheme has brought about.'[87]

Lord Derby, in attempting to implement the Legion scheme following the War Cabinet's authorisation, was now under pressure from representatives of the various Jewish organisations to abandon, alter or press on with the Jewish Regiment. He also knew that the Swaythling delegation were keen to restate their case for a change of name, their alternatives already having been minuted at the War Office. Supporters and opponents of the scheme both in parliament and the War Office had added to these pressures, and even the Foreign Office, through Sir Ronald Graham, was now attempting to influence Derby's actions. The press too, had begun to question the authorities' refusal to confirm where the regiment would serve, and publicised the fact that factions of both Zionists and anti-Zionists objected to service in Palestine.[88]

These pressures may have persuaded Derby that, whatever he did, enough objections would be raised to prevent or delay the creation of real, fighting battalions from the Russian Jewish conscripts. To add to his woes, the prime minister also became anxious at the lack of progress and, writing through his private secretary, Philip Kerr, in a confidential letter of 22 August, pressed for the rapid formation of the Jewish Regiment:

> Jewish circles, which exercise a great deal of influence all over the world, are divided with regard to the War. There is no doubt that a growing number of influential Jews are beginning to work for a premature peace. They can see no decisive end to the War and they are anxious that normal conditions of trade and industry should be re-established as soon as possible. The Prime Minister thinks that it is of great importance that some definite focus should be given to the other section of Jewry which is in favour of the Allies and the vigorous prosecution of the war. The project of creating a Jewish Legion with special reference to the liberation of Palestine, in great measure gained his support because he felt [it] would create a most valuable rallying point ... In his opinion its political importance

vastly outweighs its military importance. He understands that a good deal of opposition is being organised against the scheme in Jewish circles and he has therefore instructed me to write and express to you this hope that the creation of a definitely Jewish unit ... will be pressed forward as rapidly as possible.[89]

That Lloyd George felt it necessary to urge Derby on is evidence that the activities of the Swaythling delegation and their associates were preventing the War Office from completing the project.

The harassed Lord Derby wrote an immediate reply to Kerr, in which he sought to reassure the prime minister that the War Office was doing everything in its power to make the Jewish Legion a going concern. This correspondence with Kerr concluded with comments indicative of the extreme sensitivity of the Zionist issue in relation to British foreign policy. Lord Derby confirmed that, whilst the Russian Jews would be officially enlisted for general service, they would in fact only be employed in Palestine. He justified this subtle and devious policy by advising that the public committal of the regiment to exclusive service in Palestine 'might cause the Prime Minister and his colleagues a considerable amount of trouble', as such a step could be interpreted as a pledge to Zionism. Given that the Balfour Declaration had yet to be formulated, Derby was correct in seeking to avoid any announcement that could have prejudiced the ongoing secret negotiations.

The prime minister was well aware of the assimilationist point of view that regarded Zionism in general and the Jewish Regiment in particular, with horror. Lord Swaythling's brother, Edwin Montagu, the secretary of state for India, expressed his feelings in a memorandum, dated 23 August, addressed to his Cabinet colleagues:

> I am not surprised that the Govt. should take this step [setting up Zion] after the formation of a Jewish Regiment ... my brother a serving Captain in the Grenadier guards, will be forced by public opinion or Army Regulations to become an Officer in a Regiment which will mainly be composed of people who will not understand the only language he speaks – English. I can well understand that when it was decided, and quite rightly, to force foreign jews [sic] in this country to serve in the army it was difficult to put them into Regiments because of the language difficulty ... A Jewish Legion makes the position of all Jews in other regiments more difficult and forces a nationality upon people who have nothing in common.[90]

Furthermore, the assimilationists' efforts were now significantly strengthened by the intervention of no less a figure than Lord Reading (Rufus Isaacs), the Lord Chief Justice. Determined to have his say on the Legion, Reading, son of a middle-class Anglo-Jewish family from London, told Derby on 29 August in a conversation that was minuted at the War Office:

> that he [Reading] is opposed to the Jewish Regiment because, though nominally British, it will be mostly Russian and may not acquit itself well, in which case the discredit will be to the British and not the Russians. He realized, however, that the project has gone too far to withdraw now. The immediate difficulty is the name, and he seems to be anxious not to include in it reference to the Jews which will make it Jewish and nothing else.[91]

Given the existence of this strong lobby, it is unsurprising that Lord Derby agreed to meet another assimilationist delegation on 30 August, in order to resolve 'the immediate difficulty', despite the publication, in the *London Gazette* of 27 August, of the appointment of Patterson to command a battalion of the Jewish Regiment.

To add to Derby's difficulties, Landa, as secretary of the provisional executive committee, had begun to organise a counter-delegation to the War Office, by sending out a circular inviting supporters of the Jewish Regiment to participate in the delegation and support the following statement:

> The constitution of a Jewish Regiment will enable soldiers to serve without violence to religious scruples with regard to sabbath breaking or forbidden food. ... The large number of applications from officers, nco's and men for transfer to the regiment includes a strong sentiment in favour of the scheme ... It proves, also, that English born Jews of all classes, are anxious to be associated with their Russian Brothers ... Objection to the name can be met by styling the regiment the Maccabeans, an inspiring title which all will be proud to bear[92]

It will be recalled that Maccabeans was one of Major Rothschild's and Claude Montefiore's alternative titles (it was also the compromise choice of Lord Rothschild), but the results of their second deputation to Lord Derby demonstrated that a change of name was but one of their demands. This deputation visited the War Office on 30 August, as planned, and included Lord Swaythling, Chief Rabbi Hertz, Major Lionel Rothschild, Claude Montefiore, Edmund Sebag Montefiore (chairman of the Jewish War Services Committee), Sir Charles Henry MP, Sir Stuart Samuel (president of the Board of Deputies of British Jews), Sir Phillip Magnus MP, Ald. Louis Cohen (Liverpool), N. Laski JP (treasurer of the Board of Deputies), Arthur Franklin JP (president of the Jewish Religious Education Board), B.A. Fersht (general-secretary of the Amalgamated Orders of Achei Brith and Shield of Abraham) and L.J. Greenberg. Again, there are no available minutes of this meeting, but a collection of typewritten notes quote attributed arguments. These notes also record the opinions submitted in writing to the War Office by non-members of the delegation, an example of which is a direct quote from Lord Rothschild's letter to Lord Derby (see above) suggesting the regimental name 'The Maccabeans'. It is therefore probable that the War Office used these untitled notes as a brief, and they certainly provide a useful summation of the various points of view pertaining to the formation of a Jewish regiment. Nothing would be gained by reiterating the familiar arguments recorded in most of the attributed notes, but four contributions to the meeting are worth examining because they further illustrate the communal complexity of the Jewish Legion issue.

Firstly, Sir Charles Henry voiced his opposition to a Jewish unit, giving the usual reasons regarding segregation, military effectiveness and the damage it would do to Jews generally. In concluding his remarks, however, Sir Charles gave his opinion that, should such a unit be formed, it would 'be an example that will certainly be followed in the United States'.

Secondly, B.A Fersht summarised his meetings with representatives of Jewish Friendly Societies, and the Birmingham Trade Union of Tailors, by stating 'they were unanimous against a Jewish Regiment'. Fersht also thought that 'nine-tenths' of Jews in Britain would be opposed to the idea and, whilst it is impossible to check these findings, opposition amongst these groups – regardless of whether they consisted of British or Russian Jews – has already been demonstrated.

Thirdly, Leonard Cohen, the president of the Jewish Board of Guardians, sought to overcome the difficulties caused to British Jews by the designation 'The Jewish Regiment', by urging the War Office to give the proposed unit a less misleading and more accurate title.

Finally, there is a contribution from Henry S.Q. Henriques, a senior member of the Board of Deputies who, it will be recalled, was a leader of the 1916 campaign to secure the same opportunities for

Russian Jews to enlist in the British Army as existed for their British co-religionists. Henriques stated:

> The only specious reason which I have seen put forward for this new departure in British Military Organisation is I think founded on a total misconception of Jewish sentiment and psychology. The great mass of the Jews no doubt look forward to their restoration to their own land of Palestine ... but no Jew worthy of the name, has ever cherished the idea that restoration is to be brought about by means of a Jewish military force ... of conscripts impressed into the service by compulsion of an alien law and directed by the authorities of a foreign nation in pursuance of that nation's political aims. Such a conception seems to me to run counter to every shade of Jewish sentiment and feeling.[93]

The War Office was thus presented with an Anglo-Jew arguing in favour of a return to Palestine, but refuting the means desired by Jabotinsky.

The strength of the above arguments and the efforts of the second deputation brought about an immediate change in policy. War Office minutes confirm that this deputation won its case, and state, in the first instance to the director of organisation, that it was decided that:

> 1. The Jewish Battalions specially raised from men who come under the Anglo-Russian Convention will be known in future simply by a number, and will have no title such as 'Jewish' or otherwise. The 1st Battalion will be numbered with the number next to the last training Battalion and so on. They will wear the General Service badge.
> 2. Care must be taken that Jewish officers and N.C.O.'s serving in British regiments are not forced to serve in these Battalions. They will, of course, be liable to transfer, but the matter must be handled very carefully ...

and secondly to the Quartermaster-General:

> At a Deputation of prominent Jews received by the S. of S. in his room today, it was mentioned that men of the newly raised Jewish Battalion were receiving special food. The S. of S. informed the Deputation that these men would receive in future the ordinary rations of the British Army, and not any special kind of food. Perhaps you would kindly note in case the statement that special food was being provided was true.[94]

This change of policy was endorsed by the War Cabinet during its meeting of 3 September. It is clear that the deputation placed the greatest emphasis on the fear that Russian Jews might have proved discreditable in the performance of their military duties, and this was the reason Derby now proposed to substitute a number in place of a title:

> although he [Derby] left open the question of adding any further designation which might express the particular character or aspiration of the regiment, but which would not involve the fighting reputation of Jews in the army generally. He also insisted he could not guarantee to keep the regiment, or even a particular Battalion of it, filled up with recruits who all shared the Zionist aspirations. He hoped eventually to form four Battalions, composed in the main of Foreign Jews ... The War Cabinet decided – that for the present the Battalions to be formed from Jewish recruits should receive numbers in the ordinary way, and without any distinctive title, without prejudice to the reconsideration of the distinctive title if a definite demand in favour of the change were substantially established and circumstances favoured such a policy.[95]

Reaction by the pro-Jewish Regiment lobby to Derby's change of mind was swift, but not swift enough to prevent Patterson submitting a letter of resignation in disgust. Before this could be actioned, however, Chaim Weizmann and Leo Amery succeeded in obtaining Lord Milner's support to persuade Lord Derby to accept the counter-deputation which Landa had been organising. Jabotinsky himself obtained the support of *The Times*, which published a helpful editorial by Wickham Steed urging the War Office – and Patterson – to reconsider. Derby received the counter-deputation on 5 September: it consisted of Landa, Dr Eder, Capt. Salaman, J. Cowen MP, E. Adler, L. Greenberg, a former 'muleteer' named Bessell, and it was led by a Gentile MP, J.D. Kiley.

Lord Derby informed this counter-deputation that he was not going to go back on his word to the first deputation regarding the regimental name and, in accordance with the War Cabinet's decision (and following a suggestion by Leo Amery), he advised Landa et al. that the provision of a Jewish name and insignia would be dependent upon the unit's performance in the field. Derby did agree, contrary to the earlier instructions he had given to the Quartermaster-General, that kosher food and religious holidays would be allowed, subject to the usual exigencies of service, and that the War Office's intention was that the unit be deployed in Palestine with the same proviso. Landa realised that these concessions were final and that in accepting them the deputation had committed itself to accepting the terms offered.

On 12 September the War Office published Army Council Instruction 1415, entitled 'Formation of Battalions for the Reception of Friendly Alien Jews', confirming their establishment. This document for the first time mentioned the regimental name under which they would initially serve – the Royal Fusiliers, with the first battalion being allocated the next available service battalion number of that regiment, the 38th. There are no records or minutes that give the reason for this choice, but it appears sensible to assume that, by becoming part of an established British regiment, the fears of the assimilationists were assuaged, and the Royal Fusiliers were chosen because they were the local infantry regiment for the East End of London.

Strenuous and ultimately successful efforts were made to persuade Patterson to withdraw his resignation. In a letter to Landa from the Royal Western Yacht Club at Plymouth on 14 September, Patterson wrote:

> You will be glad to know that I have taken your advice and written to General Hutchinson that I am prepared to 'carry on'. I would not have done this only for the official announcement granting 'Shabbas' and 'Kosher'. Our enemies have done their best to damn the idea and have not succeeded – but they have done some harm by depriving us of the name and Badge. However, we will yet win both.[96]

Taking into account the difficulties surrounding the creation of the 38th Battalion, Royal Fusiliers, it is clear that Jabotinsky's success in establishing such a unit may not have been as comprehensive as he would have liked. Nevertheless he had managed, with the assistance of colleagues and friends, to secure the promise of greater, more specific recognition in return for distinguished service in the field, and it is difficult to see how he could have realistically hoped for more at this stage in the war.

It now remains to attempt to draw some conclusions from the convoluted arguments and events that have been described above. Essentially, the Jewish Legion came about because of the convergence of British policy with a type of militant Zionism, which was epitomised by Jabotinsky, for reasons of national interest. This convergence was promoted by a new prime minister who was powerful enough to put it into effect despite the considerable opposition it provoked. Religious sympathy was of secondary importance; its significance was that it did exist within the mind of Lloyd George and many of his closest advisers, and was used to provide further moral justification for their eastern policies. No evidence has been found in this research to suggest that Protestant sympathisers – including Lloyd George and Patterson – attempted to get to grips with the complexity of Judaism, which helped to close their minds against the assimilationist establishment of Anglo-Jewry, and only respond to that faction's entreaties in a limited fashion, as demonstrated by the compromise over regimental nomenclature. It is important to underline this attitude by noting that, even though the Anglo-Jewish delegations consisted of holders of high office and leading representatives of many Jewish communal bodies and organisations, supported by a cabinet minister and senior members of the House of Lords, the government were not prepared to abandon the Jewish Legion project. However, the assimilationists won a vital symbolic point when the government conceded that the unit's name would contain no reference to Jewishness.

It is hardly surprising that Derby and the War Office also seemed to be unable to distinguish between the different interpretations of Zionism, and the differences between the various Jewish communities. Thus, whilst capable of making a straightforward distinction between British and Russian or alien Jews, on nationality grounds, the War Office found attempting to fit the Legion into a traditional British Army mould an exhausting and exasperating experience. The War Office did not help itself either, in that the prejudice of some staff officers hindered an objective approach to the project, with the result that War Office policy was driven by response to the latest arguments put before it, rather than by the consistent application of principle. Perhaps this was why Lloyd George chose to manage Lord Derby through his private secretary, instead of applying more formal pressure through the War Cabinet.

Finally, as far as the Jewish community in Britain were concerned, there can be no doubt that the question of military service for alien Jews caused internecine tension which reflected religious, social and political differences cutting across any simple classification into pre- and post-1881 assimilation and immigration.

# 5
Raising the Battalions: Great Britain

The establishment of the depot at Crown Hill Plymouth provided a base at which the conscripts and volunteers (including those transferred from other units) of the 38th Battalion, Royal Fusiliers, were to train in preparation for service overseas. It is now proposed to reconstruct the regimental activities of this period from September 1917 to early February 1918, to analyse the pattern of recruitment and examine the impact of the Balfour Declaration (2 November 1917), the Bolshevik Revolution and the withdrawal of Russia from the war in December.

In the following account, the term 'Jewish Legion' refers to all or any of the Jewish battalions of the Royal Fusiliers. Three of these units, the 38th, 39th and 40th service battalions, were used for field service whilst a further battalion, the 42nd, fulfilled a permanent holding and training function at the Regimental Depot at Crown Hill barracks, Plymouth. Before this organisation was established, the 38th battalion was responsible for its own induction and training routine, but by late 1917 it quickly became clear that, despite ACI 1415 (the instruction of 12 September 1917 confirming the formation and administrative arrangements of the Jewish battalions), the anticipated rush of recruits and transferees was not forthcoming. Both Jabotinsky and Patterson considered that a high level of experienced transferees would have provided the battalion with a valuable source of commissioned and non-commissioned officers. In their respective memoirs Patterson made only an oblique reference to the obstacles placed in the way of recruitment and transfer, whilst Jabotinsky accused the chief Jewish chaplain in France, the Reverend Michael Adler, of instructing all Jewish chaplains to 'preach that it was a shameful act to Jews to serve in our regiment'.[1]

Other parties also raised the question of obstruction with the military authorities. For example, James Kiley, the pro-Legion MP, wrote to General Macready with regard to questions he alleged were being put to serving soldiers who requested a transfer to the 38th. His enquiries elicited the following denial, which ended with a comment indicating that the slowness of recruitment was not all attributable to administration:

> You have been misinformed in regard to an examination being held in Russian, Hebrew or Yiddish for men who apply for transfer from their regiments to the Jewish Regiment ... I am bound to say that after the pressure that was put upon us to make this unit, the results have hardly been what we might call encouraging as regards numbers.[2]

During this period Sergeant Jabotinsky spent most of his time in London, at the offices of the Jewish Regiment Committee, 22 Chenies Street, London WC1. Obviously aware of the recruitment situation and sensitive to the need to ensure that the tribunals sent conscripted Russian Jews to the 38th Battalion Royal Fusiliers, he embarked upon a publicity campaign highlighting its attractions. On 15 November 1917 Jabotinsky wrote to Michael Landa to enlist his assistance in securing press interviews, and asked him to liase with James Kiley, as he suspected that the War Office were continuing to obstruct the development of the battalion. (It is interesting to compare this with the special mention that Patterson makes of Colonel King, of the military secretary's department, who worked hard to ensure the smooth transfer of suitable officers from France to Plymouth).[3] Jabotinsky's correspondence with Landa also revealed evidence of opposition from Zionist sources in the East End of London; he informed Landa that the editor of the Yiddish *Zeit*, who had received copy from his own correspondent describing the condition of the battalion in Plymouth in glowing terms, had ruined the effect by prefacing the articles concerned with an expression of his anti-Legion views.[4]

That Jabotinsky was able to work with parts of the Anglo-Jewish establishment in furthering the cause of the Legion is not surprising, given that the previous chapter demonstrated the willingness of much of that body to support the unit once its existence had become a fact. This support was led by Lord Rothschild and was most apparent in the work of the Care and Comforts Committee, Canteen Committee and Entertainment Committee, which contributed much towards the well-being of the officers, other ranks and recruits at Plymouth. On its establishment the 38th Battalion had received, via *The Times*, a donation of £1,000 from a Mr Leopold Frank, and this generous contribution enabled the wives of the supporters of the Legion, including Mrs Patterson, to set up and promote the work of the committees mentioned above, ensuring that the soldiers received kosher food, facilities for recreation and, at the request of Colonel Patterson, musical instruments for a regimental band.[5]

Civilian efforts to provide comforts for this, or any, regiment were common enough, but Foreign Office papers show that the British Government was particularly sensitive to this issue as far as the Legion was concerned. The relevant papers refer to correspondence that took place in October and November 1917, between a W. Gabotonsky of Basil Mansions, Knightsbridge and M.J. Landau (formerly one of Jabotinsky's aides as mentioned earlier), then running the Jewish Correspondence Bureau in The Hague. In his letter, Mr Gabotonsky had asked Landau to 'appeal to every Jew to assist in providing comforts to the Jewish Regiment'. The machinery of censorship had managed to intercept this letter and the Army Council wrote to Gabotonsky advising him 'such appeals should not be made as they gave the wrong impression of the temper and resources of the British people'. Whilst this may have been seen as the end of the matter by the authorities, Gabotonsky decided to pass on the Army Council's letter to Jabotinsky who, in turn, despatched a letter on 16 November to Arthur Balfour, the foreign secretary. Jabotinsky made the point that Landau was well known to the British Government in general and to Colonel Buchan in particular; and took the opportunity to vent his frustration at what he saw as the burying of the Legion by 'Whitehall, with the name removed, propaganda forbidden and now plea for comforts rejected'. The foreign secretary replied on 28 November to the effect that all of Jabotinsky's points would receive 'sympathetic consideration'. Nothing further developed from this exchange as time and events overtook Jabotinsky's complaints.[6]

Meanwhile, the Jewish Regiment Committee also sought to increase its efforts by raising further membership from among the Anglo-Jewish elite but, as might have been expected, its entreaties did not always find favour with those approached for assistance. H. Hock Esq., of 61 Portland Place, London W1 rejected a nomination to the committee in the following terms: 'I have two sons serving as officers in the army and as they and other Jews are on an equal footing with every other denomination I fail to see why the Army should be divided into religious sections.'[7]

Notwithstanding such points of view, the *Jewish Chronicle* revealed, in the weeks following the issuing of the Balfour Declaration, a desire to enhance the Jewish nature of the units at Plymouth, and promote support for the soldier's welfare. For example, the leader on 7 December called for 'His Majesty's Government to put the Jewishness back into the Battalions', and it was reported, on 21 December, that 'a concert for the Judean comforts fund at the Empire, Leicester Square, raised £700.'[8]

It can therefore be seen that, through the efforts of the supporting committee, together with the concessions on kosher food and the observance of Sabbath, the ritual and cultural needs of the Jewish soldier were addressed. Similarly, it is clear that the local community also made efforts to ensure that the Jewish soldiers benefited from recreational and spiritual comforts. Lady Astor, the wife of the member of parliament for Plymouth, donated a recreation hut and the YMCA, under its local president, Sir Arthur Yapp, was very active in the provision of recreational facilities. Perhaps, however, the small Jewish population of Plymouth, led by Mr Myer Fredman, made the most significant contribution to the well-being of the unit. In addition to providing religious facilities, this community 'lost' their Rabbi, the Revd. L. A. Falk, to the 38th Battalion, which he joined as chaplain with the rank of captain, just prior to the unit proceeding overseas.[9]

Unfortunately, there is very little in the way of personal testimony with regard to life at Crown Hill. The letters of one recruit, Private Paul Epstein, have been preserved in the Anglo-Jewish archives, and make for interesting, if brief, reading. Paul was a twenty-two year old Russian conscript from London (with no Hebrew), who arrived at Crown Hill on 22 January 1918, and his early letters refer to the large numbers of East Enders in the barracks.[10]

In spite of the efforts to improve the lot of the recruits, there is evidence that Patterson was becoming increasingly frustrated at the pace of recruitment in late 1917. Early in December he was appealing to Landa to 'stir up the Tribunals at present they are a laughing stock. We are now getting no recruits, or one, 3, or 4 a day!'[11]

Although definitive figures are not available, it is reasonable to assume that Russian Jews who had not previously volunteered were quite likely to resort to appeals to the tribunals for the deferment of service, and this is underscored by press reports in *The Times, Jewish Chronicle* and other newspapers. It would be wrong, however, to assume that all appeals for deferment of service were ill-founded, as shown by the following extract taken from the *Jewish Chronicle* of 11 January 1918:

> An exceptionally interesting case of a Russian Jewish volunteer in the British Army was mentioned at the Stepney Local Tribunal on Monday. A youth of 18, Abraham Menaker, Grade 2, in applying for exemption, stated that he had an ailing mother and younger brother to support, his father being in the Army. It was explained that although a Russian and 44 years of age, the father had volunteered and had been accepted two years ago. He is now with the British Army in Palestine and has recently been granted a certificate of naturalisation. The Military Representative confirmed the facts as to the father, and the youth was given three months exemption.

One notable applicant for exemption, who failed to gain the approval of the tribunal, was the American sculptor Jacob Epstein, then aged thirty-seven and working from a studio in Cheyne Walk, Chelsea. With the United States having entered the war in April 1917, Epstein received his call-up papers in June, and although he initially succeeded in obtaining a three-month deferment, he was with the 38th at Crown Hill by the middle of September. In a recent biography, Stephen Gardiner describes the campaign mounted to have Epstein employed as a war artist, and notes how valuable this could have been in countering German propaganda in the USA. In Gardiner's view:

> Unfortunately, such a vision in amateur diplomacy was beyond the stuffed shirts at the War Office who would have merely regarded him as an American and a Jew – hardly a combination to commend him.[12]

Epstein was confident about the outcome of this campaign, and counted among his supporters C.P. Scott, and Charles Masterman. Nevertheless, he found himself in the ranks at Plymouth – a fact he ascribed to the counter-campaign run against him in the press by his professional enemies. Jacob Epstein completed his training with the 38th, but missed embarkation due to illness. Patterson wrote about him in training with some pride and affection, but did not take the story further. Epstein went missing immediately before he was due to go overseas with another draft of the 38th, and was found on Dartmoor having suffered a breakdown, which event led to his discharge on 25 July 1918.

Returning to the poor rate of recruitment, it is difficult to prove the War Office was obstructing recruitment and transfers, although the Landa papers contain copies of further correspondence between himself and Lord Rothschild on this subject. In a confusing development Jabotinsky asked Landa, on 21 December, to enlist Lord Rothschild's assistance in raising a petition to the War Office in order to secure for the battalion its own name (Judeans) and badge. This idea was initiated by Patterson who claimed that he was 'told at the WO that if the community would ask' then such a request would be granted. Unsurprisingly, this scheme came to naught and as Rothschild advised Landa 'the War Office pays little attention to civilian voices'.[13] Meanwhile, James Kiley continued to pressure General Macready, and in January 1918 finally received a response that acknowledged that some transfer requests were not being allowed. 'Applications from Jews of Category Ai are refused because a man so soon as he becomes Ai is immediately available for drafting.'[14] As Macready could demonstrate that this was not the case with other categories, and that it applied throughout the army, no allegation of deliberate obstruction could have been upheld, at that time.

If it is clear that recruitment was slow, it is also the case that the quality of the recruits did not always appear to be of the highest standard. Patterson himself commented on the keen enthusiasm but poor quality of the recruits, which he attributed to their alien, non-British nature and their predominantly sedentary way of life in the East End.[15] This situation emphasised the importance of establishing a cadre of experienced officers and NCOs, as well as indicating that a substantial training regime was required. In an internal War Office report, unsigned and dated 10 December 1917, it was reckoned that 666 men, out of a total of 925, would be ready for service overseas 'as Ai in 4 months time.' As the average number of recruits posted per week was forty, it was estimated that, in order to make the Battalion up to its full establishment of 1,000, 'the battalion will not be fit for Overseas for 5 months or more probably 6, i.e. June 1918'.[16]

The rate of recruitment and training revealed in this War Office report contradicts the official monthly returns preserved in the PRO file WO 73. According to this file, the numbers of other ranks on strength with the 38th Battalion (officers and NCOs have been excluded from this number as they were not recruits) were 152 in September 1917 (on October return), 339 in October 1917, 897 in November 1917, and 1352 in December 1917. In other words recruitment increased by 1,200 over a thirteen-week period, a rate of increase that is more than double that presented in the report, and claimed by Patterson himself (see above). Even so, the rate and quality of recruitment was of some concern to Patterson, but it is also clear that the pessimism and training prognosis put forward in the report was exaggerated. After all, a fully trained 38th Battalion was, in fact, ready for overseas duty by early February 1918, some five months ahead of the report's predicted date. It therefore seems reasonable to conclude that, since the report ignored the evidence of army statistics, its pessimistic forecast and the discredit it cast upon the battalion resulted from administrative incompetence. Patterson's low figures may well have been an example of an exaggeration designed to encourage greater action from the War Office.

Any comprehensive discussion of the recruitment of Russian Jews must also take into account the effect of the Military Service Convention, the Balfour Declaration and the second Russian Revolution. As far as the convention was concerned about 3,000 men returned to Russia; approximately 10 per cent of the estimated number of military age. The policy of paying dependants' allowances to the families of men recruited to the Legion may, in practice, have encouraged enlistment in Britain and discouraged conventionism. Thus, if they remained in Britain, the needy families of conventionists relied on the Board of Guardians and the Russian Dependants Committee,[17] whereas if they were recruited to regular army units, like the Jewish Battalions, their dependants were entitled to the normal allowances. Evidence for this treatment can be found in the *Jewish Chronicle* of 18 January 1918, which revealed that the Russian Tribunal had begun to sit twice weekly at the Guildhall (instead of Limehouse), and in opening the first session the chairman (F. Brinsley-Harper) announced that:

> Separation and dependants allowances to Russian subjects would be paid at the same rate as for British subjects. Where Russians called up for military service have been sending money to Russia, the Army allowances would be paid through the British Ambassador in Petrograd.[18]

It is evident that the issuing of the Balfour Declaration, on 2 November 1917, giving the British government's endorsement of a Jewish national home in Palestine, had little practical effect upon the rate of recruitment.[19] The real value of the declaration to the Legion lay not in recruitment in the United Kingdom, but as propaganda in the United States and Russia, where it was used to counter pro-German sentiment. One of the consequences of this propaganda was the recruiting drive for the 39th Battalion that was undertaken in the United States, and this development will be examined in the next chapter.

The Bolshevik Russian revolution, which overthrew the provisional government and inaugurated an ideologically based civil war, added further strain to intra-communal relations, and threatened the delicate balance between support for and rejection of the Russian immigrant population by the Anglo-Jewish elite. This had the dual effect of perpetuating the difficulties that had surrounded the formation and establishment of the Legion, and of heightening an atmosphere of anti-Semitism, within which all the Jewish community had to live. Of particular note was the effect on Anglo-Jewry of the general belief in the western democracies that Jewish activists dominated the revolutionary movement in Russia, which has been described in the work of Eugene Black. The Bolsheviks in particular were seen as an anti-western Jewish coterie. In comments that relate directly to inter-Jewish relations and, at the same time, reflect the fear of socialism that was engendered by events in Russia, Black states:

> Fears about East European Jewish radicalism reinforced ingrained elite prejudices about immigrants, nourishing their own sense of self-righteousness and superiority ... At the same time, the Anglo-French Jewish elite shared all class prejudices about what was happening in Russia and privately worried endlessly about property rights and expropriation.[20]

The effect of the publicity given to Jewish involvement in such activities, both in Russia and Britain, was clearly out of proportion to the numbers concerned.[21] Such propaganda only served to reinforce latent and existing anti-Semitism among some members of the army staff, a situation that was to create difficulties for the Legion in Palestine.

Returning to the more immediate problems posed by the November revolution, the armistice with Germany (5 December 1917) and Russia's withdrawal from the war could not be hidden from the Russian Jewish soldiers at Plymouth, or their compatriots who were awaiting conscription. The Military Service Convention empowered both the British representative to Russia and his Russian counterpart in London to grant exemptions from conscription. Home Office records contain copies of correspondence between M. Litvinov, the Bolshevik's representative and the British government, which demonstrate that the new regime did not recognise the convention because it had been agreed to by the previous administration.[22] Litvinov was, nevertheless, prepared to grant exemptions in response to the pleas he had received from Russian Jews living in Britain, who felt that the requirement for them to undertake military service was unjust, due to the armistice with Germany. In the true sprit of Brest Litovsk, Litvinov threatened to publish all the correspondence regarding this matter, and thus embarrass the British government that was now forced to review the whole question of Russian aliens in Britain. This pressure was compounded by the fact that France had already suspended its own Military Service Convention with Russia, and it was only a matter of time before the validity of the Anglo-Russian Convention was questioned by some of the men at Crown Hill.[23]

Patterson was able to restore the situation by pointing out to the disaffected soldiers that they were subject to military law and discipline, and the drastic penalties enforceable in wartime for disobeying orders. Jabotinsky and Weizmann were also concerned to have the 38th Battalion deployed to Palestine before any further damage could be inflicted upon the morale and efficiency of the battalion. Writing to Arthur Henderson, the Labour party leader (who had been expelled from the government in August), Jabotinsky again pressed for the renaming of the Legion (to Judeans) and its despatch to Palestine.[24] In another letter written on 12 December to Aaron Aaronson, a leading Zionist from Palestine then visiting the United States, Weizmann expressed his feeling that the 'question of the Jewish Regiment is becoming urgent', and that he too was endeavouring to obtain from the British Government a commitment to the early despatch of the unit to Palestine.[25]

Weizmann did not have to wait long for responses from the War Office and subsequently Downing Street. The War Cabinet met on 23 January 1918, and the minutes of this meeting include details of the briefings given by Arthur Balfour and General Macdonogh.[26] Balfour advised his colleagues of the difficulties posed by the attitude of the Bolshevik government and its representative in London, and Macdonogh – acknowledging the efforts of Weizmann – informed the War Cabinet of the fact that orders had now been issued to the Jewish Battalion at Crown Hill, effectively placing it at immediate notice for transport overseas.[27] In making this statement he was supported by his political chief, Lord Derby, who confirmed to the committee that

Colonel Patterson was convinced his men were now ready to serve in Palestine. Moving on to wider implications General Macdonogh went on to state that:

> there were about 25,000 of these Russians of military age in this country, of whom only about 4,000 had so far been called up. From the counter-espionage point of view, it was most desirable that these aliens should be either got into the Army, interned or deported to Russia.[28]

These estimates strongly support Sharman Kadish's research that determined that there were about 3,000 'conventionists'. If the 1,200 conscripts, identified earlier in army records as having been sent to Crown Hill by early 1918, are added to this figure, then the total approximates to General Macdonogh's official number. This means that, despite all of the Government's efforts, there were still in excess of 20,000 eligible Russian Jews in civilian life.

The War Cabinet was determined to force the issue and respond to the alarmist perceptions circulating in the East End. General Macdonogh (and by implication the Russian Jews themselves), was well aware that a shortage of shipping made the deportation option impracticable, a fact which no doubt prompted Derby to propose that those Russians who 'could not be got into the Army' should be interned in camps until transport became available. In accepting this proposal, the War Cabinet gave Derby the responsibility for working out its implementation.[29]

Within five months of establishing a Jewish regiment, Derby found himself once again embroiled in Jewish affairs, with the predictable result that the War Cabinet's hard-line decisions to deport or intern defaulters became subject to compromise. This is not surprising because of the sheer impracticality of the internment scheme with its associated costs and logistical problems; the same considerations having effectively removed the threat of deportation.[30]

The sensitivities raised by this issue are emphasised by the general lack of mention in official British and Anglo-Jewish records of anything relating to attempts to intern Russians during this confused period. There is, however, a report in the *Jewish Chronicle* voicing the concern of the Board of Deputies Foreign Affairs Committee over '8000 Russian Jews not at present soldiers, who had been kept at Maidstone in a most deplorable condition'.[31]

The immediate difficulty caused by this brief report is the number of Russian Jews mentioned therein. Although Maidstone was an established garrison with a large military encampment – but no civilian internment facilities – the presence of some 8,000 persons of Russian origin should have left a more significant record than has been discovered. If this number is reduced to 800, however, then the explanation revealed below becomes extremely plausible. The Russian Jews were friendly aliens but, whereas the Aliens Restriction Act of 1914 presumed government agencies could distinguish between enemy and friendly aliens, in practice public attitudes blurred the distinction. This confusion has made it difficult to investigate properly circumstances as described in the brief comment from the Board of Deputies. In the specific context of Russian Jews and military service, however, David Cesarani has succinctly reinforced the position argued by Sharman Kadish and agreed by this study, by writing; 'Russian Jews were amongst the aliens affected by the riots in 1915, but this was accidental as compared to the sustained animosity aroused by their reluctance to serve in the allied forces.'[32]

Returning to the concern of the Board of Deputies, an explanation of the Maidstone situation may lie within the columns of the *Kent Messenger*. The following extract is given at length so as to convey something of the atmosphere during the war and the language in which attitudes to aliens were expressed. Under the general heading 'Maidstone and the War', it was reported:

> More than usual interest was taken in Military movements in Maidstone last weekend, because they meant the removal of the organisation which had brought such a mixed population to the town during the last month or so – in other words, the 24th Recruit Distribution Battalion, which deals with the Russians, Russian Jews, Italians and other foreign elements called up under the Military Service Conventions. For a time Maidstone was a veritable gathering ground for the tailors, barbers, waiters. old clo' men, [sic] and cheap jewellery vendors who go to make up the life of the East End of London in its most Oriental aspects. Many were unwholesome and cadaverous, a few no doubt crafty and repulsive; many again quite respectable, clean members of society; but Maidstone had to take them as they came, good, bad and indifferent, and the news that the stream of them was to be diverted to another direction – not east but west – gave general satisfaction.[33]

According to War Office records the 24th Recruit Distribution Battalion, or to use its correct name, the 24th Training Reserve Battalion, had a strength (not including officers and NCOs who were British), of about 1,500 other ranks during its three months in Maidstone. It seems reasonable to assume, given that other nationalities were involved, but not reported on by the local press, that at least half of this number were Russian.[34] Finally, the *Kent Messenger* said goodbye to the British soldiers who had been posted out of Maidstone:

> The lads in khaki who also took their departure on Saturday were bidden farewell with much regret on the part of the townspeople, and the regret was mutual. There were many handshakings at the recreation rooms on Friday evening, and many tokens of appreciation were given of the efforts which had been made to make them feel at home in the town.[35]

It should also be recorded that this expression of civic appreciation had earlier been extended to the town's most notable British Jew, Sir Marcus Samuel (the co-founder of Royal Dutch Shell), who had lost his younger son killed on active service in France, whilst serving as a subaltern in the local infantry regiment.[36]

Aside from considerations of attitude, this episode also demonstrates that many Russian Jews were not automatically sent to the 38th Battalion on conscription, but were channelled through recruit battalions; it is therefore likely that this type of organisational procedure contributed to the slow recruitment at Crown Hill. The corollary is somewhat easier to prove. When the 28th Training Reserve Battalion was disbanded, through late January and early February 1918, official strength returns show the largest monthly increase of recruits into the 38th and nascent 39th Battalions Royal Fusiliers, amounting to some 755 men. This figure also adds further support to the earlier assumption that about 800 and not 8,000 Russians were encamped at Maidstone.[37]

The Maidstone episode shows that contemporary provincial anti-Semitism, particularly directed towards alien Jews, was not very different to that of the East End. The descriptions given of the Jewish and other alien conscripts in the above quotes from the *Kent Messenger* contain negative racial clichés, which contrast with the treatment of the British soldiers and even with the respect shown to the scion of established, local Anglo-Jewry. It is no surprise, therefore, to note that the GHQ of the British Army were shortly to receive an Intelligence

Summary which, under the heading 'General Public Opinion Concerning the War – Aliens', reserved its most derogatory remarks and racist language for Russian (and Polish Jews). After deriding these Jews –'this monied and artful race' – for their success in avoiding conscriptions through medical deception and the manipulation of the special tribunals, the report noted the disgust of the host population who 'saw these foreigners making continuous expeditions to the country in the already overfilled trains for the express purpose of bomb-dodging'. As if this were not enough, this section of the report finished with a criticism of the Jew ('the grabbing propensities of the Jewish Tribe') for buying businesses on the cheap where forced sales were made by Englishmen who had been called up.[38]

This report was compiled by military officers for their high command; its language leaves no doubt that anti-Semitic discourse was institutionalised. The comments on 'General Public Opinion' may suggest that anti-Semitism in the lower middle classes was linked with anxieties over the fate of 'one-man' businesses, due to the conscription of small-shopkeepers.

Returning to the survey of initial Russian recruitment, whilst it was true that the police were required to register Russian males over the age of eighteen, it was nevertheless the case that, by mid-February 1918, the War Cabinet had decided not to intern or deport Russian aliens.[39] Typically, even this was not the final twist as, in yet another effort to get the remaining Russians into the army, it was decided to place all new Russian recruits into labour battalions. This news was received by the 38th when in Italy *en route* to the Middle East (the effect of which will be examined later) but, after a short interval, recruitment into the infantry battalions was resumed and the situation appeared to settle down.[40]

It will be recalled that the order to prepare for embarkation had been received by Colonel Patterson on 20 January. In confounding the predictions made in the War Office report of 10 December, the 38th Battalion Royal Fusiliers had actually reached a trained strength of 31 officers and 859 other ranks, when this order was issued.[41] The battalion's readiness by 20 January indicates that, whilst the numbers were fewer than desired by the Legion's promoters, the recruits' training and preparation had been completed in an acceptable period. With Patterson's orders came a warning from the War Office about the increased risk of desertion. Again, there are no official figures available to indicate the number going absent without leave during the pre-embarkation period, but Private Epstein wrote to his parents advising that fifty-eight men had gone adrift immediately prior to travel.[42] Patterson himself recorded that 'when the final roll call was made there were not so many absentees, certainly no more than there would have been from an ordinary British Battalion'.[43]

To the bald figures extracted from War Office records and Patterson's memoirs can now be added the results of an analysis of the Avichail testimonies mentioned earlier. There are ninety-eight testimonials of men who joined the 38th Battalion in 1917, and who were despatched overseas in February 1918 after the completion of their training. From these records it appears that five were Gentiles, usually of drill and arms instructors, with the remainder being Jewish. The total of ninety-eight represents about 10 per cent of the battalion's strength, and their details confirm that thirty-six were born in London, thirty elsewhere in the United Kingdom and twenty-four were born in Russia, Poland or Lithuania. Thus two-thirds of this sample was British born, an unsurprising figure given their average age of twenty years, and the fact that immigration was virtually halted with the Aliens Act of 1905. Another less than surprising statistic to emerge is that, of the seventy-six recruits that recorded their address, fifty lived in London, with six each in Manchester, Leeds, and the general area of Edinburgh/Glasgow. More revealing are the figures concerned with transferees from other units and the proportion of volunteers to conscripts. The transferees amount to forty-nine (or 50 per cent of the sample), of whom thirteen had been conscripted into the army before the Legion's formation, which indicates that they were British subjects. Volunteers totalled forty-eight, consisting of twelve who joined the 38th before they were conscripted, and thirty-six (the balance of the transferees) who had enlisted in the army before the introduction of the draft. As nationality was not recorded in the testimonies, it must be assumed that the latter portion contained both British and alien subjects.

On the basis of this sample it seems probable that the 38th Battalion had a high proportion of volunteers and transferees, thus supporting the argument that Jews – particularly British Jews – did participate fully in the patriotic volunteer 'movement', and that there was a significant interest in transferring to a Jewish regiment once established. We should recall that, in addition to the numbers analysed above, the battalion included between twenty and thirty volunteers who had served with the Zion Mule Corps, which reinforces the importance of volunteers and transferees. Finally it is worth remarking that, apart from the testimony of three or four of Jabotinsky's keenest supporters, such as Harry First, none of the ninety-eight records mentions any Zionist activity, which contrasts sharply with the testimonials of the American volunteers that will be examined in the next chapter.

Behind the numbers lie the individual experiences of the soldiers of the 38th Battalion, some of which will now be used to bring to life the men behind the statistics. Several examples from the small sample of Avichail testimonies used in this research have been selected, so as to reflect the wide cross-section of men involved. They are repeated in their entirety so as to convey and preserve their original and highly personal perspective.

The first soldier is David Dobrin, who wrote his own testimony (*c*.1960) from an address in Amhurst Road, Hackney, London E8, which is, incidentally the most often featured street in the records. David, whose regimental number was J1159, completed his service in the 38th Battalion as a sergeant. Particularly noteworthy are his comments regarding being with his 'own people', despite the fact that the battalion consisted of a mixture of British and Russian subjects, with language and cultural differences, and contained both volunteers and conscripts. Note also the deference applied to officers who, whether Jewish or Gentile were credited with the peculiarly English attribute of gentlemanliness. The presence of British class and status values within a unit, designed to absorb alien and British Jews is palpable. David Dobrin's testimony reads:

> I joined the British Army in Nov.1916 at the age of 15 years and 11 months. I claimed to be 19 years of age. I served with the Rifle Brigade, Duke of Cornwallis [*sic*] Light Infantry, Royal Scots, and then got transferred to the 38th Bn. Royal Fusiliers (Jewish Battalion) and served with the Legion until demobilisation. This was the happiest time of my army service amongst my own people. I was commanded by Col. Patterson and my company commander was Capt. Harris who was Jewish. He was a great soldier and a great Jew. My officer was Lieut. Mendes who was well-known in the East End of London. I had also the pleasure of serving under Capt. Van Dyke and his brother, both of whom were great Jewish gentlemen. I was with the 38th right through from Cairo to Ludd, over the Judean hills to the Jordan valley where we went into action at Es Salt. I visited the then Jewish colonies and was greatly impressed with them. The only disappointment I had with the colonists [was] that they were intolerant with those who did not speak Hebrew. They certainly were a great people to be able to survive the Turks and the Arabs. I liked the country and if [I] only had a little encouragement would have settled

there. However, that was not to be. I am a married man with three sons. I am a taxi driver by trade. I belong to the Hackney Synagogue (United) but do not participate on account of illness. I was never a Zionist but since the Nazi atrocities I am in favour of a National Home and in Israel. I certainly would like to revisit Israel but I am afraid it could never be owing to my poor financial circumstances.[44]

David Dobrin's description of the Jews of Palestine, (who do not seem part of 'my own people') and his late conversion to Zionism, suggest the ambiguities of his Jewish self-consciousness, and indicate the difficulties historians face when trying to describe and classify Jewish identities. Assuming that he did consider settling in Palestine, this rather contradicts his non-Zionist beliefs and his non-identity with the Jewish settlers.

For the second example, a soldier from a less humble background has been chosen. Captain Samuel Horace Barnet, who died in 1950 at the age of 67, came from an established, middle-class, Anglo-Jewish family from London. The Barnet family supplied the following testimonial written at least seven years after his death:

Born 1883. Educated St. Paul's School and Corpus Christi, Oxford, where he read Classics. A versatile journalist and author, books include 'The French Default', 'Unholy Memories of the Holy Land', 'Shareholders' Money', 'Revolt by Leave', translations, poems, etc. In 1908 called to the Bar, practiced until the outbreak of war. A volunteer first in Artists Rifles, later in the 38th Royal Fusiliers (1st Judeans) where he served until the war ended. In 1918 became a military judge under the Occupied Enemy Territory Administration, but obliged to resign when he gave evidence before a Court of Inquiry into the anti-Zionist policy of the administration. After demobilization he became a leading lawyer and Judge of the First Instance in Palestine. In 1928 he went back to the Bar in England, returning to Palestine solely to defend (successfully) the accused in the famous Arlosoroff trial of 1933. Eventually left the Bar and went into the City as a 'financial consultant', a field in which his knowledge of company law, his legal training and his ready and powerful pen, found a natural outlet. Financial Times obituary 1950: 'His death leaves a ... gap ... in the City. And it will be awfully hard to fill.'[45]

Samuel Barnet's decision to testify before the anti-Zionist inquiry is evidence of his principles and loyalty, but what we are reading is virtually an obituary written by his close family. Thus, while the document's content reflects the values and status of Captain Barnet, its form makes it a problematic primary source. Nevertheless, the convening of a Court of Inquiry shows there was an anti-Zionist case to answer.

An example of a more detailed account, written by the veteran himself, is the testimony submitted by Sergeant Samuel William Wolfson J137, of Kilburn, London. What is especially notable about this account is the zeal of Sergeant Wolfson's commitment to the Jewish Legion cause. Originally a volunteer, he transferred to the Jewish Battalions and, after the war, made strenuous efforts to defend its reputation whenever this was publicly challenged. Included in his account is information that usefully shows how the Legion museum was supported by the veterans:

> Transferred after overseas service in France from 16th Bn. Royal Scots after being returned to U.K., wounded in 1916, as N.C.O. to newly formed Battalions of 38th and 39th at Plymouth. Was made orderly Sergeant by Col. Patterson and departed overseas East, with the 38th Batn. Royal Fus. Accompanied Col. Patterson and laid on behalf of the 38th Batn. Royal Fus. one of the 12 Foundation stones of the then new Jewish University in Jerusalem at the opening ceremony of that new University then[sic]. On demobilazition [sic] subsequently with telegraphic consent of Col Patterson, threatened a Four Million Pound Sterling Action against the 'News' of London, on behalf of 4,000 men of the Jewish Battalions. Correspondence & Certified Telegram of Col Patterson enclosed, together with copies of letters to the Jewish Bd. of Deputies. 'Evening News' published an apology, and retracted libellous defamations against the Jewish Regiments. Also correspondence (enclosed) of a similar libel by a so called Capt. Shaw at HOVE TOWN HALL SUSSEX, on a lecture there 'THE ALIEN MENACE', and the counter action thereon. Also have framed letter from Col. Patterson signed by him, re allegations previous to action, etc., as well as a signed copy of Col. Patterson's Books of the With the Jewish Regiments, Gallipoli etc.[sic]. These can be passed to U.K. Sec., for eventual transmission to your museum together with small [illegible] used near Jericho by the regiment on Yomim Noraim 1916/17, when I was only then A/sgt. Helped Col. Patterson, Lt. Jabotinsky on KASHRUS FOR THE BRIGADE. Confirm have promised 4 Annual Subscriptions of £50 annually from the F. & S. (Fanny and Samuel) Wolfson Foundation, total of £200, provided you are registered for Tax Reclaim, in the U.K.[46]

Unfortunately, the correspondence that was enclosed or promised has not been traced.

Next, there is the account of Lance-Corporal Abraham Jacob Robinson, J162, again written by the man himself. What is notable about his story is the fact that he was a second-generation soldier in the British army, his father having served in the Boer War. It is estimated that over twelve hundred Jews undertook military service in South Africa, within British regiments, a fact acknowledged by the attendance of Lord Roberts at the annual Maccabean ceremony at the Central Synagogue, London, on Sunday 28 December 1902.[47] Lance-Corporal Robinson recalled:

> Born in Boston England on 24th May 1899. In 1902 joined father who was fighting in the Boer War. In 1914 family returned to England and joined the army at age of 15. Discharged as under age rejoined army in 1917 and transferred to Jewish unit at Plymouth. On Feb. 5th 1918 embarked at Southampton for service in Palestine. On demobilization returned to south [sic] Africa and at the outbreak of the second world war joined local police reserves. Saw service in Ethiopia and later in Egypt. Spent two leaves in Palestine.[48]

Abraham Robinson was living in Uitenhage, Cape Province, when he wrote his testimonial.

Finally, the testimonial of a Gentile NCO, J.H. Carmell of London, the regimental sergeant-major of the 38th Battalion:

> In 1917, men of the Zion Mule Corps including Jabotinsky were posted to my Company (E comp) 20th London Regt for instruction and discipline, this delivered by my NCOs and by myself. Untill [sic] transfer [to] Plymouth to join the new formation of the 38th Royal Fusiliers including myself, and had the hard task of getting the Battalion fit for overseas service under Lt-Col. Patterson. OR's were trained in same way as the British G [illegible] in all weapons and Square Drill.[49]

It is a pity that this testimonial does not state whether RSM Carmell volunteered to transfer to the Jewish Battalion, or was compulsorily posted, but it does make military sense for him to have continued to work with the Jewish soldiers he had trained. This experience would, of course, have been extremely valuable in terms of his understanding the culture and behaviour of his future charges in the Legion.

It would be very unwise to make general conclusions from this very small sample of testimonials, even taking into account their various shortcomings. What they do confirm, however, is that the 38th attracted a number of Jews who were not alien Russians, and must have been fully prepared to serve with their conscripted co-religionists.

On Saturday 2 February 1918, the Jewish community in Plymouth hosted a farewell function for the 38th Battalion, after which it was ordered to assemble at Southampton in readiness for embarkation on the troopship *Antrim* on the 5th. Whilst half of the battalion, under the command of the recently appointed Major Ripley, proceeded directly to Southampton, Patterson and the remainder were given the honour of parading through the streets of Whitechapel and the City of London. This event was presaged by enthusiastic press coverage in the 1 February edition of the *Jewish Chronicle*, where the leader took the following line, in the tradition of sending troops off to war:

> It will be the first time that a Regiment consisting entirely of Jews will have tramped the streets of England, and the march of the Judeans will be a picturesque reminder of how history is being made in these days, here and in Palestine.

(It is interesting to note the use of the term 'Judeans' in the *Jewish Chronicle*, after the earlier dispute over nomenclature between Leopold Greenberg, the editor and the War Office. In fact, with effect from the issue of 25 January 1918, this newspaper carried a section devoted exclusively to the Jewish Battalions and entitled simply 'The Judeans').

On the morning of the parade, Monday 4 February, Jabotinsky was gazetted a lieutenant in the battalion, an event which caused amusement as well as pride. This was because, as Patterson pointed out, Jabotinsky was joining the ranks of the privileged few foreigners – like the Kaiser – who held the King's commission. After spending the night in the Tower of London, Lt.-Col. Patterson, mounted on a white horse, proudly led his men, who were marching to the music of the band of the Coldstream Guards, through the streets to the saluting base outside the Mansion House, where the salute was taken by the Lord Mayor and Sir Neville Macready.[50] The march continued on to Whitechapel and the Mile End Road, in the heart of the Russian Jewish community, after which the General Officer Commanding London District, Sir Francis Lloyd, inspected the men. This was followed by a reception given by the Mayor of Stepney, the Chief Rabbi and two of the MPs who had been most supportive of the regiment, James Kiley and Joseph Cowen, and then the detachment was given lunch at Camperdown House, Aldgate. In the afternoon, the troops marched to Waterloo where they boarded a train for Southampton to be reunited with their comrades. Commenting after the event, the *Jewish Chronicle* sought to place the Russian Jewish Battalion firmly in the context of the Jewish contribution to the British war effort as a whole. The editorial concerned reminded readers that over 40,000 Jews were serving in the armed forces and, after describing the City of London march-past, declared:

> Where, one asked oneself, were the warnings of the worldly wise; where the exaggerated torments of the sapient leaders in Israel who frowned on the idea of a regiment of Jews in the early days when Jewish volunteers were pouring by their thousands into the recruiting depots, and who did their best to spoil even the scanty and inadequate recognition of the idea by the War Office, against which we felt it our duty earnestly to protest, a few months ago?[51]

Where indeed? It has been demonstrated that the opposition to the Legion had only been defeated by the narrowest of margins, and it will be shown how this opposition continued to hamper its progress and development over the next two years.

What can be concluded from the experience of the raising of the 38th Battalion, Royal Fusiliers? In general terms, the two main points to emerge are the reluctance of the Russian Jews to serve in the British Army, and the effect of anti-Semitism generated as a response both to this avoidance and to earlier experiences and prejudice as exhibited during the Boer War. It has also been established that such anti-Semitism affected Jews of anglicised origin, regardless of whether or not they had undertaken their share of national, patriotic duty. More specifically, the linking of the Jewish Legion with Zionism gave idealists such as Jabotinsky a route towards their ultimate objective. By the same token, political realists like Weizmann were provided with an opportunity to make progress against the neutral stance of international Zionism, by aligning their interests with the sympathies of Lloyd George and his confidants. Unfortunately for Jabotinsky, and in spite of the fears of the War Office, such enthusiasm for the Zionist cause was not reflected in the ranks of the 38th. In contrast to the testimonies of the American volunteers who were to join the 39th Battalion, very few veterans, outside of Jabotinsky's own 'staff', mention any affiliation to a political body or Zionist organisation prior to enlistment.

Finally, there remains the question of the extent of anti-Semitism among the general staff and its subordinate officers. During the course of this chapter evidence of prejudice and institutionalised anti-Semitism has been demonstrated, but it should be made clear that this was not universal. In particular the Adjutant-General, Sir Neville Macready, was forthright in his support for the Legion and, given his position on the Army Council, it is perhaps entirely possible that he was responsible for pushing through the formation and deployment of the regiment in the face of the difficulties mentioned.[52]

Colonel Patterson embarked for Egypt encouraged by an interview at the War Office with Generals Macready and Hutchinson, at which they advised him that it was the intention to send out another Battalion (the 39th), when available, with the object of forming a Jewish Brigade, implying that Patterson would be its commander. The significance of these remarks is twofold. Firstly, they demonstrate that the messages emerging from the War Office were still mixed and secondly, the prospect of a brigade formation gave the Jewish Battalions an expectation of a certain independence of action and a strong voice within the Egyptian Expeditionary Force.[53]

6
Raising the Battalions: the United States

By deploying the 38th Battalion to active service in Palestine, the British government finally endorsed the idea of a Jewish Legion participating in the military conduct of the war. This commitment also guaranteed the previously noted expansion of the Legion through the addition of two further service battalions, the 39th and 40th Battalions Royal Fusiliers. These battalions relied heavily upon the recruitment of Jewish volunteers from, respectively, America and Palestine. How was this achieved? This account will examine the background to the recruitment and early progress of the volunteers from America (the Palestinian recruitment will be reviewed in the next chapter) and will address questions of propaganda, Zionism and their impact upon the motivation and expectations of these soldiers. As with the Jews from Britain, the implications of the Balfour Declaration and Russia's withdrawal from the war will be considered. Finally, the British Army's attitude will be reviewed to gauge the nature and extent of its anti-Semitism, and its effect upon recruitment.

This account begins with Britain's propaganda campaign in the United States, waged to ensure America's friendly neutrality, or ideally, co-belligerency. As we have seen, the propaganda value of raising a Jewish Legion lay mainly in its impact on American Jews, who were perceived – rightly or wrongly – as having great influence within government and business circles. In 1916, this influence had been seen as a means of countering President Wilson's peace promoting efforts as well as opposing pro-German propaganda. With America's entry into the war as an associate power in April 1917, the danger of a US-sponsored peace receded, but the problem of pro-German sentiment remained. Jewish support earlier in the war for German aggression against the detested Tsarist regime should not be underestimated (see previous chapter). Furthermore, despite the regime's collapse in March 1917, Britain remained apprehensive that Germany might persuade its Turkish ally to reconsider Jewish settlement and home rule under Ottoman aegis, an apprehension that influenced the timing of the Balfour Declaration. The British fear was that Germany might gain some credibility with Central European Jews and that Turkey would succeed in placating world opinion, following the outrage over the Armenian massacres. Viewed in this light the declaration itself was effectively a British pre-emptive strike that disregarded earlier promises to its French and Arab allies, to protect British interests in the Middle East and India.[1]

At about the same time (the autumn of 1917), the administration of official propaganda had been reorganised by the War Cabinet, so that 'Home' propaganda became the responsibility of the War Aims Committee, and propaganda for use in 'Allied, neutral and enemy countries' was controlled by the Department of Information, under its director (Colonel) John Buchan,[2] which had its headquarters at the Foreign Office. Both the committee and the department reported to Sir Edward Carson, Churchill's successor as First Lord of the Admiralty and a member of the War Cabinet. In September 1917, Buchan was instructed by Carson to prepare a report describing the organisation and methods of the Department of Information, and the following extract demonstrates the efforts made to promote the British case in the United States:

> The entry of America into the war as an Ally [sic] has enabled us to conduct our propaganda work there in a more open and businesslike manner ... Our war films have been shown throughout the length and breadth of the States, and it is calculated that in the past three months over 10,000,000 people have seen them ... Suitable pamphlets are sent regularly to over 170,000 addresses in the United States ... Copies of the chief English newspapers are sent daily to upwards of 300 papers in small American towns ... the Reciprocal News Service supplies a London letter weekly to 109 Middle Western papers.[3]

The impact of such British propaganda on American public opinion is difficult to judge from these records, but it was certainly needed if only to counter Germany's own propaganda offensive before the severance of diplomatic relations with the United States in February 1917. Buchan estimated that Count Bernstorff, head of German propaganda in the USA, had a financial budget of just under £5 million per annum, a sum that was three and a-half times his own budget for the whole of the world outside Britain.[4]

The records do reveal, however, one peculiar effect of the bureaucratic division between home and overseas propaganda, upon propaganda promoting Zionism. Towards the end of 1917, Albert Hyamson, a middle ranking civil servant and Zionist, was invited to establish a Zionist branch within the Department of Information, under the overall leadership of Colonel Buchan.[5] Because the Department's activities were restricted to 'Allied, neutral and enemy countries', Hyamson was frustrated in his ambition to counter the anti-Zionism of the League of British Jews, which eventually, thanks to its influence on Buchan's successor, Lord Beaverbrook, managed to ensure the breakup of the Zionist branch in September 1918.[6]

American public opinion during the course of the war had already swung from revulsion at German atrocities in Belgium to outrage over British 'blacklisting' of American firms for trading with the central powers in the autumn of 1916. Jewish immigrants to the United States, with their known hostility to Russia, were targeted by German propaganda, which was supported by Turko-German moves to conciliate world Zionist opinion by making promises as to the treatment of Jews in Palestine and Eastern Europe respectively.[7] However, whatever lingering sympathy for the central powers was felt among immigrant Jews in the USA, had been largely forfeited by Turkey's treatment of its minority populations during the war, as exemplified by the deportation of Zionists and Armenians within the Ottoman Empire. American missionaries in Armenia witnessed the atrocities and alerted the American public to the ensuing genocide. Britain, too, publicised the Armenian atrocities through the Bryce Report of 1916.[8] It is estimated that the Turks murdered over 600,000 Armenians and, despite the propaganda of their ally, it can be concluded that Turkey's standing in American eyes was at a very low level indeed.[9]

The central powers' effort to court Jewish influence contrasts with the wooing of the Arab and Muslim Diaspora by Britain, using material prepared in London by the Department of Information and in Cairo by the Arab Bureau. According to Buchan:

> Arrangements have been made with the British authorities in Egypt to send copies of loyal Arabic newspapers to the different South African ports, to the Netherlands East Indies, and in smaller quantities to Madagascar and other French colonies. A certain amount of

material of Moslem interest is also sent to Rio de Janeiro and Buenos Aires for the large Arab populations there.[10]

It therefore appears that, two months prior to the announcement of the Balfour Declaration, the difficulties of the British Government's changing policy towards Jewry and Palestine, in relation to the Sykes–Picot agreement, and the differences within Jewry and the Cabinet itself prevented any pro-Zionist propaganda emerging from Whitehall. In military and strategic terms, however, the efforts made towards conciliating Arab populations in the Middle East were entirely logical and understandable, since a coalition of Arab forces was being used to protect the eastern flank of the Egyptian Expeditionary Force.

The Cabinet were undoubtedly aware of the implications of their Palestine policies for Jewry in general and Zionists in particular, although the diverse Jewish attitudes towards Zionism were not well understood. Turkey's alignment with the central powers had forced the Foreign Office to abandon its traditionally pro-Ottoman stance, and Leopold Amery, Sir Mark Sykes and C.P. Scott had challenged its anti-Zionism. The influence of these individuals, in combination with the energy and ideas of Lloyd George's new administration, had led to a Middle Eastern policy that accommodated Zionist ideals. Further, their support for the Legion was crucial to the prime minister accepting the idea.

Leo Amery and Mark Sykes were members of the War Secretariat, as was William Ormsby-Gore who, having spent some time in the Arab Bureau in Cairo, wrote a series of memoranda in early 1917 to the Cabinet that described, in favourable terms, the activities and ambitions of the Zionist settlers in Palestine. Not only was this assessment contrary to the Foreign Office's view, it also indicated a change of heart among many of the settlers themselves. In a memorandum dated 14 April 1917, Ormsby-Gore advised the Cabinet that: 'It is difficult to analyse why precisely the Zionists had become more and more pro-British, save they are more and more anti Turk and anti German.'

And then added:

> I heard a good deal in Cairo about Jewish troops. Aaronson [sic] [see below] said he could get 1000 really good Palestinian Jews in Egypt. He thought America and Morocco might help as well as Whitechapel and Stepney. He expressed the view that the moral of a Jewish Brigade entering Palestine would be wonderful ...[11]

Ormsby-Gore completed his summary of the situation by commenting on the aims of Poale Zion, the socialist Zionist movement, and the Russian revolution; it will be seen how relevant his acknowledgment of these factors was to become.

Aaron Aaronson's influence, as indicated above, was pivotal to the development of British policy in the Middle East and Palestine. Aaronson was born in Rumania in 1876 and arrived in Palestine, with the rest of his family, in 1882, where he grew up in the Jewish colony of Zichron Ya'akov that had been founded by his father, among others. As a young man, Aaronson was able to attend universities in France, Germany and the United States through the support of Baron Edmund Rothschild, whose organisation was responsible for many of the Jewish areas of settlement in Palestine.

What set Aaronson apart was his pre-war conviction that Zionist settlement would benefit from a benign British administration in Palestine. In coming to this conclusion he was some four to five years ahead of the Benim, who maintained a confidence in Ottoman rule until war-time events dispelled this trust. Aaronson acted on convictions in mid-1916 establishing a covert intelligence organisation in Palestine, named 'Nili', which provided valuable information to the EEF. Secrecy was, of course, essential to this work, but Aaronson was also sensitive to the plight of the Jews remaining in Palestine, and knew that it was premature to defy openly the official, neutralist policy of the Zionist Congress. At the end of 1916 Aaronson came to London and personally briefed civil and military officials including Sir Mark Sykes, who was probably 'converted' to Zionism as a result. From London, Aaronson was sent to Cairo where his work included co-operation with Ormsby-Gore; hence the latter's reference to the former in his reports back to London.[12] The importance of Ormsby-Gore's contribution, in combination with the other 'advisers' mentioned earlier, towards the development of an alternative British Middle Eastern policy which supported Zionism, and indirectly the Legion, cannot be underestimated. Indeed, Isaiah Friedman attributes Lloyd George's eastern policy to the 'Amery, Ormsby-Gore, Sykes trio' and gives a full and detailed account of the way in which this triumvirate effectively bypassed the hostile Foreign Office.[13]

The securing of Zionist support for the campaign in Palestine, the balancing of this support against the interests of the Arab populations and the implications of the Sykes–Picot agreement, presented a series of irreconcilable differences, which the British government either ignored or allowed to take their course. These differences had to be considered by the British government against future British strategy in the Middle East and the effects of political developments in Russia. For example, the Turks sought to take advantage of Russia's weakness by attacking the Baku oilfields (despite the conclusion of an armistice with Russia on 18 December 1917), and hoped to threaten British rule in India by inciting Muslims to revolt. British intelligence had assumed, because of the armistice, that the Turks would re-deploy its troops from the Caucasus to the south (Palestine and Syria). On this basis General Allenby felt justified, after his forces had occupied Jerusalem in early December 1917, in requesting substantial reinforcements before embarking on an advance through to Damascus and Aleppo, his final objective.[14]

This strategy was endorsed by the Lloyd George but, in recent research, has been criticised by Matthew Hughes. Hughes argues that whilst the capture of Jerusalem was justified on morale-boosting and symbolic grounds, a campaign through Palestine to Syria, followed by military occupation, risked the later withdrawal of troops to France and loss of captured territory. The risk was run because at the time of Allenby's Palestine offensive no one anticipated an armistice in November.[15] The major offensive was preceded by unsuccessful raids across the Jordan in March and May 1918, and Hughes suggests that Allenby undertook these excursions in response to the pressure exerted by Lloyd George following the removal of Robertson as CIGS and the Supreme War Council's endorsement of the order directing Allenby to drive the Turks out of the war.[16] Among the reinforcements made available to Allenby were the 38th and 39th Battalions (later supplemented by the locally recruited 40th Battalion). It is now appropriate to consider the recruitment campaign in the United States, which eventually provided the majority of recruits for the 39th.

The Benim had arrived in the United States in the summer of 1915 following their detainment in Egypt by the British authorities, where they witnessed the formation of the Zion Mule Corps in Alexandria whilst awaiting passage to New York. Though impressed by Trumpeldor's vision, they were not, at that time, in favour of service with the western Allies because of their objection to the Tsarist regime and their desire to protect the Jews remaining within the Ottoman Empire. Once arrived in New York, however, the Benim realised that they were now involved with a Jewish community whose circumstances differed greatly from those found in the Pale of Settlement and the Yishuv. Indeed, intra-communal relations in American Jewry were even more convoluted than in Anglo-Jewry. In a masterful exposition of the ideology, personalities and politics that lay behind the forging of American Jewry during this period and beyond, Jonathan Frankel has analysed in great detail the complexities of the relationships between such groups as Zionists, non-Zionists, socialist Zionists and Bundists that made up the body politic of American Jewry.[17] The following brief analysis owes much to Frankel's work as a guide, and aims to provide a description relevant to recruitment to the Legion.

On the outbreak of war, the leadership of American Jewry included three men who personified the various Jewish sub-communities and the spectrum of political opinion within American Judaism. Firstly, Louis Marshall, born of German-Jewish parents in upstate New York in 1856, was a leading lawyer and president of the American Jewish Committee. Although not a Zionist, Marshall was a determined defender of Jewish minority rights throughout the world, a position that allowed him to welcome the Balfour Declaration, without compromising his position as leader of the American non-Zionist Jewish community, which had little in common with the mass of recently arrived immigrants in New York.

Secondly, Justice Louis Brandeis, born in Kentucky (also in 1856) of parents from Prague, had become in 1914 the first chairman of the Provisional Executive Committee for General Zionist Affairs, a body set up to provide assistance to the Yishuv, a practical function that was made possible by the fact that the USA's neutrality enabled it to deal directly with Turkey. The curious point about Brandeis leadership was that he did not convert to Zionism until 1911 when he met Herzl's former secretary, Jacob De Haas, though he had, through a legal case involving the rights of Jewish garment workers in New York, already been attracted to the Zionist beliefs of the Russian Jewish immigrants. His new convictions were further strengthened by chairing a conference in Boston at which Nathan Sokolow, the Russian Zionist leader (and a close friend of Chaim Weizmann) was the main speaker. Brandeis became the first Jewish Supreme Court judge in 1916, and used his influence with President Wilson to assist Weizmann by allaying American doubts over the Balfour Declaration. Incidentally, these doubts were not an expression of disapproval of Zionism, but were indicative of American suspicion of British imperialist ambitions in the Middle East.[18]

Thirdly, Rabbi Stephen Wise was a noted religious leader who founded his own synagogue in New York and co-founded, in 1897, the Federation of American Zionists. Born in Hungary in 1874, his parents brought him to America as a small child, and his later work with the federation involved attendances at pre-war Zionist congresses, as well as visits to the Yishuv in Palestine. Wise also worked with Brandeis to lobby President Wilson over the Balfour Declaration, but perhaps his greatest effort was put into the formation of the American Jewish Congress, an issue that divided American Jewry like no other.

The idea behind the American Jewish Congress was to create an organisation that democratically reflected the various Jewish constituencies, and would therefore provide a single voice to protect the interests of all Jews. As in Britain the older establishment, as represented by Marshall's American Jewish Committee, appreciated that this democratic approach threatened to overwhelm their position due to the huge numbers of eastern European immigrants, who now expected a say in Jewish affairs and who had found their champions in Brandeis and Wise. There were two main areas of disagreement, Zionism and socialism, and Marshall's initial tactics were to procrastinate and argue constitutional points, in the hope that the Congress idea would either disappear or, at least, be established as an anti-socialist body. His tactics were partly successful, in that the congress did not meet until after the war, but by then, its original ideals and purpose had been somewhat overtaken by international events.[19]

The disagreements between the Jewish sub-communities in the United States must be understood in the context of late nineteenth-century Russian Jewry. Jewish responses to chronic harassment included self-defence (of which Jabotinsky was a vocal and prominent advocate), social revolution, emigration and the pursuit of a nation state either in Israel or elsewhere. In an earlier chapter it was seen how these various responses, and their underlying philosophical differences, had divided the Anglo-Jewish and Russian immigrant populations in the United Kingdom.[20] The divisions within American Jewry were heightened by the scale of Russian Jewish immigration into the United States, where just under two million settled compared to about one hundred thousand in Britain.[21]

Particularly noteworthy was the Poale Zion movement, founded in the Ukraine in 1906 by Ber Borochov, with the aim of establishing a socialist nation state for Jews. He emigrated to the United States at the beginning of the war and, after the February 1917 revolution, he returned to Kiev, where he died prematurely at the end of the year. In 1915, Poale Zion in New York welcomed the arrival of Pinchas Rutenberg from Europe. Rutenberg's exhortations amongst the Russian Jews of the Lower East Side succeeded in generating support for Poale Zion and an American Jewish Congress, and were mainly based on anti-Russian sentiment. He also impressed some of his audience with his advocacy of the original Jewish Legion idea, despite the official Zionist opposition and fears of Poale Zion leaders such as the Benim, of the effect of the formation of a Legion upon Turkish treatment of the Jews living in Palestine. Rutenberg's leadership in this regard came to an end when he returned to Russia in September 1917 to take a position in Kerensky's provisional administration.

Support for Brandeis, Wise and the congress was also initially forthcoming from the Bundist movement, which had its foundations in the National Workmen's Committees of Poland and Russia. Unlike Poale Zion, which looked to a congress to provide a platform for the international unity of Jews, Bundists wanted to limit any congress to the discussion of domestic matters. The effect of this fundamental disagreement was that the Bundists decided, in May 1917, to boycott elections to the American Jewish Congress, a situation that isolated Poale Zion on the left and virtually ensured that the assembly of the congress would be postponed.[22]

It would appear, therefore, that the fear of public divisions over fundamental issues presented by the war contributed to the failure of the Diaspora to present an united Jewish front, in preparation for representation at the peace talks following the ending of hostilities. A further complication was provided by the secrecy of the negotiations with the British government that led to the Balfour Declaration. Louis Brandeis met Arthur Balfour in Washington in April 1917, and supported Chaim Weizmann in his pragmatic efforts to secure a Jewish homeland under the protection of Britain, a somewhat different concept to the official Poale Zion aim of achieving territorial independence in Palestine within the protection of all of the major powers. As Frankel has established, unanimity on the part of the American Jewish Congress, when faced with the reconciliation of such conflicting policies, was clearly out of the question.[23]

The proclamation of the Balfour Declaration had a profound effect. In similar fashion to Weizmann, who had defied official, international Zionist policy to secure the declaration, Ben-Gurion seized on the opportunity it presented to escape from Poale Zion's restrictive commitment to the American Jewish Congress. He finally accepted that events had overtaken the fears he had held for his co-religionists back in Palestine. Nevertheless, his attempts to persuade his colleagues to accept that the declaration, coupled with the near certainty of an Allied victory following the entry of the United States into the war, would bring the reality of Zion closer and marginalise the functions of an American Jewish Congress, fell on deaf ears. It was this rejection that finally propelled Ben-Gurion, Ben-Zvi and their supporters towards taking action designed to capitalise on the opportunity presented by the declaration. The route to Palestine they chose was to volunteer for service in the Jewish Battalions of the British Army, and fellow Poale Zion rebels and many Halutz members followed them.

It is important to note, however, that the Benim attached themselves to an existing Jewish Legion Committee in New York, and they should not therefore be credited with initiating the recruitment of the American volunteers. According to Gilner this committee was formed by eight members of Poale Zion branch No. 2, shortly before Rutenberg's departure for St Petersburg. Fearful that the loss of Rutenberg might have put paid to any chance of a Jewish Legion movement succeeding in the USA, these eight men, Pinhas Gingold, Max Gutbeter, M. Moshevitzky, Eliezer Marchaim, F. Papush, F. Rabinowitz, Jacob Ravid and A. Trotsky decided to defy the opposition and pursue their declared aim to join what was then the Jewish Legion in Britain. To this end they tried to contact Jabotinsky in London, but they never received any reply and there is no evidence to suggest that Jabotinsky was aware of their activities at this early stage. In fact, according to Jabotinsky's own testimony, he received, just a short time before sailing from Southampton in early February 1918: 'a telegram from New York, signed by Brainin, Ben-Zvi and Ben-Gurion, which informed us of the launching of the recruiting campaign for the Legion in America'.[24]

Unperturbed by their early failure to establish communication with Jabotinsky, the dissident Poale Zionists lobbied President Wilson and Congress, mainly through the good offices of Justice Brandeis, and thereby received the tacit backing of the United States government. This support would not have been forthcoming without some semblance of unity among the various Jewish organisations, presenting the president and Congress with an official American Zionist endorsement for the Legion. Chaim Weizmann's papers contain evidence demonstrating that this position was not reached until the beginning of 1918. In December 1917, Weizmann sent several cables to Aaron Aaronson in the United States asking about progress in American recruitment for the Legion. Receiving no reply, Weizmann then telegraphed Brandeis, on 27 December 1917, who was quick to respond, cabling on 31 December: 'that participation of Americans in the Jewish Legion was not possible under existing international conditions, but a ZOA (Zionist Organisation of America) statement in its favour would shortly be made'.[25]

The American government now allowed Jews residing in the United States (but not American citizens), who wished to join the Jewish Battalions, to sign up with the British recruiting mission in New York, prior to being sent to Windsor, Nova Scotia, for basic training. The British recruiting mission was headed by Brigadier-General White, and the specific responsibility for Legion recruitment, and liaison with the Legion Committee, was allocated to one of his officers, Major Brooman-White.

Gilner has described the transition from the political lobbying campaign to actual recruitment and training in great detail.[26] It is not proposed to reprise this excellent passage from Gilner's work, especially as he made full use of the appropriate War Office records. For the sake of clarity and continuity, however, due consideration must be given to four relevant facts that are apparent from the circumstances at the time and from the result of Gilner's own research and personal experience.

First, since the United States was not at war with Turkey, any notion of a Jewish unit being formed in the American army for service in Palestine was out of the question. Second, whilst the encouragement from the United States government was of practical assistance to the British recruiting mission and the Jewish Legion committee, the American authorities had no wish to dilute the requirements of their own military draft laws and regulations for American citizens. According to Isaac Ben-Zvi this restriction had a profound effect upon recruitment:

> It would have been possible to mobilise many more, had it not been for the strict prohibition of the American government against its citizens serving in a foreign army. However, many American Jews gave up their citizenship in order to join the Hebrew Battalion.[27]

It is appropriate to note at this point, that the British authorities treated American citizens in the same way as other friendly aliens, although no Military Service Convention was agreed between the two governments. This contrasts with French, Italian and, of course, Russian subjects, who did not have the choice.[28]

Third, despite continuing internal disputes, the Jewish Legion Committee and the Zionist Organisation of America began to work together, thus promoting recruitment and presenting a united front to the outside world. Finally, there is clear evidence, in War Office records, of confusing and incomplete information being sent to Brigadier General White, concerning the Jewish Battalions in Britain and the prospects of guaranteeing service in Palestine to the volunteers. As late as 14 February 1918 the War Office was informing General White that it: 'Can give guarantee that men of Jewish faith shall be employed in special Jewish Battalions, but the theatre of war in which they will be used cannot be guaranteed.'[29] Chaim Weizmann acted swiftly to correct the situation and the War Office despatched the following message to Brigadier-General White (who had also sought clarification), at Fifth Avenue on the 21 February 1918:

> For so long as the exigencies of the service admit Jewish Battalions are definitely intended for employment in Palestine ... Men may be taken irrespective of knowledge of English but the greatest care should be taken to enquire into the antecedents of all recruits as it is imperative that included in these units there should be no undesirables or men of enemy alien nationality or parentage.[30]

British concern about the background of the volunteers in America was reinforced by the fact that the Jewish Legion Committee in New York had contacted the Argentinean Zionist Federation, which had wanted to send volunteers to join the Legion in Britain. Foreign Office files reveal that Arthur Balfour was keen to discourage this activity, as he believed that the sole motive of these volunteers was to obtain a free passage to Palestine.[31] The recruitment process in Buenos Aires effectively screened them out, but 52 Argentineans were successful in obtaining passage to Britain where, despite the lack of assistance from the authorities, they eventually arrived in Plymouth and joined the Jewish Battalions.[32]

Gilner also records that Rufus Isaacs, Lord Reading, when acting as a special ambassador to America, was instrumental in obtaining the original War Office commitment to Palestine service, following Sir Cecil Spring Rice's original enquiries from the British Embassy in Washington in September 1917. On 13 February Reading had telegraphed the Foreign Office himself, asking for a public statement confirming service in Palestine, but it was not until 8 March 1918 that he was informed of the War Office decision to confirm this commitment.[33] The Foreign Office file relating to this exchange shows that the FO was against a public statement in the form of a parliamentary question and answer, as requested by Reading, and indicates that the Army Council was still fudging the issue, by refusing to give a definite assurance on Palestine, whilst maintaining that official policy was to place the Jewish Battalions with the EEF.[34]

It would therefore appear that the departmental confusion that had surrounded the formation of the Legion was still very evident after its establishment. Aside from mere bureaucratic muddle, it can be surmised that the FO's reluctance to make a public statement and the hesitancy of the War Office arose in recognition of the public sensitivities surrounding the Russian recruits, at a time when Russia was close to complete withdrawal from the war.

The Bolshevik revolution made Russia's exit from the war inevitable and effectively terminated the operation of the Military Service Convention. The British government officially suspended conscription under the convention on about the 11 February 1918, just a few days after the departure of the 38th Battalion from Southampton, a belated gesture that reflected both the impracticality and growing irrelevance of the scheme. On hearing this news, a number of legionnaires approached Patterson to express their dissatisfaction at having to continue with their service whilst their fellow Russians in Britain were no longer subject to the provisions of the convention. Patterson, who complimented his men on their 'exemplary' behaviour during the journey to Italy, telegraphed the War Office while awaiting embarkation at Taranto, and received a reply to the effect that this issue would be dealt with on arrival in Egypt.[35]

This matter was not, however, dealt with 'on arrival in Egypt', but remained under consideration by the War Cabinet until 8 April, from which date Russian Jews were to be posted to labour units only, and were specifically excluded from combatant duties. In the intervening period General Allenby, GOC Egypt, corresponded with the War Office in order to clarify the position, as it affected the troops that had recently joined his command. War Office records on this exchange are incomplete but reveal that Allenby first contacted Whitehall on 10 March 1918, in a cable marked secret, addressed to the CIGS. It is reproduced below so as to establish Allenby's understanding of this issue, and to introduce the important element of the attitude of the army in Egypt towards the Jewish soldiers, in preparation for the next chapter:

> There are a number of Russians in the Jewish Battalion, which may now be an element of danger. There may be among Jews of other nationalities some who sympathize with our enemies. I wish to have instructions as to what nationalities should remain with Jewish Battalion and how I should dispose of others. I understand that U.S.A. citizens are enlisting for Jewish Battalions. I think before such

men are included in our military forces, their antecedents should be examined, as it would be possible for German or Austrian Jews to gain access to these Battalions through this channel. It has been suggested to me by Colonel Patterson that Jews should be recruited in this country (Palestine) and Egypt. I do not consider this wise for the present and I do not propose proceeding with enlistment of Jews which is sanctioned in your 52335 cipher A.G.2.A February 15th until I know what your general policy is.[36]

The War Office replied a week later advising that:

> while it is undesirable to enlist Russian jews [sic] any further, no objection exists to those of other nationalities ... providing they are able to produce satisfactory references. This policy is being carried out in regard to those from America. Colonel Patterson ... should be able to ensure that undesirable characters do not remain undetected. If men enlisted already should not prove to be satisfactory, you should deal with them as soldiers under the Military code.[37]

The last available record in this series features Allenby's response, which recommended that the disenchanted Russian Jews of the 38th Battalion be released. He obviously realised that having such men alongside the majority who continued to serve without complaint, created a situation that imposed a heavy burden of leadership, tact and discretion upon Patterson and his officers.[38] Unfortunately, it is impossible to calculate from official records such as returns and war diaries how many men deserted or were granted a release. The constant flow of replacements, postings and the effects of sickness increase the difficulty of identifying what must have been a relatively small number of men (if any) who simply became lost in the statistics.

It also says much for Patterson's grip on his men that they carried on despite contact with German Jews and disaffected Russian soldiers during two of the frequent halts on their railway journey across France. The War Office and Allenby were blissfully unaware of these incidents, which were recorded by Rabbi Falk in a series of articles in *The Maccabean* in May 1929. These articles consisted of extracts from his book, *With the Jewish Battalions in Palestine,* and included an encounter with a German prisoner of war:

> who came forward to the barbed wire fence with his eyes fixed at the window of my compartment from which a blue and white flag

was suspended. His features did not bear any pronounced Semitic characteristics especially since 'alle Yevonim haben ein panin.' (A Yiddish proverb: 'All soldiers look alike') ... the German soldier addressed me with the following words: 'Sie fahren nach Palestina!' 'Auch ich bin ein Jude.' (You are going to Palestine also I am a Jew.) ... The German Jews were as loyal to their country as the English Jews to their's [sic] and yet what a magic hold Palestine has on the soul of the Jew!

In a later passage, Rabbi Falk noticed that the men of his battalion became excited when they saw Russian soldiers labouring under the supervision of the French:

A general conversation commenced between these Russians and our men. The mystery of their unexpected presence in France was soon explained. When news of the Russian revolution reached these soldiers who were fighting in France they refused to fight and demanded to be sent back to Russia. This demand, however, was not complied with, and instead of sending them back to Russia they were converted into Labour Battalions behind the lines. This piece of interesting information was a priceless discovery for the semi-Bolsheviks in our own Battalion whose number, thank heaven, could be counted on the fingers.[39]

As far as the Jewish soldiers back in Plymouth, with the 39th and 42nd Battalions, were concerned, the only indication of the number of desertions has been found in two short references in the Anglo-Jewish archives. Firstly, the previously mentioned correspondence of Private Paul Epstein to his family in London from Crown Hill barracks Plymouth, reveals that there were some desertions prior to the 38th Battalion's embarkation for Egypt. In letters written on 3 and 4 February, Epstein refers to the fact that his company (of the 39th) was asked for volunteers to make up the 38th's draft for Egypt, without draft leave, at which prospect 'we have 73 men who mean to get prison rather than go without draft leave'. Consequently, no volunteers were forthcoming, at which point the authorities relented and offered leave, which obtained the desired result. Unfortunately, this leave was cancelled after the volunteers had completed their medical examinations, an event that Epstein attributed to fifty-eight men who had deserted from the 38th and therefore 'we of the 39th Battalion had to suffer for their sins.' It would not be unreasonable to assume that, apart from the usual reasons for deserting before embarkation, a number of these soldiers of Russian nationality would have hoped to remain in the United Kingdom in expectation of the cancellation of the Military Service Convention.[40]

Secondly, within the Landa papers there is a letter from Lord Rothschild referring to the fact that Dr Hertz, the Chief Rabbi, had received a letter in May 1918 passing on news of 180 deserters in Plymouth, and stating that 'good name only being maintained by mass arrival of American volunteers for Palestine'.[41] The irony of this message is that the great majority of the American volunteers were of Russian nationality or background, a fact also seemingly overlooked by the War Office in their reply to Allenby's initial enquiry.

In Britain, public comment on the issue of Russian recruitment and the withdrawal of Russia from the war was mainly confined to the columns of the *Jewish Chronicle*, which printed a series of relevant items in its weekly editions from early February 1918. For example, in a leader published on 15 February, and following comments on the Treaty of Brest-Litovsk, the view was expressed:

> [T]hat the conscription of Russians was not justified mainly on the grounds that they were born in Russia. Many of their appeals are based on the point that they are not really Russian by nationality ... [but] ... having found peaceful refuge in Britain, should do the morally correct thing and join up voluntarily as the Director of National Service has intimated that further conscription of Russians in this country will not take place.[42]

Other reports mention War Office approval of a training company for Jews, under the age of eighteen and a-half, and that transfers into the Jewish Battalions had been made easier for officers and NCOs who were now permitted to leave front line units serving in France in order to join their co-religionists. Furthermore, the newspaper covered the screening of the Pathe newsreel showing the march through Whitechapel and the City, and also announced that Captain Trumpeldor had been given permission to form a Jewish unit for self-defence in Petrograd.[43]

Following up on the training and transfer news, the issues of 22 February, 1 March and 8 March emphasised the benefits of these improved arrangements. Specific mention was made of the availability of kosher food and 'Jewish surroundings' for young British Jews on call-up and Russian-born volunteers (this was before the War Cabinet decision of 8 April). The government pledge to offer naturalisation after three months service to those of alien nationality was also given coverage, as was the opening of the recruitment campaign and acceptance of Russian volunteers in America. Thereafter, reports on the Legion were mainly limited to its activities in Egypt, and there is evidence, in the form of a letter from Leopold Greenberg, the editor, to Lord Rothschild at Tring that, sometime in early April, 'the Press Bureau forbade any mention of the American Judeans'.[44]

This sensitivity, arising at the same time as the decision to restrict Russian recruits to non-combatant duties, indicates that the government were perfectly aware that many of the soldiers from America were of Russian nationality, notwithstanding their earlier message to Allenby. In any event, the British policy decision of the 8 April meant that, in practice, recruitment to the Jewish Battalions was now restricted to three sources, British Jews (volunteers and conscripts), transferees from other units and the volunteers from America. In practical terms, therefore, the Bolshevik revolution had no effect on the prospects for recruitment in the United States, but, overall, there can be no doubt that this restriction threatened the viability of the Jewish Battalions, to the extent that Nathan Sokolow remonstrated with the British government in June 1918, an intervention that was to lead to yet another change in policy in October.

In order to demonstrate the extent to which the Legion relied on the American contingent, an examination of the Legion's manpower statistics has been made. Unfortunately, official records, such as the monthly returns and the war diaries of the individual battalions, do not contain a definitive total figure for the number of soldiers that actually served in this unit.[45] Gilner and Jabotinsky, however, agreed that a total of 10,000 men enlisted in the Legion, this number being confirmed in an untraced letter to Gilner from the Army Records Centre, Hayes, and dated 4 November 1966.[46] Similar difficulties exist in determining the proportion of men from America within this total, although Isaac Ben-Zvi estimated that around 6,500 Jews – 65 per cent – volunteered in the USA.[47] Jabotinsky himself produced figures for the 5,000 members of the Legion that actually served in the Middle East, and calculated that of this number 34 per cent were from the USA, 30 per cent from Palestine, 28 per cent from Britain, 6 per cent from Canada, 1 per cent from Argentina and 1 per cent from Turkish prisoners of war.[48]

The difference between these two sets of figures was due to the fact that recruitment of Jews in America began so late into the war that a large number either failed to complete their training, or were preparing for embarkation for the Middle East, when the armistice with Turkey was concluded on 30 October 1918. Taking this factor into account, together with the known restrictions on recruitment in Britain, then it is reasonable to conclude that the American volunteers did indeed form the largest constituent part of the Legion, accounting for nearly two-thirds of the total strength employed.

Finally, it will be recalled from the previous chapter that 626 individual testimonials have been used as a primary source, and these have also been analysed. This analysis reveals that the volunteers from America are under-represented in this sample with 284 or 45 per cent of the total, but nevertheless, one third (ninety-six) of this number were members of Poale Zion. As we already know that Poale Zion had a pivotal role in Jewish recruitment in the United States, this figure indicates the significance and pervasiveness of its influence in the Legion as a whole, the consequences of which will be dealt with in the next chapter.

With the background to recruitment in the United States explained, it is now appropriate to turn to the individual experiences of some of the legionnaires, taken from their testimonials and correspondence with the author. In appreciation of the strong sentiment for Zion and Jewish nationalism that is explicit in the majority of the testimonials, the following piece entitled 'A Father's Blessing', is reproduced in its entirety. It was published in local Yiddish newspapers by H. Gordon of New London, Connecticut, the father of Maurice Gordon, a member of the first group of volunteers:

> Go, my child, and prepare the way for the liberation of your unhappy people. Go, and let your courage make your people proud. As for you, O my child, my wish is that you may rise higher and higher, until you attain the heights of Judah Maccabee. May your name be perpetuated to the end of time as a source of pride to our family and our people. I thank you, my beloved son, for having brought me so much honor. May you be able before long to receive your mother and me in the land where the sun is so warm and bright. I also wish your comrades, the heroes of the Jewish Legion, who are leaving with you on 28 February 1918, that the Guardian of Israel may watch over them and you and protect all of you so that you may reach England safely. Then, I am sure, you will fulfil the holy mission you have undertaken.

Elias Gilner quoted this 'Father's Blessing' in full and remarked that Maurice Gordon, who was employed in a clerical position at the New

London submarine base, enlisted at the age of seventeen with the necessary approval of his parents.[49] Maurice Gordon's testimonial states that he was born near Vilna on 12 October 1903 but this date must be in doubt as the other evidence contained therein, such as his regimental number (J2901), is corroborated by military records that confirm his dates of service (February 1918–November 1919), and it is unlikely that he would have been recruited at fourteen.[50]

Another volunteer was Gershon Avrunin, whose testimonial (written by his surviving family at least thirty-four years after his death in 1923, at the age of forty), shows that he was thirty-four when he enlisted in the Legion from his private law practice in Detroit. He was born in Kiev and emigrated to the United States in 1903, where he became one of the founders of the American Poale Zion movement. The family also recalls that he was the first president of the Jewish National Workers Alliance (National Arbeiter Farband), and played a major role in recruitment prior to his own departure for service overseas with the 39th Battalion.[51]

Gustave Lossos, who was born in Lithuania on 1 July 1893, arriving in America at the age of nineteen, was also involved in recruitment to the Legion. Active in the Zionist movement, Lossos states in his own testimonial that he became a charter member of the Legion branch of the Farband, and assisted well-known campaigners such as Dr H.L. Gordon, Pinhas Gingold, Kretchmar Israeli and Joshua Gordon in their efforts in New York to secure support for the Legion amongst the immigrant Jewish population. During his service with the 39th Battalion Gustave Lossos played the piano for both English and Yiddish concert parties, and continued to rally support for the Zionist cause after his return to New York.[52]

Previous reference has been made to American draft laws and the generally strict application of their provisions to volunteers who held American citizenship. One of the legionnaires who manoeuvred his way around this obstacle was Isadore Stone, who had taken American citizenship before the war, having been born near Kiev in 1888. His surviving family have recorded that he settled in the US in 1906 after brief periods of residence in Bessarabia, Warsaw and London. Isadore was able to join the Legion in Boston, in May 1918, by using his original name of Israel Chrushe, and served until demobilisation as a lance-corporal in the 39th Battalion. Without supplying an explanation, Isadore's testimonial goes on to claim that, following his return to the United States, he remained in the US Army, eventually retiring to Washington DC as a Quartermaster-Sergeant, where he died in the early 1960s.[53]

No such manoeuvres were required by two legionnaires whose personal testimonials relate that they received deferment from the draft authorities, which permitted them to volunteer for the Jewish Battalions in the British Army. Benjamin Morrow of Cleveland had been born in Russian Poland in 1893 and took out citizenship papers on the eve of the United States entry into the war in 1917.[54] His compatriot, Morris Stern, of Brooklyn, New York, also had no difficulty in joining the Legion, whilst his four brothers served in the American army. Ironically, it is interesting to note that Morris' father, Yasof Sterinshus (Morris' original name had been Moishe Sterinshus) had emigrated to the United States after making his fortune as a blanket manufacturer for the Russian Army.[55]

Two testimonials, belonging to Harvey Schwartz, a corporal of the 38th Battalion, and Nathan Newman, a private of the 39th, describe avoidance of military service in a different army, that of Imperial Russia. In the first example, Harvey Schwartz, who was born in Russia on 15 June 1898, received his conscription papers from the Tsarist government, and having decided that he was really not interested in serving this oppressive regime, fled to the United States via Siberia and Japan.[56] Born some nine years earlier, Nathan Newman was drafted into the Russian army in 1912 at the age of 21, but deserted after three months service, managing to arrive in the USA in 1913. He made a living as a shoemaker before joining the Legion in 1918.[57] A former Russian soldier with a longer period of service was Bereskin Myer, born 1878 in Propoisk, White Russia, and conscripted in 1899. Bereskin served throughout the Russo-Japanese war, after which he was discharged and emigrated to Winnipeg in Canada, where he helped to organise the local Poale Zion group. Moving to Palestine in 1908, he came under the influence of Ben-Zvi, and was sent to Britain and Canada to campaign on behalf of Jewish settlement. Eventually arriving in the USA, Bereskin joined the Legion and settled in Sioux City on his return from the war, where he died in 1957.[58]

In the next chapter the backgrounds and biographies of the Jewish volunteers from Palestine will be examined, but among the Americans there was at least one soldier who was actually born in Jerusalem. According to his brief testimonial, Jack Cohen, born in this city on 15 April 1897, travelled to the USA in 1915 after the purge of the Jewish population of Palestine. Jack reached the rank of acting sergeant, and later settled in Oklahoma. He was active in the American Legion, the Zionist Organisation of America and Br'nai Brith, becoming 'the recipient of the first Americanism medal ever awarded by the local chapter of the Daughters of the American Revolution'.[59] Isadore Schwartz, born in Rumania in 1892, also found his way to the USA in 1915, having been a member of the second Aliyah to Eretz Israel.[60] Neither Jack Cohen nor Isadore Schwartz appear to have been among those Jews whom the Turks expelled to Alexandria, unlike Maurice Frankel, who joined the Zion Mule Corps and served in Gallipoli. Maurice had been born in Warsaw in 1882 and had spent many years in Palestine until the Turkish intervention. After the Zion Mule Corps was disbanded in January 1916, Maurice joined two of his brothers, who had settled in the United States, and enlisted in the 39th Battalion on 9 April 1918 in Cleveland, Ohio.[61]

Of those that enlisted in Philadelphia, Gilner described the tribulations of William Braiterman of Baltimore, who, whilst under age and assuming the name of Cohen, joined up in opposition to his parents' wishes by employing the simple expedient of travelling to the recruitment office in Philadelphia.[62] In correspondence with the author, William, who devoted a large part of his later life to the Jewish Legion veterans group and the Legion museum at Avichail (a Hebrew place name that means my father, the soldier), enclosed copies of interviews he had given to the press in America. The following extract is reproduced from an interview by Jay Marwin in the *Concord Monitor*, dated 13 October 1983, which explains the motivation that lay behind William's desire to volunteer:

> When he immigrated with his family in 1911, Braiterman was at first relieved that America would be a safe harbor from the Russian pogroms against the Jews. Two years later, however, when he learned about the lynching of a Jew arrested in Georgia on trumped-up murder charges, he discovered that America had an anti-Semitic tradition of its own. 'I came to the conviction' he recalled, 'that the only safe place for Jews would be their own country, their own government, where they would be the majority.'[63]

It is probably appropriate at this stage to refer to the testimonial submitted by Elias Gilner himself, under his original surname of Ginsburg. Born in Wolksurysk, Russia on 5 December 1890, Gilner emigrated to the US in 1912, after a brief time spent in Baku, in the Caucasus. He joined the Legion in St Louis, Missouri and helped in the recruitment campaign conducted in the western states of the USA. After the war, Gilner served with the Zionist Commission in Jerusalem, and was later jailed for his activities with the Haganah, in which many Jewish

Legion veterans were involved. Following his release he continued to work in Palestine for the Zionist cause, before returning to New York in 1940. Acknowledged as the official historian of the Jewish Legion, Elias Gilner died on 2 February 1976, aged 85.[64]

If the evidence presented in the personal and family testimonies above is taken at face value, then it can be concluded that the volunteers from North America did contain an element of activists who were motivated by a genuine desire to advance the Zionist and nationalist causes in which they believed. It may of course, be the case that family claims on behalf of their deceased forebears were coloured by sentiment, and a desire to present the memory in the most pioneering light. Without corroborative evidence it is difficult to distinguish between the well-meaning myth, apocryphal story and reality, but it remains the case that a significant proportion of the personal testimonials of these volunteers were explicit in terms of political and nationalist affiliation. It is also quite possible that these affiliations were stated publicly as a means of reinforcing the bond between the veterans at the time the testimonials and museum were being collected and constructed. Nevertheless, correspondence with Braiterman and other veterans supports the notion of politicisation among the volunteers.[65] Furthermore, whilst recruitment was certainly concentrated on the North East coast of the USA, the testimonials examined revealed the wide geographical spread of the recruitment campaign, which is evidence in itself of a strongly supported and well-financed movement across the whole of American Jewry. In addition to New York, recruitment took place in urban centres such as Baltimore, Boston, Chicago, Cleveland, Detroit, Houston, Kansas City, Los Angeles, Oklahoma, Philadelphia and St Louis. It therefore appears to be the case that, regardless of official Zionist policy, the influence of the Benim and the determination of Poale Zion to seize an opportunity to establish Israel in Palestine – encouraged by the Balfour Declaration – resulted in the attachment of a significant number of Jewish volunteers to the Jewish Battalions of the British Army. It can also be argued that the presence of anti-Semitism in the army command did not discourage recruitment from this source, with the volunteers from America making up the largest 'group' in the Legion.

How would the young men from the USA get on with the British Army and their comrades in arms from Britain and Palestine? It is now time to examine the progress of the Jewish Legion in preparation for Allenby's final campaign against the Turks, and to deal with the raising of the local recruits from Palestine.

7
Preparation and Prejudice

According to the war diary of the 39th Battalion, this unit joined the 38th at the training camp at Helmieh, outside Cairo, on 28 April 1918, exactly two months after the latter had disembarked at Alexandria. Lt.-Col. Eliezer Margolin, who had seen the Zion Mule Corps whilst serving with the Australian forces near Alexandria, commanded the battalion. A Russian Jew by birth, Margolin had been an agricultural pioneer in Palestine before emigrating to Australia, and had received a commission and the DSO whilst serving with the Australian forces in France. While recovering in a London hospital from wounds received at the front, Margolin was visited by Jabotinsky, and later offered the command of the 39th Battalion. Colonel Margolin's background made him an eminently suitable leader of a battalion that would eventually consist of a mix of conscripts and volunteers from Britain, America and from the Jewish community in Palestine.

The 39th had a strength of thirty-one officers, six warrant officers, forty-eight sergeants and 608 other ranks – or about two-thirds of the manpower of the 38th. This number was increased by the success of recruitment in the United States (the first contingent of 295 Jewish volunteer soldiers from America were to join the Jewish Battalions in Egypt on 24 July). The prospect of substantial local recruitment was to be some consolation for Lt.-Col. Patterson following the British Government's inconsistent Russian recruitment policy. Patterson was also aware that if the promise made to him of a brigade command was to be honoured, then the sources of recruitment from outside Great Britain would become increasingly important in supplying enough manpower to sustain at least three battalions in the field.

In setting the local context for the deployment of the Jewish Battalions, account has been taken of recently released Military Intelligence records that provide an insight into the attitude of the staff of the EEF towards the peoples of Palestine. To illustrate this point, the following examples have been taken from a 'very secret' document entitled 'Personalities of South Syria. iii North Palestine', dated 20 May 1917. Although produced about a year prior to the Legion's arrival, the report nevertheless reflects the attitude of the staff officers who prepared it. The document contains brief pen sketches of local notables, organised on a town-by-town basis, with further sub-division by religion. In the case of the town of Tiberias there appears:

> Salamon Gross, 65. Banker. Orthodox Jew of the Old Type. Richest and most influential Jew in Tiberias. No European education. Speaks Yiddish and Arabic. Very Clever. Oriental standard of honesty.

> Abraham Abali, 45. Merchant. Consular Agent of France, Austria and other countries. Speaks french [sic]. Very shrewd. Has considerable influence. Indifferent character.

> The Mufti (1916, name unknown) about 50. A cynical, dishonest scoundrel.

> Eftimos, 60. Greek Orthodox priest. The leader of the community. Immoral, unscrupulous intriguer.

Similar treatment is given to the notables of Safed:

> Raful Silberman, better known as Raful Dayan, 70. Very influential, not always for the best, in the Jewish community. A narrow minded and combative fanatic.

> Haim Majoulis Kahlvansky, 50. Agent for Baron Edmond Rothschild's Jewish Colonial Association. Educated in France. Intelligent. Rather superficial. A man of great, but impracticable projects. Very influential in the district.

> Wolkomitch. Director of the School of Roshpina (a Jewish village). First rate philologist. Has had much influence on Jewish education in Palestine. A very distinguished Hebrew teacher. President of the B'nai Brith Lodge.[1]

It is the language of these sketches, which were written for senior staff officers of the EEF in preparation for the campaign in Palestine, that evokes a strong sense of the educational and cultural background of the British officer class, whose generally anti-foreigner and anti-Semitic attitude was described in an earlier chapter. Terms such as 'Oriental standard of honesty' and ' Rather superficial. A man of great, but impracticable projects', show a degree of condescension in addition to moral judgement, with the exception of the acknowledgment of Wolkomitch's distinction.

External influences upon the professional leadership of the EEF were also responsible for shaping the attitude of some officers towards the Jewish Battalions. The two most prominent events in this regard were the Balfour Declaration and the circulation of the *Protocols of the Elders of Zion*. General Allenby barred publication of the Balfour Declaration in Palestine, in the cause of maintaining good relations with his Arab allies and the local Muslim community. Interestingly, Chaim Weizmann appreciated the dilemma facing Allenby:

> [T]he Balfour Declaration, which had made such a stir in the outside world, had never reached many of Allenby's officers, even those of high rank ... They were cut off from Europe; their minds were naturally concentrated on the job in hand ... holding their own on their particular front, and not being rolled back by the Turks.[2]

Nevertheless, Allenby's efforts and the ignorance of his staff did not prevent the news of the declaration from reaching the local population, both in Jerusalem and the southern part of Palestine that had been occupied by the EEF by the spring of 1918. This was mainly due to Turkish government propaganda ensuring that the Arabs in Palestine were aware of the British support for a Jewish homeland. The publication of this information was designed to heighten Arab fears of greatly increased Jewish immigration, and reinforce their suspicion of the British.[3]

The officers whom Weizmann thought ignorant of the Balfour Declaration were however, aware of the *Protocols of the Elders of Zion*. These infamous and inflammatory forgeries were concocted out of earlier materials by the French division of the Okhrana following the 1897 Zionist conference, and were purportedly minutes of a secret session when the Zionist leaders planned a Jewish world conquest. Russian emigrants brought copies of the Protocols to western Europe at this time, and some British officers in the EEF certainly had them. As they were not published in English until February 1920, we must presume that these officers read them in the original Russian.[4] The evidence for this is contained in Weizmann's memoirs, where he recalled a conversation with Major Wyndham Deedes of the intelligence section of the EEF staff. They met in the late spring of 1918, during Weizmann's visit as head of the Zionist Commission, when Deedes, a Gentile Zionist who, like Ormsby-Gore and Meinertzhagen had been chiefly influenced by Aaronson, showed a copy of the Protocols to Weizmann and said:

> You had better read all of it with care; it is going to cause you a great deal of trouble in the future ... You will find it in the haversack of a great many British officers here – and they believe it! It was brought over by the British Military Mission which has been serving in the Caucasus on the staff of the Grand Duke Nicholas.[5]

Against this background, Lt.-Col. Patterson wrote to General Allenby, C.-in-C. of the EEF, on 5 March 1918, requesting permission to recruit from among local Palestinian Jewry, and seeking his commander's approval for Jewish officers and men, serving in other regiments, to transfer into the Jewish Battalions if they so wished.[6] The response to this communication was to leave Patterson in no doubt as to the difference between the attitude of General Macready, the pro-Legion Adjutant-General in London, and the commander and staff of the EEF in Cairo. Patterson was obviously keen to see the expansion of the Jewish Battalions, and the creation of the promised brigade (with himself as commander), and considered that Allenby, whom he had known since the second Boer War, would be willing to implement this policy.

When summoned to headquarters, the Chief of Staff, Major General Louis Jean Bols, made it clear to Patterson that the Jewish units were not welcome and that General Allenby would not grant his requests.[7] This was entirely consistent with the view put to the War Office by Allenby (see previous chapter). At a subsequent personal interview with Allenby, Patterson was told that the C.-in-C. disagreed with War Office policy with regard to the Jewish Battalions. Despite Patterson's disappointment, he refrained from any personal criticism of Allenby, choosing instead to mention that Bols told him 'quite plainly that he Bols was not favourably disposed towards Jewish aspirations'. Both Patterson and Jabotinsky believed that Bols was the 'chief opponent' of the Legion.[8]

Gilner accounted for Allenby's and Bols' defiance of Macready (and the Foreign Office) by explaining that, given the lack of unity amongst Jewry in Britain as far as the Legion was concerned, differences emerged between the Foreign Office and the War Office that effectively gave the EEF a free hand in this matter. The most telling point he makes in this regard refers to the earlier (April 1917) Army Council decision in accepting the formation of a Jewish regiment, provided that it was not associated with Zionism, a caveat that did not accord with the Foreign Office's endorsement of the scheme.[9] He then chose to explain the attitude of Allenby and Bols by arguing that they were 'followers of the "Lawrence of Arabia" line of thinking', and 'were close to Jewish assimilationist circles, titled Jews who had not swerved from their opposition to the Legion.'[10] This explanation now appears over-simplistic and is indicative of Gilner's understandably strong antipathy towards both the staff of the EEF and the assimilationists. It seems more likely that the general anti-Jewish prejudice of the British officer class, with notable exceptions such as General Macready, was a result of upbringing and education. Their attitude towards Zionism was, however, more complex. Previous chapters have demonstrated the inability of some Gentiles to comprehend and distinguish between Judaism and Zionism. Furthermore Gilner, in assuming that the staff were aligned with the assimilationists, overlooked the fact that it was their contempt for Jewish finance that lay behind much of their prejudice, and the assimilationist Jewish establishment in Britain had come from Jewish families that had generally made their fortunes by this very means.

There are two other convincing and contributory reasons for the prejudicial conduct of the British military leadership in the Middle East. Firstly, it made a great deal of sense, militarily and politically, for the British Army to favour better relations with the Arabs rather than the Jewish population, both indigenous and immigrant, of Palestine. This was because an Anglo-Arab entente facilitated Britain's need to protect the Suez Canal, the route to India, and the supply of oil from the Middle East. An important proponent of this view was Colonel A.P. Wavell who had walked into Jerusalem as one of a select band of officers accompanying Allenby's entry into the Holy City in November 1917. Wavell's opinion on this subject was summarised by his biographer, John Connell:

> He was fully aware of the considerations which had led to the issue of the Balfour Declaration, but he laid greater stress on its negative

safeguards for the Arabs than on its positive provisions for the Jews ... He believed, too, that the fulfilment of Zionist aspirations would lead to trouble in the Middle-East and – since it was the one subject on which all Arabs were united – would focus antagonism against Britain throughout the region.[11]

Secondly, Lawrence James, in his biography of Allenby, has described how the latter, in correspondence with the War Office, supported a request for European soldiers for the proposed advance to Damascus by asserting that they – as white and European – were held in higher regard by the indigenous population than the Indian and West Indian Battalions that had been added to his force.[12] (It will be seen later on, that this situation was also noted and understood by Weizmann.) Incidentally, a later cable from Allenby advised the War Office that:

> Egypt is Moslem and chiefly pro-Turkish. This renders propaganda among Indian Moslems easy, especially when they see British troops are withdrawn, as foretold by propagandists. This situation is also anxiously watched by our Arab Allies.[13]

The wording of this message highlights Allenby's concern for the morale of the Muslim soldiers of the Indian Army, and offers another indication of the political and military balance that he was required to strike in his command in Egypt and Palestine. His manpower difficulties were also observed and noted by other significant personalities in the region. Towards the end of March 1918, Chaim Weizmann arrived in Egypt at the head of the Zionist Commission; it was his meeting with Allenby and Bols at GHQ Bir Salem soon afterwards that made him aware of the aforementioned situation regarding the local censorship of the Balfour Declaration.

The Zionist Commission had been sent to the Middle East to report on Palestine in the wake of the declaration, and consisted of British, Italian and French representatives. It had been originally proposed that Russia and the United States also be represented, but with Russia's withdrawal from the world war and the outbreak of civil war, this never happened. American Zionist participation was also not forthcoming, for two major reasons. Firstly, America was not at war with Turkey and participation may have had unwelcome foreign policy consequences, for which Jewry did not want to be held responsible. Secondly, within American Zionism itself, there was a split between those in favour and those against sending a representative to join the commission. The head of World Poale Zion, Shlomo Kaplansky, had wanted either Izhak Ben-Zvi or David Ben-Gurion to join the commission. Ben-Zvi wrote from his training camp in Canada to his future wife Rahel in Palestine:

> several of the members of the American Central Committee did not agree to this and instead chose an unsuitable person – Zarr Izhak Zarr, a prominent member of Poale Zion. In the end we received word that we give our mandate outright to our haverim in Eretz Israel and suggested you Rahel [Rachel] as our candidate.[14]

Nothing came of this suggestion as the majority of the American Central Committee finally decided, in Ben-Zvi's own words, 'to abstain completely, on principle, from participation in the Zionist Commission'.[15] Weizmann's colleagues from Britain included several leading Zionist Jews whose names will be recalled from their earlier support for the formation of the Legion. They were Joseph Cowen, David Eder, Leon Simon and I.M. Sieff. Major James Rothschild, son of Baron Edmond (and a naturalised British citizen) and Major Ormsby-Gore also accompanied the commission as military liaison officers. The arrival of the commission did nothing to alleviate the political problems of Allenby, whose situation was again appreciated by Weizmann:

> In fact, I felt we could hardly have descended upon GHQ at a more inappropriate time ... The train which had brought me from Cairo had been promptly loaded with (European) officers and men being rushed to the West[ern Front] ... he was left with a small Indian Moslem force, and the Arabs, quick to sense the weakening in the British position, were showing signs of restiveness.[16]

Weizmann did not exaggerate Allenby's manpower problem: the massive German attack in France that commenced on 21 March necessarily required urgent British reinforcement. In a message dated one month (21 April) after the start of this offensive, the War Office described to Allenby the stark facts facing the army on the western front, and explained that:

> The only possible means at our disposal is by further calling on you for Battalions ... It is fully realized that this will entail loss of efficiency in your force and temporary reduction in strength ... [but] this is a risk which should be taken and we are prepared to accept it.[17]

The shortage of infantry did not, however, prevent further attempts by the EEF to diminish the role of the Jewish Legion within the British and Imperial Army in Egypt. Seeking to capitalise on the fact that Russian Jewish recruitment from Britain into the Jewish Battalions had been stopped, and no doubt presuming that the Russian Jews of the 38th did not want to fight anyway, the EEF command decided, just before the arrival of the 39th Battalion, to offer these troops the opportunity of joining a labour corps. Unfortunately for GHQ, the scheme failed because Patterson paraded the battalion, and his officers explained to their men the nature of 'their sacred duty'. This appeal to the ranks was very successful, in that only twelve men confirmed their intention to volunteer for labour units, a number that was reduced to ten after the further personal intervention of Patterson.[18]

This episode is important because it says a great deal about the leadership and morale of the 38th Battalion, which had been under a shadow since receiving the news of the stoppage of Russian recruitment, and had since been subjected to discriminatory treatment at the hands of the EEF. This latter included difficulty in obtaining kosher food for Passover despite the promises made earlier in London. It is ironic that military discipline, which, it will be recalled, had been identified by the War Office as the means by which the Russian Jews already enlisted would be controlled, had enabled Patterson to unite and fortify the men under his command, using the attitude of the EEF staff as a goad. Indeed, the commitment of Patterson's soldiers may also have been a factor in persuading General Allenby to rescind, in May 1918, his earlier decision to ban local recruitment of Palestinian Jews, a development that will be examined later.

The tribulations of the 38th also activated the Zionist organisation in Britain, on whose behalf Nahum Sokolow took action (see previous chapter) to halt the threat to recruitment and viability of the Jewish Legion. In a series of exchanges between June and October 1918, with the Foreign and War Offices, Dr Sokolow alleged that the latter had broken the conditions of the Army Council Instruction establishing the Jewish Battalions (ACI 1415 dated 12 September 1917). Sokolow also pointed out that, by a manipulation of the medical categorisation provisions, the opportunities for Jews to transfer from other units of the British Army had been reduced. As a result of these interventions the War Office relented and confirmed, in a memorandum that 'Instructions will be issued to ensure that ACI 1415 of 1917 are complied with'.[19] This memorandum was issued on 31 October 1918 – one day after the armistice with Turkey was signed at Mudros.

Whilst the Legion's supporters continued their struggle for the operation of ACI 1415 in spirit and deed, the bonding effect of military training and shared hardship maintained and improved the morale of the 38th Battalion in Egypt. The letters home of Private Epstein at around this time convey a sense of how this developed. For example, he recorded the pride of the battalion at being inspected by the Duke of Connaught (8 March), and noted that behind them marched 'a lot of Zionist organisations ... with the Jewish National Flag'. It might be surmised that this type of public display further antagonised the staff of the EEF, and reinforced their apprehension at the presence of uniformed Zionists in their army. If so, then its effect did not filter down to Private Epstein and his comrades for, in a letter home dated 22 April he wrote that there is a 'noticeable increase in good feeling towards army'. To this he added, in a letter dated 12 June that, in the process of 'hardening for war', he had participated in a '5 hour march – singing "The bells are ringing for me and my girl", a song learnt from the 39th Battalion who said it was the rage in London'.[20]

While the training of the 38th was coming to an end in Egypt, and the 39th settled into its own preparations at base camp, the induction of further recruits continued back in Plymouth. A detailed description of this period at the adopted home of the Jewish Battalions is given in the unpublished memoirs of Major Henry Myer, which include contemporaneous material in the form of a diary and the letters he wrote to his fiancé.[21] Major Myer was born in Bayswater, London on 22 April 1892, the son of Jewish middle-class parents, and was commissioned into the 6th Battalion (City of London Rifles), the London Regiment, Territorial Force in 1909, shortly after becoming articled to his father, a City solicitor. Following mobilisation, Henry Myer arrived in France in 1915 and was subsequently wounded at the Battle of Loos on 25 September. After further service on the western front, Myer opted for transfer to the Jewish Legion.[22]

It is clear from Henry Myer's writing that he had mixed feelings about his Russian co-religionists, but a strong sense of duty towards them and his country of birth outweighed these. He was well connected to the Anglo-Jewish establishment (he married, shortly after the war, Louie Solomon, a niece of Herbert Bentwich), and provides a good example of the way in which national and religious loyalties could be reconciled within this part of the British population. Myer had few doubts about his judgement when he recorded that the poor physical condition of the Jews from London, and other metropolitan areas in Britain, limited the opportunities for training. In an amusing anecdote he recalls how the CO of the 39th, Lt.-Col. Eliezer Margolin, had personally inspected each man at a sick parade:

> I asked him afterwards what the majority was suffering from, he said they replied 'Oh! It's mine heartz and mine feet'. There was some truth in this. They had led sedentary lives and their hearts were not in the job.[23]

Following Margolin's departure to the Middle East with the 39th, a replacement as CO at Plymouth had been announced in the *Jewish Chronicle* of 15 February. Lt.-Col. Fred Samuel DSO was the nephew of Sir Marcus Samuel and the brother in law of Captain Redcliffe Salaman, the medical officer of the 39th, who asked him to join the Jewish Legion. Jabotinsky acknowledged Fred Samuel as a genuine English Zionist, and among Samuel's officers were Major Daniel Hopkin MC, a barrister and transferee from the Royal Welsh Fusiliers, Lt. Rubin, an Old Etonian from the Grenadier Guards and Leon Roth, a Hebrew speaker who was to become a leading academic at the Hebrew University in Jerusalem. The senior NCOs who had transferred in provided the vital link between the officers and men of the Jewish Battalions in training. Myer is particularly appreciative of their contribution, maintaining that they:

> were of the greatest value in training men of diverse backgrounds, whose only acquaintance with discipline – and that by no means general - was religious. Here at least was some common ground. A few could also speak or understand Yiddish.[24]

Singled out by Myer are CSM 'Chick' Bitton, Sergeant Scorah, Sergeant Fries and Sergeant Joseph Cohen, who had been sent to the recruiting mission in New York. In an interesting comment, Myer noted that Cohen was 'a learned and cultured man – a Zionist and idealist – a type undreamed of in the British or any Army'. By way of contrast, CSM Bitton, another resident of Amhurst Road Hackney, had a distinguished war-time career already behind him when he transferred to the Jewish Battalions in 1918. In his testimonial, Chick Bitton wrote:

> Joined 6th London Regt Sept 5th 1914. Went to France March 19th 1915 ... Awarded Military Medal September 1916 ... Promoted CSM February1917 ... Went overseas with 40 RF. Demobbed April 5th 1919.

No doubt the conscripts from East London were suitably impressed. Chick Bitton's story does not end here, however, because his testimonial records that, 20 years after his first demobilisation, he:

> Enlisted 14th Royal Fusiliers Jan 4th 1940. Went to France Feb 1940. Left France June 17th 1940 with the last troops. Owing to contracting arthritis was discharged medically unfit Oct 1942.[25]

'Chick' Bitton's military experience prior to becoming a CSM in the 40th Battalion mirrors that of the splendidly named Max Karo, who was appointed a CSM in the 38th Battalion. Max was born in Russia on 4 May 1876, emigrated to London some twenty years later and was naturalised in 1902. His civilian occupation was in business in the City of London, where he became a member of the London Stock Exchange in 1909. He volunteered for the army, at the age of 38, in August 1914 and served in France with the 26th Battalion Royal Fusiliers (Bankers), until transferring to the 38th Battalion as a sergeant instructor. After the war Max Karo was commissioned into the Jewish Lads Brigade and subsequently founded the Stock Exchange Cadet company after which he was awarded the MBE. He finally retired in 1951.[26]

With the arrival in Plymouth of more men in the form of drafts from the USA, conscripts, transferees and volunteers, Lt.-Col. Samuel prepared a third battalion, the 40th, for later embarkation for Egypt (where it arrived at the end of August 1918). Samuel moved the 40th to a training camp in nearby Eggbuckland, where the rugged terrain was invaluable in preparing the men during their thirteen weeks of infantry training. Meanwhile, back at Crown Hill, the holding battalion (42nd) received a Commanding Officer in the shape of a South African Jew, Lt.-Col. Miller. Miller, a regular soldier who was commissioned from the ranks, had transferred from the Machine Gun Corps, and was to oversee the depot until the end of the war.

Returning to the 38th and 39th Battalions, it will be recalled that earlier mention was made of General Allenby's volte-face in May with regard to the recruitment of Palestinian volunteers into the Legion. Basing his objections on fears concerning the motivation and behaviour of Jews of Russian origin, Allenby had been firm in his refusal to consider local recruitment, even before the arrival of the Jewish Battalions from Britain. In late 1917, General Hill, the GOC 52nd division based in Jaffa, had asked permission to form a locally recruited unit, and attended a meeting in mid-February, at which 500 local Jewish volunteers offered their services. Soon afterwards their offer was amended to a request to become part of the 38th and 39th Battalions, as a militia-type unit for local defence. Unsurprisingly, GHQ denied permission. The amended offer came about after the volunteers were addressed by Jabotinsky at the Jewish settlement of Rehovoth, not far from Allenby's GHQ at Bir Salem.

Jabotinsky's intervention was required to settle the differences that had arisen between the various political factions that had formed within the Jewish settler communities. In this regard, the divisions between socialists, workers and revolutionaries were temporarily laid aside in order to present a united band of volunteers prepared to fight for a place at the peace conference. Jabotinsky convinced the volunteers that the Legion would provide the best chance for meeting this objective. Leading members of the Volunteers' Committee included Dov Hos, Eliyahu Golomb, Berl Katznelson and Rahel Yanait (later Rahel Ben-Zvi) who represented the women volunteers that are estimated to have made up about a third (500) of the total number at that time.

The three men served in the Legion. Dov Hos was an immigrant from Russia who had been educated at the Herzl Gymnazia, before holding a commission in the Turkish Army early in the war. After helping in the defence of Jewish settlements, he was sentenced to death *in absentia* by a Turkish court martial but managed to avoid capture. In due course he was to become one of the founders of the Israeli Labour Party. Eliyahu Golomb had the same background and education as Dov Hos, and after the war played a leading role in the Haganah, the Jewish defence force. Berl Katznelson, originally from Byelorussia, came to Palestine at the age of 21 in 1908 and quickly made a reputation as a labour leader, establishing co-operatives and developing the kibbutz system. He worked with Ben-Gurion to create a united Labour party and was, perhaps, the most notable advocate of Labour Zionism.[27]

If the way was now clear for the Palestinian volunteers to offer their services to the British Army, what caused Allenby's subsequent change of mind that enabled them to be enlisted? The official records indicate that Allenby wanted to demonstrate impartiality between Arab and Jewish communities, as is shown in the following extract from Allenby's 'Secret' cable to the War Office of 10 May:

> Your 55434 March 17th I wish, after further consideration, to concede principle of recruitments in Palestine for British Army. Although majority of candidates for enlistment are of Russian nationality I do not consider that this shall necessarily form a

reason for their rejection in this area ... As I am allowing recruitment of Moslems for Sherifiam [sic] Army in Palestine I am the more anxious to accord this permission.[28]

Unfortunately, there is no copy available of the War Office cable of 17 March, although there was an earlier exchange between Allenby and Horse Guards two days earlier, which confirmed that local recruits were to receive the same pay and conditions as their British comrades.[29] It would seem that a policy of even-handedness in the occupied territory, combined with the existence of so many volunteers in Jaffa, led to the granting of Patterson's wishes. In any event, the War Office concurred, in a reply sent to Egypt on 16 May:

> Approval given to your proposal to recruit in Palestine for Jewish Battalions, Royal Fusiliers on understanding that the credentials of recruits will be closely investigated in every case.[30]

General Allenby immediately permitted Palestinian recruitment, and a mission was established under the command of Major James Rothschild, a member of the Zionist commission and an officer of the 39th Battalion to which he had transferred from the Grenadier Guards. Lt.-Col. Patterson sent a Hebrew speaking party, under Lieutenant Lipsey, to Palestine to assist Major Rothschild in his work. This small party contained a number of former Zion Mule Corps veterans, such as the earlier mentioned Sergeant Nissal Rosenberg, who would be reunited with some of their former colleagues from the Herzl Gymnazia and the refugee camp at Gabbari. Major Rothschild, in consultation with the Zionist Commission and the Volunteers Committee, had a poster distributed throughout Palestine, a translation of which appears in both Gilner and Patterson's works, and is reproduced here. The evocative sentiments are simple but clear and the influence of Jabotinsky in the conjunction of British and Zionist interests are self-evident:

> HEAR, O ISRAEL!
> Hear! What does your heart prompt you to do?
> Shall we not reclaim our heritage and establish its possession in the eyes of the world?
> Hearken! What does your reason say to you?
> The British are fighting here before our eyes, and shall we remain in our houses until they return from the battle to give us our country which they have redeemed with their blood?

Hearken! What does your honour and conscience dictate?
Is it possible for us to accept from the hands of our righteous redeemers such an offering of blood?
Shall not we too, together with them, offer our lives for our country?

HEAR, O ISRAEL!

The blood of our heroic forefathers, the blood of the British who fight for us this day, and the blood of the martyrs, cry unto us from this sacred ground.

ENLIST! ENLIST!

Shoulder to shoulder, together with our saviours, to the battle let us go. And salvation is with the Lord.

BE STRONG![31]

Chaim Weizmann was already aware of the willingness of many Palestinian Jews to enlist, as illustrated by the response to Brigadier Hill's recruiting committee at Jaffa. In a letter to Nathan Sokolow in London, written on 19 June 1918, Weizmann described the local recruitment situation in the following words:

> Thirty Nine. [39th battn.] Spontaneous movement here for formation of Jewish Regiment had already taken decisive steps before Commission arrived. After considerable delay authorities agreed recruit which began last week amid great enthusiasm recalling volunteer movement in England at beginning of war.[32]

Four days later, in a further letter to Sokolow, Weizmann wrote the following passage capturing the enthusiasm of the Palestinian volunteers:

> the health of the local people is very good. Ten lads who were afraid they might have appendicitis went to a Doctor and gave him £100, asking to be operated on immediately, and they were poor workers! The British didn't see such enthusiasm amongst their best people in 1914. However, it pains me to admit that the local British here so far failed to understand or appreciate this phenomenon![33]

Weizmann's final sentence emphasises that British officers such as Brigadier Hill were very much the exception to the rule.

Jaffa, near Tel Aviv, became the major recruitment centre for Jews living in Palestine, not least because it was the scene of the establishment of the volunteers' committee. Official photographs (see Figures 7.1–7.4) show men queuing up at the reception centre and boarding trains from Jaffa to the battalion's training camp at Helmieh in Egypt. The official returns, which show that the 40th Battalion reached a trained strength of nearly 1,500 by September 1918, demonstrate the success of this mission. Allowing for turnover due to replacements, sickness, training, transfers in from the 38th and particularly the 39th, it is reasonable to conclude that between 1,500 and 2,000 volunteers were forthcoming from this source.[34] Gilner, Weizmann and Jabotinsky reckoned that the large majority of volunteers were émigré or second generation Russians from the Yishuv, which then contained about 50,000 immigrants in total. The enlistment of large numbers of young men in the British Army had a profound effect upon the longer established population of the 'older Yishuv'. Weizmann has described how the commission had to appeal to the 'relatively few young men' in this community to replace the volunteers, and the difficult relations that existed between the two parties.[35]

From the surviving records it is not possible to determine the actual number of locally born Jews who enlisted, but the volunteers included Jews from the Mediterranean and even some 106 Turkish prisoners of war who transferred their allegiance to the British Army.[36] The following four examples of individual legionnaires who volunteered in Palestine, have been taken from the Avichail testimonials. Despite their limitations, they convey a sense of human background and it is interesting to note that they all left Palestine after demobilisation in order to make a living in either Britain or the United States.

Firstly, Sergeant Aryeh Rubenstein was born in Russia in 1892, and had grown up in Palestine where he attended the Herzl Gymnasium in Tel Aviv. Sergeant Rubenstein was among the first to enlist and stayed with the battalion until its disbandment in 1921. In 1925 he emigrated to Britain, where he obtained a law degree at Manchester University and went on to a distinguished academic career, until his death in 1966.[37] Secondly, Jacob Pinchevsky (later known as Pinches) was another volunteer of Russian background. He enlisted in Jaffa on 18 July 1918 and was demobilised on 20 June 1919. Jacob also moved to Britain after the war and established his home in Dalston, East London, where he married another Russian immigrant, Gitta Kalmanoivitz and had four children.[38] Private David Ribniker joined the Jewish Battalions as a member of a contingent of volunteers from Galilee. Unlike Rubenstein and Pinchevsky, he remained in Palestine after the war but eventually left for Britain in the early 1930s, settling in Surrey.[39] Finally, a native of Palestine, Naim Freedman, who was born in Jerusalem, served in the Legion from September 1918 until his discharge in April 1920. In 1921 he emigrated to the United States and spent the remainder of his life in New Jersey.[40]

Figure 7.1 Recruits for the 40th (Palestine) Battalion, Royal Fusiliers, Jerusalem summer 1918

Figure 7.2 Major James de Rothschild enlisting Jewish volunteers for the 40th (Palestine) Battalion, Royal Fusiliers, at Jaffa summer 1918

176 *The Jewish Legion and the First World War*

Figure 7.3 Some of the 1,000 recruits for the 40th (Palestine) battalion, Royal Fusiliers, obtained in Jerusalem, summer 1918

Figure 7.4 Palestinian recruits in the narrow-gauge open-truck train *en route* from Jaffa to Helmieh, their training centre, summer 1918

Jabotinsky, Gilner and Weizmann all agree on the physical capabilities and potential of these recruits, as might be expected of pioneers, but an even more interesting indication of their intellectual, social and political make up was given by Weizmann's question to Major James Rothschild 'You have cleaned out the country. Where are we to find workers and teachers and officials?'[41] This make up was also manifested by the volunteer's formation of a Regimental Council, which consisted of elected representatives from the various factions or groups – such as Herzl Gymnasium alumni and Hashomer (watchmen) – that were to be found amongst the recruits. This council was completely unofficial, but there is no doubt that it was used as a means of communication between the battalion officers and men. It was, for instance, used to choose five private soldiers from the 40th Battalion to attend the laying of the foundation stone of the Hebrew University in Jerusalem on 24 July 1918.

Returning to the early days of recruitment, by 3 July 1918 the first and largest detachment of 700 Jaffa volunteers were ready for the journey to the training camp in Egypt. At a ceremony in Tel Aviv, Chaim Weizmann, on behalf of the Zionist commission, presented the volunteers with a flag described thus by Gilner:

> The blue and white colors [sic] bore the Union Jack in one corner, and the Star of David, a lion and an inscription lettered in gold: 'For our People and the cities of our Lord ... 5678'.[42]

The volunteers, under the command of Major Hopkin of the 39th, boarded railway cattle trucks on the following day for a protracted journey to Helmieh. Having to leave Palestine for Egypt was difficult for some of the volunteers, but they were buoyed up by Weizmann's promise of a return under British arms. The majority of these men were to become part of the 39th and 40th Battalions, and for them this promise was to remain unfulfilled.

At Helmieh, the men from Palestine joined their new comrades in the 39th, including its large contingent of American volunteers. Gilner has written how they received a warm and enthusiastic welcome from their fellow volunteers, but did not enjoy a similar relationship with the mainly conscripted soldiers from London:

> There were many emotional reunions between former Palestinians who had come from America and the Palestinian volunteers. The latter had not been getting on too well with some of the London boys who were snobbish and lacked understanding of the true

meaning of their service. The Palestinians were more tolerant of their American comrades and even produced a show with Yiddish choruses for their entertainment.[43]

Music was not the only form of entertainment produced by soldiers of the Legion. A newsletter, entitled 'The Judean', was published and issued to all ranks. In a box found in the Anglo-Jewish archives there is a folder containing programmes of entertainments and also a second edition of the 'The Judean' – price 5 piastres. This copy includes yet another example of the self-deprecating humour which was present in the Legion, and not dissimilar to the humour exhibited by their British comrades:

Joke: I met a Palestinian the other day and he had his rifle at the slope. I tried to speak to him but received no answer. 'Why didn't you reply?' I asked. 'How can I?' he answered 'when my hands are full!'[44]

The 38th had completed its training in the first week of June 1918, and proceeded to Palestine via Serafend. The battalion remained here for three days during which time they were welcomed by local Jewry, visited by Major Rothschild from Jaffa and inspected by General Allenby. Moving forward on 12 June the battalion took its place near the front line by encamping at Umm Siffah, where it formed part of the reserve for the 10th Division. For the next six weeks the Jewish soldiers gained active service experience with periods spent in and out of the line to the west of the River Jordan. They were introduced company by company to the front until on 3 July, the battalion relieved the 2nd/101 Grenadier Guards and became responsible for three to four miles of line opposite the Turks.

During their period in the line, Patterson's men undertook the building of roads and stone fortifications (sangars), work which had to be carried out during the hours of darkness. At the same time the battalion maintained a vigorous series of night patrols designed to keep the Turks under pressure and to obtain intelligence. Patterson singled out the activities of Lieutenant Abrahams and Private Angel in respect of the latter, and Jabotinsky wrote about his growing pride in the 'tailors' from London taking part in the former.[45] The battalion soon became accustomed to artillery shelling and the odd exchange of small arms fire, but the first casualty was Lieut. Wolffe who was killed by injuries received on 11 July when trying to halt two stampeding horses that were part of an ordnance team.[46]

Intelligence gathering and reconnaissance, which involved mapping no-man's land and attempting to discover the disposition of their forces by taking prisoners, were carried out in preparation for the expected advance of Allenby's army. The intentions of the commander-in-chief and the resulting offensive will be described later, but as far as intelligence was concerned, it was an activity in which the participation of Jewish soldiers was not confined to the immediate front. For example, it will be recalled from Chapter 3 that Corporal Leon Hildesheim (later Gildesgame), had served with the Zion Mule Corps in Gallipoli, after which he travelled to Britain. It can now be revealed that he then served with the Royal Horse Artillery before transfer-ring to the Royal Flying Corps as an instructor and interpreter for 100 Russian officers and cadets. Following this posting, Leon was sent to the intelligence department of the War Office in London, 'to help in preparation of Allenby's campaign in Palestine'.[47]

For Colonel Patterson and a few selected representatives of the 38th, duty in and out of the front line was temporarily relieved by their participation in the aforementioned laying of the foundation stone of the Hebrew University at Mount Scopus, Jerusalem on 24 July 1918. They were accompanied by colleagues from the 39th and 40th, the latter including one Levi Eshkol, later prime minister of Israel. Levi Eshkol had good reason to remember this occasion as he recalled in a letter written to a veteran of the 39th, Harry Levine some forty-six years later, on 28 August 1964:

> We who were in Palestine then had been treated as potential enemies by the Turks, and the Jewish settlement suffered greatly. After the British advance, many of us volunteered and formed the Palestinian Battalion of the Jewish Legion, 40th Royal Fusiliers. I did reach the rank of corporal, but I came back to camp late from the dedication of the Hebrew University and lost my stripes.
>
> The Jewish Legion stands out as an important milestone in our history. For us, it was an illustration of the potential of the independent Jewish army, which eventually followed. You can well be proud of your part.[48]

A copy of this letter (see Figure 7.5) shows that it was written by the prime minister on his official paper. As an ex-legionnaire himself, Levi

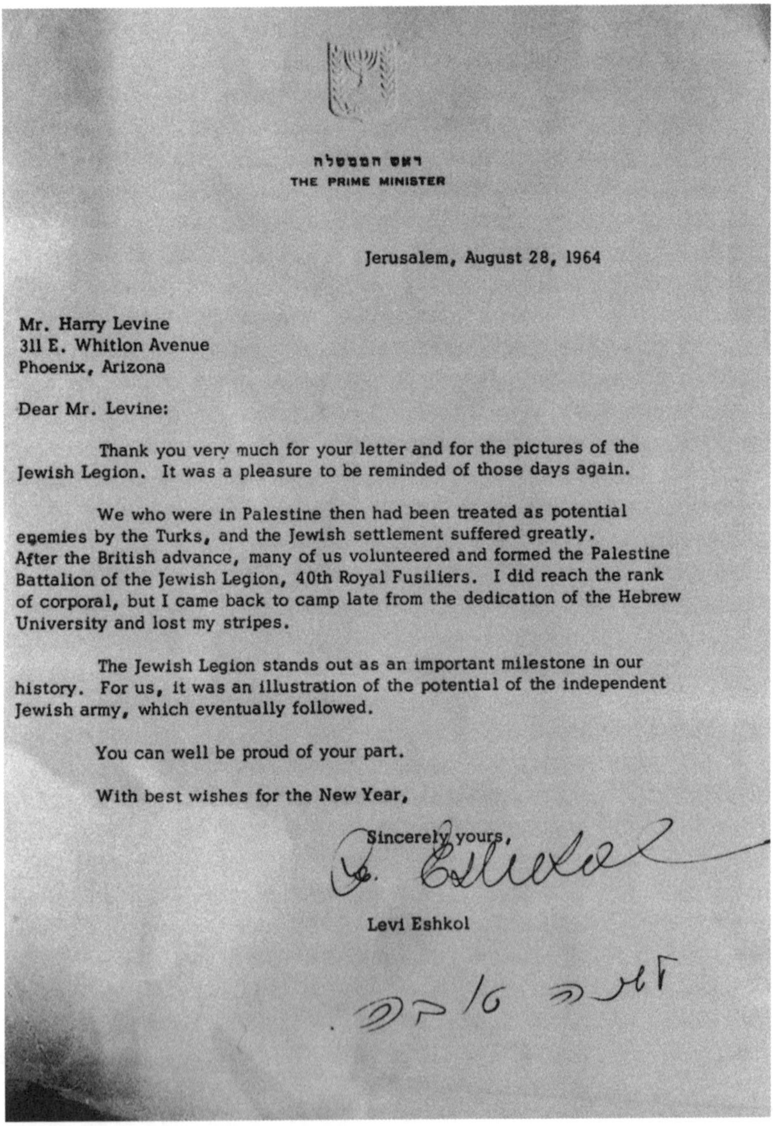

ראש הממשלה
THE PRIME MINISTER

Jerusalem, August 28, 1964

Mr. Harry Levine
311 E. Whitlon Avenue
Phoenix, Arizona

Dear Mr. Levine:

Thank you very much for your letter and for the pictures of the Jewish Legion. It was a pleasure to be reminded of those days again.

We who were in Palestine then had been treated as potential enemies by the Turks, and the Jewish settlement suffered greatly. After the British advance, many of us volunteered and formed the Palestine Battalion of the Jewish Legion, 40th Royal Fusiliers. I did reach the rank of corporal, but I came back to camp late from the dedication of the Hebrew University and lost my stripes.

The Jewish Legion stands out as an important milestone in our history. For us, it was an illustration of the potential of the independent Jewish army, which eventually followed.

You can well be proud of your part.

With best wishes for the New Year,

Sincerely yours,

Levi Eshkol

Figure 7.5 Letter to Harry Levine from Levi Eshkol, 1964

Eshkol may have been keen to publicly reinforce the linking of the origin of the Israeli army to the Jewish Legion of 1917–21.

To complete events concerning the Legion in July, mention must be made of a significant letter written on 27 July by Lord Stanhope, parliamentary secretary to the War Office. It was addressed to Major Lord Rothschild at Tring, and clarified government policy regarding the organisation and deployment of the Jewish Battalions of the Royal Fusiliers. Stanhope advised, in response to Rothschild's continuing enquiries that no decision had been made to disband the Legion, that the 40th Battalion was to proceed overseas, and that Russians were able to volunteer for combatant duties.[49] This definitive response meant that after nearly two and a half years of confusion and contradiction, the final war-time structure of the Jewish Legion was in place. Thus, by the end of July 1918 the 38th had been prepared for action, the 39th was in the final stages of its training, and the local recruits were awaiting their comrades from Plymouth to complete the 40th Battalion at Helmieh.

In conclusion, it can be argued that the Legion had reached this situation in spite of and not because of the activities of the command and staff of the EEF. Their reluctance to embrace the Legion was most markedly demonstrated by the attempt to discredit soldiers of Russian nationality, by placing them in a labour corps and effectively emasculating the Jewish Battalions as a fighting force. Other provocations included the failure to facilitate full religious observance, and the willingness of some British officers to countenance the *Protocols of the Elders of Zion*, which indicated the existence of a general, ingrained prejudice in the local army hierarchy. Furthermore, Allenby had a genuine military reason to make the Jewish Battalions unwelcome: the need to preserve good relations with the Arab coalition that protected his flank. No doubt he was aware that the threat of Zionist encroachment was one factor creating an otherwise illusory unity amongst the Arab peoples, and could not therefore afford to be seen to be arming Jewish soldiers in Palestine.

Why, then the change of policy? Perhaps the key lay in Allenby's own message to the War Office seeking sanction for Palestinian Jewish recruitment, and indicating that this could be balanced against Muslim recruitment into the Sherif's forces. This reasoning reflected the fact that Allenby, due to the manpower situation, had been forced to accept a multi-national and multi-cultural army. He had also recognised the reality of British Government policy towards Palestine and its post-war future in the light of the Balfour Declaration.

8
The Legion at War

From July until October 1918, the Jewish Legion experienced a series of events and experiences that began with the question of the proposed formation of a Jewish Brigade, and continued with the participation of the 38th and 39th in the battle of Megiddo, which included preparation in the heat of the Jordan Valley. How the Legion performed, and to what extent it was affected by prejudice, are questions that will be addressed throughout.

It will be recalled that soon after arriving in Egypt in early March 1918, Lt.-Col. Patterson had had an unpleasant confrontation with Allenby's Chief of Staff, General Bols. During this exchange it was made clear that promises given in London by the Adjutant-General (Macready), regarding the expansion of the Jewish Battalions and the formation of a Jewish Brigade, which Patterson himself was to command, counted for naught at the headquarters of the EEF. Subsequently, however, manpower and political considerations had led to Allenby's reluctant agreement to local recruitment. By early July, operational demands compelled Allenby to contact the War Office with his own proposals for incorporating the 38th and 39th Battalions in a new brigade:

> In Jordan Valley I must replace a mounted division by an infantry brigade, which I proposed [sic] to form from two British West Indian and two Jewish Battalions to enable me to concentrate sufficient troops for this purpose. Request sanction to provide locally brigade headquarters and brigade signalling section. Please allot number for the brigade.[1]

Patterson, on behalf of the Jewish Battalions, objected strongly to this proposal, on the grounds that this was yet another attempt to dilute the promises he had received in London. In his own account he also describes how he saw this brigade proposal being used by certain senior officers in his division (60th) to harm the Legion by reducing its identity.[2] It is not possible to determine with certainty the names of these officers, due to the frequency of the changes in the Legion's attachments to brigades at this time, but Patterson exempted the GOC 60th Division (Shea) from any criticism.

Prevailing upon their acquaintance, Patterson again wrote to General Allenby, reminding him of the Adjutant-General's commitments to a wholly Jewish brigade, and offering his resignation if the proposed alternative went ahead. Allenby responded immediately, rescinding the proposal both in a letter to Patterson and informed the War Office on 7 August that:

> Jewish Battalions have raised objections to being brigaded with British West Indians. The Jews are very anxious for the formation of a Jewish brigade. I consider that this is desirable politically, and that it will be feasible shortly ... I request, therefore, that for the present the 235th Brigade may consist of two British West Indian Battalions, and that a Jewish brigade of two Battalions may be formed and named 236th Jewish Brigade. The only increase involved will be one brigade headquarters, and to enable it to be divided the increase of about eight men to the brigade signal section.[3]

The wording of this extract deserves closer consideration in the context of Allenby's view on the deployment of the Jewish Legion (and the two British West Indian Battalions). Firstly, the numbers given to the proposed brigades were the next in turn; in the event there were no further infantry brigades after the 234th. Secondly, and of greater importance is the phrase 'I consider that this is desirable politically, and that it will be feasible shortly', which indicates Allenby's acceptance of the presence in his army of a distinctly Jewish force. The feasibility he mentioned involved the readiness of the 38th and 39th Battalions, the forthcoming despatch from the United Kingdom of the 40th Battalion and the prospect of the Palestinian Battalion completing its training in Egypt in the near future.[4] In addition, Allenby's willingness to form small brigades of two battalions (the standard components of an infantry brigade at this time being four battalions), and his particular use of the nomenclature Jewish Brigade, add further weight to the view that Allenby had accepted the spirit as well as the letter of War Office policy as expressed in the erstwhile promises of the Adjutant-General.

The War Office reply to this cable was immediate and unequivocal, confirming that it agreed with Allenby on the future development of the Legion, whilst indicating that the formation of a two-battalion brigade was seen to be premature:

> Regret cannot sanction formation of a second brigade headquarters. The 235th Brigade should consist ultimately of four Jewish Battalions, and for the present the West Indies Battalions remain independent units.[5]

What, therefore, can be determined from the evidence reviewed in this episode? It seems that, in spite of the continuing prejudice recorded by Patterson at staff level, both his personal contact with Allenby and the official communications demonstrate that the War Office and the responsible General Officer Commanding-in-Chief were committed to the formation of a Jewish brigade. Nevertheless, it should also be recognised that Patterson's willingness to communicate directly with the Commander-in-Chief was bound to irritate others in the chain of command, particularly Major-General Bols, and the results of this will be revealed later. Neither is there any clear evidence to suggest that Patterson's objections were themselves driven by race prejudice against the coloured soldiers of the British West Indian regiment, though the lack of evidence does not mean that such prejudice did not exist. It is worth mentioning that the Legion included two coloured Jewish soldiers, one named Lobagola from West Africa, and the other Melhado, who was a Sephardic Jew from the West Indies. There is little indication in Lobagola's autobiography of how he was treated by his comrades, although he claims to have enjoyed his period of service.[6]

The objections within the Legion to its treatment were expressed in stronger fashion by Lt.-Col. Margolin, the Commanding Officer of the 39th Battalion, who is reported to have sent the following remarks to HQ on 26 November 1918:

> Everything possible has been done to hamper, damp down, [sic] and suppress Jewish effort, both civil and military, in Palestine. This anti-Semitic policy even went so far as to attempt the elimination of the Jewish units as such by merging them into a brigade with Negroes ... This anti-Jewish attitude filtered down through all channels ... men were made to feel that they were of the 'despised race' ... No stone was left unturned in order to discredit us in every possible way.[7]

Nevertheless, it is probably true to say that the overriding motive behind Patterson's objection to the locally proposed brigade, was his desire to maintain the integrity of the Jewish Battalions, and see that the promises of Whitehall were fulfilled. In other words the brigading of Jews with West Indians would have lessened the status of the 38th and 39th Battalions in the eyes of the British Army. Similarly, since two battalions were not enough to form a viable brigade, any attempt to constitute one at this stage would have marginalised the Legion. Finally, and with hindsight, it is known that a Jewish brigade was never formed but it should not necessarily be concluded that there had been no intention to form one. The planned formation was overtaken by the speed of events that commenced with the battle of Megiddo and the rapid advance through Syria, culminating in the collapse of Turkish resistance in less than three and a-half months. It is worth noting that, in the battle of Megiddo, both Jews and West Indians fought well alongside each other and reached the objectives set them by their commanding general.

Preparations for the battle, involving the 38th and 39th Battalions were well underway by the time that the Jewish brigade controversy had passed. Megiddo itself was but a part of the final campaign planned by Allenby, which involved mounting a full-scale attack from the south through the coastal plain in the west, whilst convincing the Turkish commanders that his real intention was to send north a major force up through his eastern flank, along the Jordan valley. Furthermore, Allenby wished to retain a threat to Amman and the Hejaz railway, thus forcing the Turko-German forces opposing him to maintain troops to protect these positions, and so extending their lines of communication and supply.[8] In order to assist in the accomplishment of these objectives, the British West Indian and Jewish troops were deployed to the Jordan Valley in early and mid-August respectively.

Initially the 38th took up its position on the Wadi Mellaha, adjacent to the Jordan, where it came under the command of Major General E.W.C. Chaytor, a New Zealander. They were joined, in mid-September, by two fully trained companies of the 39th under Lt.-Col. Margolin, known as 'American' Companies, due to their consisting mainly of soldiers recruited in the USA. This command, designated 'Chaytor's Force' by GHQ, also included British West Indian (BWI) troops, the Australian and New Zealand Mountain Division, the 20th Indian Brigade (four battalions of Indian infantry) and four batteries of artillery.

The placing of the Jewish soldiers in the torrid and malaria-infested Jordan valley gave rise to more complaints from Patterson who, because his soldiers served longer (seven weeks) here than other infantry units, felt once more that his unit was being discriminated against. Again, Patterson did not criticise his local commander (Major General Chaytor) or his staff, but it is noteworthy that, on this occasion, Jabotinsky did not share his feelings. Nevertheless, there can be no doubt that conditions in this area were extremely debilitating in terms of climate and disease. To provide a better understanding of the experiences of the Jewish soldiers in this situation, they will be compared with those of the BWI Battalions who served in the valley. Before proceeding, however, the story of one fit member of the 38th who avoided this ordeal can be recounted. Private Epstein wrote a further letter to his mother on 24 July telling her that he was thankful to be in Palestine, rather than France as 'the Turks are quite demoralised as regards British methods of warfare'. He missed the opportunity to test this assertion in person because, on the afternoon of 29 July, he passed a trade test in tailoring and found himself posted to the army workshops in Jerusalem.[9]

Private Epstein was fortunate indeed to miss the sheer physical hardship involved in living and soldiering in the Jordan Valley. To set the scene it is necessary to understand the geography and climate of the area, and all sources agree on the extreme nature of both. For example, the *Official History* describes the summer months in the Valley thus:

> Week after week a shade temperature of 100°, rising sometimes to over 120°, is maintained. Yet the thermometer is no index to its horrors. Owing to its great depth and the enormous amount of evaporation from The Dead Sea, its air is leaden with moisture ... The hills on either Side of this trench act as walls to screen it, so that its atmosphere is commonly stagnant and seethed all day in the sun's rays.[10]

Wadi Mellaha, where Patterson's men were encamped, is a dried-up river bed that runs parallel to the Jordan for about ten miles, and is itself up to a mile wide. It presented all the difficulties associated with the Jordan Valley in summer, and was particularly prone to infestation and malaria. According to Wavell's account 'the most strenuous efforts of the medical staff kept at bay the most virulent type of malaria',[11] but despite this action, which involved the draining of marshland that provided mosquitoes with their breeding habitat, both West Indians and Jews suffered a high level of malarial casualty, which was attributed by the *Official History* to the negligence of the enemy: 'Yet it was impossible to prevent a certain amount of malaria in the Jordan Valley, for the enemy took few precautions or none, so that every strong breeze from his quarter blew in mosquitoes from his area.'[12]

The numbers of malarial casualties amongst the infantry serving in the Jordan valley at this time are difficult to ascertain. For example, casualty and sickness rates are not given in the 38th and 39th war diaries, and the numbers contained in the definitive *Statistics of the Military Effort of the British Empire during the Great War 1914–1920* (War Office, London 1922), summarise them within the figures for the British Army in Egypt and Palestine as a whole. Some figures have been found, however, for the 38th Battalion in Jabotinsky's book, where it is also noted that the two 'American' companies of the 39th were camped west of the Wadi and therefore suffered much less from malaria, and for the BWI Battalions in G.D. Howe's unpublished PhD thesis.[13]

Taking the figures for the 38th Battalion first, Jabotinsky stated that the battalion entered the valley (on or about 16 August) with 800 men, a figure that was reduced to 550 by the commencement of the advance (22 September), and to 150 by the time of the return to Ludd some two weeks later. In addition half of the battalion officers, some fifteen in total, had also been affected by the disease. Since only twenty officers and men were battle casualties, these figures indicate that malaria affected 645 officers and men, or just over 80 per cent of the total employed.[14] The position regarding the BWI however was even worse, according to the numbers extracted by Howe from the war diary of the BWI. These showed that, out of a total of 2,340 officers and men who were posted to the Jordan Valley, only 500 returned fit, including those that had less severe symptoms of, or had recovered from, a bout of malaria. In total it was reckoned that nearly 90 per cent of the BWI had contracted malaria during this deployment. Incidentally, Howe's thesis also contains details of their exposure to sand fly fever (206 cases between 27 July and 31 August), preceded by an outbreak of Spanish flu that affected some 700 men.[15]

To set the figures for both the Jewish and West Indian Battalions in context, it is worth looking at the compilation of statistics available in a volume of the *Medical History of the War*, originally published in 1931. Chapter xiv deals with British and Dominion casualties in Egypt and Palestine 1915–1918, and contains the following remarks within its introduction: 'The average annual sick ratio per 1,000 for other ranks in Egypt and Palestine during the war was 750.40, which compares very favourably with the post-war rates of 741.8 and 682.3 in 1921 and 1922 respectively.'[16]

It can therefore be asserted that the sickness rates for the battalions in the Jordan Valley were between 5 and 10 per cent greater than the average for the British and Dominion troops in the EEF as a whole. Further support for the relevance of the high incidence of malaria is also forthcoming from the same source. Statistics taken from the records of admission to hospital for treatment of malaria, show that in 1916 there were 1,423 cases, 8,480 in 1917 and 30,241 in 1918. According to the accompanying remarks: 'The increase of malaria cases in 1918 is due to the severe infection suffered by the troops operating in malarious areas during the advance and final operations against the Turks.'[17]

It would seem therefore that the Jewish soldiers were not disproportionately affected when compared to the troops of the BWI regiment, and that the opposite may well have been the case.

Finally, and notwithstanding Patterson's distrust of the General Staff, Wavell's account includes the assertion that Allenby had, in fact, planned to avoid the placing of troops in the Jordan Valley during the height of summer altogether. The means of achieving this were demonstrated in late April, when Allenby's forces crossed the Jordan at the Umm esh Shert ford, and captured the town of Es Salt. The occupation of this communications centre would have allowed Allenby to base troops in the surrounding area, with the same strategic effect and in a far healthier climate. Unfortunately, the Turks responded fiercely to the attack and the British and Imperial forces were forced back across the Jordan late on 4 May. To justify the object of this attack, Wavell noted that the military handbook covering Palestine remarked upon the Jordan valley in the following terms: 'Nothing is known of the climate in summer time, since no civilised human being has yet been found to spend summer there.'[18] A contrary view has been put forward by Hughes who, as mentioned in the previous chapter, has criticised the raids on Es Salt as a sop to Lloyd George and a demonstration of a lack of strategic direction.[19] Hughes does, however, acknowledge that Allenby had a need to secure his eastern flank on the Jordan and, with no other evidence available from Allenby's papers or the War Office records an exact understanding of the strategy behind these raids is impossible. Given Wavell's position as a staff officer to Allenby it is also possible that the reasoning he gives may have been influenced by their relationship. As far as this research is concerned Allenby's intentions seem consistent with the EEF's recognition and handling of the malaria problem, and the acknowledged requirement to secure the Jordan front in preparation for the coastal assault.

Returning to the preparations being made prior to the commencement of the advance of Chaytor's force on 17 September, the Jewish soldiers of the 38th Battalion undertook a number of patrols for reconnaissance and intelligence. It should be remembered that Patterson's men were at the northern end of Allenby's eastern front, with the head of the Wadi forming a salient with Turkish soldiers present on three sides. Chaytor's force objectives were the tying down of Turkish forces in the east and the taking of Umm esh Shert ford, followed by an advance to Amman via Es Salt, thus recapturing the ground lost in late spring. The patrolling activity of the 38th therefore involved movement north out of the Wadi Mellaha towards the river Jordan and the ford at Umm esh Shert.

Both Jabotinsky and Patterson describe in detail the nature of these patrols, and comment on the usefulness of their men, particularly ex-muleteers, who used their knowledge of Turkish to trick and capture enemy sentries for interrogation. Such patrols took place against a background of frequent Turkish shelling which caused casualties. The first fatality was Sergeant Levy, an English Jew who had transferred from the 20th London Regiment and who was shot dead in an ambush whilst scouting with Lieutenant Mendes on 27 August. The following day his body was recovered by a member of another patrol, Private Sepiashvili, a Georgian Jew, but this patrol also came under fire and Private Marks was hit, being carried back to camp by Private J. Gordon, where he later died from his wounds. Both Privates Sepiashvili and Gordon were decorated with the Military Medal for their gallantry. The third and final fatality of this preparatory stage was Private S. Greyman, who was shot in the head whilst exchanging fire with Turkish snipers who had approached the 38th's camp, on 16 September, the Day of Atonement. Patterson remarked upon the irony and sadness of this particular casualty:

> One of the ten men who, at Helmieh, had wished to join a Labour Battalion, but who, on reconsideration, had seen that it was his duty to remain as a fighting soldier, was Private Greyman. He was a man who disapproved of all forms of violence. He hated war and all the brutalities pertaining thereto, yet he carried out his military duties most conscientiously.[20]

Events now moved rapidly as the date of the advance of Chaytor's Force approached. The previously mentioned two companies of the 39th Battalion had now been joined by the remainder under Major Hopkin MC, a barrister in civilian life who had been decorated whilst serving in France with the Royal Welsh Fusiliers. Like the majority of the 39th's officers, he was a Gentile, and later a Labour Member of Parliament. A fellow officer recalled Hopkin's background and his links with British Jewry, through Redcliffe Salaman:

> I surmise that from a humble family background he had with the aid of scholarships and through excellence at games, distinguished himself at University and had been engaged by Redcliffe as a Tutor to his young sons. He therefore had a good acquaintance with Judaism, Zionism and Jews in general, because Redcliffe had made it a practice to entertain in his home at Royston, not only Jews of distinction, who happened to visit Cambridge, but also Jewish undergraduates.[21]

Given the above, it is no great surprise that Hopkin volunteered for the Jewish Battalions, and served amongst those middle-class intellectuals with whom he had socialised before the war.

Returning to the deployment of the 39th, Major Hopkin's detachment encamped at the Auja River, behind the 38th, on 14 September, leaving behind in Egypt a small number of Palestinian members of the battalion and, although no mention of this fact is made in surviving official records, it is important to mention that none of the Palestinians in this or the 40th Battalion were permitted to leave Egypt prior to the armistice with Turkey at the end of October 1918.

At the commencement of the battle, therefore, one Jewish Battalion was at the front and one in reserve. The advance of Chaytor's force and the seizure of its objectives relied on the moves of his immediate opponent, the Turkish Fourth Army. The basic idea behind Allenby's plan for this sector was that the Fourth Army would be compelled to retreat to the north as the main thrust proceeded up the coast to the west. Initially, this meant that Chaytor's force was faced with an unmoving enemy for three days, and activity was limited to demonstrations along the front. These probes, supported by artillery, had the effect of unsettling the Turkish defenders, who began to withdraw on the 22nd, following their realisation of the massive attack on their comrades near the coast. Unfortunately for the Turks this delay had not only played into Chaytor's hands, but had allowed the Arab forces of Prince Feisal to disrupt railway communications and to place themselves in way of Deraa, thus threatening their line of retreat.

The 38th played its full part in mounting these demonstrations on every one of the four nights involved (18–21 September inclusive). Patterson's men probed harder each night, provoking an increasing response from the Turkish positions, including artillery and machine gun fire that caused some wounds but no fatalities. On the night of the 20th, however, firmer resistance was encountered, prompting Patterson to commence a heavy mortar barrage against the Turkish positions by employing No. 6 Trench Mortar battery RA. Over the subsequent forty-eight hours, Turkish resistance weakened so that Patterson was able to inform Chaytor that the 38th were now in a position to take the ford:

> I galloped off as dawn was breaking, scrambled up the cliffs and across the ground from which the Turks had fled, and arrived in time to go down with Major Neill, Captain Julian and Lieutenants Jabotinsky and Cross, to take possession of the coveted passage across the Jordan.[22]

Patterson was accompanied by his batman, Private Philip Bratt, who had emigrated to London from Poland in 1914 at the age of 16. He was demobilised in 1919 and returned to Bethnal Green, where he lived until his death in 1975. Although unable to remain in Palestine himself, his son and family took up permanent residence in Israel after the Second World War.[23]

By the morning of the 23rd, Jabotinsky and his company had dug in around the ford, and it was soon crossed by the mounted troops of the 1st Australian Light Horse Brigade, *en route* to Es Salt. In order to consolidate their position, a reconnaissance patrol from the 38th was sent out, under the battalion's Irish transport officer Captain Julian and the Anglo-Jewish Lieutenant Cross, towards the woods to the north and east of the river. Unfortunately, this patrol was ambushed, and Private S. Mildemer was killed and both officers wounded. Lt. Cross was taken prisoner but Captain Julian was rescued from the field by Lance-Corporal M. Elfman, who later received the Military Medal in recognition of his bravery under fire. A reinforced company of the 38th was sent to the scene of the ambush, but the Turks had gone and Private Mildemer was buried with due ceremony and honour.

Meanwhile, the 39th Battalion had moved up the Wadi Mellala, in support of the 38th and, on the afternoon of the 22nd, received the attention of both Turkish artillery and a lone German aircraft for its troubles. One casualty of the aerial bombing was Maurice Gordon, who was wounded in the leg. The 39th was then moved up to Es Salt, via the Jordan River crossing to the south of Umm esh Shert at Ghoranijeh, whilst the 38th held the ford and acted as rearguard to the continuing advance of Chaytor's command. On 22 September Chaytor placed both battalions under the command of Patterson, and designated this new formation 'Patterson's Column'.

For the 38th, their rearguard activity involved a great deal of marching and countermarching in very hot and arduous conditions, between the Jordan river and Es Salt, and beyond on the road to Amman. Ralph Share, a Jewish soldier from the North of England who had transferred to the 38th from the Yorkshire Imperial Infantry, was one of those who did not complete the march. According to his testimonial 'Contracted malaria just three miles before Es Salt after gruelling forced march from Wadi Aujah'.[24] Fortunately, Private Share recovered and returned to the regiment, completing his service on demobilisation in June 1920. A soldier who did complete the march to Es Salt was Lance Corporal Yehuda Furst who, under the anglicised name of Harry First, had played, as described earlier, a significant role in assisting Jabotinsky to raise the Legion in Whitehall and Whitechapel. He died shortly before the Avichail testimonies were compiled, so the following résumé of his life was completed by his family, who were obviously keen to assert his Zionism and close association with Jabotinsky:[25]

> Born in Russia and came to Palestine with the second Aliyah. Was in England at the outbreak of World War 1 and became Jabotinsky's chief lieutenant in the campaign for a Jewish Legion. When 38th Bn Royal Fusiliers was formed he was among the first recruits. Participated in the march to Es Salt, Transjordan. Served with the Sanitary Squad in Jerusalem and on demobilisation returned to Great Britain, making his home in Glasgow. Was very active in ranks of Poale Zion. Untimely death [30th December 1956] disrupted plan to settle in Israel. Body re-interred in Avichail.[26]

By 1 October the 38th Battalion had been relieved, and Patterson's column had been disbanded as a formation. The headquarters of the 38th Battalion were relocated to Jerusalem. Meanwhile, the 39th had continued to garrison Es Salt until it too was relieved on 1 October, when they escorted about 1,500 Turkish prisoners to the rear. This duty was recalled by Lieutenant Arthur Cowen, an Anglo-Jewish officer from Northumberland, who transferred to the 39th after seeing service in France with the Northumberland Fusiliers:

> served all though the campaign helping to push Turks & Germans out of Palestine. Finished at Es Salt, helped to capture German troops (Wurtembergers) & led 700 back to Jerusalem as prisoners of war, with men of B Coy. Jewish Regiment.[27]

Lance Corporal (later Sergeant) Samuel Dratch of 'C' Coy, who had been one of the advance scouts of the 39th Battalion, also 'helped to escort Turkish prisoners and German officers' to captivity in the rear. Like Yehuda Furst:

> In Jerusalem I was attached to the 123rd Sanitary Section as an Inspector, and in this capacity I had access to all religious places. When Justice Brandeis, Chaim Weizmann and Chief Rabbi Gock came to Jerusalem I was in the guard of honor.

Sergeant Dratch returned to his home in New York in December 1919, and wrote at the end of his testimonial:

> I served in the Legion for one year and 10 months and consider it an honor to have been priviledged [sic] to have had some small part in the initial ground work towards the establishment of a Jewish homeland.[28]

The participation of the Jewish Battalions in the battle of Megiddo earned the Royal Fusiliers the battle honours 'Megiddo' and 'Nablus', and contributed to the considerable success achieved by Chaytor's force. All of Chaytor's objectives were reached at small cost, with 139 fatalities out of an approximate total of 15,000 troops engaged, and the 38th and 39th had fulfilled their orders to the satisfaction of the Commander-in-Chief, who acknowledged their efforts in his cables and reports to the War Office.[29] That Allenby and his staff made no public statement in Palestine and Egypt regarding the performance of the Jewish Battalions upset Patterson, Jabotinsky and others. Again, from the Legion's point of view this seemed like deliberate slight on the part of the authorities, who had publicly lauded the Arab contribution to the twin advances to Amman and Damascus. As with retaining the Palestinian volunteers in Egypt, it indicated a desire to keep the profile of Jewish troops as low as possible, whilst conforming to the pro-Zionist policy of the British Government.

The duties (guarding POWs and lines of communication) that were allocated to Patterson and his men, following the conclusion of fighting, offered no respite from the effects of the summer spent in the Jordan valley, and deepened Patterson's exasperation with the staff of the EEF. It will be recalled that the 38th Battalion had, by the time it reached the encampment at Ludd, been reduced to a fit strength of about 160 officers and men, having commenced the campaign in the Jordan with a total strength of nearly 900. Patterson was infuriated by seeing his men having to spend the night of their arrival at camp, in the open, on rain-sodden ground. To add insult to injury, it was about this time that Allenby's General Staff contacted Patterson's GOC, Major-General Chaytor, to voice their displeasure at Patterson's earlier, direct contact with London (General Macready and the welfare committee of the Jewish Battalions), with regard to the provision of Jewish hospital facilities in Jerusalem. At the same time, the 38th lost the services of its Medical Officer, Captain Davis, through sickness, and a permanent replacement was not available for almost a year. In the meanwhile, Capt. Redcliffe Salaman, who had arrived with the 39th Battalion, ably attended to Patterson's men.[30]

The militarily active part of the service of the Jewish Battalions was now at an end, but the four months that had passed since the initial frontline deployment of the 38th on 12 June had not been without further incident. Additional arrivals of Jewish soldiers, mainly recruited in the USA, from the depot in Britain, and their training alongside their Palestinian comrades continued throughout this period. The two 'American' companies of the 39th deployed to the front, where they were soon joined by the remainder of the battalion, except – as noted earlier – for the Palestinian recruits, who were left behind at Helmieh. Before this movement took place the Palestinians, who were obviously concerned about the effect on their home communities in northern Palestine of Allenby's forthcoming offensive and the Turkish response, consulted their commanders through the Regimental Council. They proposed that their local knowledge be used by the British to prepare the Jewish communities for defence against the retreating Turks, and to provide guides for the offensive. At the same time, it should be remembered that the British high command had already established an intelligence network through Aaron Aaronson and the Nili organisation, and such division seriously reduced the influence and effectiveness of the Regimental Council's intentions. Gilner's account of this episode, beginning with the selection of legionnaires for the organisation of local defence and guiding for the EEF, is concise and to the point:

> Noah Sunin, Saul Kerbel and Hayim Feinberg were chosen on behalf of Hashomer; Eliahu Kamenetzky, Zvi Rabin and Nahum Gelman represented the Herzlia High School alumni. The nature of these appointments required secrecy and the secrecy aroused suspicion. But the Council still thought in terms of factions rather than in terms of an unified army ... The Council suggested that there should be no contact between the chosen men and Aaronson, but GHQ turned this down. The result was that no contact was established with the Jews of the Galilee at that time; and for the guides to the north Aaronson chose only Zvi Rabin from the appointed group.[31]

It is difficult to predict what might have been the effect upon the Palestinian members of the Jewish Legion had they succeeded in gaining greater, official endorsement for their proposed activities. The fact remains that the local British military administration chose to rely on its relationship with Aaronson, and to deny the Palestinians the opportunity to serve with the EEF in Palestine. Before the consequences of this restriction are examined, however, it is necessary to provide further context noting the experiences of the Jewish soldiers who were still arriving in Egypt from America, Britain and Palestine for the completion of their training. In this respect, the recollections and letters of Major Myer and Private Izaak Ben-Zvi are useful in portraying the day-to-day existence of the Legion as seen from two very different cultural, personal and political viewpoints.

Henry Myer, as second-in-command to Lt.-Col. Samuel, saw off many reinforcements from the depot at Plymouth, before embarking himself with the 40th on 16 August 1918. He recalled some of his more notable charges from amongst the volunteer contingents from America, in somewhat forthright manner:

> One of the later contingents from America brought, among others, Joseph L. Cohen, David Ben-Gurion, Isaac Ben-Zvi and Dov Hos. Of all these, unquestionably Ben-Gurion was the most thrusting. He constituted himself the prime agitator, leader, demagogue, advocate, preacher and mouth-piece for and of nationalistic militarism.[32]

Following arrival in Egypt on 29 August, camp was established at the site of Tel-el-Kebir, after which Myer was sent with the adjutant, Captain

196 *The Jewish Legion and the First World War*

Hodgson (a Gentile and, according to Myer, an excellent administrator) to Cairo in order to purchase equipment for the battalion. On 1 September the opportunity was taken to visit Major Hopkin and his detachment of the 39th at Helmieh, which he described as follows:

> we walked to Helmieh where we saw the detachment of our Regiment, recruited for the most part in Palestine and also in Egypt. Some of them are Jews who have been recruited as prisoners from the Turks ... I believe they are turning out well. The main difficulty with the Regiment is the language question. As far as I can see the only solution is for all ranks to learn Hebrew and for all the words of command to be given in English. ... I am utterly and hopelessly ignorant of it [Hebrew] at present and I can see much hard work ahead if I am to become at all proficient.[33]

This solution was to be put to the test after the Palestinian element of the 39th joined the 40th on 19 September, heralding the complete formation of the 40th as the 'Palestinian' Battalion. When this process was eventually completed in November, the war diary of the 40th recorded that the battalion had grown to five companies. A, B and C companies were Palestinian, E was HQ and company D was used for those who were under-aged and Palestinian recruits. Myer's continuing remarks and observations regarding his Palestinian charges are reminiscent of Patterson's view of the differences between the Alexandrian Jews and the Russian Jews who served in the Zion Mule Corps. On 26 September he wrote:

> I'd like to see something of Palestine ... Parts must be pretty good otherwise they would not have produced the splendid types that are to be found amongst the Palestine Detachment here. They compare favourably with the average Anglicised-East-End-Jew and vastly excel the Cairenes and Alexandrines who are not of a very high order of intelligence or physical development. The agricultural life of the Colonists has made them hardy and strong and much more amenable to discipline than other Jews with whom I have been brought into contact ... I think they are worthy representatives of the race.[34]

These comments reveal the values of a professional, British middle-class Jew brought up in an imperial age, and reflect western society's exultation of the pioneer or 'frontier' spirit. Myer, a metropolitan type to his fingertips, felt an affinity with the 'Colonists' that he did not share with the working-class conscripts from Hackney and Whitechapel, despite sympathy for his co-religionists and Zionism. In the complex ethical geography of the time, agricultural labour on the 'frontier' could be assimilated to the core values of the professional middle class; sweatshop labour in the East End could not.

Social differences notwithstanding, the British Army imposed its training regime on the Jewish Battalions in Egypt. Both Myer and Ben-Zvi mention the daily routine in letters written, coincidentally, on the same day, 6 September 1918. Myer wrote: 'I rise at any time between 4.30 and 5 a.m. and am busy at work with the exception of an hour, which I usually manage to keep free for slacking after lunch, until dinner time in the evening.'[35]

Writing to his wife Rahel in Palestine, Ben-Zvi first attested to his safe arrival at Tel-el-Kebir where:

> We are living in tents. The 40th Battalion which now has about 1400 men, among them 800 Americans ... In general the per centage of Poalei Zion is the determining one in relation to the number of the 'non-affiliated'. In absolute terms, there must be about 200 ... The vast majority belong to no party at all ... there is a great difference between the Americans, all of whom are volunteers, and the English, most of whom are doing compulsory military service ... the English who are with us, however, are influenced considerably by the Americans.[36]

Something may have been lost in translation, but it seems curious that Ben-Zvi should have referred to the soldiers from Britain, the majority of Russian background or indeed nationality, as 'English'. Nevertheless there is no escaping his main point about the commitment to Zionism and the element of politicisation present amongst the American volunteers, something that gave both Ben-Zvi and Ben-Gurion much encouragement in their contemplation of the future of Palestine. For example, Ben-Zvi went on to say that it was important to put together a social and cultural programme for the evenings. In this he was particularly referring to the popularity (in America) of the Legion and the consequently broad range of background and education of the men attracted to it. In what can only be described as a politician's remark, he expressed the view that if the energies and talents of 'those men of social awareness and public conscience do not gain the upper hand, other forces will,' implying that the opponents of Poale Zion had to be forestalled.

Major Myer had no such political machination in mind. Organising the camp and training programme were his main concerns, including the efforts he had to make in selecting a concert party from amongst the many volunteers with their various talents, and how proud he was of the Magen David flag, made by his fiancé, which now flew alongside the Union Flag outside his headquarters. This flag, which also flew at the training depot in Canada, consisted of a light blue Star of David (Magen David) on a white background, with one light blue horizontal stripe above and one below the emblem, later becoming the national flag of the independent state of Israel.

Henry Myer was accompanied to Palestine by his batman, Harry Freeman, whose story is evidenced, in addition to Myer's own recollections, by his Avichail testimonial and an interview with the author in 1987. At interview and in his testimonial, Harry Freeman stated that his father was a Yiddish-speaking Lithuanian Jew who came to Britain in 1889, settling in London, where Harry was born on 11 November 1899. His father needed to look for work in 1904 and found employment in the coalfields of South Wales, to where the whole family moved. Harry was conscripted into the 4th Royal Welsh Fusiliers, his local infantry regiment, at the end of 1917, later responding to the appeal for volunteers for the Jewish Battalions. Harry was very proud of his boxing skills and of his later promotion to sergeant as a drill and musketry instructor, but the former was more important to him, as he considered 'My Israeli comrades will probably recall me as a Boxing instructor when in Tel el Kebir.'[37] Other memories were less pleasant and involved the poor food and water leading to the constant presence of disease.[38] This evidence gives some idea of camp life for the soldiers of the Legion after the cessation of hostilities, their active service behind them.

In conclusion, the period covered by this chapter saw the trained soldiers of the 38th and 39th Battalions participate in their only major battle of the war. The Jewish soldiers achieved their objectives and did all that was required by their commanders. Their gallantry led to the award of a DSO to Major Neill, the Military Cross to Captains Brown and Leadley, Lieutenants Flingelstone, Cameron (with bar) and Bullock (with bar). A DCM was awarded to CSM Plant with the Military Medal going to Corporal Bloom, Lance-Corporal Elfman and Privates Angel and Robinson. In addition there were eight awards of Mentioned in Despatches. General Chaytor presented the decorations after the battalion had moved to Rafa. The price that the Legion paid, six killed in action, twenty-six dying as a result of wounds or disease and four wounded in action, reflected

Figure 8.1 Platoon of 'A' Company 38th at Giza, 1918

the relatively small scale of the engagement. Battle casualties were trifling when compared to losses due to disease.

This chapter has also shown that the Jewish units performed well against what Patterson and his fellow commanders maintained was a continuing background of prejudice on the part of some Staff Officers at EEF HQ. Their force commander, General Chaytor, fully appreciated their military contribution to the battle of Megiddo, and later expressed his feelings in a letter to Patterson:

> So few people have heard of the Battalion's good work, or of the very remarkable fact that in the operations that we hope have finally reopened Palestine to the Jews, a Jewish force was fighting on the Jordan, within a short distance of where their forefathers, under Joshua, first crossed into Palestine, and all who hear about it are anxious to hear more ... The way you smashed up the Turkish rearguard when it tried to counter-attack across the Jordan made our subsequent advance up the hills of Moab an easy matter.[39]

The alleged discrimination has been difficult to prove beyond question, but the circulation of the *Protocols of the Elders of Zion* and the

200 *The Jewish Legion and the First World War*

refusal to pay public tribute to the Legion support the existence of anti-Semitism. It can be argued that prejudice is often hard to detect because it involves a lived relationship rather than, say, a set of written and obviously discriminatory rules. In this respect it is important to note the strength of feeling amongst the legionnaires, as recorded in their testimonials and represented by their own commanders.

The armistice with Turkey saw the Legion preparing for the post-war period and the early years of the British Mandate in Palestine, with newly trained soldiers and recruits still arriving from Britain and the recruiting camps in Palestine. It now remains to examine this final part of the Jewish Legion's history from November 1918 until May 1921; a period involving demobilisation, re-organisation, riot and disbandment.

9
Disturbance and Decline

On 11 November 1918, Lieutenant Vladimir Jabotinsky wrote a reply to a letter he had received from Leo Amery, then political secretary to the War Cabinet, celebrating the end of the military campaign against the Turks. Jabotinsky opened his note with remarks concerning the Britishness of the victory in Palestine. The fact that the Legion had large numbers of 'Americans' was also credited to 'British magnetism', an assertion that does not take into account the independent actions of the Zionist Jews in the United States. This lack of understanding may have been due to his limited contact with the American volunteers, the early drafts of whom arrived in the 39th Battalion whilst he was at the front with the 38th. On the other hand it also demonstrates his pro-British attitude, especially as he appreciated that Britain, notwithstanding the vicissitudes caused by the local military, had, through the Balfour Declaration and victory, placed itself in a very strong and influential position regarding the future of the Jews in Palestine.

Jabotinsky then explained what he considered lay behind 'British magnetism', and attributed it, and the creation of the Jewish Legion, to Lloyd George and his 'young secretariate [sic]', including Amery and Sir Mark Sykes. He then informed Amery:

> Do not think that I am trying to pay compliments. I really think that the high moral pitch which has helped all the entente countries to keep their morale through difficult days was due to the influence of six or seven young politicians behind the scenes.[1]

The remainder of the letter concerns Jabotinsky's real purpose, which was to ask Leo Amery for his assistance in seeing that Lord Derby's pledge, with regard to name and badge, was honoured, and that Patterson be granted his brigade. As far as the former was concerned, he pointed out that the Legion's participation in the Battle of Megiddo had fulfilled Lord Derby's condition that these honours were to be earned. As for the brigade, it can be argued that Jabotinsky was keen to see a strengthened and more independent Legion firmly established in post-war Palestine; an idea in line with his concept of Jewish self-defence. Jabotinsky's keenness to achieve this was evidenced by the following strongly worded passage in his letter to Amery:

> The formation of the brigade has been delayed, and there are some unknown forces working against Col. Patterson ... If you can straighten things and get justice for him and place him in the post which is his creation even much more than of any of the Jewish initiators, do it.[2]

Leo Amery's response was swift. He wrote to the Adjutant-General (Major-General Macdonogh) on 4 December, and reminded him that he (Amery), had been present at the meeting at which Lord Derby had agreed to Amery's compromise suggestion that the name and badge be earned 'by good service in the field'. The question of the raising of a full brigade was not addressed so definitely, as this would depend upon post-war policy with regard to garrison and recruiting arrangements.[3]

During December 1918 Macdonogh had his staff research the matter so that he could prepare a reply to Amery. This research was summarised in a two-page minute submitted on 13 December and signed by Lt-Col. C.G. Liddell, an Assistant-Adjutant General (AAG) at the War Office. The minute summarises the gestation of the Jewish Battalions and correctly states: 'As a compromise it was decided to raise Battalions of the Royal Fusiliers and organise these especially for the reception of Jews.'[4] Col. Liddell goes on to confirm the current status of the battalions and refers, interestingly to 'a proposal on War Office paper 212/Mediteranean [sic] /3764 to form them into a Brigade'. Unfortunately no trace of this paper has been discovered, but a later handwritten minute has been found that adds some substance to this remark. The minute, written by Major O.C Williams of the Adjutant-General's staff, on 3 January 1919 contains the following statement: 'The policy, subject to financial approval, is to form a Jewish Bde of 3 Battalions *now*, and to include 1 Jewish *Battalion* in the ultimate post-war garrison.'[5]

Subsequent events, however, would suggest that this was but one of many different proposals relating to the post-war organisation of the army, although the fact that the War Office was contemplating the formation of a Jewish Brigade contrasts with the rejection of the idea prior to the battle of Megiddo. This change of approach may well have come about due to considerations of demobilisation and the need to replace British and Indian troops who had been in the Middle East theatre for some time. Returning to Colonel Liddell, his final recommendation to his superiors was to do nothing:

> At present the Battalions are largely filled with American Jews whom we can hardly expect to attract later, and our experience of the English Jews is, that whilst those who are over Military age are enthusiastic, those who are eligible for service, either do not share this enthusiasm, or prefer to enlist into other Regiments.
>
> We think the question as to the formation of a Jewish Regiment should stand over until the general policy regarding the post-bellum Army has been decided, just as the question of the conversion of the London Regiment into a Corps is being held over.[6]

Colonel Liddell's submission made the logical point that, in order to sustain a Jewish Regiment, the source of post-war recruits needed to be clarified. Whilst rightly noting that reliance could not be placed on further American recruitment, he appears not to have taken into account the existence of the Palestinian element that had already been active in the Legion for nearly six months. This omission prompts the question as to whether or not the War Office, despite its agreement to local recruitment, had already discounted the role of Palestinian recruits.

Major General Macdonogh accepted his brief and responded to Amery on 17 January 1919. This elicited a prompt reply from Amery, on 25 January. Amery corrected Macdonogh's version of events surrounding the various deputations and counter-deputations that were received by Lord Derby:

> But there was after that a third deputation which appealed very strongly for a distinctive name ... He [Derby] sent away the deputation, without satisfying them, but afterwards on my representations and *after a short talk with your predecessor* [my italics; M.W.] (Macready) agreed that he would hold out to them the hope of earning both a distinctive name and badge if they did well in the

field. This was incorporated in the official version of the interview with the deputation which appeared next day.[7]

At the end of the typescript Amery added, in fountain pen, 'It was a very distinct pledge', thus emphasising the force of his argument. Amery's remarks concerning the post-war situation included the fact that he could see no reason why a name and badge could not be given on a 'pro-tem' basis, and quoted the Imperial titles that had been used for temporary regiments in the Boer War. At the end of this particular passage he also stated that the unit may be transferred 'to whatever local unit of Volunteers may be raised under the British Protectorate after the war'. There could therefore have been no doubt, in Amery's mind that, at this early stage (in terms of the post-war treaty negotiations), Britain was certain to become the mandatory power in Palestine. Finally, Amery advised Macdonogh that he did not consider that the Jewish Battalions had a role in the regular British Army, unless they were linked to other units that recruited locally and concluded: 'In that case the Regiment might be useful as a means of settling British minded and militarily trained Jews in Palestine.'[8]

The portent of this conclusion will become evident in the latter part of this chapter; what effect such a sentiment had upon the War Office is unknown. After the cessation of hostilities with Turkey the British authorities, both in Whitehall and in the Middle East, had to consider and deal with such issues as the military and civil administration of the occupied territories, logistics and the protection of lines of communication, prisoners of war and demobilisation. By examining the deployment and experience of the Jewish Legion, it is possible to see how the policy of the British government and of the military administration of Palestine affected its operations, and vice versa.

At the time of the armistice with Turkey, some of the Jewish volunteers from America were still receiving their initial training in Newfoundland. The war diary of the 39th Battalion shows that the last draft from Britain, consisting of 541 men, arrived in Palestine on 6 January 1919. Members of these later groups (see Figures 9.1 and 9.2 depicting American volunteers) could look forward, in most cases, to a military career of less than eighteen months before demobilisation. By the time the last groups arrived from Britain, the legionnaires had been reorganised around their initial post-war duties. The war diaries and the official manpower statistics[9] confirm the dispositions shown in Table 9.1.

Table 9.1: Disposition October 1918

Battalion	Location/activity	Officers	NCOs/ORs	Total
38th	Ludd, garrison	32	999	1031
39th	Ludd, garrison	38	995	1033
40th	Tel el Kebir, training camp	30	1413	1443
42nd	UK depot	46	1676	1722
Totals		146	5083	5229

One important feature of this deployment was that, since none of the Legion's units had taken part in the advance after Megiddo into Galilee, they had no presence in the northern part of Palestine. Whilst this caused some discontent, because Arab forces had been allowed into Damascus, the continued encampment of the 40th Battalion in Egypt gave Jabotinsky and others further cause for annoyance over the behaviour of the local General Staff. By now the 40th Battalion mainly consisted of volunteers from America and Palestinian recruits, both of which groups were desperate for a promise of service in Palestine to be honoured. These feelings were heightened when a small draft of seventy-one soldiers, consisting of older men, was sent to the 38th Battalion at Ludd in Palestine, leaving the vast majority of Palestinians behind. Gilner has described what happened when, due to this treatment, the Palestinians threatened to strike, a protest that was taken up by their families:

> Eliahu Golomb, Dov Hos, Ben-Gurion and Ben-Zvi conferred with Colonel Samuel, who sympathised with them but apparently was not strong enough to overcome the obduracy of General Headquarters ... Meanwhile in Palestine, mothers of volunteers ... decided to take action ... Impervious to representations from men, Allenby was amenable to the pleas of women. Two weeks later, the Palestinian and American 40th Royal Fusiliers were on their way to Palestine.[10]

The bringing together of the three battalions in Palestine came as a result of the general redeployment of the EEF. War Office records released after Gilner published allow for an examination of some of the relevant cables exchanged between GHQ and Whitehall. This exchange was initiated by a message to London, marked 'Secret', sent from GHQ Egypt, on 20 November 1918. It is quoted here in full as it

Figure 9.1 Private Aaron Gitelson, 1919

Figure 9.2 Private Aaron Gitelson and comrades, 1919

also neatly summarises the organisation of the battalions, following the movements mentioned above:

> The following is situation as regards Jewish Battalions. 40th Battalion R.W.F. [*sic*] has been converted into Palestinian (?) Battalion retaining its staff and 500 of its men who originally came from Palestine. Its strength is being completed by Palestinians who were enlisted locally. We have transferred remaining men who came out with 40th Battalion to 38 and 39th Battalions. There are 100 ex-prisoners of war and 150 men who enlisted in Cairo and Alexandria whom it was proposed to utilize to form Labour Companies. I recommend that they be discharged as they speak many different languages and are not suitable for inclusion in Battalions. Do you concur. After the war what is to be the policy (?) re Jewish Battalions.[11]

This cable was sent in response to an original enquiry by the War Office, and it is interesting to note the mis-spelling of the regimental name, RWF being the abbreviation for the Royal Welsh Fusiliers, and the apparent uncertainty over the Palestinian description. Such errors and uncertainties provide a further indication of the general administrative confusion that continued to surround the Legion, which was exacerbated by the dislocation caused by demobilisation. The cable itself contains a handwritten annotation concurring with Allenby's recommendation to discharge the misfits, a decision which was telegraphed to Allenby on 24 November, along with a commitment that he would be 'informed as soon as the policy re Jewish Battalions is decided'.[12] In fact, this policy was not decided upon for several months.

After the end of hostilities with Turkey, Palestine became Occupied Enemy Territory Administration (OETA) South, under the local command of Major-General Sir Arthur Money, with overall responsibility falling to Allenby as commander-in-chief. According to Wavell, his biographer, Allenby's policy was to ensure that the administration of Palestine was carried out in compliance with international law. This meant that 'no avoidable change in the existing laws and arrangements' could be made until a treaty had been reached, a principle that Allenby felt was threatened by Zionist pressure.[13] If, as Wavell asserts, this was the case, then it is easy to understand Allenby's irritation at the continuing presence of the Zionist Commission, and his enquiries to the War Office regarding the future of the Jewish Legion. Allenby's view did not coincide with the pro-Zionist policy of Lloyd George's government, founded on the Balfour Declaration, a situation that led to the dismissal of his political officer Colonel Meinertzhagen, who, in protest, had gone behind his back to the Foreign Office.

Allenby's difficulties were compounded by the liaison between the Zionist Commission and the British Government. These are well illustrated by messages exchanged between the War Office and Allenby's GHQ, the first of which, dated 28 November 1918, came from the director of military intelligence in Whitehall. This message was relayed on behalf of the Zionist organisation in Britain to the Zionist commission in Jerusalem, headed by Chaim Weizmann:

> Following from Eder to Weizmann: – 'We are submitting to Government definition of meaning of National Home ... Please explain Sykes and authorities that according to latest information Jewries of the world, especially America, whole-heartedly supporting British trusteeship; greatly disappointed moderation and timidity our demands. They rightly think that in new Arabo-Syrian State Arab national ambitions fully realized; Palestine ... placed under British trusteeship must form political administrative organism, where all opportunities should be afforded for ultimate

development of Jewish Commonwealth. Pan-Arab threats and appeals to violence ... will not intimidate Jews ... Legitimate interests of Palestinian peasantry always safeguarded by suzerain power and Jewish population.'[14]

Before relaying Weizmann's reply on 6 December, Allenby sent a strongly worded message to the War Office, refuting some of the statements made by the commission and seeking to acquaint his superiors with the facts on the ground as he saw them. In this message he requested that the statements be treated as confidential because Weizmann's public pronouncements, based on the moderate and timid demands of the commission, had already succeeded in arousing distrust and suspicion among the local non-Jewish populace, who wanted to maintain their position in Palestine. He was also concerned as to the accuracy of the assumption that the Arabs would be satisfied with a Syrian state, and noted that both Zionists and Arabs would now be adopting public positions in advance of the peace negotiations. This appreciation was followed by a warning that 'anti-Jewish action might be taken by Arabs', and the message ended with the following appraisal and recommendation:

> In Palestine non-Jews number approximately 573,000 as against 66,000 Jews ... consider it essential that Zionists should avoid increasing apprehension by indiscreet declarations of policy ... and laying them open to charge of securing their arms [aims?] by force. The Zionists [can?] realize their legitimate aspirations provided that they carry out their programme patiently and show sympathy for what is today a very large majority of Palestine's population. If they force the pace now ... insecure foundations will be the basis of whole structure.[15]

This message reveals that Allenby, whilst wishing to dampen Zionist enthusiasm, also recognised their 'legitimate aspirations', and used this telegram to convey to the War Office the threat to local peace that he felt would follow unbridled Zionist activity.

Allenby's interpretation, however, was certainly not shared by the Commission. Eder's reply to Weizmann, via the director of military intelligence, was unequivocal:

> the Commission would be very disappointed if our just demands in shaping of political future under British tutelage were timid

and moderate and urge that they be not abated ... The universal Zionist organisation under British trustees should receive definite guarantees of due share in control?(s)[sic], while rights of local population are safeguarded. We are convinced that you should not allow yourself to be intimidated by either the threats of Pan-Arabs here or their acts.[16]

Military routine within the Jewish Battalions continued, in spite of the political situation, and men were transferred between battalions in accordance with the deployment arranged by GHQ towards the end of the year. Ben-Zvi and Ben-Gurion were allowed leave to visit the Zionist Commission (to where Jabotinsky had already been seconded), and the 'Palestinians' were now in Palestine. Colonel Patterson objected to a large draft of 'Palestinians' who were received into the 38th as he regarded it as a dilution of his fully trained and experienced battalion, but to no avail. Other transfers had also or were about to take place, which meant that the 'Americans' became widely spread between the units, and the final large draft from Britain, consisting of 541 officers and men, and mainly American in origin, joined the 39th on 6 January 1919.

It is now time to examine the question of what was to be the post-war future of the Jewish Legion, within the context of demobilisation and the occupation of former enemy territory, and a political background dominated by British foreign policy and Zionism. The whole question of immediate post-war deployment and demobilisation was addressed in army orders published in February 1919. As far as armies of occupation were concerned, the introduction to Army Order 55, 1919, confirmed government policy that, whilst the Regular Army was being reconstructed:

> All those retained in the Armies of Occupation, or who may volunteer for such armies, may be called upon to serve in any corps or arm of the Service or in any of the Armies of Occupation. No soldier under the age of 20, however, will be required to serve elsewhere than in the Home Army or the Army of the Rhine.[17]

It has already been seen that there were a small number of volunteers from the Jewish Legion who transferred to other fronts, and a number of the American recruits also volunteered to participate in the army of occupation in Palestine, no doubt expecting to remain to build and protect their 'homeland'. It will be seen that the local authorities discouraged their presence, which led to indiscipline and disillusion with serious consequences for those affected.

At the time that this army order was being promulgated, Allenby's headquarters and the War Office were exchanging cables regarding the make-up of the army of occupation for Egypt and Palestine. The first cable in this series was sent from the War Office on 1 February, and listed thirteen Battalions of British infantry who were to be retained, including the 38th Battalion, Royal Fusiliers.[18] From the contents of the cables that are available in the archives, it appears that one possibility was that the 38th might be used as part of the British element in an Indian brigade in Egypt, a proposal which did not suit Allenby, as was made clear in his reply of 4 February:

> In my opinion 38th Battn. Royal Fusiliers is not suited to represent British troops in an Indian brigade as it is not sufficiently smart or efficient to uphold in the eyes of Indian Battalions the credit of British infantry. It is advisable that it should not be employed in Egypt but in Palestine. Therefore I suggest that Jewish Battalion be retained till their future is settled for employment on Lines of communication and that another Battalion be detailed to replace 38th.[19]

The inference of this cable is clear. Whilst GHQ did not want the Jewish Legion in Egypt, its employment in Palestine was certainly most desirable from its own point of view, and the War Office agreed to Allenby's suggestion.[20] It is notable in Allenby's message that, rather than give a positive reason concerning the desire of the Jewish Battalions to serve in Palestine, Allenby's reason is expressed in negative and discriminatory terms. Before this message was received in London, however, the War Office cabled Allenby:

> With concurrence of Foreign Office it has been agreed that one Jewish Battalion shall be included in the garrison of Palestine when latter definitely constituted. Meanwhile recruiting in Palestine of Jews should cease.[21]

This is the first indication of an intention to reduce the Jewish Legion to one Battalion, a process that would take some ten months to complete. It will be noted that the battalion referred to in this exchange of cables is the 38th, which originally consisted of soldiers who were either conscripts (both British Jews and friendly aliens enlisted under the terms of the Military Service Convention), or volunteers from Britain. As 1919 progressed, however, the drafting in of 'Palestinian' and 'American' recruits, who replaced the men lost through sickness, demobilisation and the general wear and tear, diluted the 38th. This change in character was to present Patterson with disciplinary problems, and thereby reinforce the views of those members of the local General Staff who wished to accelerate the disbandment of the Legion. This situation will be examined in more detail, as events in Egypt and the occupied territories unfold, but it is important to establish the ultimate direction of this policy, so that the fragmentary evidence provided by the remaining public records, testimonials and secondary sources can be seen in political context and administrative perspective.

Further cables exchanged between Allenby and the War Office continued to indicate that a policy of reduction and demobilisation was emerging. For example, the War Office informed Allenby that the 39th and 40th Battalions were to be reduced to cadres, with 'retainable personnel being posted to the 38th Battalion', although this decision was put on hold in May, thus delaying the final reduction of the three original battalions.[22] Nevertheless, some demobilisation occurred at a relatively early stage, as witnessed by Major Myer of the 40th Battalion and recorded in a diary entry dated 16 January 1919:

> We sent off today our first party to be demobilised. It consisted of what is known as 'Group 43'. They are the teachers and students ... The Colonel is in hopes of the Battalion being demobilised and we await news to this effect from GHQ ... We have now no role and so the sooner we are demobilised the better.[23]

The implications of Myer's views are clear. With the future of Palestine remaining unsettled, he believed the Palestinian volunteers would be better employed at home whilst awaiting the outcome of the peace negotiations.

Allenby himself made suggestions to rid his command of some of the Jewish troops, as evidenced in a cable to the War Office sent on 12 February:

> A number of men in 40th Palestinian Battalion, (?) Royal Fusiliers, own farms or have definite employment in this country to which they are anxious to return; it is important that they should. Recommend, therefore, that men having definite employment to go to be demobilized.[24]

No reply to this recommendation has been found but it is clear that, six months after urging the War Office to sanction the local recruitment of Jews in Palestine for the 40th Battalion, Allenby no longer required their services.

The situation facing Allenby in the immediate post-war period was completely different to that which existed prior to the final advance against the Turks. The tensions of the time, which were heightened by the prolonged nature of the peace negotiations in Paris, created a fragile situation in Egypt. It is interesting to note that whilst Allenby advised the British Government that 'President Wilson is blamed for rising in Egypt',[25] there was resentment in Egypt over British exploitation of local resources during the campaign against the Turks.[26] Thus, although there were more than sufficient military resources available to deal with disturbances in Egypt, including the presence of troops *en route* to Britain for demobilisation, continued British control was under threat. This situation became complicated by morale problems in the army caused by unsatisfied expectations of demobilisation.

The very military resources that GHQ had at its disposal to deal with the policing and administration of the region, at a time when local populations were seeking to assert their independence, were being undermined. Morale difficulties manifested themselves in the form of unrest and mutiny, in units of British, Indian and Imperial forces, in the Middle East and other theatres, and these have been well documented elsewhere.[27] A message sent by Allenby to the War Office succinctly summarised the state of mind of some of the forces under his command:

> It has been discovered that efforts are being made throughout the country [Egypt] to form a Soldiers Union. Men state that their contract ends 6 months after hostilities, i.e., 10th May. Endeavours are to be made after that date to make all troops refuse to work. A mass meeting of troops is intended at Alexandria. I must be in a position to tell troops certain dates when they can expect release on replacement by Army of Occupation soldiers. Especially my 1914–1915 men should go home quickly. Men want to know dates of sailing, capacity and number of ships. Commanding officers should be able to inform troops on which date they are likely to go. Telegraph fullest particulars.[28]

Colonel Patterson also recognised the significance of 10 May 1919, when he recalled: 'All through the early days of May I saw chalked up everywhere – on the Railway Station, signal boxes, workshops, on the engines, trucks and carriages – the mystic words, "Remember the 11th May."'[29] Fearing that this unrest might spread to his own men, Patterson spoke to each member of his battalion and was proud that 11 May passed without incident for the 38th. Back in Kantara, Egypt, mass mutiny and outbreaks of violence amongst British and Imperial troops occurred, with the authorities forced to adopt a pragmatic attitude in its resolution. The militant elements of the local population in Egypt added to the pressure on the British administration, which had taken its compliance during the war for granted.[30]

The 5,000 trained soldiers of the Jewish Legion comprised, according to Jabotinsky, approximately one-sixth of the forces available for army of occupation duties. With two months of mutinies and Arab unrest requiring the transfer of British and Indian troops from Palestine to Egypt, Jewish legionnaires were left to garrison parts of Palestine alone. For example, Patterson's memoirs recall that during March troops of the 38th Battalion, then based at Rafa, were sent to the Arab town of El Arish. Working in co-operation with aircraft of the Royal Air Force, men of the Legion, led by Captain Jaffe, succeeded in preventing Egyptian nationalists from causing trouble in the town. The success of this operation was a source of pride to Patterson who, in addition to commanding his battalion, was also the local area commander, and thereby relieved to be away from the petty discrimination experienced at their previous location.[31]

With Jewish troops now fulfilling an internal security role, it can be appreciated that Jabotinsky considered that this was the time to take advantage of the military administration's difficulties, and promote the expansion and prolonged employment of the Legion in Palestine.[32] Similar thinking lay behind Chaim Weizmann's communications with the Chief of the Imperial General Staff, Sir Henry Wilson, whom he met at the peace conference in Paris. In an undated letter written from the Zionist Delegation offices in Paris, Weizmann referred to 'our conversation of Saturday, March 29th' and enumerated three specific issues: demobilisation, housing and the purchasing of army stores and material. Weizmann remarked that he understood the Jewish soldiers could stay in Palestine, provided they volunteered to re-enlist after demobilisation. He added: 'As we [the Zionist Delegation] are desirous that a great number of these soldiers should settle definitely in Palestine we shall call for volunteers and submit the list of names to the Commander in Chief.'[33]

With regard to the housing question, Weizmann acknowledged that this was a critical problem that could be overcome if the commander in-chief would permit the Zionists:

> to import building material [so that] we could build several hundred houses on land belonging to us in Jerusalem and Jaffa ... We could also make preparations for the erection of several buildings on the University site.[34]

Weizmann's charm must have had some effect on Wilson, because he sent copies of the correspondence to the War Office and Allenby. In an extract of the covering letter he sent to the latter, Wilson mentioned that, subject to Allenby's approval, the housing and stores requirements were reasonable, but as far as re-enlistment was concerned:

> I do not quite know what the AG will say about enlisting Jewish soldiers only for service in Palestine ... and it seems to me that the simplest way will be for Weizmann to get all his Jews to settle in Palestine and then have them formed into a local corps of territorials or some such body for service in their own country. How does this smile on you?[35]

From this letter it can be seen that Wilson's understanding of the Balfour Declaration and government policy can be interpreted as meaning a truly national home for the Jews, as evidenced by his remark 'for service in their own country'. In his reply to the CIGS, Allenby was cautious and circumspect, perhaps in recognition of the distance between circumstances in Palestine and the peace conference in Paris, and between himself and his political masters. Allenby was also aware that a commission was to be sent to Palestine, to assist in determining the nature of the League of Nations mandate, and this allowed him to assert that no decision on Jewish immigration be made in the interim. As for the questions of re-enlistment and stores, he included the following remarks in his reply:

> the time has not come for the formation of a Jewish territorial corps, nor should Jewish soldiers be enlisted for service solely in Palestine. If Jewish soldiers now in Palestine wish to settle there and are suitable and desirable men I see no objection ... With regard to the purchasing of stores ... these things are sold in open market, and the Zionists have the same opportunity of buying as have others.[36]

The conciliatory tone of Allenby's correspondence with Wilson was inconsistent with the hostility shown towards the Jewish Legion, but Allenby soon revealed to the War Office his case against assisting the Zionists. On 2 May he sent a cable containing Money's report, prepared in the light of the impending commission to Palestine. The opening paragraphs of this report asserted that the Palestinian Arabs, who were the overwhelming majority in the region, feared the pro-Zionism of the British Government, and would therefore be more likely to support an American or French mandate. He also remarked that this attitude had been encouraged by French and Arab propaganda and reinforced through the fact that:

> Egypt and India are quoted as example of the tenacity of Great Britain's hold on countries on which she once lays her hand. More speedy autonomy is expected from United States. Moreover the people of Palestine have been greatly impressed by recent events in Egypt. Nevertheless fear of Zionism by Moslems and Christians is the main issue, and a large majority would vote for a British mandate if this were removed ... In conclusion any local request for a British mandate will be precluded by the idea that Great Britain is the main upholder of the Zionist programme, and except by force and in opposition of the wishes of the large majority of the people of Palestine no mandatory power can carry through Zionist programme.[37]

Allenby fully endorsed this report and completed the cable with this warning to his superiors in Whitehall:

> The indefinite retention in the country of a military force following occupation of that now in Palestine [sic] will be the result of a British mandate for Palestine on the lines of the Zionist programme.[38]

There can be no doubt that Allenby's prediction of the need to maintain a military garrison in Palestine did not envisage the inclusion of Jabotinsky's enlarged Legion. Money's appreciation and Allenby's endorsement demonstrate that British government policy and the local military authority were at odds with respect to the Zionist question. Furthermore, confirmation of Money's anti-Jewish prejudices can be found in Bernard Wasserstein's detailed research, which includes the following extract from a personal letter written by Money, who retired to

Britain in the summer of 1919: 'I am the more inclined to go since I see every prospect of the edifice I have built with some labour being pulled down by Messrs. Balfour, Lloyd George, and their long-nosed friends.'[39] Whatever encouragement Weizmann might have received in Paris from General Wilson, and whatever opportunities Jabotinsky might have foreseen in Palestine, local events involving the Jewish Legion undermined their efforts. From just prior to the feast of Passover in early April through to the end of the summer, tension between the Legion and GHQ escalated, reaching a climax with the courts martial of over 90 Jewish soldiers and the reduction of the Legion to a single battalion. Before reviewing this summer of difficulties for the Legion, it should be remembered that it was preceded by relative quiet in Palestine, as compared to Egypt, which Jabotinsky attributed to the presence of the Jewish Legion. There were, however, sporadic outbreaks of violence between Jewish soldiers and members of the local population, which Jabotinsky considered was due to some Palestinian legionnaires being over-familiar with some of the local Arabs, whom they had known since childhood and whose language they understood.[40] Another, more sinister explanation for these outbreaks of violence was offered by Gilner, who was convinced that, following Allenby's failure to acknowledge publicly the Jewish Legion's contribution to the war, anti-Semitic behaviour by certain officers was allowed to flourish, and that militant Arabs took their cue from this attitude.[41]

The following account of the troubled summer of 1919 has been compiled from primary sources, which include British public records that were made available between 1969 and 1993, and records from the US State Department.

The first notable event occurred at the end of March 1919, when a company of the 39th, who were engaged in shooting practice on a beach near Jaffa, were ordered back to camp before completing their course. With the rest of the battalion they were assigned to labour duties in place of the Egyptian Labour Corps who were on strike. GHQ had evidently decided that the presence of Jewish troops was provocative at a time of heightened feelings amongst the local Arab population, and that they would use non-Jewish soldiers to defend Jewish citizens against attack. This decision enraged the legionnaires, who were doubly slighted by being denied the opportunity to defend those they regarded as their own, and being forced to perform labouring duties. In the event the men refused to carry out the tasks they had been set, but Lt.-Col. Margolin managed to smooth things over with GHQ, thus maintaining a fragile peace, and the *status quo* was soon restored.[42]

218 *The Jewish Legion and the First World War*

The experience of the 39th contrasted, at this time, with that of the 40th Battalion. On 4 March command of the 40th Battalion passed from Lt.-Col. Samuel to Lt.-Col. Michael Scott, a Gentile who, like Patterson, held firm Christian beliefs and supported Zionism. He soon acquired the respect of his men. The war diary of the 40th notes that there were disturbances involving Muslims in Haifa on 11 March, and this continuing threat was met on the 23rd by the formation of a picket, comprising three officers and 100 men, who were to be available at fifteen minutes notice 'in case of trouble with ELC (Egyptian Labour Corps) or Moslems in the area'. Major Myer's diary contains some very strong remarks about the growing distrust between the battalion, the local population and the military authorities. For example, part of his entry for 12 March reads:

> We have had a little trouble too, as the result of the accusations made by the natives against one or two of our men, which I am well-nigh certain will prove utterly baseless. The native Christians and some of the Arabs are most unscrupulous swine [sic] and in every respect untrustworthy ... This sort of thing is rather harassing to every member of the Battalion and I think that under the circumstances the good behaviour of the men up till now is extraordinarily praiseworthy. ... I am still beaten by the intricacies of demobilisation and can't understand why one man gets home and another with precisely similar circumstances and authorities is turned down.

And on 14 March:

> I don't think the Battalion is being fairly dealt with by the Authorities and the situation is most aggravating. The swines of Syrians make every kind of lying accusation they can think of and the Authorities seem quite ready to punish us without investigating the charges at all ... Only English good-nature or rank anti-Semitism could permit of anyone listening to the charges that have been made. Really one is now face to face with anti-Semitism in a form that I have never met before. Whether the Authorities know that they are countenancing it or not, I am not clear, but the situation gives me food for thought.[43]

Major Myer's views, whilst reinforcing the general impression given by the sources covered in this section, are difficult to substantiate with unequivocal evidence. An examination of the recently released (1996)

Court Martial Register, however, has revealed that two soldiers of the 40th were tried on 24 March for 'Offence against inhabitant' and were acquitted, which outcome supports Myer's contentions.[44] As for the Jewish soldiers' opinion of the Arab population, Jabotinsky, Gilner et al. were very careful not to be explicit in their writing, but the evidence above of disrespect for members of the Egyptian Labour Corps, and Myer's obvious contempt for the 'Syrians', convey an impression of Jewish superiority. In essence, Jabotinsky and his comrades would tolerate Arabs provided they did not interfere with the formation of a Jewish state in Palestine.[45]

On 28 March the men were warned by their officers to avoid holding political meetings, an indication that the command was strengthening its attempt to maintain discipline and calm. Three days later, however, an outlet was found for some of the men, by the decision to send a party of three officers and 138 men to Samaria, 'to protect the inhabitants against Moslem threats'. The detachment returned on 2 April with no reported incidents.[46] This episode would seem to support Jabotinsky's assertion (see above) that the Legion was responsible for keeping the peace in Palestine. The 40th's reward for this achievement was to be returned by GHQ to Rafa in order to relieve the 38th Battalion, following further unrest in the Haifa area.

The transfer of the 40th was preceded by further provocation that had a particular effect on both the 39th and 40th, due to their location. General Money issued an order, on 6 April, forbidding the Jewish soldiers to enter the old walled city of Jerusalem during Passover week. Although it can be argued that this order was issued to pre-empt trouble between Arabs and Jews, the legionnaires thought otherwise. The operative part of the order read:

JERUSALEM
The Walled city is placed out of bounds to all Jewish soldiers from the 14th to 22nd April inclusive. They may, however, visit the Colonies and suburbs and should be encouraged to visit Jewish Colonies.
JAFFA
The town of Jaffa is to be avoided and Jewish soldiers granted leave there should be instructed that by Jaffa is meant Tel-Aviv.[47]

The Legionnaires regarded the denial of access to the Wailing Wall, which was within the old city, as an act of great prejudice, compounded by the fact that many Jewish soldiers had friends in old Jaffa and not in the wealthy area of Tel Aviv. More importantly, the issuing of this order prompted British soldiers, especially members of the Military Police, to display their anti-Semitism. In Jabotinsky's own words:

> But the worst of this order was the fact that its execution had naturally to be left to the discretion of the rank and file of the Military Police. A regular Jew-hunt followed. Lieut. Nutty, a Christian officer in charge of a Passover leave party of the 38th R.F. in Jaffa, stated that for his men and him 'this was not a holiday but a torture.' Soldiers wearing the R.F. badge were stopped at every turning, while no questions were asked from men of other units, even when former and latter were walking together. Inaugurated during Passover week this practice has ever since continued ... So it followed that soon after this unfortunate Passover week the whole atmosphere of the EEF became strongly poisoned with anti-Semitism.[48]

In order to avoid the harassment of the Military Police the legionnaires began to discard their badges when proceeding on leave, replacing them with those of other units. Whilst this action achieved its object, it can also be said that it represented a loss of self-respect and *esprit de corps*; officers could do little but make every effort to keep their men out of trouble. Their efforts were successful in that no great difficulties were experienced during Passover 1919, but the seeds of discontent were certainly sown. It is as well to remember that the Jewish Battalions were at this time experiencing the daily grind of guard and sentry duty, relieved by their own theatrical and musical entertainments, and by the occasional participation in army sporting events, especially boxing. Even then prejudice was never far away, as recalled by Lance-Corporal A. Goldfarb:

> I am an amateur boxer. In March last [1919] I was sent to the General Sports Meeting of the EEF at Kantara to fight for the 38th R.F. I regret to say that while fighting in the ring I heard many shouts from among the audience insulting me as a Jew.[49]

Neither did the Jewish soldiers escape from the other types of pest that existed in their desert quarters. Private Harry Levine wrote the following postcard to his sister in New York City on 2 March 1919:

> Hello Sis, I'm allright [*sic*] and are you so? When you send me a letter, send along a fly swatter. There are millions of them in my

tent and I am desperate. They bit my nose and oh! I look *not* like a respectable soldier. As soon as I get a chance, I'll take a bus home. Yours with love. Pte. H. Levine.[50]

Being struck down with disease, and having to spend time in hospital, did not provide any respite from the anti-Semitism to which the legionnaires were subjected. Private W. Bronstein of C Company 38th Battalion, sent the following complaint to his company commander, which was corroborated by Private J. Goodman of the same unit:

> Sir, I wish to make a complaint against the Colonel of the 24th Stationary Hospital, Kantara. I was admitted into the CCH Ludd, on May 22nd 1919, from where I was sent down to the 24th Stationary Hospital, Kantara, on 31st May 1919 with a recommendation for a medical board. On being paraded before the O.C. of the 24th S.H., he asked me if I belonged to the 38th R. Fus. Immediately on answering in the affirmative, he made the following statement: 'Clear out the 38th, I have had enough of you!'[51]

A further example taken from Jabotinsky's petition further highlights the nature of the discrimination. Private Lichtenfeld of the 38th:

> Early in June I was travelling by train from Kantara East. I was wearing my sun helmet when I showed my movement order to the Sergeant on the platform. As I speak good English he did not recognise me for a Jew. He indicated to me a carriage containing other British soldiers. A little later I took off my helmet and put on my cap, and so the R.F. badge was revealed. The same Sergeant, passing by the carriage, looked at my badge and ordered me to go to another truck half-filled with merchandise.[52]

This incident speaks for itself but it is worth noting that Private Lichtenfeld had probably removed the Magen David from his sleeve, and that the Sergeant would have been aware that the Jewish Battalions were the only Royal Fusiliers serving in the area.

Matters came to a head in July 1919, when serious outbreaks of disobedience and mutiny occurred amongst all three battalions at their various locations. Not content with having removed the 40th Battalion to Rafa, GHQ issued an order, in breach of the conditions of engagement of the Palestinian majority of the battalion, requiring members of the battalion to be posted to guard duties in Egypt and Cyprus. The men refused to obey this order, and under the leadership of Sergeant-Major Dov Hos, Sergeant Kivashni and Private Golumb, presented their commanding officer, Lt.-Col. Scott, with a dangerous and volatile situation, that could well have resulted in bloodshed, had other troops been called in to force the issue. Fortunately, Scott's compassion and understanding of his men led him to take a firm but tactful course of action, which involved an invitation to Dr David Eder, the Anglo-Jewish Zionist leader, to address the men in his capacity as the acting chairman of the Zionist Commission (Weizmann being absent in Paris).

At no time during the ensuing discussions – it was not a negotiation as Scott insisted that the men obey orders at all times – did Eder appear to make much progress, but he was in touch with GHQ and able to propose a compromise. This was not enough, however, and all but 200 of the men refused orders once again, after his departure. On this occasion Scott sent the three ringleaders to Kantara where they were detained. At risk of being personally court-martialled, Scott wrote to GHQ putting his men's case and testifying to their otherwise excellent behaviour. This clever and sensible two-pronged approach capitalised on Dr Eder's efforts and achieved the desired effect; an entry in the battalion's war diary dated 5 August 1919 confirmed that GHQ had decided that it was all a misunderstanding. The ringleaders were released and, in accordance with Eder's advice, a token number of legionnaires agreed to be posted for temporary duty and the matter was allowed to close, with the battalion remaining in Palestine. On a less positive note, Dr Eder had been unable to confirm to the legionnaires that the Zionist commission would be in a position to guarantee employment for those who wished to remain in Palestine after demobilisation. It can therefore be reckoned that this was another major factor contributing to the particular disillusionment of the volunteers from Canada and the United States, whose idealistic dreams were being replaced by economic and political reality.[53]

There is, however, another point of view that should encourage caution in ascribing actions to high-minded motives. Dr Eder's activity has been recently recounted in Tom Segev's *One Palestine, Complete*, and it is evident from this research that Eder did not consider the legionnaires to be motivated by patriotic feelings.[54] Rather, he attributed their behaviour to grievances arising out of discriminatory treatment. It is also argued that Eder was far from taken with the attitude of Ben-Gurion, who asked him to issue false commitments to employment in order to satisfy the British authorities, thus permitting discharged legionnaires to remain in the country. Eder refused to do so and strongly disapproved of any action that would bend the rules and thereby discredit the work of the Zionist Commission. The existence of this rift clearly showed the difference between the instinctive approach of Ben-Gurion and the pragmatism of Weizmann and Eder, with the Jewish Legion again providing a focal point for the development of Zionist policy in Palestine.[55]

The next serious incident involved a detachment of the Legion that had been sent to Belah on outpost duty, under the command of Major Smolley, Lt.-Col. Margolin's deputy in the 39th. The detachment included the American volunteers who had offered their services to remain in the army of occupation, and had been disappointed by the authorities' failure to allow them to do so, simply by making the procedure difficult. This further discriminatory treatment combined with the Zionist Commission's failure to assist the men to settle in Palestine, prompted them to give notice to Patterson that they wished to be demobilised and repatriated. This demand was accompanied by a deadline after which the men stated that they would no longer turn out. Desperate to avoid the inevitable consequences of a threatened mutiny, Patterson, who had already requested GHQ to demobilise the disaffected members of his command, asked the men to be patient, as he understood that their request would soon be granted. Regrettably, his advice was ignored by about fifty men and he was left with no choice but to remand them for court martial.[56]

Gilner's account of the reasons for this mutiny contains the additional factor of the abuse by Major Smolley of his own men. This allegation was supported by Jabotinsky who considered that Smolley was the one Gentile officer in the Legion who 'openly hated us'. Jabotinsky also made an interesting argument as to why the Major behaved in the way he did:

> I am certain that had he [Smolley] been just an official in the War Office, and given the affairs of the Jewish Battalions to handle, he would have treated us in the friendliest manner possible. But coming into daily contact with a psychology absolutely strange to his own, he could not find the right attitude to adopt. It is precisely this that is the trouble with many of the British officials in Palestine today.[57]

This passage acknowledges that discriminatory behaviour may not be entirely and necessarily attributed to anti-Semitic beliefs, but may be caused by social and cultural differences that create mutual misunderstanding and foster clashes in attitude, temperament and behaviour.

Shortly after the events at Belah, a further incident occurred also involving Major Smolley, Margolin's deputy while he was on leave. This dispute involved the transport section of the 39th Battalion at Sarafend, who had taken exception to the severe field punishment handed out to one of their members for neglect of a mule. The punishment, which consisted of the wretched soldier being tied to the wheel of an artillery piece, was taken as a racial slight by the remainder of the men. Major Smolley addressed the section on parade in an effort to restore discipline. During the course of this parade he is alleged to have insulted and sworn at the men, whose insubordinate response resulted in the arrest and court martial of over forty of their number.[58] This latter incident is also mentioned in the Avichail testimonial of Private Isaac Lichtenstein (later known as Edward Stone) that reads:

> When Major Smalley [sic] took command of Battalion after our Colonel Margolin left for his leave, and when Major Smalley began to show his anti-Semitism towards our Section, (for which he was well known); we protested and he had us court-martialled, and found guilty of mutiny and sentenced to 5 years hard labor in the Citadel of Cairo, Egypt. After serving 10 months, our Colonel interceded on our behalf, and we were pardoned.[59]

The fragmentary and conflicting nature of the coverage given to these serious incidents in the secondary sources, combined with a lack of public record, has meant that the details of the above account may be inaccurate. The two primary public records used, the Court Martial Register and Jabotinsky's petition to the King do, however, support the finding that mutiny and insubordination did occur at Belah and Serafend, and that its basic cause was the accumulation of discriminatory and anti-Semitic treatment, inflicted upon the increasingly disaffected volunteers from North America.

Further examination of these records has demonstrated that the trials of the mutineers took place in August as shown in Table 9.2. It can be seen that a total of fifty-four men from the 38th and forty-four from the 39th were arraigned, of whom forty-four were acquitted. It will also be noticed that the charge of mutiny was not put to the men of the 38th, a change brought about by the skill of Jabotinsky at the initial hearing, when he pointed out a flaw in the papers. Lesser charges of disobedience and miscellaneous misconduct were substituted, although the resultant prison terms issued to those found guilty turned out to be the same as those given to the men of the 39th who were convicted of mutiny.[60] What makes these prison terms (five to seven years) appear particularly severe is that earlier – post hostilities – cases of mutiny or disobedience, involving men of the Jewish Battalions, resulted in sentences of six months or one year only. It is therefore difficult to disagree with Patterson's statement that:

> Be it noted that the mutineers of other British units, the men who had openly defied all authority and set Kantara on blaze, were not even put on trial![61]

It therefore seems clear that the Jewish soldiers were treated in a discriminatory manner by the military authorities that indicates, yet again, the presence of an underlying anti-Semitism within the OETA South command.

Table 9.2: Courts martial summary August 1919

Date	No. charged	Bn.	Main charge	Outcome
11-Aug-19	7	38	disobedience	5 years prison, commuted to 2
12 & 13-Aug-19	11	38	quitting post	1 sentenced to 7 years commuted to 2 2 sentenced to 5 years, later quashed 8 found 'not guilty'
14-Aug-19	9	38	disobedience	5 years prison, commuted to 2
16-Aug-19	27	38	misc. (40)	5 sentenced to 5 years commuted to 2 22 found 'not guilty'
22 & 23-Aug-19	44	39	mutiny	30 sentenced to 5/6 years commuted to 1 14 found 'not guilty'
Total	98			
Guilty	54			
Not guilty	44			

Source: PRO WO 213 29–34. Field General Court Martial Registers 1919–1921

Court martial proceedings were terminated towards the end of August and the fifty-four guilty men were imprisoned in the military jail in Cairo. Jabotinsky's efforts on behalf of all the defendants had not gone unnoticed by GHQ, to whom – without taking Patterson into his confidence – he had personally written in July pleading for a fair deal for the Legion and the honouring of the earlier promises made by the War Office. Patterson and Gilner have recorded how GHQ responded, not by replying, but through the use of a staff officer to interview Jabotinsky under a pretext, which resulted in the lodging of a confidential and damning report to the staff. No details or trace of the contents of this report have been discovered, but whatever its part in the proceedings, the fact was that the Hon. Lieut. Vladimir Jabotinsky received his demobilisation papers at the end of August, and by early September his military service in the British Army was at an end.[62]

Choosing to remain in Palestine, Jabotinsky accepted the post of editor of the *Hadshot Haaretz*, a Hebrew newspaper published in Jerusalem. On 7 October he wrote a letter to Arthur Balfour, enclosing a copy of the petition he had submitted to the King, pleading for mercy for the fifty-four convicted and imprisoned legionnaires. Jabotinsky had also taken the precaution of sending copies to influential sympathisers such as Leo Amery and General Smuts. There is no date on the petition, but as Jabotinsky addressed himself on this document as the 'Hon. Lieutenant V. Jabotinsky, 38th Royal Fusiliers, counsel for the defence', the original must have been submitted prior to his discharge and demobilisation. In any event, his letter was received at the Foreign Office on 23 October and this communication, together with the accompanying petition, has provided the basis for some of the examples of discriminatory treatment as described above.[63]

Apart from the evidence presented in the petition, further insights into the social position, political purpose and military status of the Jewish Battalions can be gleaned from comments made in Jabotinsky's letter, and the remarks placed on file by officials at the Foreign Office. After emphasising to Balfour that there were wider political implications of the imprisonment of the mutineers, Jabotinsky stated:

> I can only add that, as perhaps your advisers, especially Sir Ronald Graham, might know, I had done my best to call my London friends' attention to the course things in Palestine were taking ever since Gen. Money's appointment – a course driving Jews to despair and leaving Arabs to arrange a pogrom. As one of the men responsible for the pro-British orientation among Jewry, I have no right to

be silent when thousands begin to accuse me, together with a few others, of having deceived and betrayed them into unfriendly hands. I have still a faint hope that perhaps the situation can be saved before we have a clean cut between betrayal on one side and betrayed on the other.[64]

Jabotinsky's strong words to the issuer of the Balfour Declaration read almost as a threat. Politically speaking, his remarks can be interpreted as meaning that Britain's commitment to the promises it made in the declaration would be undermined, unless the injustice to the Jewish soldiers were corrected, and the Jewish homeland established after the removal of the local military administration. It is also clear that, far from being a force able to defend Jews in Palestine and generally maintain the peace, Jabotinsky felt that the continued discrimination against the Jewish Legion would create a divided unit unable to fulfil any useful military or political purpose.

The Foreign Office formally acknowledged receipt of Jabotinsky's communication on 5 November 1919, in the name of Lord Curzon, who had recently become foreign secretary following Balfour's resignation. The file reveals that, whilst Jabotinsky had addressed Balfour personally, Balfour's secretary advised the Foreign Office, which considered this to be mainly a military matter, that:

> Mr Balfour thinks that Mr. Jabotinsky's letter was intended to be addressed to him as Foreign Secretary: it was written on Oct. 7-, before he resigned. In any case, he holds the view that it would be best for the reply to be sent from the F.O.[65]

Aside from the formal acknowledgment, no record of any further response from the Foreign Office has been discovered, and it is certain that Balfour himself stayed at arms length. Nevertheless, comments made on the file contain some interesting and revealing remarks. Major Scott, writing the first minute on 24 October, acknowledged that offence had been occasioned on the Jewish soldiers, but attributed the blame for this on their own conduct:

> The opinion of the rank and file is generally pretty correct, and though I should have never expected a warm welcome for these Battalions, if they had proved their worth they would have lived down their unpopularity. The attitude of the general staff towards them was prompted more by apprehension of trouble with the

Moslems than tact demanded. We might discuss this complaint with a representative of the W.O. But I don't think it is any good corresponding with them about it.[66]

The next official to comment, N.D. Peterson, followed Scott's lead, beginning with the observation that Jabotinsky had not described the mutinies, and had not substantiated the alleged anti-Semitism practised by the army staff. Rank and file opinion was then succinctly summarised 'As for the British private soldier, he is apt to lack a sense of political values and is usually brought up to detest the Jew!'[67] This comment appears to attribute the British private soldier's anti-Semitism to ignorance and a poor upbringing, which begs the question as to why so many officers held the same prejudice. The effect of this shared sentiment only served to reinforce the racism evidenced by the practice of officers turning a blind eye to the treatment meted out to the legionnaires by military policemen.

Peterson was also aware of political reality, but, as the following extract shows, remained determined that any advancement of Zionist aspirations be effected begrudgingly:

> Most of the trouble has probably arisen from the fact that these Jews – like many of their seniors holding for [sic] more responsible positions in the Zionist movement – have been in too much of a hurry to enter upon their heritage ... The Zionists do not lack advocates in the W.O. itself (to which the original petition addressed to H.M. will no doubt be referred) and I do not think we should 'butt in' at this stage. But we might suggest an amnesty a little later on, when the mandate is given if not before.[68]

This passage shows an appreciation of Jabotinsky's position and the reluctant acceptance by the Foreign Office of the inevitability of Lloyd George's policy, with the proviso that Britain needed to gain the mandate if the Balfour declaration was to mean anything. The proposal that an amnesty be arranged is also consistent with this policy and does at least suggest that it was recognised that there was some merit in Jabotinsky's application. Within months it would become clear that Britain would have its mandate and an amnesty for all fifty-four mutineers was indeed forthcoming.

Jabotinsky's petition and the influence of his British pro-Zionist allies was not the only point of pressure upon the authorities to release the mutineers. As mentioned earlier, some of the mutineers were from Canada and others were American citizens, and they or their families wasted no time in contacting servicemen's organisations and their representatives in the US Senate. The families were concerned as to the fate of their menfolk and issues regarding pay, allowances and pensions.

One documented example of the treatment given in these circumstances relates to Lance-Corporal Nemchek, one of the convicted mutineers of the 39th Battalion, whose situation was described in a letter from the Canadian Patriotic Fund, a charitable foundation that had been aiding the dependants of the legionnaires, to the OC of the Transport Section, Ludd on 16 July 1919:

> Dear Sir, On the 23rd March 1919, you sent us a certificate that Lance Cpl. M. Nemchek, J8076, 39th Battalion, Royal Fusiliers was doing transport duty with the Transport Section of this Battalion, but did not state whether he had assigned his pay to his mother. According to the information we have been securing, this boy was her sole support since the death of his father in 1913, and although we have forwarded Army Forms 01839 and 01840 to the proper authorities, we have been informed by the Officer Paying Imperial Pensions at Ottawa, that the War Office in England states that the conditions under which the soldier enlisted do not permit of any allowance from Army Funds being granted Mrs. Nemchek. Can you give us any reasons for this decision? ... We have had the same trouble with all our families of men who enlisted in this unit and do not think they have been treated fairly by the Imperial Authorities.[69]

Such grievances contributed to the outbreak of mutiny at Belah (see below). Allowances would have been suspended on conviction and, regrettably there is no irrefutable evidence they were eventually granted. We can reasonably assume they were because of the granting of an amnesty and the mention in a small number of testimonials of war pensions and grants.[70]

It is very important to state that all of the fifty-four convicted mutineers were either American citizens, Russian citizens who had enlisted in the USA or Jewish volunteers from Canada. Their clear motivation for joining the Legion has already been established, and it is therefore reasonable to assert that frustration, disillusionment and the continued denial of what they had believed would be their destiny made mutiny highly likely. Perhaps the mutineers thought that their actions would either prompt GHQ to facilitate their establishment and settlement in Palestine or speed up their repatriation. The families of some of the American citizens duly contacted their elected state and national representatives. Enquiries were then made through the Department of State, which contacted the Foreign Office in London. Brief details of these communications are contained in an US Department of State summary file, the contents of which have been reviewed and can be commented upon as follows.[71]

The first mention of the problems in Egypt is made following acknowledgment of an enquiry from the governor of Minnesota, on behalf of Private B.D. Levin, and dated 10 April 1919. The purport of this enquiry, as listed in the summary by the State Department reads: 'Discrimination by the British authorities in Egypt against Am. citizens in the Egyptian Expeditionary Forces. To be brought to the attention of the proper authorities.'[72]

It is clear that the US authorities were alerted to the difficulties and frustrations of the American legionnaires early on, but most of their enquiries, at this time, concerned relatives wishing to get their sons home, especially if they had enlisted under age. Minors identified in this file are Privates Schannon, Isaac Rotblatt, Harry Levine and Samuel Fleischer, whose discharges took about four months to complete.[73] Although they could obtain an immediate discharge by proving their age, nationality and by furnishing the necessary documentation, slow transatlantic diplomatic communications and transport delays added to the processing time.

In the case of the few mutineers mentioned in the file, the delays in communication between the Foreign Office and the State Department were longer than average. Families who had anticipated seeing their sons discharged and home in August and September 1919 were informed, after several promptings, that these men were imprisoned in Egypt for mutiny and advised of the sentences handed down by the courts martial. Included in this group was Private Max Dubin whose father, Rabbi Harry Dubinsky, had based his original enquiries on the basis that his son had enlisted under age. It took four months for him to be finally informed as to the details of his son's whereabouts and fate as a participant in the Belah mutiny, which had occurred after the Rabbi had first sought his son's discharge.[74] The families of Privates David Tobias (alias Tobin), Ed Siegel (alias Murray) and Abe Shereshevsky shared a similar experience, with requests for early discharge being transformed into petitions for early release once their situation had been revealed.[75] Finally, the file shows that it was not until 9 April 1920 that the Foreign Office finally confirmed to the State Department that the prisoners were amnestied and released on 31 March 1920; their repatriation took place over the next eight weeks.

The demobilisation and repatriation of the convicted men formed only a small part of the decline in numbers of the Legion throughout that year. It will be recalled that the War Office and Allenby exchanged cables with regard to post-war deployment in January–February. On 17 May 1919, GHQ Egypt received a cable from the War Office advising that the 'reduction of the 39th and 40th Bns. Royal Fusiliers' was to be 'held in abeyance'.[76] A further message, arranging the deployment and relief duties of the three battalions to Haifa, Ramleh and Rafa, the bases at which the troubles were to occur, was sent two days later.[77] There is no direct evidence as to why this suspension of policy occurred, but it has already been demonstrated that Weizmann and Amery were trying to persuade the government to retain Jewish troops in post-war Palestine. What is clear is that this question was far from resolved for, on 2 June, the War Office asked Allenby outright for his 'views on the advisability of a permanent increase of Jewish troops in Palestine', immediately followed by the statement that 'it may be assumed that a corresponding decrease of British troops would not accompany any such increase'.[78] The wording of this cable is interesting. On the one hand it provided Allenby with an opportunity to state his views unequivocally, whilst on the other it confirmed that Jewish troops would not be used as substitutes for British soldiers. Allenby did not hesitate: on 6 June he replied in the following concise terms:

> The measure would be interpreted as a preparation to enforce the claim of the Jewish minority on rest of population. The present distrust of Zionist aims among non-Jewish population would be greatly increased. There have been already incidents between Jewish soldiers and non-Jewish inhabitants, especially Moslems, and an increase in number of Jewish troops would certainly lead to riots and widespread trouble with Arabs.[79]

Allenby's prediction of difficulties with the Jewish troops under his command may have been justified, although his main problem at this time was mutiny and disobedience and not trouble with the Arab population. Court martial records for 1919 show that, out of a total of 188 legionnaires that appeared before the courts, only five were charged with 'offence against inhabitant', resulting in two acquittals and three convictions which carried a penalty of two years imprisonment. This can be compared with the 113 that were charged with mutiny or disobedience (including the ninety-eight involved at Belah or Serafend).[80] It is, perhaps, not surprising that Allenby failed to mention that the commanding officers (and Jabotinsky) of the Jewish Battalions had warned him of the consequences of the anti-Semitism of some British officers and men. Instead, he chose to justify the reduction of the Legion on the grounds of the likelihood of civil unrest, and made the most of the Zionist threat. Events were to make this a self-fulfilling prophecy.

The records do not contain an explicit War Office response to Allenby's views but a draft army council instruction (ACI), drawn up in June, indicates that the army had finally made up its mind. This draft confirmed that a decision had been made to re-designate the 38th Battalion Royal Fusiliers (City of London Regiment) as the 38th Battalion Royal Fusiliers (1st Judeans), thus creating the single Battalion with its own promised name. This is supported by War Office correspondence of 21 June which deals with the closure of the Plymouth depot and the transfer of the remaining 300 fully trained recruits (all under the age of twenty and conscripted in Britain), to the 47th Bn. Royal Fusiliers in France, for the relief of soldiers due to be demobilised.[81] The administrative depot for the battalions in Palestine was transferred to Hounslow; it may well be the case that some of the problems encountered with pay and allowances could have been due to this disruption.

Almost inevitably, the draft ACI remained just that, until the end of the year. Weizmann's persistent efforts to increase a Jewish military presence in Palestine continued to such effect that the War Office was again obliged to cable Allenby on 28 August 1919:

> It has been proposed by Dr. Weizmann that (a) in view of the necessity for a future garrison in Palestine the Jews should take larger share in producing the necessary man power. In his opinion it would be possible to recruit 10 to 15 thousand Jewish volunteers of good physical standard principally from Georgia, Transylvania, Czecho-Slovak prisoners in Siberia and Polish-Jew [sic] prisoners of war in Italy.
>
> (b) In order to facilitate dealing with questions regarding Jewish Battalion a Jewish liaison officer should be attached to your headquarters. For this duty he recommends Colonel F.D. Samuel.[82]

This message not only shows that Weizmann continued to exert considerable influence, but raises the question of how much was known in Whitehall of the courts martial of the mutineers, which were held in

Egypt two weeks before the cable was despatched. Whatever the case Allenby certainly would have known and he wasted no time in sending a terse reply 'I consider this most undesirable (see my (earlier) telegram).' He also added that he would accept Fred Samuel as liaison, but this appointment was never made.[83] Allenby's response seems to have settled the matter and Whitehall appears to have made no further efforts on the Government's or Weizmann's behalf to do anything other than reduce the Legion to a single battalion. Against the background of continuing demobilisation and the events at Belah and Serafend, it is perhaps a sign of desperation that Weizmann resorted to the suggestion of such outlandish recruitment schemes. With the army unable or unwilling to confront the issue of prejudice and discrimination the fate of the Legion was sealed.

Demobilisation had begun in early 1919, by when many of the American recruits were disillusioned and discouraged from attempting to remain in Palestine. Army order 236, of July 1919, further accelerated this process by confirming that soldiers who had been conscripted under the Military Service Convention were no longer required to serve in armies of occupation, and would be discharged upon the ratification of peace.[84] Although this did not take place until the Treaty of Sèvres in August 1920, which itself was preceded by the allocation of the Palestine Mandate at the Council of the Allied Powers at San Remo in April, the official manpower figures show that the drift of men out of the Legion continued throughout 1919. In summary, official records show that at the end of February 1919, the number of men serving in Palestine and at the depot in Plymouth had reached its highest figure of 5,910. By the end of June this number had declined to 5139 and by the end of November to 3,079. At this point the 39th and 40th Battalions were disbanded and all 'non-demobilisable' troops were placed into the 38th Battalion under Lt.-Col. Margolin, and only then granted its own name and cap badge (1st Judeans and the Menorah in place of the Fusiliers Grenade), thus belatedly fulfilling Lord Derby's promise of August 1917. As for Patterson, after handing over to Margolin, he left Palestine at the end of the year and returned to Britain, where he wrote to the Government and the US State department urging an amnesty for the imprisoned mutineers.

The process of establishing the new unit took three months to complete, and the first full monthly return for the 38th Battalion Royal Fusiliers (1st Judeans) shows that, at the end of March 1920, the battalion consisted of a total of 1,216 men including sixty-eight officers, nine warrant officers and fifty sergeants.[85] Unfortunately for Margolin's battalion, its date of formation, 1 December 1919, was shared with the appointment of Major-General Bols as the chief administrator in Palestine. This appointment might have been counterbalanced by the fact that Meinertzhagen had returned to Palestine as chief political officer in September. Regrettably their personalities clashed and Bols was provided with an excuse for continuing to ignore the declared policy of the British Government. As Wasserstein's research into this important episode shows, the change in identity of the Legion had no effect upon the attitude of the local administration towards it. On 31 December Meinertzhagen wrote to Bols, remarking that he had:

> been much struck by the unsympathetic attitude of a great many Englishmen, both of the official and unofficial classes, which I can only trace to ignorance regarding Zionism which they regard in very much the same light as the native inhabitants of Palestine ... Meinertzhagen urged Bols to publish a declaration which would show Zionism in its true light, and dispel, not only amongst the native classes, but also amongst the Europeans, the very erroneous and harmful appreciation of the policy of HMG.

Bols refused and asked Meinertzhagen to substantiate his charges against OETA and then continued:

> There exists, of course, a fear of the power of the Jews which it is not possible to eradicate. I am still of the opinion that the publication of the policy of HMG can do no good and that such publication is likely rather to create antagonism than to reduce friction.[86]

This exchange soured relations between the two men and Bols' comments confirm the paranoia about Jewish 'power' that overrode the spirit of Lloyd George's government's policy.

Allenby's headquarters could see no future for the battalion. Whilst acknowledging that the battalion 'is now composed of promising material', GHQ did not consider that the expense of retaining this unit was justified:

> In case of internal disturbances, which are most likely to arise from inter-racial feeling, use of Jewish troops would tend to inflame such feeling, and would, therefore, be dangerous ... They could not be used in Egypt or elsewhere; therefore for use either in case of internal or external troubles in either countries [sic] Battalion

rather than a source of strength will be a source of embarrassment, and unless political reasons for retention are very strong, I recommend in due course the personnel of the Battalion be demobilised, and the Battalion be disbanded.[87]

The administration's fears of inter-communal disturbances were soon realised. On 1 March the small Jewish settlement of Tel Hai was approached by a number of Arabs who were looking for a group of French soldiers with whom they had been in dispute. Tel Hai is situated in remote Northern Galilee, which had a reputation as bandit country. Although the details of what happened are not clear, shots were fired and the Jews called for help, which arrived under the leadership of Joseph Trumpeldor. In the ensuing fight Trumpeldor was mortally wounded along with five other Jews and five Arabs, and he became a martyr and Tel Hai a mythic symbol for the Zionist cause. Two of the Jewish dead were American citizens who had been discharged from the 1st Judeans only two weeks beforehand, and were buried with their comrades at Tel Hai. Their names were William Sherf and Jack (Jacob) Tucker, both former privates in the 39th with twenty-two and eight months service respectively.[88]

Tel Hai increased tension between the Jewish and Arab communities, and it led Jewish leaders to warn the authorities that further trouble could be expected in Jerusalem in April during the Muslim festival of Nebi-Musa and the Jewish Passover. The authorities (Bols and Storrs) reassured Weizmann and Jabotinsky and refused to permit Jews to carry arms in order to protect themselves. Notwithstanding this order, Jabotinsky and Rutenberg continued to train and arm Jewish volunteers (including former legionnaires) illicitly, using weapons that had been procured during the reduction of the Legion. Furthermore, and according to a history of the Palestinian police, immediately before the Arab riot, Jewish youths who had recently arrived from Europe paraded through Jerusalem demanding a Jewish defence force, in a demonstration organised by Jabotinsky.[89]

On 4 April, following the procession that marked the commencement of Nebi-Musa, Arabs began rioting and looting through the Jewish part of the city. Jabotinsky's further request to aid the Jewish residents was again rejected, while the all-Arab civil police were removed from their duties after siding with the rioters. This left the authorities with no choice but to deploy the army (not the 1st Judeans) and by the time they arrived all they could do was to surround the area and enforce a curfew. This involved arresting Jews who attempted to enter the Jewish quarter in order to provide relief, an action that persuaded Weizmann that the riot was a pogrom. It took four days for relative quiet to be restored, with casualties amounting to nine deaths (five Jewish), 244 wounded (211 Jews), and seven injured British soldiers.[90]

Peace only lasted one day, then, on 9 April, 'five men, dressed in the uniform of Royal Fusiliers (1st Judeans) approached house of Grand Mufti and fired six rounds at his son, nevertheless no damage was done'.[91] They were neither found nor arrested and, if they were legionnaires, then they must have been in Jerusalem on leave. This was indeed the opinion of Bols, as he reported to Allenby in a message that was transmitted, together with Allenby's reply, to the War Office on 12 April:

> 1. Strong protest was to-day made by deputation of Ulemas and Sherifs against reported attack on Grand Mufti's house by Jewish troops which they consider to be an insult to Moslem religion ... Kadi in name of all asked for Zionist Commission to be removed from the country within 5 days or else serious trouble must ensue ... I think Zionists' Commission should be broken ... [Zionist Commission] which has gradually grown into an Administration cannot continue within Occupied Enemy Territory South must continue to irritate ... Owing to the action of Jewish soldiers on leave in Jerusalem during riots, feeling against this Battalion is very strong. Also reported from Jaffa three incidents of maltreatment of inhabitants by these soldiers.[92] I recommend Battalion be sent to Kantara and demobilised.
> 2. (Allenby's) Answer. Idea of removal of, or any change as to Zionist Commission cannot be entertained ... Jewish soldiers on leave must be dealt with in ordinary course by military authorities. Not prepared to accept recommendation that Jewish Battalion be moved to Kantara and demobilised.[93]

Bols' efforts to disband the Legion thus came to end, but the military authorities were quick to arrest some of the perpetrators of the violence in Jerusalem and, following a search of his apartment, where illicit arms were discovered, Jabotinsky himself was arrested and tried by a military court. Justice was meted out at speed as demonstrated by the report that Allenby sent to London on 23 April:

> Following are cases tried so far by military courts and sentences confirmed:
> 1. Jabotinsky, convicted of (a) Possession of firearms, (b) Instigation to disobedience by arming populace, (c) Conspiracy and preparing means to carry out riot acts. Sentenced to 15 years' penal servitude ...

2. Nineteen Jewish confederates of Jabotinsky convicted of possession of firearms, sentenced to 3 years' penal servitude each.
3. Jews convicted of shooting at and wounding Moslems, sentenced to 15 years' penal servitude.
4. Seven Moslems arrested in possession of firearms, awaiting trial. Two Moslems convicted of rape, sentenced to 15 years' penal servitude.[94]

The gaoling of Jabotinsky caused consternation in London and among the Zionists in Palestine. As an indication of the extraordinary circumstances which surrounded his confinement, however, the War Office record of messages to and from GHQ contain many questions asking after Jabotinsky's welfare; he appears to have been held in comfortable conditions and was transported from the court to Acre prison in a first class railway compartment.[95] In any event, following the appointment of Sir Herbert Samuel in July 1920, as the first civil high commissioner, Jabotinsky and the other Jews and Arabs who had been gaoled were released.

When Samuel took over from Bols, the 1st Judeans were languishing at Ludd and their strength had declined to a total of 719, including thirty-three officers. Although it was clear, from Allenby's response to Bols' recommendation to disband, that their existence was politically expedient, there can be little doubt that the events of April did nothing for their reputation. Once again, through their inability to be usefully employed, they had fulfilled earlier anti-Zionist prophecies, and nothing was done to replace those who were demobilised or otherwise discharged throughout the remainder of 1920. The pro-Zionist policies of Samuel, which opened the door to Jewish immigration and land ownership, also reduced the symbolic need for a Jewish Legion; the Haganah was now the effective Jewish fighting force. Nevertheless, the unit continued in its less than useful existence into 1921 and by the end of April was awaiting a decision on future British military requirements in Palestine. Effective strength at this time consisted only of Margolin and about thirty men.

The final incident of the Legion's unhappy post-war existence took place during the Jaffa riots of 1–3 May 1921. May Day had been the occasion of an officially sanctioned parade of Jewish socialists that was expected to pass without incident. Unfortunately, Jewish communists disrupted the parade and some Arabs took advantage of this internecine disturbance to attack Jewish premises. A full-scale riot ensued and the Jews sent for help, a call that was answered by the remnants of the 1st Judeans. On hearing of his men's departure for Jaffa, Margolin followed them and obtained approval for their participation in the defence of the Jewish community. This action only succeeded in escalating the situation, particularly when the legionnaires were joined by a number of their former comrades; the sight of British uniforms intermingled with the Haganah could only inflame the situation.

The authorities declared martial law on 3 May and moved in a large number of British troops to quell the trouble, which had resulted in fifty-seven deaths (forty-three Jewish) and 183 wounded (134 Jews). Both the Arab police and the 1st Judeans were disarmed.[96] Margolin submitted his resignation but Herbert Samuel offered him only the choice of court martial or exile. Margolin chose the latter and returned to Australia where he lived until his death on 22 June 1944, his body being re-interred in Israel after independence.[97] His men were returned to camp and, on 31 May 1921, the 1st Judeans were formally disbanded, thus bringing the existence of the Jewish Legion to an end.

In conclusion, the evidence used in this chapter demonstrates that the Legion was maintained in Egypt and Palestine after the armistice in order that British troops, with longer overseas service, could be demobilised. It was gradually run down and isolated as a result of the continued confusion over policy between Allenby and Whitehall and its awkward political presence culminating in its identification with Jewish self-defence. The Legion's post-war existence was also clearly marked by the anti-Semitism of the OETA South command which, when added to the difficulties caused by its presence near to Arab disturbances, ensured its demise.

10
Conclusions: Legacy of the Legion

In Chapter 1, certain substantive questions were raised in respect of the founding and subsequent history of the Jewish Legion, and the relation of this work to ongoing debates within Anglo-Jewish historiography. In concluding, it is therefore appropriate to revisit both the substantive and historiographical issues.

The idea of the creation of a Jewish Legion came from two individuals, Vladimir Jabotinsky and Pinhas Rutenberg, who both saw an opportunity for achieving a Jewish national state through military participation in the First World War, and it was Jabotinsky who emerged as the main driving force behind the Legion's foundation. For them, and colleagues such as Weizmann and the Benim, the Legion was instrumental in pursuit of a larger political aim – the establishment of Israel as an independent nation. This role led later to the Legion being celebrated as the forerunner of the modern Israeli Army, with the historical lineage running through the Mandate via the Haganah. This kept alive the Legion's memory, and enabled a mythology to be constructed around it but, apart from providing some of the original members (and equipment), the Haganah shared nothing of the Legion's existence. It can therefore be asserted that the historical significance of the Legion lies mainly in its symbolism and not its military effectiveness. However, mythmaking is itself a matter for historical investigation. The evidence produced in this book clearly shows the veterans' determination to sustain a collective memory of the Legion that emphasised its political purpose. That memory was embodied in the significant number of founding fathers of the Israeli state who served in its ranks, as exemplified by Ben-Gurion whose letter to another veteran, Harry Levine, is shown in Figure 10.1.

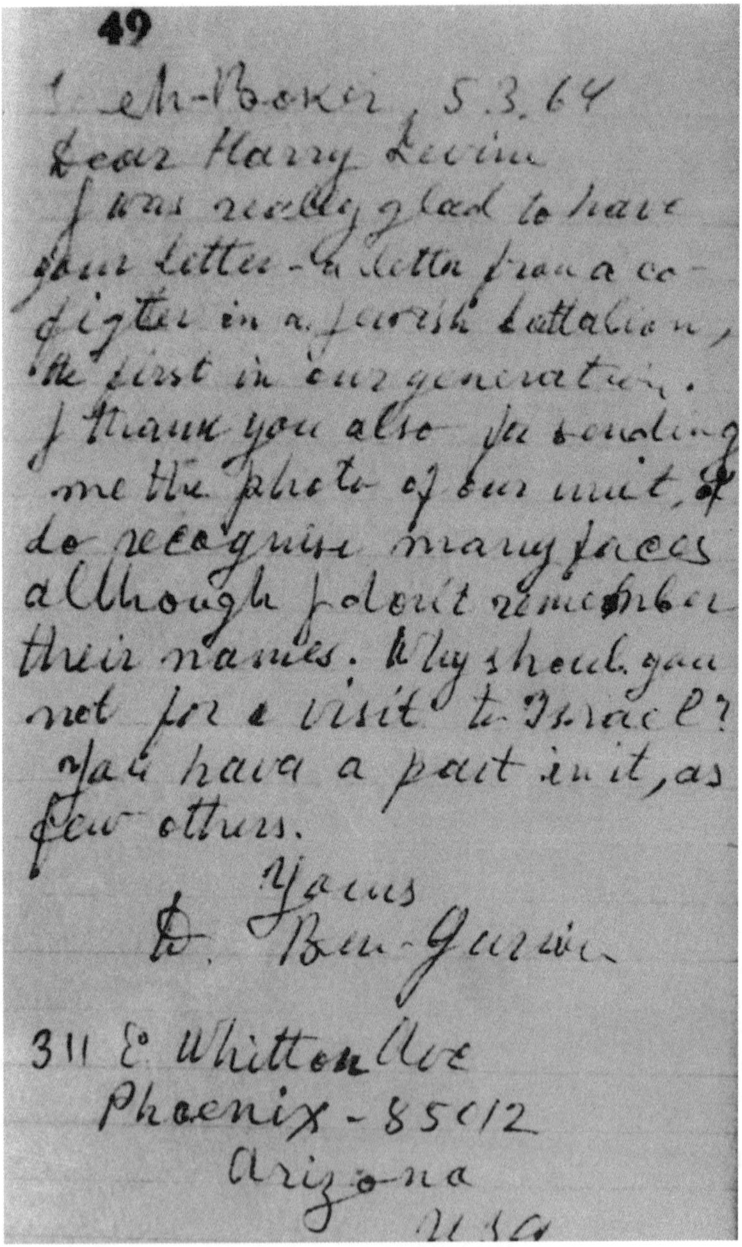

49

Sde-Boker, 5.3.64
Dear Harry Levine
I was really glad to have
your letter - a letter from a co-
fighter in a Jewish battalion,
the first in our generation.
I thank you also for sending
me the photo of our unit, I
do recognise many faces
although I don't remember
their names. Why should you
not for a visit to Israel?
You have a part in it, as
few others.
Yours
D. Ben-Gurion

311 E. Whitton Ave
Phoenix - 85012
Arizona
USA

Figure 10.1 Letter to Harry Levine from D. Ben-Gurion, 1964

Conclusions: Legacy of the Legion 241

Why did Britain agree to the formation of the Legion, when it was so atypical of British military practice and so opposed within Anglo-Jewry? The evidence makes clear that the personal, philo-Semitic sympathies of Lloyd George and his 'kitchen cabinet', combined with their assessment of Britain's strategic interests in the Middle East, determined that the unit was formed against considerable odds. Without Lloyd George as premier, the efforts of Zionist Gentiles like Amery and Smuts would have been to no avail. Neither should it be forgotten that geo-political interests were served by the British Government informally allying itself with the Jewish lobby in the United States. It helped cement the association with American democracy. During the war, Jabotinsky and Weizmann played a weak hand very adroitly. With few political assets of their own, they extracted every ounce of support from sympathisers in British politics by exploiting sentiment and establishing congruence between Britain's imperial interests and their own nationalist agenda. This was a transitional moment between Jewry's existence solely as a Diaspora and the formation of a Jewish nation state being placed on the international political agenda. As the collective representative of militant Zionism fighting on the Allied side, the Legion made a considerable contribution to that transition. This explains its pivotal role in contemporary Jewish politics.

Turning to the military performance of the Legion, this study has established that in limited operations, the Jewish soldiers achieved all that was asked of them, despite the hostile attitude of some of the staff of the EEF and the failure of the War Office to honour all its promises. As far as relations with other troops are concerned, it has been demonstrated that the Zion Mule Corps earned respect for its endeavours in Gallipoli; endeavours that were not solely confined to behind the lines logistics. The Legion in Palestine, in spite of the anti-Semitism experienced in the EEF, did settle down reasonably well with the ANZAC troops of Chaytor's force, and earned the praise of their commander for their small part in the decisive battle of Megiddo. In both Gallipoli and Palestine the lesson learned was that respect is best earned within the shared, extreme experience of action under fire, and not in encampments or headquarters.

This study has confirmed the pervasive nature of anti-Semitism in early twentieth-century Britain, but its more novel and unexpected finding concerns the deep divisions between the Jewish sub-communities in Britain. (Similar fissures in American Jewry were also revealed.) The complexity of intra-communal relations was such that Jewish Zionists and non-Zionists alike were on both sides of the Legion debate. Similarly, working-class Jews both supported and opposed the Legion. Its most obdurate opponents were assimilated, middle- and upper-class Jews who prized their English national identity above a political attachment to their religious community. (I say 'English' rather than British because that is how assimilated upper-class Jews such as Montagu identified themselves.) This illuminates the essential and unanswered question as to whether Jewishness is a religious or ethnic ascription. The evidence examined here indicates that it was a matter both of individual consciousness and the cultural circumstances of one's upbringing. Major Myer and his batman, Harry Freeman, were worlds apart.

Within the limits of the available evidence, the demography of the Legion has been established and the social origins of the legionnaires have been explored. Of the main constituents, it can be said that the volunteers from America were more highly motivated politically, but less amenable to military discipline. This discipline, however, was crucial in maintaining the morale and effectiveness of the reluctant conscripts from the East End. As far as the Palestinian recruits were concerned, their isolation from the action meant that their military value was not tested, but there is significance in the scale of local volunteering that indicates strong support for Zionism. The consideration of the Legion's constituents has illuminated its internal dynamics and its decline after the armistice, which served to reveal its growing irrelevance to the occupation forces. The marginalisation of the Legion by OETA was a major factor in its demoralisation.

In relation to the historiographical debates touched on in the Introduction, this work has drawn on insights from both the 'modern' school of Anglo-Jewish scholars and their most prominent critics, W.D. and H.L. Rubinstein. The latter's study of philo-Semitism, although evidently hurriedly written and occasionally superficial, rightly emphasises the existence of a tradition of sympathy and support for Jews within the British political class.[1] Rather oddly, the authors do not discuss the formation of the Jewish Legion within the context of this philo-Semitic tradition, though by any assessment it should have been grist to their mill. As we have seen, philo-Semitism within the political class was a necessary, though not sufficient, condition for the Legion's existence. That it proved to be an efficient military unit was largely due to Patterson, a philo-Semite who surely deserves more than a single, unilluminating entry in the Rubinsteins' index. Though acknowledging the indispensability of Gentile support, this research has documented a climate of prejudice directed against 'alien', unassimilated Jews, and a suspicion of Jewish 'power', which obstructed the

Legion's formation and meant that it existed under a cloud. The British Army, or at least the senior officers who dealt with the Legion, were distinctly uncomfortable with a formation having a Jewish identity. To this extent, the historiographical emphases of the 'modern' school are confirmed.

Finally, we should ask how this work has offered new perspectives on Anglo-Jewish relations in the early twentieth century. Viewed through the prism of military service in the First World War, questions of anti-Semitism, citizenship, nationality, conscription and assimilation presented an unprecedented challenge to Anglo-Jewish relations in Britain. Militarily, the challenge produced a unique unit of three battalions recruited from a single religious base. Politically, Anglo-Jewish relations at the governmental level were raised to a new level: the deputations and counter-deputations resulted in the full range of Jewish opinion being exposed to the executive, and secured greater recognition of Jewish interests and influence, particularly where they coincided with British foreign policy. Socially, the operation of the Military Service Convention linked conscription to the granting of citizenship, but expectations that the Legion's foundation would redeem the reputation of 'alien Jews' were largely disappointed. Similarly, the fears of the Anglo-Jewish community, which was over-represented in the army,[2] that a poor performance on the part of reluctant conscripts would tarnish the reputation of Jews in general, were equally confounded. Post-war anti-Semitism in Britain paid little heed to Jewish war service either by Anglo-Jewry or 'alien Jews'.[3]

These conclusions indicate that the Legion itself had little or no effect on established anti-Semitic attitudes in Britain, notwithstanding that the debate over its formation did reflect the hostility towards the 'alien' Jews' reluctance to serve. The contribution of the Legion to Zionism however, should not be underestimated, for its existence opened Palestine to the founders of Israel.

Appendix I

Table A.I.1   Strength returns March 1918–May 1921

Battalion	Date	Offs	Wo's	Sgts	Drum	Or's	Total
38 Egypt	Mar-18	30	5	44	0	922	1001
39 Depot	Mar-18	19	8	0	0	660	687
42 Depot	Mar-18	14	0	0	0	652	666
Total	Mar-18	63	13	44	0	2234	2354
38 Egypt	Apr-18	30	5	44	0	919	998
39 Depot	Apr-18	30	8	28	0	542	608
42 Depot	Apr-18	19	1	25	0	742	787
Total	Apr-18	79	14	97	0	2203	2393
38 Egypt	May-18	30	5	44	0	919	998
39 Egypt	May-18	31	6	48	0	455	540
42 Depot	May-18	28	3	39	0	1223	1293
Total		89	14	131	0	2597	2831
38 Egypt	Jun-18	32	6	44	0	914	996
39 Egypt	Jun-18	31	6	48	0	455	540
42 Depot	Jun-18	40	6	53	16	1177	1292
Total		103	18	145	16	2546	2828
38 Egypt	Jul-18	32	6	44	0	918	1000
39 Egypt	Jul-18	33	6	48	0	757	844
42 Depot	Jul-18	50	6	48	16	1633	1753
Total		115	18	140	16	3308	3597
38 Egypt	Aug-18	33	7	43	0	935	1018
39 Egypt	Aug-18	33	6	49	0	919	1007
42 Depot	Aug-18	58	10	48	16	2123	2255
Total		124	23	140	16	3977	4280
38 Egypt	Sep-18	32	6	42	0	943	1023
39 Egypt	Sep-18	33	6	48	0	930	1017
40 Egypt	Sep-18	30	7	49	0	1357	1443
42 Depot	Sep-18	43	7	31	15	937	1033
Total		138	26	170	15	4167	4516
38 Egypt	Oct-18	32	6	51	0	942	1031
39 Egypt	Oct-18	38	7	47	0	941	1033
40 Egypt	Oct-18	30	7	49	0	1357	1443
42 Depot	Oct-18	46	9	37	15	1615	1722
Total		146	29	184	15	4855	5229

Appendix I 245

Battalion	Date	Offs	Wo's	Sgts	Drum	Or's	Total
38 Egypt	Nov-18	36	7	48	0	921	1012
39 Egypt	Nov-18	37	6	43	0	1877	1963
40 Egypt	Nov-18	30	6	54	0	1341	1431
42 Depot	Nov-18	56	8	42	16	1676	1798
Total		159	27	187	16	5815	6204
38 Egypt	Dec-18	37	6	48	0	888	979
39 Egypt	Dec-18	42	6	46	0	1823	1917
40 Egypt	Dec-18	30	6	51	0	1340	1427
42 Depot	Dec-18	39	12	42	24	2515	2632
Total		148	30	187	24	6566	6955
38 Egypt	Jan-19	37	8	49	0	951	1045
39 Egypt	Jan-19	41	8	44	0	1797	1890
40 Egypt	Jan-19	35	7	43	0	1250	1335
42 Depot	Jan-19	39	13	48	24	2442	2566
Total		152	36	184	24	6440	6836
38 Egypt	Feb-19	46	8	55	0	1360	1469
39 Egypt	Feb-19	38	7	47	0	1278	1370
40 Egypt	Feb-19	34	7	42	0	1465	1548
42 Depot	Feb-19	31	9	55	16	2412	2523
Total		149	31	199	16	6515	6910
38 Egypt	Mar-19	43	8	53	0	1890	1994
39 Egypt	Mar-19	39	9	62	0	1801	1911
40 Egypt	Mar-19	32	7	47	0	1495	1581
42 Depot	Mar-19	25	9	37	16	990	1077
Total		139	33	199	16	6176	6563
38 Egypt	Apr-19	30	7	46	0	1682	1765
39 Egypt	Apr-19	37	6	39	0	1657	1739
40 Egypt	Apr-19	29	7	36	0	1314	1386
42 Depot	Apr-19	23	9	32	16	955	1035
Total		119	29	153	16	5608	5925
38 Egypt	May-19	27	6	43	0	1515	1591
39 Egypt	May-19	35	6	48	0	1581	1670
40 Egypt	May-19	26	3	32	0	1234	1295
42 Depot	May-19	25	6	10	16	737	794
Total		113	21	133	16	5067	5350
38 Egypt	Jun-19	24	6	34	0	1491	1555
39 Egypt	Jun-19	35	6	36	0	1558	1635
40 Egypt	Jun-19	29	3	28	0	1259	1319
42 Depot	Jun-19	24	4	11	16	575	630
Total		112	19	109	16	4883	5139
38 Egypt	Jul-19	24	6	35	0	1472	1537
39 Egypt	Jul-19	35	6	36	0	1517	1594
40 Egypt	Jul-19	32	3	24	0	1254	1313

Appendix I

Battalion	Date	Offs	Wo's	Sgts	Drum	Or's	Total
42 Depot	Jul-19	19	4	22	16	556	617
Total		110	19	117	16	4799	5061
38 Egypt	Aug-19	24	6	35	0	1425	1490
39 Egypt	Aug-19	28	6	36	0	1438	1508
40 Egypt	Aug-19	29	3	24	0	1252	1308
42 Depot	Aug-19	12	3	22	16	254	307
Total		93	18	117	16	4369	4613
38 Egypt	Sep-19	21	5	36	0	1413	1475
39 Egypt	Sep-19	19	5	32	0	1401	1457
40 Egypt	Sep-19	26	5	23	0	1225	1279
42 Depot	Sep-19	5	5	18	16	95	139
Total		71	20	109	16	4134	4350
38 Egypt	Oct-19	21	5	36	0	1272	1334
39 Egypt	Oct-19	19	5	34	0	1336	1394
40 Egypt	Oct-19	26	5	23	0	1075	1129
42 Depot	Oct-19	1	0	5	16	69	91
Total		67	15	98	16	3752	3948
38 Egypt	Nov-19	20	4	24	0	864	912
39 Egypt	Nov-19	17	4	27	0	1092	1140
40 Egypt	Nov-19	24	3	18	0	982	1027
Total		61	11	69	0	2938	3079
38 Egypt	Dec-19	24	4	24	0	734	786
39 Egypt	Dec-19	27	4	24	0	485	540
40 Egypt	Dec-19	28	3	12	0	865	908
Total		79	11	60	0	2084	2234
38 Egypt	Jan-20	21	4	24	0	729	778
39 Egypt	Jan-20	25	3	22	0	358	408
40 Egypt	Jan-20	26	4	12	0	858	900
Total		72	11	58	0	1945	2086
38 Egypt	Feb-20	43	3	27	0	1501	1574
39 Egypt	Feb-20	9	5	18	0	509	541
40 Egypt	Feb-20	16	1	5	0	63	85
Total		68	9	50	0	2073	2200
38 Egypt	Mar-20	46	4	24	0	1046	1120
39 Egypt	Mar-20	4	0	2	0	57	63
40 Egypt	Mar-20	8	0	5	0	20	33
Total		58	4	31	0	1123	1216
38 Egypt	Apr-20	43	4	24	0	1050	1121
38 Egypt	May-20	40	4	22	0	761	827
38 Egypt	Jun-20	33	4	20	0	662	719
38 Egypt	Jul-20	34	3	19	0	644	700
38 Egypt	Aug-20	34	3	18	0	548	603
38 Egypt	Sep-20	34	3	16	0	482	535

Battalion	Date	Offs	Wo's	Sgts	Drum	Or's	Total
38 Egypt	Oct-20	32	2	12	0	292	338
38 Egypt	Nov-20	23	1	8	0	199	231
38 Egypt	Dec-20	22	0	0	0	146	168
38 Egypt	Jan-21	19	0	0	0	146	165
38 Egypt	Feb-21	21	0	0	0	101	122
38 Egypt	Mar-21	23	0	0	0	101	124
38 Egypt	Apr-21	22	0	0	0	96	118
38 Egypt	May-21	12	0	0	0	0	12

Source: PRO WO 73 107

Appendix II: Maps

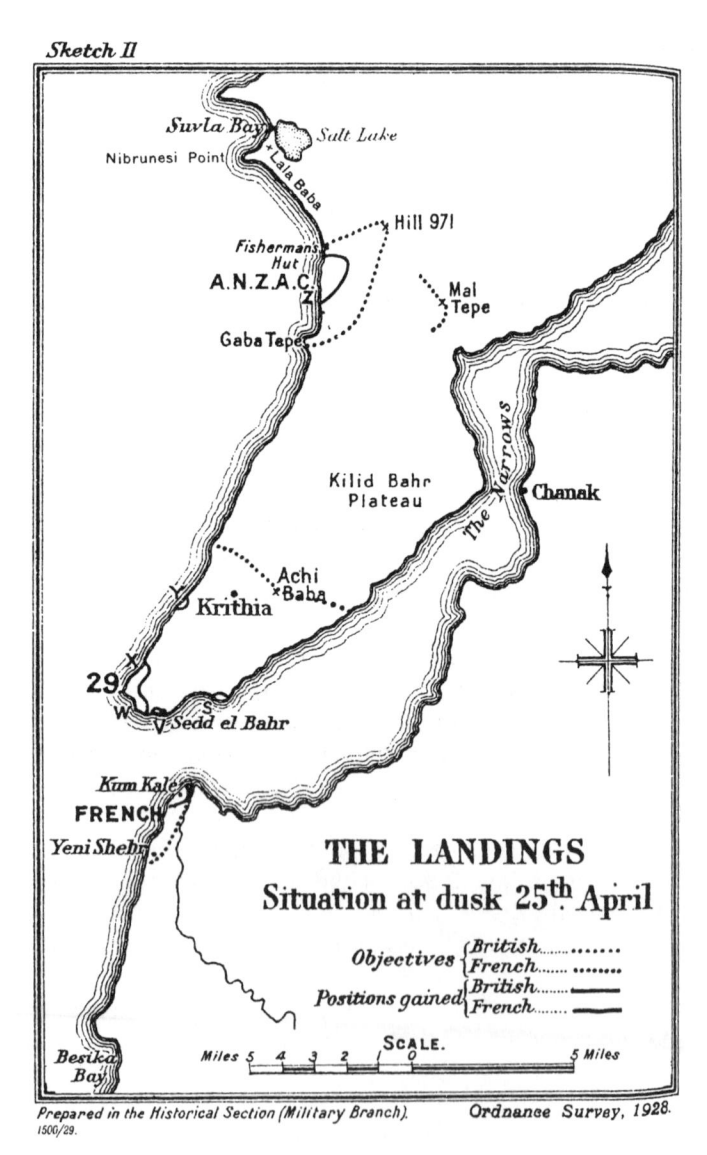

Map A.II.1 The landings at Gallipoli

Appendix II 249

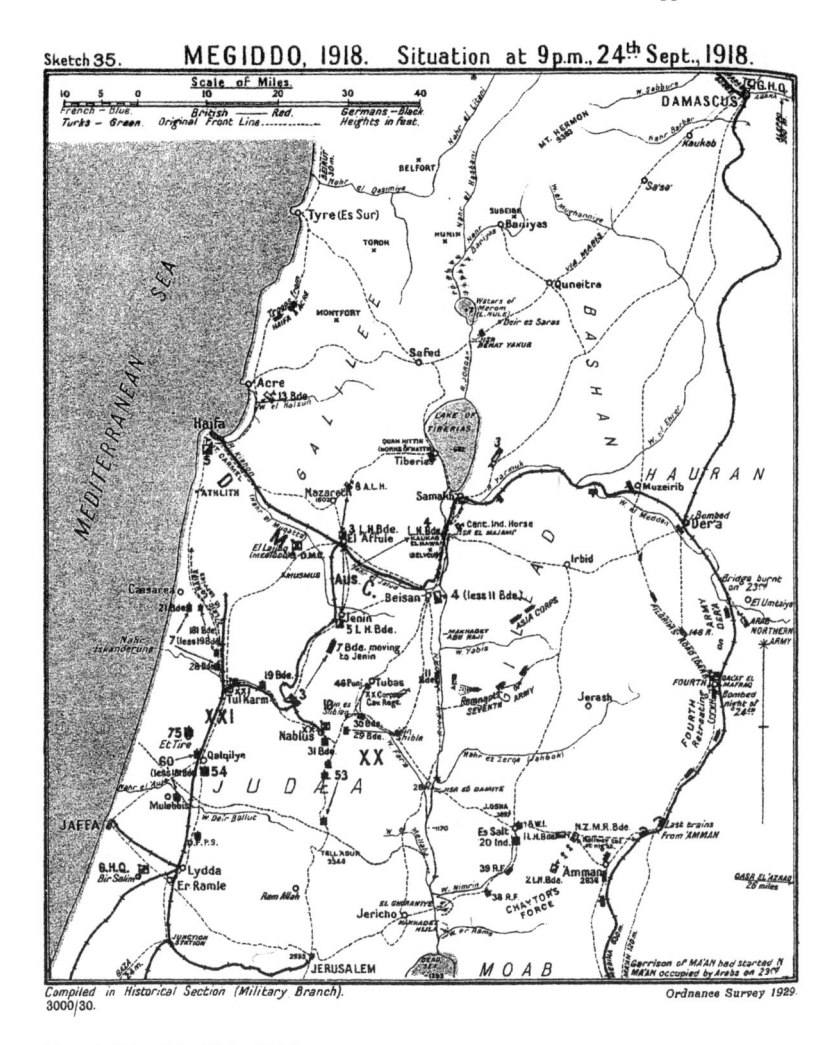

Map A.II.2   Megiddo 1918

Notes

1 Introduction: a Matter of Record

1. Lt.-Col. W.G. Pettifar MBE, *The Fusilier*, 5, 2, June 1985, p. 125.
2. As acknowledged by the official museum of the Jewish Legion, the Beit Hagudim Museum, Avichail, Israel, run by the Israel Department of Defence.
3. David Vital, *The Origins of Zionism* (Oxford: Clarendon, 1975), ch. 8.
4. Chaim Weizmann, *Trial and Error* (London: Hamilton, 1949), p. 190.
5. Ibid., p. 214.
6. *Chaim Weizmann Papers Series A Vol. VII August 1914–November 1917*, ed. L. Stein (London: Oxford University Press, 1975), p. 12.
7. Weizmann, *Trial and Error*, p. 215.
8. Ibid., pp. 446–7.
9. B. Gardner, *Allenby* (London: Cassell, 1965), p. 286.
10. Vital, *Origins of Zionism*, p. 373.
11. Eugene C. Black, *The Social Politics of Anglo-Jewry 1880–1920* (Oxford: Blackwell, 1988), p. 217.
12. Stuart Cohen, *English Zionists and British Jews* (Princeton: Princeton University Press, 1982), pp. 314–23.
13. Ben Halpern, 'The Americanisation of Zionism 1880–1930', in J. Reinharz, and A. Shapira (eds), *Essential Papers on Zionism* (London: New York University Press, 1995), pp. 319–36.
14. Ibid. p. 331.
15. Weizmann, *Trial and Error*, pp. 256–62.
16. See Anita Shapiro, 'Introduction' in J. Reinharz, and A. Shapira, pp. 20–1.
17. L. Stein, *The Balfour Declaration* (London: Vallentine Mitchell, 1961).
18. Isaiah Friedman, *The Question of Palestine, British–Jewish–Arab Relations 1914–1918*, 2nd expanded edn (New Jersey: Transaction, 1992).
19. Friedman, *Question of Palestine*, Foreword.
20. Rashid Ismail Khalidi, *British Policy towards Syria and Palestine 1906–1914* (Oxford: Ithaca, 1980).
21. Mark Levene, 'The Balfour Declaration: a Case of Mistaken Identity', *English Historical Review*, cvii, 422, January 1992.
22. Ibid., pp. 70–1.
23. Cecil Roth, *A History of the Jews in England* (Oxford: Oxford University Press, 1941).
24. D. Cesarani (ed.), *The Making of Modern Anglo-Jewry* (Oxford: Blackwell, 1990), pp. 1–11.
25. Peter Stansky, 'Anglo-Jew or English/British? Some Dilemmas of Anglo-Jewish History', *Jewish Social Studies*, 2, 1, Fall 1995.
26. David S. Katz, 'The Marginalisation of Early Modern Anglo-Jewry History', *Immigrants and Minorities*, 10, March/July 1991.
27. Tony Kushner, 'Heritage and Ethnicity: an Introduction, *Immigrants and Minorities*, 10, March/July 1991.

28. Todd Endelman, 'English Jewish History', *Modern Judaism*, 1, 1, 1991.
29. Colin Holmes, *Anti-Semitism in British Society 1876–1939* (London: Arnold, 1979), pp. 222–32.
30. Bryan Cheyette, *Constructions of 'The Jew' in English Literature and Society: Racial Representations, 1875–1945* (Cambridge: Cambridge University Press, 1993), p. 268.
31. D. Feldman, *Englishmen and Jews* (London: Yale University Press, 1994).
32. Thomas Weber, 'Anti-Semitism and Philo-Semitism among the British and German Elites: Oxford and Heidelberg before the First World War', *English Historical Review*, cxviii, 475, February 2003. William D. Rubinstein, *A History of the Jews in the English-Speaking World: Great Britain* (Basingstoke: Macmillan – now Palgrave Macmillan, 1996). See also William D. Rubinstein and Hilary L. Rubinstein, *PhiloSemitism: Admiration and Support in the English-Speaking World for Jews 1840–1939* (Basingstoke: Macmillan – now Palgrave Macmillan, 1999).
33. Rubinstein, *History*, p. 109.
34. David Cesarani, 'An Embattled Minority: the Jews in Britain during the First World War', *Immigrants & Minorities*, Special Issue, March 1989.
35. Rubinstein, *History*, p. 198.
36. Rubinstein, *History*, p. 196.
37. W.D. and H.L. Rubinstein, *Philosemitism*.
38. J.H. Patterson, *With the Judeans in the Palestine Campaign* (London: Hutchinson, 1922).
39. J.H. Patterson, *With the Zionists in Gallipoli* (London: Hutchinson, 1918).
40. Vladimir Jabotinsky, *The Story of the Jewish Legion* (New York: Ackerman, 1945).
41. Elias Gilner, *War and Hope: a History of the Jewish Legion* (New York: Herzl, 1969).
42. Harold Pollins, 'Jews in the British Army in the First World War', *Jewish Journal of Sociology*, 37 (1995), pp. 100–11.
43. PRO, WO 73/107–114. Monthly Returns July 1917–December 1921, Jabotinsky, p. 145 and Gilner, p. 278.
44. Imperial War Museum Department of Sound Records, Plotzker, tape 12506. Adler's correspondence is in the Anglo-Jewish archive, Southampton University, MS125.
45. Major H.D. Myer, *Soldiering of Sorts*, unpublished typescript (London: 1978?)
46. Mark Levene, 'Going Against the Grain: Two Jewish Memoirs of War', *Jewish Culture and History*, 2, 2, 1999. The other memoir was that of Arnold Harris, a Whitechapel Zionist who evaded military service.
47. WO 32 11352 Series.
48. See, for example, Lyn Macdonald, *Somme* (London: Penguin, 1983); John Keegan, *The Face of Battle* (London: Cape, 1976); and Martin Middlebrook *The First Day on the Somme* (London: Penguin, 1971).
49. Peter Simkins, 'Everyman at War', in *The First World War and British Military History*, ed. Brian Bond (Oxford: Clarendon, 1991), pp. 220–7.
50. Peter Simkins, *Kitchener's Army: the Raising of the New Armies, 1914–1916* (Manchester University Press, 1988). There is a growing scholarly literature on the social experience of the mass armies; see, *inter alia*, Ian Beckett and Keith Simpson (eds), *A Nation in Arms: a Social Study of the British Army in*

the First World War (Manchester University Press, 1985); Keith Simpson, 'The British Soldier on the Western Front', in Peter H. Liddle (ed.), *Home Fires and Foreign Fields: British Social and Military Experience in the First World War* (London: Brassey's, 1985); J.G. Fuller, *Troop Morale and Popular Culture in the British and Dominion Armies* (Oxford University Press, 1990); John Bourne, 'The British Working Man in Arms', in Hugh Cecil and Peter H. Liddle (eds), *Facing Armageddon: the First World War Experienced* (London: Leo Cooper 1996); Gary Sheffield, *Leadership in the Trenches: Officer–Man Relations, Morale and Discipline in the British Army in the Era of the Great War* (Basingstoke: Macmillan – now Palgrave Macmillan 2000); and various contributions to John Bourne, Peter H. Liddle and Ian Whitehead (eds), *The Great World War 1914–45*, 2 Vols (London: Harper Collins, 2000 and 2001).
51. Antony Beevor, *Stalingrad* (London: Viking 1988) and *Berlin: the Downfall 1945* (London: Viking, 2002).
52. Arthur Marwick, *The Deluge*, 2nd edn (Basingstoke: Macmillan – now Palgrave Macmillan 1991).
53. Using Dr G.D. Howe, 'A Social History of the British West Indies Regiment', Unpublished Ph.D., University of London, 1994.

2 The Zion Mule Corps

1. R. St. John, *Ben-Gurion* (London: Doubleday, 1959), p. 31.
2. For a fuller explanation of Ahad Aha'am's book see D. Vital, *The Origins of Zionism*, Oxford: Clarendon, 1975), from p. 108.
3. R. St. John, *Ben-Gurion*, p. 32.
4. Shabtai Teveth, *Ben-Gurion: The Burning Ground 1886–1948* (Boston: Hale, 1987), p. 92.
5. For further details on Trumpeldor, see P. Lipovetzky, *Joseph Trumpeldor* (Jerusalem: World Zionist Organisation, 1953).
6. Vladimir Jabotinsky, *The Story of the Jewish Legion* (New York: Ackerman, 1945), p. 32.
7. Elias Gilner, *War and Hope. A History of the Jewish Legion* (New York: Herzl Press, 1969), p. 35.
8. Gilner, *War and Hope*, pp. 36–7.
9. Ibid. p. 46.
10. Ibid. p. 41.
11. PRO Cabinet records. CAB 19/33, Report of the Dardanelles Commission.
12. Eugene C. Black, *The Social Politics of Anglo-Jewry 1880–1920* (Oxford: Blackwell, 1988), p. 335.
13. Gilner, *War and Hope*, p. 41.
14. General Sir Alexander Godley GCB, KCMG, *Life of an Irish Soldier* (London: Murray, 1939).
15. Avichail Testimonial, Pte. No. 164 I.C. Korman, Zion Mule Corps.
16. PRO, WO95/4670, War Diary, Directorate of Transport, EEF, 30 March 1915. See also J.H. Patterson, *With the Zionists in Gallipoli* (London: Hutchinson, 1922) p. 12.
17. Army List 1903–1912.
18. PRO, CAB 19/33, Report of the Dardanelles Commission.

Notes 253

19. *JC*, 24 March 1916.
20. At the time of writing, Mr Denis Brian of West Palm Beach USA, was researching a biography of John Patterson. For discussion of the roots of philo-Semitism see David S. Katz, *Philo-Semitism and the Readmission of Jews to England* (Oxford: Clarendon, 1982); and William D. Rubinstein and Hilary L. Rubinstein, *PhiloSemitism: Admiration and Support in the English-Speaking World for Jews 1840–1939* (London: Hamilton, 1999).
21. PRO, WO 158/966.
22. Jabotinsky, *Story of the Jewish Legion*, Foreword.
23. PRO, WO 95/4670, War Diary, Directorate of Transport EEF.
24. *British Jewry Book of Honour*, ed. Rev. M. Adler (London: Claxton, 1922), p. 63.
25. Liddell Hart Archives, Kings College London, Hamilton Papers, File 19/3.
26. General Sir Ian Hamilton, *A Staff Officer's Scrapbook*, 2 Vols (London: Arnold, 1906/7).
27. General Sir Ian Hamilton, *Gallipoli Diary*, 2 Vols (London: Arnold, 1920), Vol. 1 p. 84.
28. LHA, Hamilton Papers, File 6/10 Letter No. 40.
29. PRO,WO 95/4269, War Diary, Command Paymaster MEF.
30. PRO, WO 32/18541, Zion Mule Corps Compensation.
31. PRO, WO 95/4350, War Diary Administrative Staff of NZ and Australian Division.
32. LHA, Hamilton Papers, File 5/12.
33. PRO, WO95/4326, War Diary General Staff 1st Australian Division.
34. PRO, WO 95/4350.
35. C.E.W. Bean, *The Story of ANZAC* (Sydney: Official History, 1921), p. 78.
36. PRO, WO 95/4269.
37. Ibid.
38. Major J. Gillam, *Gallipoli Diary* (London: [1918], Strong Oak Press edn, 1989), p. 45.
39. Gilner, *War and Hope*, p. 98.
40. LHA, Hamilton Papers, File 5/12.
41. Gildesgame/Watts correspondence, November/December 1987.
42. Gilner, *War and Hope*, ch. 8. Patterson, *Zionists*, p. 120.
43. Gilner, *War and Hope*, ch. 8.
44. Gilner, *War and Hope*, p. 65.
45. J.G. Fuller, *Troop Morale and Popular Culture in the British and Dominion Armies 1914–1918* (Oxford: Clarendon, 1990), pp. 85–7.
46. Major A.H. Mure, *With the Incomparable 29th* (London: Chambers, 1919) p. 185.
47. Hamilton, *Diary*, Vol. II, p. 249.
48. PRO, WO 95/4270, War Diary Deputy Director Supply and Transport, EEF.
49. PRO, WO 32/18544, C.-in-C. Cairo – Units raised in Egypt for MEF – pension arrangements.
50. PRO, WO 32/18541.
51. PRO, WO 32/18541.
52. Correspondence Watts/Mrs Sarah Conn (daughter), September 1987.
53. PRO, WO 95/4269
54. Ibid.
55. *JC,* 24 March 1916.

56. PRO, WO 158 966, Zion Mule Corps, misc. correspondence.
57. *Linns Stamp News*, 4 May 1987. Translation by Dr Emile Diskstein.
58. Jabotinsky, *Story of the Jewish Legion*, p. 44.
59. Bernard Wasserstein, *The British in Palestine*, 2nd edn (Oxford: Blackwell, 1991), pp. 44–5.
60. Jabotinsky, *Story of the Jewish Legion*, p. 45.

3 The Founding of the Legion: Part One

1. Vladimier Jabotinsky, *The Story of the Jewish Legion* (New York: Ackermann, 1945), p. 48.
2. Ibid., p. 51.
3. Chaim Weizmann, *Trial and Error* (London: Hamilton, 1949), p. 211.
4. Ibid., p. 217.
5. Jabotinsky, *The Story of the Jewish Legion*, p. 57.
6. Public Record Office, Foreign Office papers, FO 371 2835/18095.
7. PRO, FO 371 2835/18995, Correspondence FO/WO (Propaganda Bureau).
8. Eugene C. Black, *The Social Politics of Anglo-Jewry 1880–1920* (Oxford: Blackwell, 1988). See also D. Feldman, *Englishmen and Jews* (London: Yale University Press, 1994).
9. Black, *Social Politics*, p. 374.
10. David Cesarani (ed.), *The Making of Modern Anglo-Jewry* (Oxford: Blackwell, 1990), p. 118.
11. Feldman, *Englishmen and Jews*, pp. 382–3.
12. Weizmann, *Trial and Error*, p. 191.
13. See especially John Gordon Little, 'H.H. Asquith and Britain's Manpower Problem 1914–1915', *History*, **82**, July 1997, 397–409.
14. According to the British Jewry Book of Honour, 50,000 Jews served in the British armed forces in the First World War.
15. David Cesarani, 'An Alien Concept? The Continuity of Anti-Alienism in British Society before 1940', in David Cesarani and Tony Kushner (eds), *The Internment of Aliens in Twentieth Century Britain* (London: Cass, 1993), p. 36.
16. *JC*, 19 Nov 1915.
17. Greater London Records Office, Archive of the Board of Deputies of British Jews, File BDBJ ACC 3121 A/17. London Committee Minutes October 1915–July 1921.
18. PRO, FO 371 2835/18995.
19. Ibid.
20. Thomas Weber, 'Anti-Semitism and Philo-Semitism among the British and German Elites: Oxford and Heidelberg before the First World War', *English Historical Review*, **cxviii**, 475, February 2003, 104.
21. PRO, FO 371 2835/18995.
22. Ibid.
23. PRO, FO 371 2835/18995.
24. Ibid.
25. PRO, FO 371 2835/18995.
26. William D. Rubinstein, 'The Secret of Leopold Amery', *History Today*, **49**, 2, February 1999, 17–26.

Notes 255

27. PRO, FO 371 2816.
28. PRO, FO 371 2816.
29. Ibid.
30. Jabotinsky, *Story of the Jewish Legion*, p. 65.
31. PRO, FO 371 2816.
32. GLRO, BDBJ File ACC 3121 C11/3/1/2, Confidential Memoranda Wolf to Committee.
33. Black, *Social Politics*, p. 33.
34. Ibid., p. 23.
35. Anglo-Jewish Archive, Southampton University, File MS137, Conjoint Committee Foreign Branch Vol. 1.
36. AJA, MS137, Conjoint Committee Foreign Branch Vol. 2.
37. Viscount Samuel, *Memoirs* (London: Cresset, 1945) p. 141.
38. Bernard Wasserstein, *Herbert Samuel: a Political Life* (Oxford: Clarendon, 1992), p. 214.
39. *JC*, 14 April 1916.
40. Jabotinsky, *Story of the British Legion*, p. 67.
41. *JC*, 28 April 1916.
42. PRO, FO 371 2835/98116.
43. Mark Levene, *War, Jews and the New Europe: the Diplomacy of Lucien Wolf, 1914–1919* (Oxford: University Press, 1992), p. 118.
44. *JC*, 26 May 1916.
45. PRO, WO 32 11352, Foreign Legions: Discussion as to formation of Jewish Legion for service in Palestine, 1916–1917.
46. GLRO, BDBJ ACC 3121 C11/2/9, Wolf's correspondence.
47. GLRO, BDBJ ACC 3121 C11/2/9/2, Wolf's correspondence.
48. PRO, WO 293, ACI 1156, 8 June 1916.
49. Bod. Lib., Asquith Papers, MS Asquith 127. Folio 229.
50. PRO, WO 293.
51. GLRO, BDBJ, ACC 3121 A/17.
52. *JC*, 25 June 1916. Lord Sandhurst; House of Lords debate 2 August 1916.
53. *JC*, 7 July 1916.
54. *JC*, 30 June 1916.
55. B. Wasserstein, *Herbert Samuel: a Political Life* (Oxford: Clarendon Press, 1992), p. 214.
56. GLRO, BDBJ ACC 3121 A/17.
57. *The Times*, 15 July 1916.
58. *The Times*, 15 July 1916.
59. GLRO, BDBJ ACC 3121 C11/2/9/1. Wolf to B. Zusman.
60. PRO, FO 800/99. See also India Office Papers, MSS Eur. D 591. Unpublished typescript, Sir David Waley KCMG CB MC, *Life of Edwin Montagu*. For a more detailed account of the differences between Samuel and Montagu, which includes an extract from this letter, see Wasserstein, *Hebert Samuel*, p. 224.
61. AJA, MS137, Vol. 1. (Report 27/6/16–18/9/16).
62. Black, *Social Politics*, p. 375 (notes).
63. GLRO, BDBJ ACC 3121/C11/2/9. Wolf to Rothschild 23/8/16.
64. PRO, WO 32 11352. WO reply to a proposal from a Mr Reuben Cohen to form a Jewish Legion.

256 Notes

4 The Founding of the Legion: Part Two

1. It will be recalled from the previous chapter that 'Home' referred to the Jews defending their homes in Britain, and 'Heim' to the liberation of Palestine and the creation of a Jewish home there.
2. GLRO, BDBJ ACC 3121/C11/2/9, Wolf to Samuel 1 September 1916.
3. Vladimir Jabotinsky, *The Story of the Jewish Legion* (New York: Ackerman, 1945), p. 75.
4. Mark Levene, *War, Jews and the New Europe: the Diplomacy of Lucien Wolf 1914–1919* (Oxford: Oxford University Press, 1992), p. 146.
5. GLRO, BDBJ ACC 3121/C11/2/9. Wolf to Rothschild 23 August 1916.
6. GLRO, BDBJ ACC 3121/C11/2/9. Wolf to Jabotinsky 4 September 1916.
7. GLRO, BDBJ ACC 3121/C11/2/9. Wolf to Henderson 6 September 1916.
8. Jabotinsky, *Story of the Jewish Legion*, p. 76.
9. *JC*, 8 September 1916.
10. Sharman Kadish, *Bolsheviks and British Jews: the Anglo-Jewish Community, Britain and the Russian Revolution* (London: Cass, 1992), p. 205.
11. Eugene C. Black, *The Social Politics of Anglo-Jewry 1880–1920* (Oxford: Blackwell, 1988); L. Stein, *The Balfour Declaration* (London: Vallentine Mitchell, 1961); Isaiah Friedman, *The Question of Palestine, British-Jewish-Arab Relations 1914–1918*, 2nd expanded edn (New Jersey: Transaction, 1992); and B. Wasserstein, *Herbert Samuel, A Political Life* (Oxford: Clarendon, 1992).
12. PRO HO 45 10819/318095 Special Branch Reports 1916.
13. PRO, HO 45/10819/318095/112a. Special Branch Report, 18 October 1916.
14. Jabotinsky, *Story of the Jewish Legion*, p. 77.
15. PRO, CAB 41/37/39, Bill to compel the enlistment of unnaturalised aliens of allied countries, 1916 Nov. 7. See also Wasserstein, *Herbert Samuel*, p. 219.
16. Jabotinsky, *Story of the Jewish Legion*, p. 80.
17. Chaim Weizmann, *Trial and Error* (London: Hamilton, 1949), p. 255.
18. An extract from a typescript dated 10 November 1952, in the author's possession, of articles for the *Jewish Observer* and *Middle Eastern Review*.
19. Kadish, *Bolsheviks and British Jews*, p. 140.
20. L. Stein, *The Balfour Declaration*, p. 324.
21. *JC*, 24 November 1916.
22. For further reading see Colonel A.P. Wavell, *The Palestine Campaigns* (London: Constable, 1932), pp. 58–67.
23. See Chapter 1. The files are located in PRO WO 32 11352.
24. PRO, CAB 24/ 9, Memoranda GT Series.
25. PRO, WO 32 11352.
26. PRO, WO 32 11352.
27. *Chaim Weizmann Papers Series A*, Vol. VII, Letters 306 and 307.
28. PRO, FO 371 3094 1917, Letter to Foreign Secretary from C.G.E. Fletcher, Town Clerk, Metropolitan Borough of Islington, 14 March 1916.
29. PRO, WO 32 11353. Files Infantry (Code 15 (E)) and General Code 110 (A), relating to the raising of Jews for service in Palestine following Jabotinsky's proposals, and designation of units specially raised for Jews in Royal Fusiliers 1917–19.

30. PRO, WO 32 11353.
31. PRO, FO 371 3101. Jabotinsky to Sykes 25 March 1917.
32. PRO, FO 371 3101. Memo. Sykes to War Council 7 April 1917.
33. PRO, WO 32 11353. Amery to Lord Derby 5 April 1917.
34. *Chaim Weizmann Papers Series A*, Vol. VII, Notes to Letter 492.
35. PRO, WO 32 11353. Trumpeldor & Jabotinsky to Lloyd George 3 April 1917.
36. Jabotinsky, *Story of the Jewish Legion*, p. 87.
37. Ibid., p. 83.
38. PRO, FO 371 3101. Letter from Army Council to FO 16 April 1917.
39. PRO, WO 32 11353.WO minute dated 18 April 1917.
40. PRO, WO 32 11353. Memo. Tagart to Woodward 13 April 1917.
41. PRO, WO 32 11353. Jabotinsky to Sir Eric Drummond 20 April 1917.
42. PRO, WO 32 11353. Jabotinsky to Lloyd George 29 April 1917.
43. PRO, WO 32 11353. P.H. Kerr to War Office 5 May 1917.
44. For a detailed explanation of the dual foreign policy situation see L. Stein, *The Balfour Declaration*, pp. 383–5, and Friedman, *Question of Palestine*, pp. 14–143.
45. PRO, WO 32 11353. Memorandum (Secret) from Lord Derby to War Cabinet 23 May 1917, which indicates Imperial War Cabinet endorsed Lloyd George's view.
46. Ibid.
47. PRO, WO 32 11353. WO minute sheet Geddes to Hutchinson 12 June 1917.
48. PRO, WO 32 11353. WO minute sheet Geddes to Hutchinson 12 June 1917.
49. PRO, WO 32 11353. WO minute sheet Geddes to Hutchinson 12 June 1917.
50. Ibid.
51. Jabotinsky, *Story of the Jewish Legion*, p. 88.
52. General the Rt. Hon. Sir Nevil Macready Bart. GCMG KCB, *Annals of an Active Life* (London: Hutchinson, 1924) 2 Vols, 1, p. 280.
53. See Keith Surridge, 'All you Soldiers are what we call pro-Boer: the Military Critique of the South African War, 1879–1901', *History*, **82**, 268, October 1997. For further comment see Cecil Bloom, 'Colonel Patterson: Soldier and Zionist', paper to the Jewish Historical Society of England, April 1990.
54. PRO, WO 32 11353. Samuel to Jabotinsky, 14 June 1917.
55. Elias Gilner, *War and Hope: a History of the Jewish Legion* (New York: Herzl, 1969), p. 103.
56. PRO, WO 293/7, ACI 1470 and FO 371 3094 1917.
57. For a brief description and catalogue of the relevant Home Office files see D. Englander (ed.), *A Documentary History of Jewish Immigrants* (Leicester: Leicester University Press, 1994), pp. 310–33.
58. Kadish, *Bolsheviks and British Jews*, pp. 208–9.
59. *The Times*, 25 July 1917. See also reports in the *Daily Telegraph*, 25 September 1917 and *Pall Mall Gazette*, 24 September 1917.
60. *The Times*, 9 August 1917.
61. PRO, FO 371 3094 1917. Letter from C. Read, Hon. Sec., Tottenham ILP to General-Secretary ILP, 24 April 1917.
62. See Bruce Millman's *Managing Domestic Dissent in First World War Britain* (London: Cass, 2000). He shows that militant, working-class patriotism was the major force bearing down on dissent.

258 Notes

63. Black, *Social Politics*, p. 368.
64. For a fuller explanation see Levene, *War, Jews and the New Europe*, p. 147.
65. See D. Cesarani, 'The Transformation of Communal Authority in Anglo-Jewry, 1914–1940', in D. Cesarani (ed.), *The Making of Modern Anglo-Jewry* (Oxford: Blackwell, 1990); also Geoffrey Alderman, *Modern British Jewry* (Oxford: Clarendon, 1992).
66. AJA, MS185, Landa Papers/AJ320, Letter from Grand-Secretary of the Grand Order of Israel Friendly Society, 24 August 1917.
67. For further reading, reflecting modern research, that describes the complexities of the relationship between the practice of Judaism and assimilation into European society, see J. Frankel & S. Zipperstein (eds), *Assimilation and Community: the Jews in Nineteenth Century Europe* (Cambridge: Cambridge University Press), 1992).
68. For a fuller account of the politicisation of Russian Jewry in the East End, see Kadish, *Bolsheviks and British Jews*, ch. 5.
69. Ahad Ha'am/Trumpeldor correspondence November 1916 as quoted in Lipovetzky, P., Joseph *Trumpeldor* (Jerusalem: World Zionist Organisation, 1953).
70. *JC*, 20 April 1917.
71. *JC*, 3 August 1917.
72. *JC*, 17 August 1917.
73. PRO, WO 32 11353. WO Internal minutes 5–27 July 1917.
74. PRO, WO 32 11353. Letter from Tagart to Director of Organisation, 3 August 1917.
75. PRO, WO 32 11353. WO Internal minutes 6–11 August 1917.
76. *The Times*, 8 August 1917.
77. Jabotinsky, *Story of the Jewish Legion*, p. 94.
78. PRO, WO 32 11353. WO Minutes, and AJA, Landa Papers/AJ320, MS185, Letters 1/1.
79. Jabotinsky, *Story of the Jewish Legion*, p. 96.
80. PRO, WO 32 11353. Patterson to Lord Chichester, 14 August 1917 and AJA, Landa Papers/AJ320, MS185, Letters 1/1.
81. PRO, WO 32 11353. Patterson to Lord Chichester, 14 August 1917.
82. PRO, WO 32 11353. WO minutes 15–23 August 1917.
83. Ibid.
84. AJA, MS185, Landa Papers/AJ320, Rothschild to Landa 17 and 19 August 1917.
85. PRO, WO 32 11353. Lord Rothschild letter to Lord Derby 22 August 1917.
86. PRO, FO 371 3101. Jabotinsky to Graham 19 August 1917.
87. PRO, FO 371 3101. Graham to Jabotinsky 21 August 1917.
88. *The Times*, 21 August 1917 and *JC* 24 August 1917.
89. PRO, WO 32 11353. P.H. Kerr to Lord Derby 22 August 1917.
90. PRO, CAB 21/58. Memo. From E.S. Montagu, Sec. of State for India, 23 August 1917.
91. PRO, WO 32 11353. WO Internal minutes 20–9 August 1917.
92. AJA, MS185. Landa Papers/AJ320, Landa and Adler circular issued 24 August 1917.
93. PRO, WO 32 11353. 'Members of the Deputation to Lord Derby' 30 August 1917.

94. PRO, WO 32 11353. WO Internal minutes 30 August 1917.
95. PRO, WO 32 11353. Copy of minutes of War Cabinet 227, 3 September 1917.
96. AJA, MS185. Landa Papers/AJ320, Joseph Cowen also considered Patterson as essential to the future of the regiment, see PRO, WO 32 11353, letter Cowen to Amery 7 September 1917.

5 Raising the Battalions: Great Britain

1. Vladimir Jabotinsky, *The Story of the Jewish Legion* (New York: Ackerman, 1945), p. 101. For further insight see also M. Adler, *A Jewish Chaplain on the Western Front* in Revd. M. Adler (ed.), *The British Jewry Book of Honour* (London: Caxton, 1922), which also receives a mention in D. Englander (ed.), *A Documentary History of Jewish Immigrants* (Leicester: Leceister University Press, 1994), pp. 345–6.
2. AJA, MS 185, Landa Papers/AJ320, Macready to Kiley 16 October 1917.
3. J.H. Patterson, *With the Judeans in the Palestine Campaign* (London: Hutchinson, 1922), pp. 37 & 38.
4. AJA, MS 185, Landa Papers/AJ320, Jabotinsky to Landa 15 November 1917.
5. AJA, MS 185, Landa Papers/AJ320, Letters 1/1.
6. PRO, FO 371 3104, Jabotinsky to Balfour 16 November 1917.
7. AJA, MS 185, Landa Papers/AJ320, Letters 1/1.
8. *JC*, 7 December and 21 December 1917.
9. See Patterson, *With the Judeans*, p. 46 also correspondence Gerald Falk OBE, JP (son) and the author, October 1987, and Avichail testimony compiled by Jean Falk (widow). After the war, Leib Falk emigrated to Australia, where he served as chaplain to the Australian military forces between both World Wars and throughout the Second, whilst acting as minister at the Great Synagogue, Sydney for 33 years until his death in 1956, aged 68.
10. AJA, MS 124. Letters and diary of Private Paul Epstein, 1918–19.
11. AJA, MS 185 Landa Papers/AJ320, Patterson to Landa 7 December 1917.
12. Stephen Gardiner, *Epstein* (London: Michael Joseph 1993), p. 84.
13. AJA, MS 185 Landa Papers/AJ320, Rothschild to Landa 27 December 1917.
14. AJA, MS 185 Landa Papers/AJ320/2, Macready to Kiley 29 January 1918.
15. Patterson, *With the Judeans*, p. 32.
16. PRO, WO 32 11353. Minute headed '38th Battalion, Royal Fusiliers'.
17. For longer-term consequences see PRO MH/57/204 – a detailed report by the committee's chairman covering the plight of those left behind.
18. *JC*, 18 January 1918.
19. For a modern discussion of the political background see Mark Levene, 'The Balfour Declaration: a Case of Mistaken Identity', *English Historical Review*, cvii, 422, January 1992. Levene argues that the declaration was made not on British strategic interest, but on a perception of Jews based on anti-Semitism, and ends his article with a specific reference to the deportation element of the Military Service Convention with Russia.
20. Eugene C. Black, *The Social Politics of Anglo-Jewry 1880–1920* (Oxford: Blackwell, 1988), p. 377.
21. S. Kadish, *Bolsheviks and British Jews* (London: Cass, 1992), pp. 238–9.

260 Notes

22. PRO, HO 45/10819/318095/558. Aliens: Russian subjects – military service and associated problems.
23. Ibid.
24. PRO, HO 45/10822. Jabotinsky to Henderson 12 December 1917. Henderson had been forced to leave the government because of his support for the Stockholm conference, but remained influential as the most respected leader of 'patriotic Labour'.
25. *Chaim Weizmann Papers Series A*. Vol. 1. Letter 24.
26. PRO, CAB 23/5 WC 329. War Cabinet Minutes 23 January 1918.
27. Ibid.
28. Ibid.
29. Ibid.
30. For War Cabinet 'final' decision, see PRO HO 45/10822/545.
31. *JC*, 25 January 1918.
32. David Cesarani, 'An Alien Concept?', in D. Cesarani & T. Kushner (eds), *The Internment of Aliens in Twentieth Century Britain* (London: Cass, 1993), p. 36. Also see the introduction by both editors, remarking upon the lack of research and understanding of this topic.
33. *Kent Messenger*, 9 February 1918.
34. PRO, WO 73 107.
35. *Kent Messenger*, 9 February 1918.
36. See also Robert Henriques, *Marcus Samuel First Viscount Bearsted and Founder of The 'Shell' Transport and Trading Company 1853–1927* (London: Barrie and Rockliff, 1960).
37. PRO, WO 73 107.
38. PRO, AIR 560 16 15. Intelligence summary Part II. Week ending Monday, 22 April, 1918.
39. The instruction to Chief Constables is contained in a Home Office Circular, of 5 March 1918,which can be found in PRO HO 45/10839/333052.
40. AJA, MS 185 Landa Papers/AJ320/1/1, correspondence Lord Rothschild/Landa 12 February 1918.
41. Royal Fusiliers Archive (Regimental HQ, HM Tower of London), War Diary 38th Battalion.
42. Gardiner, *Epstein*, p. 92.
43. Patterson, *With the Judeans*, p. 43.
44. Avichail testimonial J1159 Sergeant D. Dobrin 38th Battalion R.F.
45. Avichail testimonial Captain S.H. Barnet 38th Battalion R.F.
46. Avichail testimonial J137 Sergeant S. Wolfson 38th Battalion R.F.
47. For further reading on the acknowledgement of the Jewish soldier in the Boer War see David Englander (ed.), *Documentary History*, pp. 340–5.
48. Avichail testimonial J162 Lance Corporal A. Robinson 38th Battalion R.F.
49. Avichail testimonial RSM J.H. Carmell 38th Battalion R.F.
50. The film archive of the Imperial War Museum has a print of newsreel coverage of the march-past, showing Patterson leading his men through cheering crowds and on past the saluting base.
51. *JC*, 8 February 1918. The parade was also reported, with a photograph, in The *Daily Graphic* of 5 February 1918.
52. For an insight into Macready's attitude on race and officer commissions see PRO WO 163/23. Precis No. 937, 2 October 1918.
53. Patterson, *With the Judeans*, p. 42.

6 Raising the Battalions: the United States

1. Michael Bar-Zohar, *Ben-Gurion* (New York: Delacorte, 1978), p. 37. For further reading see Isaiah Friedman, *The Question of Palestine: British–Jewish–Arab Relations 1914–1918*, 2nd expanded edn (New Jersey: Transaction, 1992).
2. John Buchan has been accused of anti-semitism in his novels, especially the comments on the international Jewish conspiracy by the character Scudder in *The Thirty-Nine Steps*, but this may also be regarded as reflecting a contemporaneous view of the world from an imperialist standpoint.
3. PRO, T102/16, Scheme of Working of Department of Information, September 1917.
4. PRO, T102/16.
5. AJA, MS170 Stein Papers/AJ244. Hyamson to L. Stein, 18 December 1917.
6. PRO, 371 3409/118764, Hyamson to Ormsby-Gore, 11 September 1918. For a fuller account see Friedman, *Question of Palestine*, p. 297.
7. Ibid., p. 298.
8. It is an interesting reflection on the struggle for 'world opinion' that the British government had used the Bryce Report to distract attention from the odium attaching to Tsarist Russia because of the mistreatment of Jews in western Russia during the 'great retreat' of 1915; see W.H. McNeill, *Arnold Toynbee: a Life* (Oxford: Oxford University Press, 1989).
9. J.M. Winter, *The Experience of World War 1* (London: Guild Publishing, 1988), p. 215. For more details see R.G. Hovannisian (ed). *The Armenian Genocide: History, Politics, Ethics* (New York: St. Martins Press – now Palgrave Macmillan, 1992).
10. PRO, T102/16.
11. PRO, CAB24/10 447, Memo. Ormsby Gore to War Cabinet, 14 April 1917.
12. For more on Aaron Aaronson see Friedman, *Question of Palestine*, and Chaim Weizmann, *Trial and Error* (London: Hamilton, 1949). For a detailed examination of Nili activities, see Anthony Verrier (ed.), *Agents of Empire, Anglo-Zionist Intelligence Operations 1915–1919, Brigadier Walter Gribbon, Aaron Aaronson and the Nili Ring* (London: Brassey, 1995).
13. Friedman, *Question of Palestine*, ch. 8.
14. Lawrence James, *Imperial Warrior: the Life and Times of Field Marshal Viscount Allenby 1861–1936* (London: Orion, 1993), pp. 147–8.
15. See Matthew Hughes, 'Lloyd George, the Generals and the Palestine Campaign', *Imperial War Museum Review*, 11 November 1997, pp. 12–13; and for a fuller exposition, Matthew Hughes, *Allenby and British Strategy in the Middle East, 1917–1919* (London: Frank Cass, 1999).
16. Matthew Hughes, 'General Allenby and the Palestine Campaign', *Journal of Strategic Studies*, **19**, 4, December 1996, pp. 14–15.
17. Jonathan Frankel, *Prophecy and Politics, Socialism, Nationalism and the Russian Jews, 1862–1917* (Cambridge: Cambridge University Press, 1981).
18. Weizmann, *Trial and Error*, p. 239.
19. Frankel, *Prophecy and Politics*, pp. 512–14.
20. For further background see S. Kadish, *Bolsheviks and British Jews* (London: Cass, 1992); and Eugene Black, *The Social Politics of Anglo-Jewry 1880–1920* (Oxford: Blackwell, 1988).
21. Kadish, *Bolsheviks and British Jews*, p. 3.

22. For a detailed explanation of the arguments behind these decisions and disagreements see Frankel, *Prophecy and Politics*, pp. 548–51.
23. Ibid., p. 538.
24. Vladimir Jabotinsky, *The Story of the Jewish Legion* (New York: Ackerman, 1945), p. 109.
25. *Chaim Weizmann Papers*, Telegrams 18 and 44.
26. Elias Gilner, *War and Hope: a History of the Jewish Legion* (New York: Herzl, 1969), pp. 148–58.
27. Isaac Ben-Zvi, *The Hebrew Battalions: Letters* (Jerusalem: Yad Ben-Zvi, 1969), p. 30.
28. PRO, WO293 9, ACI 859, August 1917.
29. PRO, WO32 11353/151. War Office to General White, 14 February 1918.
30. PRO, WO32 11353/148. War Office to General White, 21 February 1918.
31. PRO, FO 371 3399, FO minutes March 1918.
32. Dr H.L. Gordon, 'From Zion Mule Corps to Jewish Legion', in the *Bulletin of the Veterans Jewish Legion*, **1**, 5, May 1976. (Hirsch Loeb Gordon was the organiser and commander of the American Palestine Jewish Legion.) See also Gilner, *War and Hope*, pp. 204–06.
33. Gilner, *War and Hope*, pp. 148–58.
34. PRO FO 371 3399, FO minute 21 February 1918.
35. J.H. Patterson, *With the Judeans in the Palestine Campaign* (London: Hutchinson, 1922), p. 49.
36. PRO, WO32 11353. Message No. E.A. 946, 20 March 1918.
37. PRO, WO32 11353. Message 54424 cipher A.G.13, 17 March 1918.
38. PRO, WO32 11353. Message No. E.A. 946, 20 March 1918.
39. Extract from Revd. L.A. Falk, 'Memoirs', *The Maccabean*, 10 May 1929 – with thanks to Gerald Falk (son).
40. AJA, MS124 AJ15/1, Epstein Papers.
41. AJA, MS185 AJ320, Landa Papers, letter 23 June 1918.
42. *JC*, 15 February 1918.
43. *JC*, 22 February 1918.
44. AJA, MS185 AJ320, Landa Papers, Greenberg to Rothschild, 10 April 1918.
45. PRO, WO73 107.
46. Gilner, *War and Hope*, ch. 35, fn. 15.
47. Ben–Zvi, *Hebrew Battalions*, p. 29.
48. Jabotinsky, *Story of the Jewish Legion*, p. 164.
49. Gilner, *War and Hope*, pp. 168–9. See also record of visit to Norman A. Cohen and Major Charles R. Piver, 'Soldiers' Mail – The Jewish Legion', *BAPIP Bulletin*, **81**, Winter 1974/75.
50. Avichail testimonial J2901 Pte. M. Gordon 39th Battalion R.F.
51. Avichail testimonial J-Pte. G. Avrunin 39th Battalion R.F.
52. Avichail testimonial J-Pte. G. Lossos 39th Battalion R.F.
53. Avichail testimonial J-Pte. I. Stone 39th Battalion R.F.
54. Avichail testimonial J- Pte. B. Morrow 39th Battalion R.F.
55. Avichail testimonial J2989 Pte. M. Stern 39th Battalion R.F.
56. Avichail testimonial J-Corporal H. Scwartz 38th Battalion R.F.
57. Avichail testimonial J4294 Pte. N. Newman 39th Battalion R.F.
58. Avichail testimonial J3101 Pte. B. Myer 39th Battalion R.F.
59. Avichail testimonial J-A/Sgt. J. Cohen 39th Battalion R.F.

Notes 263

60. Avichail testimonial J-Pte. I. Schwartz 39th Battalion R.F.
61. Avichail testimonial J-Pte. M. Frankel 39th Battalion R.F.
62. Gilner, *War and Hope*, p. 173.
63. Correspondence Braiterman/Watts, September/October 1987.
64. Avichail testimonial J5833 Corporal E. Ginsburg 39th Battalion R.F.
65. Correspondence Braiterman/Watts, September/October 1987, Ash/Watts, April 1988, Gast/Watts, September 1987.

7 Preparation and Prejudice

1. PRO, WO 160/23, Military Intelligence Dept., Memo. to GHQ, EEF, 20 May 1917.
2. Chaim Weizmann, *Trial and Error* (London: Hamilton, 1949), p. 272.
3. Ibid., p. 273.
4. According to *The Times*, 8 May 1920, the first English publication was made in February 1920 in an appendix to a book entitled *The Jewish Peril* by S.A. Nilus, originally published in Russian in May 1917.
5. Weizmann, *Trial and Error*, p. 273. For further background on the *Protocols* see Norman Cohn, *Warrant for Genocide, the Myth of the Jewish World Conspiracy and the Protocols of the Elders of Zion* (London: Eyre & Spottiswode, 1967). See also Richard S. Levy's Introduction to Binjamin W. Segel, *A Lie and A Libel: the History of the Protocols of the Elders of Zion* (Lincoln, NB: University of Nebraska Press, 1995, first published 1926.).
6. J.H. Patterson, *With the Judeans in the Palestine Campaign* (London: Hutchinson, 1922), p. 54.
7. Ibid.
8. Ibid. p. 55, and Vladimir Jabotinsky, *The Story of the Jewish Legion* (New York: Ackerman, 1945), p. 112.
9. Elias Gilner, *War and Hope: a History of the Jewish Legion* (New York: Herzl, 1969), pp. 212–15.
10. Gilner, *War and Hope*, p. 215.
11. John Connell, *Wavell: Scholar and Soldier* (London: Collins, 1964), pp. 189–90.
12. Lawrence James, *Imperial Warrior: the Life and Times of Field-Marshall Allenby* (Weidenfeld, 1993), p. 149. See also PRO, WO33/935/782, Telegrams European War: Egypt, 1917.
13. PRO, WO 33/946 Telegrams European War: Egypt, 1917–1918 No. 9760, 26 June 1918.
14. Izhak Ben-Zvi, *The Hebrew Battalions: the Letters*, trans. T. Baker and M. Benaya (Jerusalem: Yad Ben-Zvi, 1969), pp. 56–7.
15. Ibid.
16. Weizmann, *Trial and Error*, p. 272.
17. PRO, WO33/946 81467, No. 9438, War Office to Allenby 21 April 1918.
18. Patterson, *With the Judeans*, pp. 64–5 and Gilner, *War and Hope*, pp. 215–16.
19. PRO FO 371 3399, WO to Sokolow, 15 August 1918.
20. AJA, MS124 AJ15/1, Epstein papers.
21. Major H.D. Myer, *Soldiering of Sorts*, unpublished typescript (London: 1978?). See also Mark Levene, 'Going Against the Grain: Two Jewish Memoirs of War', *Jewish Culture and History*, **2**, 2, 1999.

22. Myer, *Soldiering of Sorts*, p. 20.
23. Myer, p. 98.
24. Ibid., pp. 97–8.
25. Avichail Testimonial J3777 'Chick' Bitton, CSM 40th Battalion.
26. Avichail Testimonial J192 Max Karo, CSM 38th Battalion. See also his autobiography, Max Karo, *City Milestones and Memories* (London: Weidenfeld and Nicolson, 1962).
27. This paragraph constructed from Elias Gilner, *War and Hope*; D. Ben-Gurion, *Letters to Paula* (London: Vallentine Mitchell, 1971); Izhak Ben-Zvi, *The Hebrew Battalions*.
28. PRO, WO32 11353, 112A Allenby/ WO 10 May 1918.
29. PRO, WO32 11353, 110A Allenby/ WO 14–16 April 1918.
30. PRO, WO32 11353, 111A WO/Allenby 11 May 1918.
31. Patterson, *With the Judeans*, p. 61 and Gilner, *War and Hope*, p. 225.
32. Weizmann, Letters, No. 214, in L. Stein (ed.), *The Letters and Papers of Chaim Weizmann Series A* (London: Oxford University Press, 1975).
33. Ibid. No. 217.
34. See Appendix A for full manpower statistics.
35. Weizmann, *Trial and Error*, pp. 286 and 287.
36. PRO, WO 33/960 81467. Cables No. 9845 & 9898.
37. Avichail testimonial J-Sergeant A. Rubenstein, 40th Battalion.
38. Avichail testimonial J4506 Pte. J. Pinchevsky 40th Battalion.
39. Avichail testimonial J5028 Pte. D. Ribniker 40th Battalion.
40. Avichail testimonial J5432 Pte. N. Freedman 40th Battalion.
41. Jabotinsky, *Story of the Jewish Legion*, p. 117.
42. Gilner, *War and Hope*, p. 238.
43. Ibid., p. 240.
44. AJA, MS185 AJ320, Landa Papers, Box 2.
45. Jabotinsky, *Story of the Jewish Legion*, pp. 123–9.
46. Ibid., p. 131.
47. Avichail Testimonial, J-Corporal Leon Hildesheim (Gildesgame) ZMC.
48. From copy of letter sent to author by Helen Finkel of New Jersey (niece of Harry Levine), 1988/90 (see Figure 7.5).
49. AJA, MS185 AJ320, Landa Papers.

8 The Legion at War

1. PRO, WO 33/960/ 81467. GHQ Egypt /WO No. 9872 18 July 1918.
2. J.H. Patterson, *With the Judeans in the Palestine Campaign* (London: Hutchinson, 1922), p. 88.
3. PRO, WO 33/960/ 81467. GHQ Egypt/WO No. 9961 7 August 1918.
4. See also PRO, WO 33/960 81467. GHQ Egypt/WO No. 9938 & No. 9952 August 1918.
5. PRO, WO 33/960 81467. WO/GHQ Egypt No. 9971 9 August 1918.
6. Pte. Lobagola is mentioned in a note in File R40 in the Regimental Archives, and wrote a colourful autobigraphy entitled: *Lobagola: an African Savage's Own Story* (New York: Knopf, 1930). Melhado is mentioned in Myer, *Soldiering of Sorts*, p. 97.

7. Quotation from Bernard Wasserstein, *The British in Palestine* (Oxford: Blackwell, 1991), pp. 45–6. Wasserstein's reference is 'Colonel Margolin ... to HQ, 26 Nov. 1918, marked "Very Private" (CZA L4/36)'. CZA is the Central Zionist Archive in Jerusalem.
8. For a detailed explanation of Allenby's strategy see Major-General Sir G. Macmunn and Captain C. Falls, *Official History of the War, Egypt and Palestine Vols 1 and 2*, Vol. 2, ch. xx. Also see A.P. Wavell, *The Palestine Campaigns* (London: Constable, 1928), pp. 173–203; and for a modern critique of Allenby's strategy and tactics see Matthew Hughes, *Allenby and British Strategy in the Middle East, 1917–1919* (London: Frank Cass, 1999), 'General Allenby and the Palestine Campaign', *Journal of Strategic Studies*, **19**, 4, December 1996, and 'Lloyd George, the Generals and the Palestine Campaign', *Imperial War Museum Review*, 11 November 1997.
9. AJA, MS124 AJ15/1, Epstein papers.
10. Official History, ch. xx, p. 423.
11. Ibid. p. 423.
12. Ibid., p. 425.
13. G.D. Howe, 'A Social History of the British West Indies Regiment', unpublished Ph.D. thesis, University of London 1994, p. 137.
14. Vladimir Jabotinsky, *The Story of the Jewish Legion* (New York: Ackerman, 1945), pp. 131–2.
15. Howe, 'Social History', p. 202.
16. T.J. Mitchell and M.B.E. Smith, *Medical History of the War: Casualties and Medical Statistics* (HMSO 1931), pp. 208–17.
17. Ibid., p. 217.
18. Wavell, *The Palestine Campaigns*, fn. p. 184.
19. Matthew Hughes, 'General Allenby and the Palestine Campaign', *Journal of Strategic Studies*, **19**, 4, December 1996, pp. 73–80.
20. Patterson, *With the Judeans*, p. 119.
21. Myer, *Soldiering of Sorts*, p. 96.
22. Patterson, *With the Judeans*, p. 129.
23. Avichail testimonial J1149 Pte. Philip Bratt 38th Battalion RF.
24. Avichail testimonial J894 Pte. Ralph Share 38th Battalion RF.
25. See Jabotinsky, *Story of the Jewish Legion*, pp. 64–5.
26. Avichail testimonial J1991 L/Cpl, Yehuda Furst 38th Battalion RF.
27. Avichail testimonial Lieut. Arthur Cowen, 39th Battalion RF.
28. Avichail testimonial J3123 L/Cpl. Samuel Dratch 39th Battalion RF.
29. See, for example, PRO, WO 33/960 81467. GHQ Egypt to WO No. 10148, 24 September 1918.
30. For full details of the Staff correspondence see Patterson, *With the Judeans*, pp. 159–67.
31. Elias Gilner, *War and Hope: a History of the Jewish Legion* (New York: Herzl, 1969), pp. 242–3.
32. Myer, *Soldiering of Sorts*, p. 101.
33. Ibid., p. 115.
34. Ibid. p. 125.
35. Ibid. p. 118
36. Izhak Ben-Zvi, *The Hebrew Battalions: the Letters*, trans. T. Baker and M. Benaya (Jerusalem: Yad Ben-Zvi, 1969), p. 72.

37. Avichail testimonial, J3821 Sgt. H. Freeman 39th Battalion RF.
38. Interview with author 20 November 1987. Another Legion boxer, J227 Pte. Alexander Berger was also in touch with the author in November 1987, and a picture of Alexander and his comrades visiting the Pyramids can be seen in Figure 8.1.
39. Patterson, *With the Judeans*, p. 192. General Chaytor's letter to Patterson from his home in Wellington, New Zealand, written on 9 March 1920.

9 Disturbance and Decline

1. PRO, WO 32 11353/11113. Jabotinsky/Amery 11 November 1918.
2. PRO, WO 32 11353/11113. Jabotinsky/Amery 11 November 1918.
3. PRO, WO 32 11353/111A. Amery/Major-General Macdonogh 4 December 1918.
4. PRO, WO 32 11353/112. Minute sheets nos. 37 and 38, Lt.-Col. Liddell 13 December 1918.
5. Ibid.
6. PRO, WO 32 11353. Minute sheet no. 121.
7. PRO, WO 32 11353/115A. Amery/Major-General Macdonogh 25 January 1919.
8. Ibid.
9. PRO WO 73 107. Figures relating to the Legion from its inception to disbandment are tabulated in Appendix I. War diaries in the Regimental Archive, HM Tower of London.
10. Elias Gilner, *War and Hope: a History of the Jewish Legion* (New York: Herzl, 1969), pp. 271–2.
11. PRO, WO 32 11353/110. Cable No. EA 1917 20 November 1918. Also printed on summary in WO 33/960 81467 No. 10457A.
12. PRO, WO 33/960 81467 No. 10470A, 24 November 1918.
13. A.P. Wavell, *Allenby in Egypt* (London: Harrap, 1943), pp. 27–34. See also later chapters in Lawrence James, *Imperial Warrior: the Life and Times of Field-Marshal Allenby* (London: Weidenfeld, 1993).
14. PRO, WO 33/960 81467 No. 71693, 28 November 1918.
15. PRO, WO 33/960 81467 No. 10518, 5 December 1918.
16. PRO, WO 33/960 81467 No. 10520, 6 December 1918.
17. PRO, WO 123/61 Army order 65, February 1919.
18. PRO, WO 33/960/81467. Message No. 74774 WO/GOC in C, Egypt, 1 February 1919.
19. PRO, WO 33/960/81467. Message No. EA2185 GHQ Egypt/WO, 4 February 1919.
20. PRO, WO 33/960/81467. Message No. 75054 WO/GHQ Egypt, 7 February 1919.
21. PRO, WO 33/960/81467. Message No. 79430 WO/GHQ Egypt, 4 February 1919.
22. PRO, WO 33/960/81467. Message No. 75716 WO/GHQ Egypt 27 February 1919.
23. H.D. Myer, *Soldiering of Sorts*, unpublished typescript (London: 1978?), p. 159.
24. PRO, WO 33/960/81467. Message No. EA2211 GHQ Egypt/WO 12 February 1919.

25. PRO, WO 33/960/81467. Message No. IS 2/438 GHQ Egypt/WO 3 May 1919.
26. For a brief but illuminating explanation see E. Monroe, *Britain's Moment in the Middle East 1914–1971* (London: Chatto & Windus, 1981), pp. 55–9.
27. See, for example, J. Putkowski, *British Army Mutineers 1914–1922* (London: Boutle, 1999); G. Oram, *Death Sentences Passed by Military Courts of the British Army 1914–1920* (London: Boutle, 1998).
28. PRO, WO 33/960/81467. Message No. C189 GHQ Egypt/WO 28 April 1919.
29. J.H. Patterson, *With the Judeans in the Palestine Campaign* (London: Hutchinson, 1922), p. 205.
30. Wavell, *Allenby in Egypt*, pp. 50–2.
31. Patterson, *With the Judeans*, pp. 193–5.
32. Vladimir Jabotinsky, *The Story of the Jewish Legion* (New York: Ackerman, 1945), pp. 146–7.
33. PRO, WO 33 11353. Correspondence Weizmann/Wilson.
34. Ibid.
35. PRO, WO 33 11353. Wilson/Allenby 2 April 1919.
36. PRO, WO 33 11353. Allenby/Wilson 21 April 1919.
37. PRO, WO 33/981/81467. Message No. C214 GHQ Egypt/WO 2 May 1919.
38. PRO, WO 33/981/81467. Message No. C214 GHQ Egypt/WO 2 May 1919.
39. Bernard Wasserstein, *The British in Palestine* (Oxford: Blackwell, 1991), p. 48. Letter written 9 June 1919 in private possession of Mr. J.H. Money. In the same passage Wasserstein reveals a document from the CZA which records his view that 'their (Jews) manner wherever they are given authority is often domineering and objectionable to others'.
40. Jabotinsky, *Story of the Jewish Legion*, p. 150.
41. Gilner, *War and Hope*, p. 297.
42. Ibid., pp. 299–300.
43. Myer, *Soldiering of Sorts*, p. 171.
44. PRO, WO 213 29–34. Field General court martial registers 1919–1921.
45. Jabotinsky, *Story of the Jewish Legion*, pp. 147–50.
46. PRO, WO 95 4470 War Diary 40th Battalion RF.
47. PRO, FO 371 4238 Jabotinsky's petition to the King 7 October 1919.
48. Ibid.
49. Ibid., statement made to Jabotinsky by J5842 L/Cpl A. Goldfarb 38th Battalion RF.
50. From copy of postcard sent to author by Helen Finkel of New Jersey (niece of Harry Levine), December 1987.
51. PRO, FO 371 4238 Jabotinsky's petition to the King 7 October 1919. Statement of J840 Pte. W. Bronstein 38th Battalion RF and J1563 Pte. J. Goodman 38th Battalion RF.
52. PRO, FO 371 4238 Jabotinsky's petition to the King 7 October 1919. Statement of J5231 Pte. A. Lichtenfeld 38th Battalion RF.
53. Patterson, *With the Judeans*, pp. 204–5, Jabotinsky, *Story of the Jewish Legion*, p. 155; Gilner, *War and Hope*, pp. 303–305; Wasserstein, *Story of British in Palestine*, p. 47 and PRO, WO 95 4470 War diary 40th Battalion RF.
54. Tom Segev, *One Palestine Complete*, trans. Haim Watzman (London: Henry Holt, 2001), pp. 99–100.
55. Ibid. pp. 100–01.

268   Notes

56. Patterson, *With the Judeans*, pp. 221–4. See also PRO, WO 213 29–34. Field General Court martial registers 1919–1921.
57. Jabotinsky, *Story of the Jewish Legion*, p. 158.
58. Gilner, *War and Hope*, pp. 313–14.
59. Avichail testimonial J8038 Pte. Isaac Lichtenstein, 39th Battalion RF.
60. PRO, WO 213 29–34. Field-General court martial registers 1919–1921.
61. Patterson, *With the Judeans*, p. 225.
62. Patterson, *With the Judeans*, pp. 252–8, Gilner, *War and Hope*, pp. 316–19.
63. PRO, FO 371 4238 Jabotinsky's petition to the King 7 October 1919.
64. Ibid.
65. Ibid. Note from W.M. Short to Mr Campbell 1 November 1919.
66. Ibid. File minutes Turkey A No. 144798, 24 October 1919.
67. Ibid.
68. Ibid.
69. Ibid., italics as in original. *War and Hope*, see also Gilner, pp. 312–13.
70. In addition, a copy of a telegram from Cairo to the War Office (PRO WO 32 11353) dated 23 October 1919 confirms that the 40th Battalion were refusing to draw pay as their war bonus had been stopped on 21 March. Apparently, serious trouble was avoided when this was corrected.
71. US State Department File 841.2226(1919). Key = 8 (Internal affairs of State) 41 (UK). Subject: Discharge of enlisted men from British Army (author's note: includes Canadian Army).
72. USSD 841 2226 (1919) Sub. No. 7253.
73. USSD 841 2226 (1919) Sub. Nos. 7261, 7267, 7269 & 7293.
74. USSD 841 2226 (1919) Sub. Nos. 7295 and 7360.
75. USSD 841 2226 (1919) Sub. Nos. 7360, 7323 and 7241.
76. PRO, WO 33/981/81467. Message No. 11122 WO/GHQ Egypt 17 May 1919.
77. PRO, WO 33/981/81467. Message No. 11128 WO/GHQ Egypt 19 May 1919.
78. PRO, WO 33/981/81467. Message No. 11185 WO/GHQ Egypt 2 June 1919.
79. PRO, WO 33/981/81467. Message No. 11194 GOC.-in-C. Egypt/WO 6 June 1919.
80. PRO, WO 213 29–34. Field-General court martial registers 1919–1921.
81. PRO, WO 11352 Draft ACI June 1919 and letter from director of organisation to GOC.-in-C. Southern and Eastern Commands 21 June 1919.
82. PRO, WO 33/981/81467. Message No. 11351 WO/Allenby 28 August 1919.
83. PRO, WO 33/981/81467. Message No. 11362 GHQ Egypt/WO 1 September 1919.
84. PRO, WO 123/61 Army orders July 1919. No. 236.
85. PRO, WO73 107 Monthly returns of the Army. Royal Fusiliers HM Tower of London, war diary 39th Battn.
86. Wasserstein, *The British in Palestine*, pp. 58–9.
87. PRO, WO 33/981 81467 Message No. 11739 GHQ Egypt/WO, 16 February 1920.
88. I am indebted to Herut Shlomiff of the Tel Hei Museum for this information.
89. Edward Horne, *A Job Well Done: a History of the Palestine Police Force* (London: Anchor, 1982).
90. Wasserstein, *The British in Palestine*, pp. 58–70, Segev, *One Palestine Complete*, pp. 129–38 and PRO, WO33 981 81467 Messages WO/GHQ Egypt April 1920.

91. PRO, WO 33/981 81467 Message No. 11815 GHQ Egypt/WO 12 April 1920.
92. None of these three incidents led to a court martial – see PRO, WO 213 29–34. Field-General court martial registers 1919–1921, which show only 5 legionnaires court martialled between January 1920 and disbandment in 1921, with none committing 'acts against inhabitants'.
93. PRO, WO 33/981 81467 Message No. 11815 GHQ Egypt/WO 12 April 1920.
94. PRO, WO 33/981 81467 Message No. 11838 GHQ Egypt/WO 23 April 1920.
95. PRO, WO 33/981 81467 – April/May/June 1920.
96. Wasserstein, *The British in Palestine*, pp. 101–02, and Segev, *One Palestine Complete*, ch. 8, and correspondence Watts/Dr Oscar Kraines of Miami Beach (lecture notes published in *Temple Beth Sholom*, December 1–15 1985).
97. Avichail testimonial Lt.-Col. Eliezer Margolin.

Conclusions: Legacy of the Legion

1. William D. Rubinstein and Hilary L. Rubinstein, *Philosemitism: Admiration and Support in the English Speaking World for Jews 1840–1939* (Basingstoke: Macmillan – now Palgrave Macmillan, 1990).
2. S. Kadish, *Bolsheviks and British Jews* (London: Cass, 1992) p. 51. Kadish calculates that 14 per cent of Anglo-Jewry (i.e. naturalised) served in the armed forces, compared with the national average of 11.5 per cent.
3. For a detailed discussion on post-war anti-Semitism see Tony Kushner, 'The Impact of British Anti-Semitism 1918–1945', in David Cesarani (ed.), *The Making of Modern Anglo-Jewry* (Oxford: Blackwell, 1990), pp. 198–9.

Bibliography

Unpublished primary sources

Anglo-Jewish Archive, Southampton University
AJA, MS116/115. Album of photographs of the Egyptian expeditionary force, 1918–19.
AJA, MS 124. Letters and diary of Private Paul Epstein, 1918–19
AJA MS125. Papers of Revd. Michael Adler, 1915–18
AJA, MS137. Archives of the Anglo-Jewish Association, 1871–1983
AJA, MS185. Papers of M.J. Landa relating to the 'Jewish regiment', 1916–44

Beit Hagudim Museum, Avichail, Israel
Zion Mule Corps and Jewish Legion veterans testimonials

Bodleian Library, Oxford
Asquith Papers
MS Asquith 28, Folio 45
MS Asquith 127, Folio 229

Greater London Record Office (now Metropolitan Record Office)
Board of Deputies of British Jews
ACC 3121 A/17
ACC 3121 C11/2/9
ACC 3121 C11/3/1/2

Imperial War Museum
Department of Film
IWM 651c
Department of Photographs
IWM Q12670–Q12673   IWMQ12679–Q12680
Department of Sound Records
IWM 12506 Audio tape Plotzker

Liddell Hart Archive, Kings College, London
Allenby Papers
1/8–1/14   2/1 2/2 2/5   4/ Press Cuttings
Hamilton Papers
19/3.
Robertson Papers
4/4/99   4/4/103–108   4/4/112   4/5–4/5/10
4/6   7/5/84   7/5/86   7/5/89
8/1/02   8/1/63

Miscellaneous
Myer, Major H.D., *Soldiering of Sorts*, unpublished typescript (London: 1978?)
Waley, Sir David, KCMG CB MC, *Life of Edwin Montagu*, unpublished typescript India Office Papers (now in PRO) MSS Eur. D 591

Public Record Office, London
Air Ministry
AIR 560 16 15
Cabinet Office

CAB 19/1	CAB 19/33	CAB 21/58
CAB 23/5	CAB 24/ 9	CAB 24/10 447
CAB 41/37/39	T102/16	

Foreign Office

FO 371 2816	FO 371 2835/18095	FO 371 2835/18995
FO 371 2835/98116	FO 371 3094 1917	FO 371 3101
FO 371 3104	FO 371 3399	FO 371 3409/118764
FO 371 4238	FO 800/99	

Home Office

HO 45/10819/318095/91	HO 45/10819/318095/112a	HO 45/10819/318095/558
HO 45/10822	HO 45/10839/333052	MH/57/204

War Office

WO 95/4670	WO 123/61	WO 127/10
WO 158/966	WO 160/23	WO 163/23
WO 213	WO 293	WO 293/7
WO 293/9	WO 32 11352	WO 32 11353
WO 32/11347	WO 32/18541	WO 32/18543
WO 32/18544	WO 33/935/782	WO 33/946
WO 33/960	WO 338	WO 73/107
WO 95/4269	WO 95/4270	WO 95/4309
WO 95/4311	WO 95/4326	WO 95/4350
WO 95/4470		

Royal Regiment of Fusiliers Archive, HM Tower of London
Royal Fusiliers Archive (Regimental HQ, HM Tower of London)
War Diary and Nominal Rolls 38th Battalion
War Diary and Nominal Rolls 39th Battalion
War Diary and Nominal Rolls 40th Battalion
War Diary and Nominal Rolls 42nd Battalion

United States of America: State Department Files
USSD 841 2226 (1919) Sub. No. 7253
USSD 841 2226 (1919) Sub. Nos. 7261, 7267, 7269 and 7293
USSD 841 2226 (1919) Sub. Nos. 7295 and 7360
USSD 841 2226 (1919) Sub. Nos. 7360, 7323 and 7241

Theses

Cesarani, Dr D., 'Zionism in England 1917–1939', D.Phil. thesis, Oxford University, 1986
Howe, Dr G.D., 'A Social History of the British West Indies Regiment', unpublished Ph.D. thesis, University of London, 1994

Published primary sources

Ben-Gurion, D., *Letters to Paula* (London: Vallentine Mitchell, 1971)
Ben-Zvi, Izhak, *The Hebrew Battalions: the Letters*, trans. T. Baker and M. Benaya (Jerusalem: Yad Ben-Zvi, 1969)
Gilner, Elias, *War and Hope: a History of the Jewish Legion* (New York: Herzl, 1969)
Jabotinsky, Vladimir, *The Story of the Jewish Legion* (New York: Ackerman, 1945)
Karo, Max, *City Milestones and Memories* (London: Weidenfeld and Nicolson, 1962)
Patterson, J.H., *With the Zionists in Gallipoli* (London: Hutchinson, 1918)
Patterson, J.H., *With the Judeans in the Palestine Campaign* (London: Hutchinson, 1922)
Stein, L. (ed.), *The Letters and Papers of Chaim Weizmann Series A* (London: Oxford University Press, 1975)
Weizmann, Chaim, *Trial and Error* (London: Hamilton, 1949)

Contemporary Newspapers and Periodicals

Jewish Chronicle
Kent Messenger
The Times
Daily Telegraph
Pall Mall Gazette
Daily Graphic

Secondary sources

Articles and papers

Bloom, Cecil, 'Colonel Patterson, Soldier and Zionist', presented to the Jewish Historical Society of England, April 1990
Cesarani, David, 'An Embattled Minority: the Jews in Britain During the First World War', *Immigrants and Minorities*, Special Issue, March 1989
Endelman, Todd, 'English Jewish History', *Modern Judaism*, 1, 1, 1991
Falk, Revd. L.A., 'Memoirs', *The Maccabean*, 10 May 1929
Gordon, Dr H.L., 'From Zion Mule Corps to Jewish Legion', in the *Bulletin of the Veterans Jewish Legion*, 1, 5, May 1976
Hughes, Matthew, 'General Allenby and the Palestine Campaign', *Journal of Strategic Studies*, 19, 4, December 1996
Hughes, Matthew, 'Lloyd George, the Generals and the Palestine Campaign', *Imperial War Museum Review*, 11 November 1997
Katz, David S., 'The Marginalisation of Early Modern Anglo-Jewry History', *Immigrants and Minorities*, 10, March/July 1991

Kushner, Tony, 'Heritage and Ethnicity: an Introduction', *Immigrants and Minorities*, **10**, March/July 1991
Levene, Mark, 'The Balfour Declaration: a Case of Mistaken Identity', *English Historical Review*, CVII, 422, January 1992
Levene, Mark, 'Going Against the Grain: Two Jewish Memoirs of War', *Jewish Culture and History*, **2**, 2, 1999
Little, John Gordon 'H.H. Asquith and Britain's Manpower Problem 1914–1915', *History*, **82**, July 1997
Pettifar, Lt.-Col. W.G., *The Fusilier*, **5**, 2, June 1985
Pollins, Harold, 'Jews in the British Army in the First World War', *Jewish Journal of Sociology*, **37** (1995)
Rubenstein, William D., 'The Secret of Leopold Amery', *History Today*, **49**, 2, February 1999
Stansky, Peter, 'Anglo-Jew or English/British? Some Dilemmas of Anglo-Jewish History', *Jewish Social Studies*, **2**, 1, Fall 1995
Surridge, Keith, 'All you Soldiers are what we call pro-Boer: the Military Critique of the South African War, 1879–1901', *History*, **82**, 268, October 1997
Sugarman, Martin, 'The Zion Muleteers', *The Orders and Medals Research Society*, Winter 1995
Weber, Thomas, 'Anti-Semitism and Philo-Semitism among the British and German Elites: Oxford and Heidelberg before the First World War', *English Historical Review*, CXVIII, 475, February 2003

Lectures and seminars

Connelly, Mark, 'Assimilation and Integration: the Jewish ex-servicemen of the East End, the memory of the Great War and the fight against fascism'. Institute of Historical Research, Contemporary History seminar, 29 May 1996
Hickey, Colonel M., 'Gallipoli', Imperial War Museum, London, 17 April 1996

Books

Adelson, Roger, *London and the Invention of the Middle East* (London: Yale University Press, 1995)
Adler, Revd. M. (ed.), *British Jewry Book of Honour* (London: Claxton, 1922)
Alderman, G., *Modern British Jewry* (Oxford: Clarendon, 1992)
Andrews, E.M., *The Anzac Illusion: Anglo-Australian Relations During the First World War* (Cambridge: Cambridge University Press, 1993)
Ascoli, David, *A Companion to the British Army* (London: Harrap, 1993)
Ashmead-Bartlett, E., *Uncensored Dardanelles* (London: Hutchinson, 1933)
Aspinall-Oglander, Brigadier-General C.F., *Official History of the War: Gallipoli Vols 1 and 2* (London: HMSO, 1929)
Bacon, J. and Gilbert, M. (eds), *The Illustrated Atlas of Jewish Civilisation* (London: Deutsch, 1990)
Baker, A., *Battle Honours of British and Commonwealth Armies* (London: Allan, 1986)
Barnes, J., and Nicholson, D. (eds), *The Leo Amery Diaries Vol. 1. 1896–1929* (London: Hutchinson, 1980)
Barnett, Corelli, *Britain and her Army 1509–1970* (London: Allen Lane, 1970)
Bar-Zohar, Michael, *Ben-Gurion*, trans. P. Kidron, (New York: Delacorte, 1978)

Bayley, C.C., *Mercenaries for the Crimea* (Montreal: McGill, 1977)
Bean, C.E.W., *The Story of ANZAC* (Sydney: Official History, 1921)
Bean, C.E.W., *Official History of Australia in the Great War*, 3rd edn (Queensland: Angus & Robertson, 1944)
Beckett, Ian F.W. and Simpson, Keith (eds), *A Nation in Arms: a Social History of the British Army in the First World War* (Manchester: Manchester University Press, 1985)
Beevor, Antony, *Stalingrad* (London: Viking, 1988)
Beevor, Antony, *Berlin: the Downfall 1945* (London: Viking, 2002)
Ben-Gurion, D., *Israel: a Personal History* (New York: Funk & Wagnalls, 1971)
Black, Eugene C., *The Social Politics of Anglo-Jewry 1880–1920* (Oxford: Blackwell, 1988)
Bond, Brian (ed.), *The First World War and British Military History* (Oxford: Clarendon, 1991)
Bourke, Joanna, *An Intimate History of Killing: Face-to-Face Killing in Twentieth-Century Warfare* (London: Granta, 1999)
Bourne, John, Liddle, Peter and Whitehead, Philip (eds), *The Great World War 1914–45*, 2 vols (London: Harper Collins, 2000 and 2001)
Briggs, Asa, *A Social History of England* (London: Weidenfeld & Nicolson, 1994)
Brown, Malcolm, *The Imperial War Museum Book of the First World War* (London: Sidgwick & Jackson, 1991)
Bruce, A., *An Illustrated Companion to the First World War* (London: Joseph, 1989)
Bullock, David L., *Allenby's War* (London; Blandford, 1988)
Bush, J., *Behind the Lines* (London: Merlin, 1984)
Carlyon, L.A., *Gallipoli* (London: Doubleday, 2002)
Carsten, F.L., *The Rise of Fascism* (London: Batsford, 1980)
Carver, Field-Marshal Lord, *Britain's Army in the Twentieth Century* (Basingstoke: Macmillan – now Palgrave Macmillan, 1998)
Cecil, Hugh and Liddle, Peter (eds), *Facing Armageddon: the First World War Experienced* (London: Leo Cooper, 1996)
Cesarani, D. and Kushner, T. (eds), *The Internment of Aliens in Twentieth Century Britain* (London: Cass, 1993)
Cesarani, D. (ed.), *The Making of Modern Anglo-Jewry* (Oxford: Blackwell, 1990)
Cheyette, Bryan, *Constructions of 'The Jew' in English Literature and Society: Racial Representations, 1875–1945* (Cambridge: Cambridge University Press, 1993)
Cohen, M., *Zion and State* (Oxford: Blackwell, 1987)
Cohen, Stuart, *English Zionists and British Jews (*Princeton: Princeton University Press, 1982)
Cohn, Norman, *Warrant for Genocide, the Myth of the Jewish World Conspiracy and the Protocols of the Elders of Zion* (London: Eyre & Spottiswode, 1967)
Connell, John, *Wavell: Soldier and Scholar* (London: Collins, 1964)
Cumming, H.H., *Franco-British Rivalry in the Post-War Near East* (Oxford: Oxford: University Press, 1938)
Duncan, Andrew, and Opatowski, Michel, *War in the Holy Land: From Megiddo to the West Bank* (Stroud: Sutton, 1998)
Edelman, Maurice, *Ben-Gurion: a Political Biography* (London: Hodder & Stoughton, 1964)
Englander, D. (ed.), *A Documentary History of Jewish Immigrants* (Leicester: Leicester University Press, 1994)

Falls, Captain Cyril, *Official History of the War, Egypt and Palestine Vol. 2* (London: HMSO, 1929)
Feldman, D., *Englishmen and Jews* (London: Yale University Press, 1994)
Ferguson, Niall, *The Pity of War* (London: Allen Lane, 1998)
Fishman, W.J., *East End Jewish Radicals 1875–1914* (London: Duckworth, 1975)
Fishman, W.J., *East End 1888. A Year in a London Borough among the Labouring Poor* (London: Duckworth, 1988)
Foss, M., *The Royal Fusiliers* (London: Hamish Hamilton, 1967)
Fox, Sir Frank, *The Royal Inniskilling Fusiliers in the World War* (London: Constable, 1928)
Frankel, Jonathan, *Prophecy and Politics: Socialism, Nationalism and the Russian Jews 1862–1917* (Cambridge: Cambridge University Press, 1981)
Frankel, J. and Zipperstein, S., *Assimilation and Community: the Jews in 19th Century Europe* (Cambridge: Cambridge University Press, 1992)
Freulich, Roman, *Soldiers in Judea* (New York: Herzl Press, 1964)
Friedman, Isaiah, *The Question of Palestine: British–Jewish–Arab Relations 1914–1918*, 2nd expanded edn (New Jersey: Transaction, 1992)
Fuller, J.G., *Troop Morale and Popular Culture in the British and Dominion Armies, 1914–1918* (Oxford: Oxford University Press, 1990)
Gardiner, S., *Epstein* (London: Michael Joseph, 1993)
Gardner, Brian, *Allenby* (London: Cassell, 1965)
Gilbert, Martin, *Exile and Return* (London: Weidenfeld and Nicolson, 1978)
Gilbert, Martin, *Routledge Atlas of the First World War* (London: Routledge, 1994)
Gilbert, Martin, *First World War* (London: Weidenfeld and Nicolson, 1994)
Gilbert, Martin, *Israel: a History* (London: Doubleday, 1998)
Gillam, Major J., *Gallipoli Diary* (Stevenage: Strong Oak, 1989)
Godley, General Sir Alexander, *Life of an Irish Soldier* (London: Murray, 1939)
Grey, Major W.E. (*2nd City of London Regiment in the Great War* (London: Regimental HQ, 1929)
Hamilton, General Sir Ian, *A Staff Officer's Scrapbook*, 2 vols (London: Arnold, 1906/7)
Hamilton, General Sir Ian, *Gallipoli Diary*, 2 vols (London: Arnold, 1920)
Hammond, J.L., *C.P. Scott and the Manchester Guardian* (London: Bell, 1934)
Haythornwaite, P., *The WW1 Source Book* (London: Arms & Armour, 1992)
Henriques, Robert, *Marcus Samuel First Viscount Bearsted and Founder of the 'Shell' Transport and Trading Company 1853–1927* (London: Barrie and Rockliff, 1960)
Herzog, Chaim, *Heroes of Israel: Profiles of Jewish Courage* (London: Weidenfeld and Nicolson, 1989)
Hickey, Michael, *Gallipoli* (London: Murray, 1995)
Holmes, Colin, *Anti-Semitism in British Society 1876–1939* (London: Arnold, 1979)
Horne, Edward, *A Job Well Done: a History of the Palestine Police Force* (London: Anchor, 1982).
Hovannisian, R.G. (ed.), *The Armenian Genocide: History, Politics and Ethics* (New York: St. Martins Press – now Palgrave Macmillan, 1992)
Hughes, Matthew, *Allenby and British Strategy in the Middle East, 1917–1919* (London: Frank Cass, 1999)
James, Lawrence, *Imperial Warrior: the Life and Times of Field-Marshal Allenby* (Weidenfeld and Nicolson, 1993)

Kadish, S., *Bolsheviks and British Jews* (London: Cass, 1992)
Khalidi, Rashid Ismail, *British Policy towards Syria and Palestine 1906–1914* (London: Ithaca, 1980)
Katz, David S., *Philo-Semitism and the Readmission of Jews to England* (Oxford: Clarendon, 1982)
Katz, David S., *The Jews in the History of England* (Oxford: Clarendon, 1994)
Keegan, John, *The Face of Battle* (London: Cape, 1976)
Kramer, Gudrun, *The Jews in Modern Egypt 1914–1952* (London: Tauris, 1990)
Laffin, J., *Damn the Dardanelles* (London: Doubleday, 1980)
Laquer, Walter, *A History of Zionism* (London: Weidenfeld & Nicolson, 1972)
Lawrence, T.E., *Seven Pillars of Wisdom* (London: Book Club Associates, 1976)
Lebzelter, Gisela C., *Political Anti-Semitism in England 1918–1939* (London: Macmillan, 1978)
Levene, Mark, *War, Jews and the New Europe: the Diplomacy of Lucien Wolf 1914–1919* (Oxford: Oxford University Press, 1992)
Liddell-Hart, B.H., *History of the First World War* (London: Cassell, 1970)
Liddle, P., *Men of Gallipoli* (London: Allen Lane, 1976)
Liddle, P. (ed.), *Home Fires and Foreign Fields: British Social and Military Experience in the First World War* (London: Brassey's, 1985)
Lipovetzky, P., *Joseph Trumpeldor* (Jerusalem: World Zionist Organisation, 1953)
Litvinoff, Barnet, *Ben-Gurion of Israel* (London: Praeger, 1954)
Lloyd-George, David, *War Memoirs*, 2 vols (London: Odhams, 1938)
Lobagola, *An African Savage's Own Story* (New York: Knopf, 1930)
Macready, General the Rt. Hon. Sir Nevil Macready, *Annals of an Active Life*, 2 vols (London: Hutchinson, 1924)
Marwick, Arthur, *The Deluge*, 2nd edn (Basingstoke: Macmillan – now Palgrave Macmillan, 1991)
Macdonald, Lyn, *Somme* (London: Penguin, 1983)
McNeill, W.H., *Arnold Toynbee: a Life*. (Oxford: Oxford University Press, 1989)
Meinertzhagen, R., *Middle East Diary 1917–1956* (London: Cresset, 1956)
Messinger, Gary S., *British Propaganda and the State in the First World War*, (Manchester: Manchester University Press, 1992)
Middlebrook, Martin, *The First Day on the Somme* (London: Penguin, 1971)
Millman, B., *Managing Domestic Dissent in First World War Britain* (London: Cass, 2000)
Mitchell, T.J. and Smith, M.B.E., *Medical History of the War, Casualties and Medical Statistics* (London: HMSO, 1931)
Monroe, E., *Britain's Moment in the Middle East 1914–1971* (London: Chatto & Windus, 1981)
Moorehead, A., *Gallipoli* (New York: Harper & Row, 1956)
Morton, F., *The Rothschilds* (London: Secker and Warburg, 1962)
Mure, Major A.H., *With the Incomparable 29th* (London: Chambers, 1919)
O'Neill, H.C., *The Royal Fusiliers in the Great War* (London: Heinemann, 1922)
Oram, G., *Death Sentences passed by the British Army 1914–1920* (London: Boutle, 1998)
Parkes, Revd. Dr James, *The Foundations of Judaism and Christianity* (London, 1955)
Putkowski, J., *British Army Mutineers 1914–1922* (London: Boutle, 1999)
Reinharz, J. and Shapira, A. (eds), *Essential Papers on Zionism* (London: New York University Press, 1995)

Bibliography

Rhodes, James, R., *Gallipoli* (London: Batsford, 1965)
Rogers, C., *The Battle of Stepney: the Sidney Street Siege: its Causes and Consequences* (London: Hale, 1981)
Rose, N., *Chaim Weizmann: a Biography* (London: Weidenfeld and Nicolson, 1987)
Roth, Cecil, *A History of the Jews in England* (Oxford: Oxford University Press, 1941).
Rubinstein, William D., *A History of the Jews in the English-Speaking World: Great Britain* (Basingstoke: Macmillan – now Palgrave Macmillan, 1996)
Rubinstein, William D. and Rubinstein, Hilary L., *Philosemitism: Admiration and Support in the English-Speaking World for Jews 1840–1939* (Basingstoke: Macmillan – now Palgrave Macmillan, 1999)
Samuel, Raphael and Thompson, Paul (eds), *The Myths We Live By* (London: Routledge, 1990)
Samuel, Viscount, *Memoirs* (London: Cresset, 1945)
Sanders, M.L. and Taylor, Philip M., *British Propaganda during the First World War 1914–1918* (London: Macmillan – now Palgrave Macmillan, 1982)
Segel, Binjamin W., *A Lie and A Libel: the History of the Protocols of the Elders of Zion* [1926] (Lincoln, NE: University of Nebraska Press, 1995)
Segev, Tom, *One Palestine Complete*, trans. Haim Watzman (London: Henry Holt, 2001)
Sheffield, Gary, *Leadership in the Trenches: Officer-Man Relations, Morale and Discipline in the British Army in the Era of the Great War* (Basingstoke: Macmillan – now Palgrave Macmillan, 2000)
Sheffy, Yigal, *British Intelligence in the Palestine Campaign 1914–1918* (London: Cass, 1997)
Sidebotham, H., *Great Britain and Palestine* (London: Macmillan, 1937)
Simkins, Peter, *Kitchener's Army: the Raising of the New Armies, 1914–1916* (Manchester University Press, 1988)
Steel, N., and Hart, P., *Defeat at Gallipoli* (Basingstoke: Macmillan – now Palgrave Macmillan, 1994)
Stein, L., *The Balfour Declaration* (London: Vallentine Mitchell, 1961)
Stone, Norman, *The Eastern Front 1914–1917* (London: Hodder & Stoughton, 1975)
Teveth, Shabtai, *Ben-Gurion the Burning Ground, 1886–1948* (Boston: Houghton Mifflin, 1987)
Trumpener, U., *Germany and the Ottoman Empire 1914–1918* (Princeton: Princeton University Press, 1968)
Udelson, Joseph H., *Dreamer of the Ghetto: the Life and Works of Israel Zangwill* (Alabama: Alabama University Press, 1990)
Verrier, A. (ed.), *Agents of Empire, Anglo-Zionist Intelligence Operations 1915–1919, Brigadier Walter Gribbon, Aaron Aarohnson and the Nili Ring* (London: Brasseys, 1995)
Vital, D., *The Origins of Zionism* (Oxford: Clarendon, 1975)
Wasserstein, Bernard, *The British in Palestine* (Oxford: Blackwell, 1991)
Wasserstein, B., *Herbert Samuel: a Political Life* (Oxford: Clarendon, 1992)
Wavell, A.P., *The Palestine Campaigns* (London: Constable, 1928)
Wavell, A.P. *Allenby in Egypt* (London: Harrap, 1943)
Wavell, Field-Marshal A.P., *Allenby: Soldier and Statesman* (London: Harrap, 1974)

Weightman, G., and Humphries, S., *The Making of Modern London* (London: Sidgwick & Jackson, 1984)

Winter, J.M., *The Experience of World War 1* (London: Guild Publishing, 1988)

Correspondents

Frank Adam, Manchester, UK
Mr and Mrs P. Ash, New York, USA
Mr W. Blumfield, Haifa, Israel
Mr W. Braiterman, Baltimore, USA
Dr J. Caditz, Los Angeles, USA
Benjamin Cohen, Tucson, Arizona, USA
Norman Collins, Merseyside, UK
Mrs Sarah Conn, London UK
Mr H. Davis, New York, USA
Mr Gerald Falk, Sydney, Australia
Helen Finkel, New Jersey, USA
Doreen and Eddie Flaxman, Leeds, UK
David M. Gordon, Leeds, UK
Cyril Franks, UK
Cyril Gallant, London, UK
Mr L. Gildesgame, New York, USA
Mr and Mrs Herbert Goldsmith, London, UK
Mr Laurence Hoppen, London, UK
Joyce Rose, London, UK
Jack H. Schwartz, Michigan, USA
Peter White, London, UK

Interviews

Harry Freeman, London, UK 20th November 1987
Mrs Irene White, UK 11th April 1991

Index

Aaronson, Aaron   125, 141, 142, 147, 194–5
Achi Baba, Turkey   35, 37
Adler, Revd. Michael   117
Albers, Police Sergeant   79–80
Aleppo, Syria   143
Alexander, David Lindo   56, 62, 67, 100–1
Alexandria   21–33 passim, 41–2, 45–6
  see also Egypt
Alexandrian Jews, in Zion Mule Corps   38, 44–5
Aliens Act (1905)   130
Aliens Restriction Act (1914)   56, 127
Allenby, Edmund H.H., Viscount   1, 4, 26, 93, 143, 151
  biographical details   xiv
  disturbance/decline of Legion   208–16 passim, 231–6 passim
  Legion at war   182, 183–4, 185, 188–9, 194–5
  Legion preparation and prejudice   162–72 passim, 178, 182, 183–4
American Jewish Congress   145–7
American Jewish soldiers   204–5, 233, 242
  recruitment   148–59, 160, 177–8
American Jewry   143–4, 165–6, 241
Amery, Leopold C.M.S.   54, 55, 57, 59–60, 141
  biographical details   xiv
  disturbance/decline of Legion   201–2, 203–4, 226
  founding of Legion   82, 83, 85, 88, 105, 114
Amman, Jordan   185
Anglo-Arab alliance   164–5
Anglo-Jewish Association   62, 90, 101
Anglo-Jewish community   4, 5, 17, 51–3, 56, 61, 62, 66, 100–1
Anglo-Jewish relations   2, 8–13, 243
Anglo-Turkish relations   7

anti-Semitism   2, 9, 10–11, 12, 15–17, 199–200, 234–5, 242–5
  in Britain   63, 128–9
  British Army   29–30, 96, 103, 217–32 passim
  Egyptian Expeditionary Force (EEF)   161–2, 163, 164, 167, 168, 181, 230
ANZAC Corps   30–4
Arab Forces   190–1, 205
Arab newspapers   140–1
Arabs
  Anglo-Arab alliance   164–5
  Egyptian   214
  Palestinian   209, 216, 217, 218–19, 235, 237–8
Argentinean Jewish recruitment   149
Armenia   140
Army Act (1908)   68
Army Council   90, 91, 103, 119
  Instruction (ACI)   1156, 1916 68
  Instruction (ACI)   1415, 1917 82–3, 115, 167–8
  Instruction (ACI), draft   1917 232
Asquith, H.H.   55, 68, 80, 83
Assheton Pownall, Lt. Col.   82
assimilationists   9–10, 12, 52, 53
  vs. Zionists   53–4, 61–3, 71–2, 77–9, 81–2, 94–5, 100, 110–11, 241–2
Assyrian Refugee Mule Corps   26, 29
Australian Light Horse Brigade, 1st   191
Australian and New Zealand Army Corps (ANZAC Corps)   30–4
Australian and New Zealand Mountain Division   185
Avrunin, Gershon   156

Baku oilfields   143
Balfour, Arthur   6–7, 9, 54, 88, 119, 125, 149, 226–7
Balfour Declaration   6–7, 54, 117, 120, 123, 139, 141, 208, 215

279

Balfour Declaration *continued*
  American perspective 144, 145, 146
  publication in Middle East 162
Bargman, Private Samuel 37
Barnet, Captain Samuel Horace 132–3
Beit Hagudim (Avichail) museum, Israel 14–15
Belah 223–4, 229, 230–1, 233
Ben-Gurion, David 1, 20, 21, 146, 147, 166, 171, 205, 210, 222–3, 239–40
  biographical details xiv-xv
Ben-Zvi, Isaac 1, 20, 21, 147, 148, 154, 166, 197, 205, 210
Benenson, Gregory 73, 76
Beneson Recruitment Committee 76, 77
Benim 20, 21, 22–3, 143, 146–7
  see also Ben-Gurion, David; Ben-Zvi, Isaac
Bernstorff, Count 139–40
Bezalele, Abraham (Solly Abrahams) 97, 103
Birdwood, General Sir William 31, 50–1, 55, 84
Bitton, CMS 'Chick' 169–70
Black, Eugene 5, 25, 52–3, 61, 62, 73, 100, 124
Board of Deputies of British Jews 56, 62, 69, 100–1, 106, 112–13, 127
Board of Guardians 123
Boer War (Second) 96, 163
Bols, Major-General Louis Jean 163, 164, 182, 184, 233–4, 236
Bolshevik Revolution 97, 117, 124, 150, 154
Brandies, Justice Louis 144, 145, 146, 147
bravery awards 189, 191, 198
  Zion Mule Corps 36, 37, 40, 47
Bridges, Major-General William 33
Britain 49–75, 117–37
  see also East End Jews
British Army 1, 2, 14
  anti-Semitism 29–30, 96, 103, 217–32 *passim*
  and Zion Mule Corp 21, 23, 24, 26, 27–8, 30

British Government 4, 6–7, 17, 21, 22–3, 50, 54–5, 57–8
  Home Office 73–4, 76, 77, 79, 124–5
  support for Zionism 85–6, 241
  see also Foreign Office (FO); War Office
British interests 7–9
British recruiting mission, USA 148
British West Indies Battalion 182–5
Brooman-White, Major 148
Buchan, Colonel John 139–40
Bund(ists) 146

Cape Helles 30, 33–4, 37, 41, 44, 45
Carson, Sir Edward 139
casualties/fatalities 178–9, 186–8, 189, 191, 192, 193, 198–9
  Jaffa riot 238
  malaria 186–7, 188
  Nebi-Musa riot 236
  Tel Hai 235
  ZMC 35, 36, 37–8, 41, 42, 46
Cecil, Lord Robert (FO) 57, 58, 59–60
Cesarani, David 9, 11, 12, 53, 56, 127
Chaytor, Major General E.W.C./GOIC Chaytor's Force 185, 189, 190–1, 192, 193, 194, 198, 199
Cheyette, Bryan 10–11
Chicherin, George (Gregory) 104
Churchill, Winston 29
Cohen (Braiterman), William 158
Cohen, Jack 157–8
Conjoint Committee Foreign Branch 62–3, 64, 66, 101
conscription (compulsion) 55, 57, 63, 70, 72–3, 94
Constantinople (Istanbul) 21, 22
conventionists 97–8, 126
Court Martial Register 224
courts martial 217, 218–19, 224–7, 231–2
Cowen, Joseph 54, 76, 135–6, 166
Cowen, Lt. Arthur 192–3
Crown Hill, Plymouth 117, 118–19, 120, 121, 125, 128, 152, 170

Daily Chronicle 78
Damascus 143, 205

Dardanelles Commission   24, 26–7, 43–4
Deedes, Major Wyndham   163
Defence of the Realm Act (1914)   56
della Pergola, Raphael   26
demobilisation   231, 233, 234–5, 236
deportation   80
Deraa   190–1
Derby, Lord   56, 125–6
disturbance/decline of Legion 201–2, 203–4
founding of Legion   88–91 passim, 107–16 passim
Derby Scheme   55, 56–7
desertions   152–3
Division(s)
  10th   178
  29th   30–1, 33–6, 37
  60th   183
  Australian and New Zealand Mountain   185
Dobrin, David   131–2
Dratch, Lance Corporal/Sergeant Samuel   193
Drummond, Sir Eric (FO)   89, 91–2

East End Jews   56, 122, 126, 196–7, 242
  founding of Legion   56, 63–103 passim
East End Recruiting Committee   73
Eder, Montague   54, 209–10, 222–3
Egypt   1, 8, 78, 83–4, 137, 140–1, 213–14, 216, 220
  Alexandria   21–33 passim, 41–2, 45–6
  Alexandrian Jews, in Zion Mule Corps   38, 44–5
  Benim in   143
  Jewish Battalions in   150–1, 154, 160, 195–6, 197, 198, 211
  unrest among Army of Occupation 213–14, 230
  Zion Mule Corps   21, 23, 26–7, 28, 41–2
Egyptian Expeditionary Force (EEF) 1, 13, 83, 93–4, 137, 141
  anti-Semitism   161–2, 163, 164, 167, 168, 181, 230

Hamilton, General Sir Ian GOC 24, 28–9, 31, 32, 36, 41, 46, 57, 84
Maxwell, General Sir John GOC 23, 24–5, 26, 27, 28–9, 30, 32, 36, 41, 42, 46
  and Nili organization   142, 194
  redeployment   205
  see also Allenby, Edmund H.H., Viscount
Egyptian Labour Corps   217, 218
El Arish, Egypt   214
Epstein, Private Jacob   121
Epstein, Private Paul   120, 152–3, 168, 186
Erchovitz, Sergeant Meyer   40
Es Salt   188, 191, 192
Eshkol, Levi   179–81
Ettinger, Akiva   23
Ettinger, J.   104

Falk, Rabbi L.A.   151–2
Foreign Jews Protection Committee (FJPC)   79, 97
Foreign Office (FO)
  disturbance/decline of Legion 226, 227, 230–1
  founding of Legion   57, 58–61, 85, 88–94 passim
  raising the battalions   119, 139, 141, 149, 150
France   48–9, 84–5, 103
  see also Paris
Frank, Farrier-Corporal Abram   37, 42
Frank, Mrs   37, 42–3
Freedman, Naim   174
Freeman, Sergeant Harry   198
Friedman, Isaiah   7–8, 66
Furst, Lance Corporal Yehuda   192
The Fusilier (magazine)   1

Gaba Tebe   30
Gabrilevitz, Hanoch   44
Gallipoli   13, 24, 30, 30–8, 44–5, 46–7, 50
Geddes, Brigadier General, Director of Recruitment   89, 94, 95–6, 104, 105

282 Index

Gilner, Elias 13-14, 15, 26, 38, 164, 177-8, 194-5, 205, 226
  raising the battalions, USA 147, 148, 149, 154, 155-6, 158-9
Ginsburg, Asher (Ahad Ha'am) 3, 4, 20, 50, 101-2
Gluskin, Victor 23
Godley, Major-General A.J. 25
Golomb, Eliyahu 171, 205
Gordon, Maurice 155-6, 192
Gorodissky, Lt. Alexander 28, 43
Graham, Sir Ronald 23, 108, 109
Grand Mufti 236
Greenberg, Leopold 154
Greenberg, Police Constable 79, 104
Grossman, Meir 76-7, 80
Groushkovsky, Private M. 36, 41
Gye, Lt. 28, 41, 45

Haganah 158-9, 237, 239
Halpern, Ben 6
Hamilton, General Sir Ian GOC MEF 24, 28-9, 31, 32, 36, 41, 46, 57, 84
Hebrew University 177, 179
Hejaz railway 185
Helmieh 177, 196
Henderson, Arthur 125
Henriques, H.S.Q. 56, 62, 112-13
Herzl Gymnasium 172, 174, 177
Hildesheim, Corporal E. (Leon Gildesgame) 36-7, 179
Hill, Brigadier General 170, 173
HM Transport *Anglo Egyptian* 30, 31
HM Transport *Antrim* 135
HM Transport *Dundrennan* 33-4
HM Transport *Hymettus* 30-1
HMS *Queen Elizabeth* 31
'Home and Heim' 65, 76, 78, 80, 81, 84, 97, 104
Hopkin, Major 169, 177, 190
Hos, Dov 171, 205, 221-2
Hunter-Weston, Major-General Aylmer GOC 29th Division 35-6
Hutchinson, General, Director of Organisation 94, 107, 137
Hyamson, Albert 140

Indian Brigade, 20th 185
Indian Mule Corps 32, 33-4

Israel 14-15, 239
Italy 48, 49
  Taranto 150

Jabotinsky, Vladimir 13, 14, 15, 160, 171, 191, 239
  biographical details xv
  disturbance/decline of Legion 201-2, 214, 219, 226-7
  founding of Legion 49-74 *passim*, 76-115 *passim*
  imprisonment 236-7
  raising the battalions 117, 118, 122, 135, 147, 154
  Zion Mule Corps 20, 21-3, 24, 28, 47
Jacobs, Philip, Captain 14, 16
Jaffa 170, 172, 173-4, 215, 219
  May Day riot 237-8
  Turkish pogroms 93
Japan 21
Jerusalem 21, 215, 219
Jewish Brigade 182-5
Jewish Chronicle
  founding of Legion 54, 55, 56, 64-5, 66-7, 69-71, 72, 78, 79, 81, 83, 86, 102
  raising the battalions 120-1, 123, 126, 135, 136, 153
  Zion Mule Corps 26, 27, 45
Jewish Legion Committee (USA) 147, 149
Jewish Recruiting Committee 56, 63, 69, 72, 73, 90, 97
Jewish Regiment Committee 118, 119
Jewish Territorial Organisation (JTO) 25
Jordan Valley 182, 185, 186-7, 188

Kantara, Egypt 214, 221, 222, 225
Karo, Max 170
Katzenjoh, Private B. 37
Katznelson, Berl 171
Kent Messenger 127, 128
Kerr, Sir Philip 93, 109-10
Khalidi, Rashid Ismail 8
Kiley, James MP 118, 122, 135-6
King, Joseph 65-6

Index   283

Kirzner, Private I.   37
Kitchener, F-M Lord   8, 29–30, 45
Korman, Israel   25–6
Krithia, Turkey   35, 36, 37
Kum Kale   30

labour units   74, 207
Landa, Myer   104–5, 107–8, 111
Lawrence, Colonel T.E.   164
legacy of the Legion   239–43
Lemnos   30
Levene, Mark   9, 17, 66, 77
Levontin, Z.D.   23, 28
Litvinov, M.   124–5
Lloyd George, David   6, 9, 54–5, 83–4, 88–9, 92–3, 109–10, 116, 141, 143
Lobagola, Private   184
local tribunals   129
London Regiment, 20th Battalion   82–4, 87, 96, 189, 203
Lossos, Gustave   156
Ludd, Palestine   205, 229

Maccabeans   111–12
Macdonagh, General   125, 126, 202, 203, 204
Macready, Major-General Sir Neville, Director of Military Intelligence   85, 96, 107, 118, 122, 137, 163, 164, 182
Maidstone   126–8
malaria   186–7, 188–9
Manchester Guardian   54, 81
Margolin, Lt.-Col. Eliezer   160, 168–9, 184, 185, 217, 233–4, 236
Margolis, Mordecai   23
Marshall, Louis   144, 145
Masterman, Charles   58–9, 60–1, 121
Maxwell, General Sir John GOC EEF   23, 24–5, 26, 27, 28–9, 30, 32, 36, 41, 42, 46
Mediterranean Expeditionary Force (MEF)   24, 27, 30, 41–2, 44
Megiddo, Battle of   182, 185, 193, 199, 202, 203
Meinertzhagen, Colonel Richard   208, 234
Metropolitan Police, Special Branch   79–80

Military Police   219–20
Military Service Convention   64, 68–9, 80, 86, 94, 96–8, 124, 127, 233, 243
Miller, Lt.-Col.   170
Money, Major General Sir Arthur   208, 216–17
Monro, General Sir Charles GOC MEF   45
Montagu, Edwin   6, 71–2, 107, 110
Montefiore, Claude G.   62, 67, 90–1, 100, 103, 105, 107, 111
morale   242
Zion Mule Corps   33, 34, 38, 40
Morrow, Benjamin   157
Mudros Bay   30–1
Murray, General Sir Archibald   83
Muscovitz, Private David   35
mutineers   213–14, 222–33
Myer, Bereskin   157
Myer, Major Henry   17, 168–9, 195–7, 198, 212, 218–19

National Registration Act (1915)   55
Nebi-Musa riot   235–6
neutrality policy   49–50, 66
New York   4, 21, 48
Newman, Nathan   157
Newton, Lord   60–1
Nili organization   142, 194
Nordau, Dr Max   22

Occupied Enemy Territory Authority (OETA)   208, 225, 234, 236, 242
Ormsby-Gore, Major W.   105, 141–2, 166
Ottoman Empire   6, 7, 20–1, 22

Pale of Settlement   2, 3, 5, 143
Palestine   1, 2, 3, 4, 13
  38th Battalion   125, 138, 178, 233–4
  40th Battalion   205–8
  Benim in   20, 21, 22–3
  distubances and decline of Legion   217–33
  as Jewish homeland   63
  mandatory period   6, 200, 215, 216, 233

284 Index

Palestine *continued*
  Occupied Enemy Territory Authority (OETA)   208, 225, 234, 236, 242
  role of Legion   58, 83–5, 87, 89, 92–3, 102, 108–10, 114–15, 148–9
  Sykes-Picot Agreement   85, 93–4, 141
  Yishuv   6, 143, 144–5, 174
  Zion Mule Corps   24–6
  Zionist Commission poster   172–3
  see also Balfour Declaration
Palestinian Jewish soldiers   195, 196, 203, 204, 205, 210, 211–13, 242
  recruitment   171–7, 181
Paris
  peace conference   213
  Zionist Delegation   214–15
Pasha, Kattawi   23
Patterson, Lt.-Colonel John H.   13, 14
  biographical details   xv-xvi
  disturbance/decline of Legion   202, 213–14, 225, 226, 233
  founding of Jewish Legion   50–61 *passim*, 82, 96, 103, 104–5, 106–7, 115, 116, 122
  Legion at war   182–3, 184, 185, 186, 189, 191
  Legion preparation and prejudice   160, 163, 167, 172, 178, 179
  raising the battalions   117, 119, 122–3, 125–6, 129, 130, 135, 137, 151
  Zion Mule Corps   25–47 *passim*
'Patterson's Column'   192
personal testimonies   13–17
Petrov, Count   22–3
philo-Semitism   2, 11–12, 27, 242
Pinchevsky, Jacob   174
Plymouth, Crown Hill   117, 118–19, 120, 121, 125, 128, 152, 170
Poale Zion   142, 145–6, 147, 155, 156, 166, 197
Prince Feisal   190–1
propaganda   138–41
Protocols of the Elders of Zion   162–3, 181, 199–200

Rafa   219
Reading, Lord   111, 149
recruitment   55–7, 58, 61, 64, 66–73
  American Jews   148–59, 160, 177–8
  Argentinean Jews   149
  Palestinian Jews   171–8, 181
  Russian Jews   48, 51, 64–5, 68–74, 78, 79–80, 84, 86–7, 88, 89–91, 98–102, 104, 105–6, 123
refugee camps   22–3, 33, 37, 41–2
Regimental badge and name   201–2, 220, 221
Ribniker, Private David   174
Robertson, General Sir William, Chief of the Imperial General Staff   85, 143
Robinson, Lance-Corporal Abraham Jacob   134
Rollo, 2nd Lt. Claude   35, 37, 38, 40, 41
Roosevelt, Theodore   26, 41, 57
Rosenberg, Private Nissel   40, 82, 172
Rothschild, Leopold   56, 67, 73–4, 77
Rothschild, Lionel W., 2nd Lord   6–7, 104, 105, 106, 107–8, 111, 122, 181
  biographical details   xvi
Rothschild, Major James   172, 177, 178
Rothschild, Major Lionel   90–1, 103, 105, 107, 111
Rottman, Private Jacob   37
Rouah, Private Joseph   37
Royal Fusiliers Battalions   1
38th
  at war   182–94 *passim*,   199
  disturbance/decline   205, 210, 211–12, 214, 217, 220, 221, 226, 232, 233–4
  preparation and prejudice   160, 167, 168, 169–70, 174, 178, 179, 181
  raising   115–34 *passim*, 150–1, 152–3
39th
  at war   182, 183, 187, 190, 191–2, 194

disturbance/decline 204, 210, 211, 223, 224–5, 229, 233
  preparation and prejudice 160, 167–74 passim, 177–8, 179, 181
  raising 124, 128, 138, 152
  40th 138, 174, 177, 179, 181
  at war 183, 190, 195, 196, 197
  disturbance/decline 205, 212–13, 218–19, 233
  47th 233
Royal Inniskilling Fusiliers, 1st 36
Rubenstein, Sergeant Aryeh 174
Rubinstein, William 11–13, 59
Russia
  abdication of Tsar 87, 92
  Bolshevik Revolution 97, 117, 124, 150, 154
  provisional government 87, 92, 97
  Revolution 4, 9, 142
  Tsarist regime 2, 3, 21, 52, 53, 68, 71
Russian Jews 3–4, 12
  in Britian 51, 52, 53, 56–7, 63, 128–9
  and British Jews 52–3, 61–2, 63, 66–7
  conventionists 97–8
  recruitment 48, 51, 64–5, 68–74, 78, 79–80, 84, 86–7, 88, 89–91, 98–102, 104, 105–6, 123
  in USA 144, 145, 150–3
  Zion Mule Corps 20, 21–3, 28, 29, 38, 44–5, 47
Russian Monitor 50
Russian Tribunal 123
Russo-Japanese War 21, 29
Rutenberg, Pinhas 3–4, 20, 23, 48, 146, 147, 239

Salaman, Captain Redcliffe 104–5, 190, 194
Samaria 219
Samuel, Herbert 237, 238
  founding of Legion 54–5, 62–3, 67–83 passim, 96
Samuel, Lt.-Col. Fred 169, 170
Samuel, Sir Stuart 104

Schwartz, Harvey 157
Schwartz, Isadore 158
Scott, C.P. 54, 57, 88, 121, 141
Scott, Lt.-Col. Michael 218, 221–2
Serafend 224, 233
Shea, Major-General GOC 60th Division 183
Sinai 83
Smolley, Major (Smalley) 223, 224
Smuts, General Jan 88, 89, 226
Sokolow, Nathan 50, 73, 144, 154, 167, 173
  biographical details xvi
SS *Arcadia* 29
SS *River Clyde* 34
Stansky, Peter 9
Steed, Henry Wickham 81–2, 114
Stein, Leonard 82
Stein, Private Hirsch 37
Stern, Morris 157
Stone, Isadore 156
Suares, Edgar 22–3
Suvla Bay 44
  see also Gallipoli
Swaythling, Edwin S., 2nd Baron xvi, 107–8
Sykes, Sir Mark xvii, 85, 87–9, 93, 105, 141
Sykes-Picot Agreement 85, 93–4, 141
Syria 1, 8, 208–9
  Aleppo 143

Tagart, Major-General, Adjutant-General 90–1, 103, 109
Taranto, Italy 150
Tel Hai 235
Tel-el-Kebir 195–6, 197, 198
Thomson, Commander Basil (Special Branch) 79
The Times 58–9, 70–1, 81, 98, 100, 104, 114
Training Reserve Battalion, 28th 128
Treaty of Brest-Litovsk 153
Treaty of Sèvres 233
Trumpeldor, Joseph 14, 78, 82, 83–4, 87, 88–9, 90, 96–7, 101–2, 153
  biographical details xvii
  mortally wounded at Tel Hai 235

Trumpeldor, Joseph *continued*
　Zion Mule Corps　21, 23–4, 25, 30, 31, 33, 34, 38, 39, 41, 44, 45, 46
Turkey　1, 3, 8, 27–8, 30, 92, 93
　Achi Baba　35, 37
　Armistice with　200, 201, 204
　Gallipoli　13, 24, 30, 30–8, 44–5, 46–7, 50
　Krithia　35, 36, 37
　Ottomans　6, 7, 20–1, 22
　Russian Jews in　20
　Turkish Army　21, 83, 188, 189, 190–1, 213
Turkish pogroms (Jaffa)　93
Turkish propaganda　162
Turkish-German alliance　139, 140

Umm Esh Shert　188, 192
United Council of Jewish Friendly Societies　101
United States of America (USA)　6, 41, 58, 59, 60, 61
　entry into war　87, 92, 121, 138, 139
　New York　4, 21, 48
　raising the battalions　138–59
　State Department　230–1
Unsere Tribune　76–7

Vital, David　4–5

Wadi Mellaha　185, 189, 191–2
War Office　26–7, 29, 41, 42–3, 44, 45, 47
　disturbance/decline of Legion　202–16 *passim*, 231
　founding of Legion　51, 56–7, 58, 67, 68, 74, 78, 82–5, 89–93 *passim*, 102–16 *passim*
　Legion at war　183–4
　Legion preparation and prejudice　165, 166, 171–2, 179, 181
　raising the battalions　118, 122, 125–6, 128, 129, 137, 150, 151
Wavell, Colonel A.P.　164–5, 186, 188, 208
Weber, Thomas　11
Weitz, Dr　23
Weizmann, Chaim　3–4, 6, 7, 13
　biographical details　xvii–xviii
　disturbance/decline of Legion　208–10, 214–15, 232–3
　founding of Legion　48–50, 54, 66, 73, 74, 76, 81–2, 83, 85, 88–9, 93, 104, 114
　Legion preparation and prejudice　162, 163, 165, 166, 173, 174, 177
　raising the battalions　125, 144, 147
White, Brigadier-General　148–9
Wilson, General Sir Henry, CIGS　214, 215, 216
Wilson, President　138, 145, 147
Windsor, Nova Scotia　7
Wise, Rabbi Stephen　144–5, 146
Wolf, Lucien　61–2, 63, 64, 66, 67, 71, 73–4, 76, 77–8, 100, 101
　biographical details　xviii
Wolfe, Lt.　178–9
Wolfson, Sergeant Samuel William　133
Wortheimer, Private　46

Yanait, Rahel *see* Ben-Zvi, Isaac
Yehuda, Corporal Nehemiah　40
Yishuv, Palestine　6, 143, 144–5, 174

Zangwill, Israel　25, 54, 67
Zion Mule Corps　13–14, 15, 20–47
　at Gallipoli　30–8
　bravery awards　36, 37, 40, 47
　casualties/fatalities　35, 36, 37–8, 41, 42, 46
　compensation and pension arrangements　41–4
　development　20–9
　division　30–1, 32
　former members volunteer　82
　indiscipline/punishment　38–9, 40, 41
　London Regiment, 20th Battalion　83–4
　morale　33, 34, 38, 40
　officers　30, 43
　petition to take offensive role　35–6
　proposal to raise status to Jewish Legion　50–1, 55, 57
　treatment of mutineers　39
　uniform　27–8
　veterans　104, 160, 172, 179

Zionism 1–2, 4–8, 13
　American perspectives 143–7
　British perspectives 85–6, 93–4, 109–10
　objections to Legion 49–50, 51
　support for 59–60, 64–5, 71, 74, 85–6, 93–4, 109–10
　vs. assimilationists 53–4, 61–3, 71–2, 77–9, 81–2, 94–5, 100, 110–11, 241–2
Zionist Bureau 141
Zionist Commission 165, 172, 177, 208–10, 222–3, 236
　poster 172–3
Zionist Council 3
Zionist Delegation, Paris 214–15
Zionist Organisation of America (ZOA) 14, 147